CHILD ABUSE AND DOMESTIC VIOLENCE

ISSN 1935-1216

CHILD ABUSE AND DOMESTIC VIOLENCE

Stephen Meyer

INFORMATION PLUS® REFERENCE SERIES
Formerly Published by Information Plus, Wylie, Texas

GALE
CENGAGE Learning·

Farmington Hills, Mich • San Francisco • New York • Waterville, Maine
Meriden, Conn • Mason, Ohio • Chicago

GALE
CENGAGE Learning·

Child Abuse and Domestic Violence

Stephen Meyer

Kepos Media, Inc.: Steven Long and Janice Jorgensen, Series Editors

Project Editors: Tracie Moy, Laura Avery

Rights Acquisition and Management: Ashley M. Maynard

Composition: Evi Abou-El-Seoud, Mary Beth Trimper

Manufacturing: Rita Wimberley

Gale
27500 Drake Rd.
Farmington Hills, MI 48331-3535

ISBN-13: 978-0-7876-5103-9 (set)
ISBN-13: 978-1-57302-640-6

ISSN 1935-1216

This title is also available as an e-book.
ISBN-13: 978-1-57302-676-5 (set)
Contact your Gale sales representative for ordering information.

Printed in the United States of America
1 2 3 4 5   19 18 17 16 15

TABLE OF CONTENTS

This chapter presents various definitions of child abuse and domestic violence and explains how changing family compositions have expanded the definitions beyond their historical contexts. It discusses major federal and state laws and programs and illustrates the roles that are played by the civil and criminal courts. Social and public health issues related to child abuse and domestic violence are also addressed. Finally, it examines the debate over corporal punishment.

Different methods of detecting and measuring child abuse, as well as the findings of various studies designed to measure the incidence and prevalence of abuse in American society, are outlined in this chapter. It also covers mandatory reporting laws and looks at how child protective services agencies respond to reports of child maltreatment. Court actions and the foster care system are also detailed. The chapter concludes with a discussion of government programs that aid impoverished children and families.

This chapter explores issues that contribute to child abuse, including factors that put mothers, fathers, and other caregivers at risk for abusing children, and common characteristics that are shared by child victims. The chapter also delves into the consequences of childhood maltreatment, with focus on biological, emotional, social, and behavioral effects.

The sexual abuse of children takes various forms and is particularly troubling to society. As with other types of abuse, sexual abuse has short-term and long-term effects. Retrospective studies in which adults are surveyed about childhood sexual abuse provide researchers with much-needed information about the long-term consequences of this type of abuse. The extent of abuse by different categories of perpetrators is also investigated.

Child abuse cases present special challenges in civil and criminal court proceedings. This chapter reports on children's legal rights during child protection cases and analyzes the major constitutional issues that affect child abuse investigations and prosecutions. Also tracked are the legal issues surrounding child pornography, prenatal drug use, the legal loophole of the incest exception, and the statute of limitations.

Estimates of how much domestic violence occurs are enumerated here, using the National Crime Victimization Surveys, the National Intimate Partner and Sexual Violence Survey, and the National Violence against Women Survey. The chapter also includes data on domestic violence incidents that ended in homicide.

This chapter offers several theories about the causes of domestic violence and profiles victim risk factors that have been identified by researchers. It also assesses the short-term and long-term effects of domestic violence and their physical and mental health consequences. It ends with an examination of prevention measures and considers the question of why someone would stay in a violent relationship.

The incidence, causes, and attitudes about rape by intimate partners (i.e., former and current spouses, boyfriends, and girlfriends), acquaintances, and dates are studied in this chapter. It also describes stalking, with special attention to the decreased barriers to stalking on the Internet.

Since the 1980s the criminal justice system has approached domestic violence cases with increasing seriousness, and some of the results are noted here. Factors involved in reporting and prosecuting cases of domestic abuse, the police response to domestic violence calls, and the effectiveness of arrest and protective orders in deterring future assaults are considered. Also highlighted is key domestic violence legislation. Lastly, this chapter provides a summary of some of the important legal cases that have helped define judicial responsibility and have influenced policies and practices to protect abuse victims.

PREFACE

Child Abuse and Domestic Violence is part of the *Information Plus Reference Series*. The purpose of each volume of the series is to present the latest facts on a topic of pressing concern in modern American life. These topics include the most controversial and studied social issues of the 21st century: abortion, capital punishment, care for the elderly, crime, the economy, energy, health care, immigration, national security, social welfare, women, youth, and many more. Even though this series is written especially for high school and undergraduate students, it is an excellent resource for anyone in need of factual information on current affairs.

By presenting the facts, it is the intention of Gale, Cengage Learning, to provide its readers with everything they need to reach an informed opinion on current issues. To that end, there is a particular emphasis in this series on the presentation of scientific studies, surveys, and statistics. These data are generally presented in the form of tables, charts, and other graphics placed within the text of each book. Every graphic is directly referred to and carefully explained in the text. The source of each graphic is presented within the graphic itself. The data used in these graphics are drawn from the most reputable and reliable sources, such as from the various branches of the U.S. government and from private organizations and associations. Every effort was made to secure the most recent information available. Readers should bear in mind that many major studies take years to conduct and that additional years often pass before the data from these studies are made available to the public. Therefore, in many cases the most recent information available in 2015 is dated from 2012 or 2013. Older statistics are sometimes presented as well, if they are landmark studies or of particular interest and no more-recent information exists.

Although statistics are a major focus of the *Information Plus Reference Series*, they are by no means its only content. Each book also presents the widely held positions and important ideas that shape how the book's subject is discussed in the United States. These positions are explained in detail and, where possible, in the words of their proponents. Some of the other material to be found in these books includes historical background, descriptions of major events related to the subject, relevant laws and court cases, and examples of how these issues play out in American life. Some books also feature primary documents or have pro and con debate sections that provide the words and opinions of prominent Americans on both sides of a controversial topic. All material is presented in an evenhanded and unbiased manner; readers will never be encouraged to accept one view of an issue over another.

HOW TO USE THIS BOOK

Every year millions of American adults are subjected to physical, sexual, verbal, or emotional abuse by their intimate partners or family members. Perhaps even more disturbingly, millions of children suffer from such abuse at the hands of the people who are supposed to care for them. Many more have their basic needs neglected. This volume provides the best information available on the prevalence, causes, and devastating consequences of family violence. The challenges that domestic violence and child abuse pose to the legal system are also covered in detail.

Child Abuse and Domestic Violence consists of nine chapters and three appendixes. Each chapter covers an aspect of the problems of child abuse and domestic violence in the United States. For a summary of the information that is covered in each chapter, please see the synopses that are provided in the Table of Contents. Chapters generally begin with an overview of the basic facts and background information on the chapter's topic, then proceed to examine subtopics of particular interest. For example, Chapter 2: Detecting, Measuring, and Preventing Child Abuse opens with an overview of federal publications and other resources that compile statistics on child abuse. A presentation of recent child abuse data follows, which includes information on numbers of maltreatment cases, demographic characteristics of child abuse victims, types of maltreatment, and child fatalities stemming from abuse. The chapter proceeds to discuss traits of child maltreatment perpetrators, focusing on the relationship between abusers and victims, while also analyzing socioeconomic, cultural, and other factors that may contribute to abusive situations. The legal framework surrounding child abuse cases, including mandatory reporting laws and the foster care system, are examined. The chapter concludes with an assessment of the child welfare system, while listing a range of federal child abuse prevention resources. Readers can find their way through a chapter by looking for the section and subsection headings, which are clearly set off from the text. They can also refer to the book's extensive Index, if they already know what they are looking for.

Statistical Information

The tables and figures featured throughout *Child Abuse and Domestic Violence* will be of particular use to readers in learning about these issues. These tables and figures represent an extensive collection of the most recent and important statistics on child abuse and domestic violence. For example, graphics include statistics on the prevalence of child maltreatment, sexual abuse, and neglect. They also cover the link between caregiver alcohol abuse and child maltreatment, rape by intimate partners and nonintimates, and the relationship between stalkers and their victims. Gale, Cengage Learning, believes that making this information available to readers is the most important way to fulfill the goal of this book: to help readers understand the issues and controversies surrounding child abuse and domestic violence in the United States and reach their own conclusions about them.

Each table or figure has a unique identifier appearing above it, for ease of identification and reference. Titles for the tables and figures explain their purpose. At the end of each table or figure, the original source of the data is provided.

To help readers understand these often complicated statistics, all tables and figures are explained in the text. References in the text direct readers to the relevant statistics. Furthermore, the contents of all tables and figures are fully indexed. Please see the opening section of the Index at the back of this volume for a description of how to find tables and figures within it.

Appendixes

Besides the main body text and images, *Child Abuse and Domestic Violence* has three appendixes. The first is the Important Names and Addresses directory. Here, readers will find contact information for a number of organizations that study child abuse and domestic violence, fight these crimes, or advocate influential positions on these issues. The second appendix is the Resources section, which is provided to assist readers in conducting their own research. In this section, the author and editors of *Child Abuse and Domestic Violence* describe some of the sources that were most useful during the compilation of this book. The final appendix is the Index. It has been greatly expanded from previous editions and should make it even easier to find specific topics in this book.

COMMENTS AND SUGGESTIONS

The editors of the *Information Plus Reference Series* welcome your feedback on *Child Abuse and Domestic Violence*. Please direct all correspondence to:

Editors
Information Plus Reference Series
27500 Drake Rd.
Farmington Hills, MI 48331-3535

CHAPTER 1
DEFINING CHILD ABUSE AND DOMESTIC VIOLENCE

Child abuse and domestic violence are crimes in which the victims suffer harm that is inflicted by people who are personally close to them. There is no one legal definition of either crime. In general, child abuse involves cases in which a child is harmed by a parent, other family member, or caregiver. As will be explained in later chapters, child abuse often includes physical violence and sexual abuse, as would be expected, but it also includes psychological abuse and neglect, such as failure to provide for a child's basic needs for food, shelter, medical care, and so forth. Domestic violence is a broad term that refers to violence that is committed by adults against adults with whom they are relationally bound by family ties, by marriage, or by some kind of romantic or sexual involvement. Some definitions of domestic violence focus only on intimate partners, which are current and former spouses, boyfriends, and girlfriends. Domestic violence takes many forms. Although most definitions include physical and sexual assaults, other definitions also consider behaviors that are psychologically abusive, coercive, or threatening in nature. Child abuse and domestic violence are not only crimes but also social and public health problems. Researchers are increasingly focusing on the prevalence of violent environments in the United States and their negative consequences, particularly on children.

CHANGING FAMILY STRUCTURES

Child abuse and domestic violence are linked by the close personal nature of the victim-offender relationship. These problems occur within families and are sometimes collectively called family violence. During the 20th century the notion of what constitutes a family began to change dramatically. Traditionally, a "family" was considered to be a nuclear family, which Merriam-Webster defines in its online dictionary (2014, http://www.merriam-webster.com/dictionary/nuclear%20family) as "the part of a family that includes only the father, mother, and children." However,

nuclear families are increasingly giving way to other arrangements in which adults live together and/or engage in romantic and/or sexual relationships without getting married. This social change has led to fundamental changes in the definition of family violence.

In the past domestic violence was known as spousal abuse, or more commonly wife beating, because the vast majority of intimate partners were married to each other. In addition, wives were assumed to be the only victims of spousal violence. Changing social conditions and greater awareness that women sometimes engage in violence against their intimate partners have made the broader term of domestic violence more popular. The growth in nontraditional families means that children increasingly live in households with adults who are not their biological parents. In addition, as women have joined the workforce in larger numbers, children are often looked after by someone other than their mother, including their mother's intimate partners, relatives, and hired caregivers. Thus, society has expanded its definition of child abusers beyond biological parents to other people who are entrusted with child caregiving responsibilities.

The chapters that follow will describe studies that have examined the prevalence of child abuse and domestic violence in the United States. Many of the researchers assessed demographic factors, such as household composition, during their analyses to compare prevalence rates between different population subsets. Thus, it is informative to understand how household composition has changed over time.

In *America's Family and Living Arrangements: 2012* (August 2013, http://www.census.gov/prod/2013pubs/p20-570.pdf), Jonathan Vespa, Jamie M. Lewis, and Rose M. Kreider of the U.S. Census Bureau examine shifts in household compositions between 1970 and 2012. As Figure 1.1 shows, married couples with children accounted for just over 40% of all American households

FIGURE 1.1

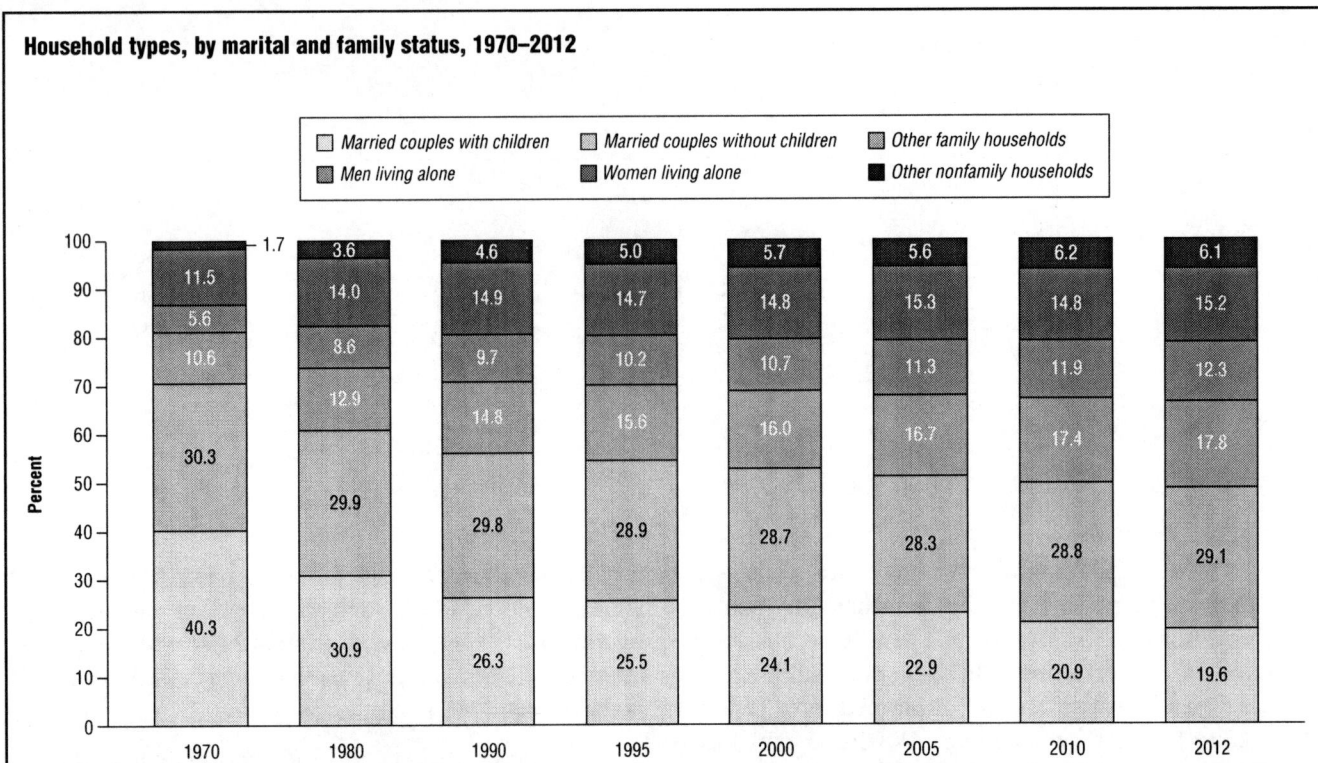

Household types, by marital and family status, 1970–2012

SOURCE: Jonathan Vespa, Jamie M. Lewis, and Rose M. Kreider, "Figure 1. Households by Type, 1970 to 2012: CPS," in *America's Families and Living Arrangements: 2012*, U.S. Department of Commerce, Economics and Statistics Administration, U.S. Census Bureau, August 2013, http://www.census.gov/prod/2013pubs/p20-570.pdf (accessed July 17, 2014)

in 1970. By 2012 this figure had dropped to fewer than 20 percent of all households. During this same span, the proportion of "other family households" (a category that includes single-parent families) rose substantially, from 10.8% of all U.S. households in 1970 to 17.8% in 2012.

As Table 1.1 displays, birth rates among girls between the ages of 15 to 19 years rose during the 1980s, from 32 births per 1,000 girls in 1980 to a peak of 61.8 per 1,000 girls in 1991. Since the early 1990s, however, the rate of teenage pregnancies has fallen dramatically in the United States. Figure 1.2 shows the decline in birth rates among adolescent girls between 1991 and 2013, by race and ethnicity. As presented in Figure 1.2, in 1991 there were more than 60 births per 1,000 girls between the ages of 15 and 19 overall; by 2013 this figure had been cut in half, dropping to approximately 30 births per 1,000 girls aged 15 to 19 years. The most dramatic decrease in teenage births during this span occurred among African American girls, from 120 births per 1,000 girls in 1991 to roughly 40 births per 1,000 girls in 2013.

According to the U.S. Census Bureau, there were approximately 73.9 million children under the age of 18 years living in the United States in 2013. (See Table 1.2.) Of these, 50.6 million, or just over 68%, lived in households with both parents; 47.6 million children lived with

both parents who were married to each other, and 3 million children lived with both parents who were not married to each other. Of children under the age of 18 years living in single-parent households in 2013, 17.5 million lived with their mothers only, and just under 3 million lived with their fathers only. Another 2.7 million American children lived in households where neither parent was present in 2013. (See Table 1.2.) As Vespa, Lewis, and Kreider report, there appears to be a strong link between household composition and the economic status of children. Of the roughly 16.4 million children living below the poverty line in 2012, more than half (8.7 million, or 53%) lived in single-parent households. (See Table 1.3.)

LEGAL ISSUES

As will be explained in later chapters, child abuse and domestic violence incidents that are reported to authorities are often handled by criminal courts (courts that deal with offenders who are accused of committing criminal offenses) and/or civil courts (courts that deal with noncriminal matters). The jurisdiction of the courts over child abuse and domestic violence cases is spelled out in the laws that have been passed by the federal and state governments. This jurisdiction has been slow in coming because historically these offenses were considered to be a private matter to be settled within families. Authorities were reluctant to get involved, except in the most egregious cases. During

TABLE 1.1

Birth rates for adolescent females, by age, race, and Hispanic origin, 1980–2012

[Live births per 1,000 females in specified age group]

Characteristic	1980	1981	1982	1983	1984	1985	1986	1987	1988	1989	1990	1991	1992	1993	1994	1995	1996
All races																	
Ages 10–14	1.1	1.1	1.1	1.1	1.2	1.2	1.3	1.3	1.3	1.4	1.4	1.4	1.4	1.4	1.4	1.3	1.2
Ages 15–17	32.5	32.0	32.3	31.8	31.0	31.0	30.5	31.7	33.6	36.4	37.5	38.6	37.6	37.5	37.2	35.5	33.3
Ages 18–19	82.1	80.0	79.4	77.4	77.4	79.6	79.6	78.5	79.9	84.2	88.6	94.0	93.6	91.1	90.2	87.7	84.7
Ages 15–19	53.0	52.2	52.4	51.4	50.6	51.0	50.2	50.6	53.0	57.3	59.9	61.8	60.3	59.0	58.2	56.0	53.5
White, total																	
Ages 10–14	0.6	0.5	0.6	0.6	0.6	0.6	0.6	0.6	0.6	0.7	0.7	0.8	0.8	0.8	0.8	0.8	0.7
Ages 15–17	25.5	25.4	25.5	25.0	24.3	24.4	23.8	24.6	26.0	28.1	29.5	30.5	29.9	30.0	30.4	29.6	28.0
Ages 18–19	73.2	71.5	70.8	68.8	68.4	70.4	70.1	68.9	69.6	72.9	78.0	83.3	83.2	81.5	81.2	80.2	77.6
Ages 15–19	45.4	44.9	45.0	43.9	42.9	43.3	42.3	42.5	44.4	47.9	50.8	52.6	51.4	50.6	50.5	49.5	47.5
White, non-Hispanic																	
Ages 10–14	0.4	—	—	—	—	—	—	—	—	0.4	0.5	0.5	0.5	0.5	0.5	0.4	0.4
Ages 15–17	22.4	—	—	—	—	—	—	—	—	—	23.2	23.6	22.7	22.7	22.7	22.0	20.6
Ages 18–19	67.7	—	—	—	—	—	—	—	—	—	66.6	70.6	69.8	67.7	67.6	66.2	64.0
Ages 15–19	41.2	—	—	—	—	—	—	—	—	39.9	42.5	43.4	41.7	40.7	40.4	39.3	37.6
Black, total																	
Ages 10–14	4.3	4.0	4.0	4.1	4.4	4.5	4.7	4.8	4.9	5.1	4.9	4.7	4.6	4.5	4.5	4.1	3.5
Ages 15–17	72.5	69.3	69.7	69.6	69.2	69.3	69.3	72.1	75.7	81.9	82.3	83.5	80.5	78.9	75.1	68.5	63.3
Ages 18–19	135.1	131.0	128.9	127.1	128.1	132.4	135.1	135.8	142.7	151.9	152.9	157.6	156.3	150.2	146.2	135.0	130.5
Ages 15–19	97.8	94.5	94.3	93.9	94.1	95.4	95.8	97.6	102.7	111.5	112.8	114.8	111.3	107.3	102.9	94.4	89.6
Black, non-Hispanic																	
Ages 10–14	4.6	—	—	—	—	—	—	—	—	5.2	5.0	4.9	4.8	4.6	4.6	4.2	3.6
Ages 15–17	77.2	—	—	—	—	—	—	—	—	—	84.9	86.1	82.9	81.1	77.0	70.4	64.8
Ages 18–19	146.5	—	—	—	—	—	—	—	—	—	157.5	162.2	161.1	154.6	150.4	139.2	134.1
Ages 15–19	105.1	—	—	—	—	—	—	—	—	111.9	116.2	118.2	114.7	110.5	105.7	97.2	91.9
American Indian or Alaskan Native																	
Ages 10–14	1.9	2.1	1.4	1.9	1.7	1.7	1.8	1.7	1.7	1.5	1.6	1.6	1.6	1.4	1.8	1.6	1.6
Ages 15–17	51.5	49.7	52.6	55.2	50.7	47.7	48.7	48.8	49.7	51.6	48.5	51.9	52.3	51.5	48.4	44.6	42.7
Ages 18–19	129.5	121.5	127.6	121.4	124.7	124.1	125.3	122.2	121.1	128.9	129.3	134.2	130.5	126.3	123.7	122.2	113.3
Ages 15–19	82.2	78.4	83.5	84.2	81.5	79.2	78.1	77.2	77.5	82.7	81.1	84.1	82.4	79.8	76.4	72.9	68.2
Asian or Pacific Islander																	
Ages 10–14	0.3	0.3	0.4	0.5	0.5	0.4	0.5	0.6	0.6	0.6	0.7	0.8	0.7	0.7	0.7	0.7	0.6
Ages 15–17	12.0	13.4	14.0	12.9	12.6	12.5	12.1	12.6	13.6	15.0	16.0	16.3	15.4	16.1	16.3	15.6	14.7
Ages 18–19	46.2	49.5	50.8	44.5	40.7	40.8	38.8	37.0	39.6	40.4	40.2	42.2	41.9	41.2	41.3	40.1	36.8
Ages 15–19	26.2	28.5	29.4	26.1	24.2	23.8	22.8	22.4	24.2	25.6	26.4	27.3	26.5	26.5	26.6	25.5	23.5
Hispanic*																	
Ages 10–14	1.7	—	—	—	—	—	—	—	—	2.3	2.4	2.4	2.5	2.6	2.6	2.6	2.4
Ages 15–17	52.1	—	—	—	—	—	—	—	—	—	65.9	69.2	68.9	68.5	69.9	68.3	64.2
Ages 18–19	126.9	—	—	—	—	—	—	—	—	—	147.7	155.5	153.9	151.1	147.5	145.4	140.0
Ages 15–19	82.2	—	—	—	—	—	—	—	—	100.8	100.3	104.6	103.3	101.8	101.3	99.3	94.6

Characteristic	1997	1998	1999	2000	2001	2002	2003	2004	2005	2006	2007	2008	2009	2010	2011	2012
All races																
Ages 10–14	1.1	1.0	0.9	0.9	0.8	0.7	0.6	0.6	0.6	0.6	0.6	0.6	0.5	0.4	0.4	0.4
Ages 15–17	31.4	29.9	28.2	26.9	24.5	23.1	22.2	21.8	21.1	21.6	21.7	21.1	19.6	17.3	15.4	14.1
Ages 18–19	82.1	80.9	79.1	78.1	75.5	72.2	69.6	68.7	68.4	71.2	71.7	68.2	64.0	58.2	54.1	51.4
Ages 15–19	51.3	50.3	48.8	47.7	45.0	42.6	41.1	40.5	39.7	41.1	41.5	40.2	37.9	34.2	31.3	29.4
White, total																
Ages 10–14	0.7	0.6	0.6	0.6	0.5	0.5	0.5	0.5	0.5	0.5	0.5	0.4	0.4	0.3	0.3	0.3
Ages 15–17	26.6	25.6	24.4	23.3	21.4	20.4	19.6	19.4	18.8	19.2	19.5	19.1	17.8	15.8	14.1	13.0
Ages 18–19	75.0	74.1	73.0	72.3	70.4	67.7	65.6	64.4	64.0	66.7	67.2	64.0	60.2	54.8	50.8	48.3
Ages 15–19	45.5	44.9	44.0	43.2	41.0	39.2	38.0	37.4	36.7	37.9	38.4	37.3	35.3	31.9	29.1	27.4
White, non-Hispanic																
Ages 10–14	0.4	0.3	0.3	0.3	0.3	0.2	0.2	0.2	0.2	0.2	0.2	0.2	0.2	0.2	0.2	0.2
Ages 15–17	19.3	18.3	17.1	15.8	14.0	13.1	12.4	12.0	11.5	11.8	11.9	11.6	11.0	10.0	9.0	8.4
Ages 18–19	62.1	60.9	59.4	57.5	54.7	52.0	50.0	48.6	48.0	49.4	50.4	48.6	46.2	42.5	39.9	37.9
Ages 15–19	36.0	35.3	34.1	32.6	30.3	28.6	27.4	26.7	26.0	26.7	27.2	26.7	25.7	23.5	21.7	20.5

the late 20th century, victim advocates and other actors for social change successfully increased public awareness about family violence and spurred calls for greater involvement of the legal system.

Child Abuse Legislation

It is important to understand that child abuse laws pertain only to people who abuse or neglect children under their care. The abusers can be parents, stepparents,

TABLE 1.1

Birth rates for adolescent females, by age, race, and Hispanic origin, 1980–2012 [CONTINUED]

[Live births per 1,000 females in specified age group]

Characteristic	1997	1998	1999	2000	2001	2002	2003	2004	2005	2006	2007	2008	2009	2010	2011	2012
Black, total																
Ages 10–14	3.1	2.8	2.5	2.3	2.0	1.8	1.5	1.6	1.6	1.5	1.4	1.3	1.1	1.0	0.9	0.8
Ages 15–17	59.3	55.4	50.5	49.0	43.7	39.5	37.5	36.3	34.5	35.3	34.7	33.5	30.9	27.3	24.7	22.0
Ages 18–19	127.7	124.8	120.6	118.8	112.9	106.3	101.3	101.3	101.2	105.6	105.2	99.5	92.9	84.8	78.8	74.4
Ages 15–19	86.3	83.5	79.1	77.4	71.3	65.8	62.5	61.7	60.1	62.2	62.1	60.1	56.5	51.1	47.3	44.0
Black, non-Hispanic																
Ages 10–14	3.2	2.9	2.6	2.4	2.1	1.9	1.6	1.6	1.6	1.5	1.4	1.4	1.1	1.0	0.9	0.8
Ages 15–17	60.7	56.8	51.7	50.1	44.8	40.6	38.2	36.4	34.1	35.2	34.6	33.6	31.0	27.4	24.6	21.9
Ages 18–19	131.0	128.2	123.9	121.9	115.9	109.5	103.4	101.6	100.2	105.1	105.2	100.0	93.5	85.6	78.8	74.1
Ages 15–19	88.3	85.7	81.0	79.2	73.1	67.7	63.8	61.9	59.4	61.9	62.0	60.4	56.8	51.5	47.3	43.9
American Indian or Alaskan Native																
Ages 10–14	1.5	1.5	1.4	1.1	0.9	0.8	0.9	0.8	0.8	0.7	0.7	0.7	0.6	0.5	0.5	0.5
Ages 15–17	41.0	39.7	36.5	34.1	30.2	28.8	27.9	26.7	26.3	25.9	26.1	25.8	23.6	20.1	18.2	17.0
Ages 18–19	107.1	106.9	98.0	97.1	92.7	85.3	82.1	79.9	78.0	80.8	86.3	80.2	73.5	66.1	61.6	60.5
Ages 15–19	65.2	64.7	59.9	58.3	54.5	50.9	49.0	47.2	46.0	46.9	49.3	47.3	43.7	38.7	36.1	34.9
Asian or Pacific Islander																
Ages 10–14	0.5	0.5	0.4	0.3	0.2	0.3	0.2	0.2	0.2	0.1	0.2	0.2	0.1	0.1	0.1	0.1
Ages 15–17	14.0	13.8	12.4	11.6	10.1	8.8	8.5	8.4	7.7	8.2	7.4	7.0	6.3	5.1	4.6	4.1
Ages 18–19	34.9	34.5	33.9	32.6	32.0	29.9	27.3	26.6	26.4	25.4	24.9	23.0	20.9	18.7	18.1	17.7
Ages 15–19	22.3	22.2	21.4	20.5	19.3	17.7	16.4	16.0	15.4	15.3	14.8	13.8	12.6	10.9	10.2	9.7
Hispanic*																
Ages 10–14	2.1	1.9	1.9	1.7	1.5	1.4	1.3	1.2	1.3	1.2	1.2	1.1	1.0	0.8	0.7	0.6
Ages 15–17	61.1	58.5	56.9	55.5	51.9	49.3	47.6	47.3	45.8	45.1	44.4	42.2	37.3	32.3	28.0	25.5
Ages 18–19	132.4	131.5	129.5	132.6	131.3	127.1	124.8	124.8	124.4	128.7	124.7	114.0	103.3	90.7	81.5	77.2
Ages 15–19	89.6	87.9	86.8	87.3	84.4	80.6	78.4	78.1	76.5	77.4	75.3	70.3	63.6	55.7	49.6	46.3

—Not available.

*Persons of Hispanic origin may be of any race. Trends for Hispanic women are affected by expansion of the reporting area in which an item on Hispanic origin is included on the birth certificate, as well as by immigration. These two factors affect numbers of events, composition of the Hispanic population, and maternal and infant health characteristics. The number of states in the reporting area increased from 22 in 1980 to 23 and the District of Columbia (DC) in 1983–1987, 30 and DC in 1988, 47 and DC in 1989, 48 and DC in 1990, 49 and DC in 1991–1992, and 50 and DC in 1993. Rates in 1981–88 were not calculated for Hispanics, Black, non-Hispanics, and White, non-Hispanics because estimates for these populations were not available.

Notes: The 1977 Office of Management and Budget (OMB) standards for data on race and ethnicity were used to classify persons into one of the following four racial groups: white, black, American Indian or Alaskan Native, or Asian or Pacific Islander. CA, HI, OH (for December only), PA, UT, and WA reported multiple-race data in 2003, following the revised 1997 OMB standards. In 2004, the following states began to report multiple-race data: FL, ID, KY, MI, MN, NH, NY State (excluding New York City), SC, and TN. Multiple-race data were reported by 19 states in 2005: FL, ID, KS, KY, NE, NH, NY State (excluding New York City), PA, SC, TN, TX, VT (beginning July 1), WA, CA, HI, MI (for births at selected facilities only), MN, OH, and UT. In 2006, 23 states reported multiple-race data: CA, DE, FL, ID, KS, KY, NE, NH, NY State (excluding New York City), ND, OH, PA, SC, SD, TN, TX, VT, WA, WY, HI, MI (for births at selected facilities only), MN, and UT. In 2007, 27 states reported multiple-race data: CA, CO, DE, FL, GA (partial year only), ID, IN, IA, KS, KY, MI (for births at most facilities), NE, NH, NY State (excluding New York City), ND, OH, PA, SC, SD, TN, TX, VT, WA, WY, HI, MN, and UT. In 2008, 30 states reported multiple-race data: CA, CO, DE, FL, GA, HI, ID, IN, IA, KS, KY, MI, MN, MT, NE, NH, NM, NY, ND, OH, OR, PA, SC, SD, TN, TX, UT, VT, WA, and WY. In 2009, 32 states and the District of Columbia (partial year only) reported multiple-race data: CA, CO, DE, FL, GA, HI, ID, IN, IA, KS, KY, MI, MN, MT, NE, NH, NM, NV (partial year only), NY, ND, OH, OK (partial year only), OR, PA, SC, SD, TN, TX, UT, VT, WA, and WY. In 2010, 38 states and the District of Columbia reported multiple-race data: CA, CO, DE, FL, GA, HI, ID, IL, IN, IA, KS, KY, LA, MD, MI, MN, MO, MT, NE, NH, NM, NV, NY, NC, ND, OH, OK, OR, PA, RI, SC, SD, TN, TX, UT, VT, WA, and WY. In 2011, 40 states and the District of Columbia reported multiple-race data: CA, CO, DE, FL, GA, HI, ID, IL, IN, IA, KS, KY, LA, MA (partial year), MD, MI, MN, MO, MT, NE, NH, NM, NV, NY, NC, ND, OH, OK, OR, PA, RI, SC, SD, TN, TX, UT, VT, WA, WI, and WY. In 2011, 41 states and the District of Columbia reported multiple-race data: CA, CO, DE, FL, GA, HI, ID, IL, IN, IA, KS, KY, LA, MA, MD, MI, MN, MO, MT, NE, NH, NM, NV, NY, NC, ND, OH, OK, OR, PA, RI, SC, SD, TN, TX, UT, VA (partial year only), VT, WA, WI, and WY. The multiple-race data for these states were bridged to the single-race categories of the 1977 OMB standards for comparability with other states. Note that data on race and Hispanic origin are collected and reported separately. Data for all years are final. Data for 2001–2009 have been revised since previous publication in *America's Children*. The revised rates use intercensal population estimates based on the 2000 and 2010 Censuses to provide more accurate rates for the period.

SOURCE: "Table FAM6. Adolescent Births: Birth Rates by Mother's Age and Race and Hispanic Origin, 1980–2012," in *America's Children in Brief: Key National Indicators of Well-Being, 2014*, Federal Interagency Forum on Child and Family Statistics, 2014, http://www.childstats.gov/americaschildren/tables/fam6.asp?popup=true (accessed July 16, 2014)

foster parents, other relatives, or other caretakers as spelled out in the law of each jurisdiction. People who victimize children who are not under their care are not considered to have committed child abuse, but they can be prosecuted for other crimes, such as assault. In addition, child abuse laws cover victims younger than 18 years old. Thus, teenagers within this age group, a population subset that is not typically considered to be "children" in other contexts, are covered.

FEDERAL LEGISLATION. At the federal level Congress has passed laws that provide funding and facilitate operation of the nation's child protection system. This legislation dates back to the passage of the Social Security Act of 1935. The act authorized funding at the federal level for grants to states for "the protection and care of homeless, dependent, and neglected children and children in danger of becoming delinquent." The Social Security Amendment Act of 1961 required each state to make child welfare services available to all children. The law further required states to provide coordination between child welfare services and social services, which served families on welfare. The law also revised the definition of child welfare services to include the prevention and remedy of child abuse. Since then the law has been amended

FIGURE 1.2

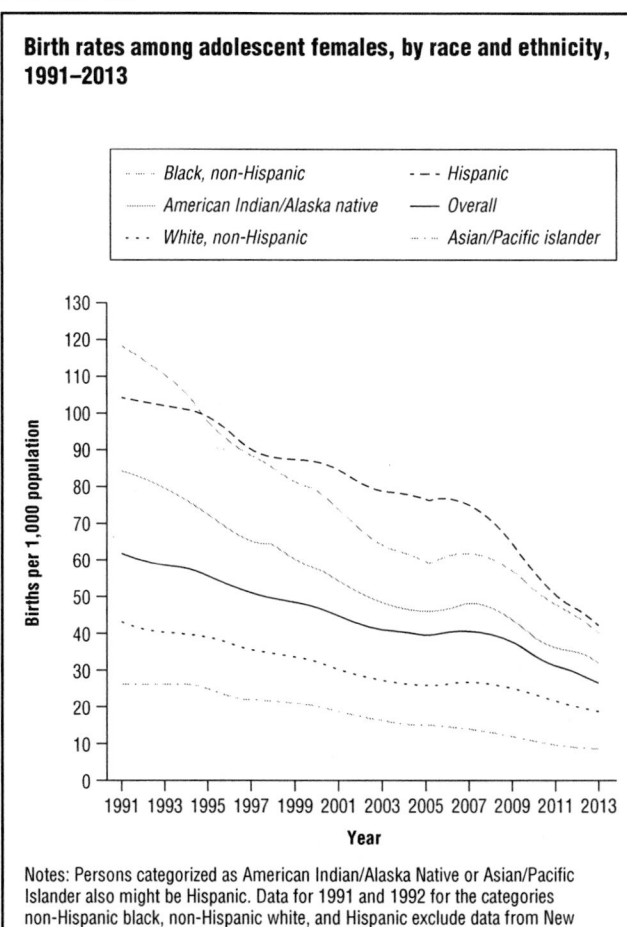

Birth rates among adolescent females, by race and ethnicity, 1991–2013

Notes: Persons categorized as American Indian/Alaska Native or Asian/Pacific Islander also might be Hispanic. Data for 1991 and 1992 for the categories non-Hispanic black, non-Hispanic white, and Hispanic exclude data from New Hampshire, which did not report Hispanic ethnicity. Includes only U.S. residents. Data for 2013 are preliminary.

SOURCE: "QuickStats: Birth Rates for Females Aged 15–19 Years, by Race/Ethnicity—National Vital Statistics System, United States, 1991–2013," in *Morbidity and Mortality Weekly Report*, vol. 63, no. 28, July 18, 2014, http://www.cdc.gov/mmwr/preview/mmwrhtml/mm6328a6.htm (accessed July 21, 2014)

to provide for additional funding for state foster care programs and child abuse prevention and treatment services. The funding programs are administered by the U.S. Department of Health and Human Services (HHS), which operates the Children's Bureau, a federal agency created in 1912 that is devoted to issues related to children.

In *Major Federal Legislation Concerned with Child Protection, Child Welfare, and Adoption* (April 2012, http://www.childwelfare.gov/pubs/otherpubs/majorfedlegis.pdf), the Children's Bureau notes that the programs authorized under the Social Security Act are "the largest federally funded programs that support State and Tribal efforts for child welfare, foster care, and adoption activities." The programs are commonly identified by the sections of the act that authorize them and include the following:

- Title IV-B Child Welfare Services and Promoting Safe and Stable Families (formerly known as Family Preservation) programs

- Title IV-E Foster Care Program

- Title IV-E Adoption Assistance Program

- Title IV-E Chafee Foster Care Independence Program

- Title XX Block Grants to States for Social Services, which is more commonly known as the Social Services Block Grant Program

Another key piece of federal legislation is the Child Abuse Prevention and Treatment Act (CAPTA), which was originally passed in 1974 and has been substantially amended since then. The Children's Bureau describes in *Major Federal Legislation Concerned with Child Protection, Child Welfare, and Adoption* the original CAPTA and its subsequent amendments as well as dozens of other related federal laws that concern child protection, child welfare, and adoption. The agency notes that the original CAPTA created the National Center on Child Abuse and Neglect to undertake the following tasks:

- Administer grant programs

- Identify issues and areas needing special focus for new research and demonstration project activities

- Serve as the focal point for the collection of information, improvement of programs, dissemination of materials, and information on best practices to States and localities

As of November 2014, CAPTA was most recently reauthorized in December 2010 through the CAPTA Reauthorization Act, which extended the legislation through the year 2015. In *About CAPTA: A Legislative History* (July 2011, http://www.childwelfare.gov/pubs/factsheets/about.pdf), the Children's Bureau lists the functions of CAPTA:

- Provides federal funding to states to support prevention, assessment, investigation, prosecution, and treatment activities

- Provides federal grants to public agencies and nonprofit organizations, including Native American tribes and tribal organizations, for demonstration programs and projects

- Identifies the federal role in supporting research, evaluation, technical assistance, and data collection activities

- Mandates operation of the Child Welfare Information Gateway (https://www.childwelfare.gov), a clearinghouse for data and information related to child abuse and the child protection system

- Sets forth a minimum definition of child abuse and neglect

The Children's Bureau notes in *Definitions of Child Abuse and Neglect* (February 2011, http://www.child

TABLE 1.2

Living arrangements of children under 18, by sex, age, race and Hispanic origin, marital status of parents, and other characteristics, 2013

[Numbers in thousands]

	Total	Living with both parents		Living with mother only					Living with father only					Living with neither parent
		Married to each other	Not married to each other	Married spouse absent	Widowed	Divorced	Separated	Never married	Married spouse absent	Widowed	Divorced	Separated	Never married	No parent present
All children	73,910	47,611	3,034	898	516	5,250	2,479	8,389	135	131	1,314	501	917	2,733
Male	37,788	24,287	1,607	493	252	2,709	1,178	4,208	69	76	722	257	472	1,457
Female	36,122	23,325	1,427	405	264	2,540	1,301	4,181	65	55	593	245	446	1,276
Both sexes														
Total	73,910	47,611	3,034	898	516	5,250	2,479	8,389	135	131	1,314	501	917	2,733
Age of child														
Under 1 year	3,873	2,444	508	42	4	58	84	554	—	—	13	8	59	99
1–2 years	7,994	5,144	662	75	27	205	186	1,243	11	3	38	23	127	248
3–5 years	12,171	7,782	662	142	51	506	382	1,804	10	1	134	88	180	428
6–8 years	12,290	7,979	477	161	51	794	452	1,459	30	30	191	90	161	414
9–11 years	12,224	8,039	289	122	76	1,065	428	1,271	34	23	239	92	139	407
12–14 years	12,491	8,060	261	170	122	1,261	476	1,035	28	27	301	108	140	504
15–17 years	12,866	8,164	176	187	184	1,360	471	1,023	21	47	398	92	112	632
Race														
White alone	54,227	38,135	2,168	555	355	3,873	1,650	3,596	84	85	1,065	358	563	1,739
Black alone	11,086	3,813	490	190	107	930	563	3,809	29	21	114	84	257	678
Asian alone	3,591	2,983	64	89	23	121	53	99	9	13	31	26	11	69
All remaining single races and all race combinations	5,006	2,680	313	64	32	325	212	885	12	12	104	33	86	246
Hispanic*	17,709	10,300	1,221	385	121	1,096	939	2,394	31	22	144	120	253	684
Presence of siblings														
None	15,238	7,217	764	158	125	1,134	374	2,475	32	35	424	130	441	1,931
One sibling	28,971	19,832	1,125	352	213	2,188	867	2,792	49	58	587	177	279	451
Two siblings	18,027	12,665	643	228	92	1,237	734	1,739	41	23	215	101	115	194
Three siblings	7,143	4,877	269	95	55	438	327	774	9	16	52	51	70	111
Four siblings	2,659	1,682	139	40	20	171	130	392	3	—	25	22	8	27
Five or more siblings	1,873	1,340	95	26	12	82	46	217	—	—	12	20	5	18
Presence of parent's unmarried partner														
Child's parent does not have opposite sex partner	68,624	47,611	261	877	466	4,439	2,333	7,577	124	105	1,037	449	613	2,733
Child's parent has opposite sex partner	5,286	—	2,773	22	50	811	146	812	11	26	278	52	305	—
Partner is also other parent	2,773	—	2,773	—	—	—	—	—	—	—	—	—	—	—
Partner is not other parent	2,513	—	—	22	50	811	146	812	11	26	278	52	305	—
Highest education of either parent														
No parents present	2,733	—	—	—	—	—	—	—	—	—	—	—	—	2,733
Less than 9th grade	2,329	1,386	146	73	28	105	138	357	9	9	17	24	36	—
9th to 12th grade, no diploma	4,917	1,907	274	149	70	308	376	1,475	11	7	89	112	140	—
High school graduate	15,535	8,095	1,145	234	136	1,219	746	2,932	43	58	384	163	381	—
Some college or AA degree	20,761	12,317	1,073	269	167	2,214	892	2,884	45	42	491	126	243	—
Bachelor's degree	15,719	13,104	293	107	74	1,004	242	532	21	10	210	43	78	—
Prof. or graduate degree	11,916	10,804	104	65	41	400	86	209	5	6	123	34	40	—
Presence of adults other than parent														
Other relatives only	17,206	8,923	525	358	185	1,200	739	2,733	51	28	233	93	234	1,904
Non relatives only	3,814	396	103	35	58	828	177	923	13	23	264	59	323	612
Both relatives and non relatives	1,074	199	49	19	9	135	70	245	2	4	61	26	39	216
No other relatives or non relatives	51,815	38,093	2,358	486	264	3,087	1,492	4,487	69	77	757	323	321	1

TABLE 1.2

Living arrangements of children under 18, by sex, age, race and Hispanic origin, marital status of parents, and other characteristics, 2013 [CONTINUED]

[Numbers in thousands]

	Total	Living with both parents — Married to each other	Living with both parents — Not married to each other	Living with mother only — Married spouse absent	Mother only — Widowed	Mother only — Divorced	Mother only — Separated	Mother only — Never married	Living with father only — Married spouse absent	Father only — Widowed	Father only — Divorced	Father only — Separated	Father only — Never married	Living with neither parent — No parent present
Child support receipt—Mom														
Parent not present	5,731	—	—	—	—	—	—	—	135	131	1,314	501	917	2,733
Does not receive child support	60,949	45,898	2,678	788	463	2,818	1,844	6,459	—	—	—	—	—	—
Receives child support	7,229	1,713	356	110	53	2,432	635	1,930	—	—	—	—	—	—
Child support receipt—Dad														
Parent not present	20,265	—	—	898	516	5,250	2,479	8,389	—	—	—	—	—	2,733
Does not receive child support	53,239	47,423	3,005	—	—	—	—	—	134	131	1,194	475	876	—
Receives child support	406	188	29	—	—	—	—	—	1	—	120	27	41	—
Stay at home married mom														
Child 15 or over, or not with two parents	34,462	8,164	3,034	898	516	5,250	2,479	8,389	135	131	1,314	501	917	2,733
Parent in labor force (LF) 1 or more weeks last year	25,507	25,507	—	—	—	—	—	—	—	—	—	—	—	—
Parent not in LF (NILF) 52wks lst yr caring for family, spouse in LF 52wks	10,818	10,818	—	—	—	—	—	—	—	—	—	—	—	—
Parent NILF 52wks lst yr caring for family, spouse NILF 1 or more wks	1,281	1,281	—	—	—	—	—	—	—	—	—	—	—	—
Parent NILF 52wks lst yr for other reason	1,841	1,841	—	—	—	—	—	—	—	—	—	—	—	—
Stay at home married dad														
Child 15 or over, or not with two parents	34,462	8,164	3,034	898	516	5,250	2,479	8,389	135	131	1,314	501	917	2,733
Parent in labor force (LF) 1 or more weeks last year	36,932	36,932	—	—	—	—	—	—	—	—	—	—	—	—
Parent not in LF (NILF) 52wks lst yr caring for family, spouse in LF 52wks	434	434	—	—	—	—	—	—	—	—	—	—	—	—
Parent NILF 52wks lst yr caring for family, spouse NILF 1 or more wks	240	240	—	—	—	—	—	—	—	—	—	—	—	—
Parent NILF 52wks lst yr for other reason	1,843	1,843	—	—	—	—	—	—	—	—	—	—	—	—
Parents labor force status														
Father in labor force, mother not present	2,678	—	—	—	—	—	—	—	123	105	1,219	424	807	—
Father not in labor force, mother not present	321	—	—	—	—	—	—	—	11	26	96	78	111	—
Mother in labor force, father not present	13,167	—	—	642	286	4,385	1,854	6,000	—	—	—	—	—	—
Mother not in labor force, father not present	4,365	—	—	256	230	865	625	2,390	—	—	—	—	—	—
Mother and father in labor force	30,402	28,803	1,599	—	—	—	—	—	—	—	—	—	—	—
Father in labor force, mother not in labor force	16,131	15,114	1,017	—	—	—	—	—	—	—	—	—	—	—
Mother in labor force, father not in labor force	2,527	2,293	234	—	—	—	—	—	—	—	—	—	—	—
Father not in labor force, mother not in labor force	1,586	1,401	184	—	—	—	—	—	—	—	—	—	—	—
No parents present	2,733	—	—	—	—	—	—	—	—	—	—	—	—	2,733
Family income														
Under $2,500	2,988	494	492	119	31	198	214	711	6	3	10	14	41	655
$2,500 to $4,999	884	150	94	40	15	113	72	311	2	2	9	10	10	55
$5,000 to $7,499	1,145	195	113	47	6	137	108	453	—	5	4	9	17	52
$7,500 to $9,999	1,229	258	120	30	19	158	139	404	4	4	14	8	19	50
$10,000 to $12,499	1,932	477	194	50	26	180	200	608	7	5	30	10	43	104
$12,500 to $14,999	1,523	380	134	55	30	185	103	508	2	2	8	12	27	76
$15,000 to $19,999	3,637	1,122	242	74	40	441	267	1,026	16	—	91	82	96	139
$20,000 to $24,999	3,630	1,476	269	73	35	388	254	799	16	11	55	30	65	157
$25,000 to $29,999	3,429	1,515	223	77	44	361	211	621	8	9	101	26	62	170
$30,000 to $39,999	6,813	3,540	341	53	89	821	241	979	25	20	210	87	153	255

TABLE 1.2

Living arrangements of children under 18, by sex, age, race and Hispanic origin, marital status of parents, and other characteristics, 2013 [CONTINUED]

[Numbers in thousands]

	Total	Living with both parents		Living with mother only					Living with father only					Living with neither parent
		Married to each other	Not married to each other	Married spouse absent	Widowed	Divorced	Separated	Never married	Married spouse absent	Widowed	Divorced	Separated	Never married	No parent present
$40,000 to $49,999	5,673	3,429	181	77	38	635	185	583	4	16	149	56	110	211
$50,000 to $74,999	12,274	8,911	316	77	65	946	305	736	15	11	305	77	142	367
$75,000 to $99,999	9,277	7,768	193	69	36	310	97	304	8	15	149	44	65	219
$100,00 and over	19,475	17,895	122	57	41	376	83	346	22	30	180	38	67	220
Health insurance coverage														
Covered by health insurance	67,360	44,091	2,682	764	444	4,815	2,174	7,576	107	112	1,171	449	812	2,164
Not covered by health insurance	6,550	3,520	353	134	72	435	305	814	27	20	143	53	106	568
Poverty status														
Below 100% of poverty	16,428	5,249	1,447	471	183	1,492	1,238	4,436	31	28	183	152	242	1,277
100% to 199% of poverty	16,131	8,896	829	195	147	1,580	703	2,293	55	25	360	130	275	645
200% of poverty and above	41,350	33,466	759	233	186	2,178	538	1,661	48	79	771	220	400	811
Household food stamp receipt														
No	58,264	42,453	1,945	501	367	3,661	1,337	3,721	97	98	1,133	354	683	1,912
Yes	15,646	5,159	1,089	397	149	1,588	1,142	4,668	37	33	181	148	234	820
Household public asst receipt														
No	70,978	46,989	2,826	814	485	5,003	2,235	7,302	121	119	1,276	478	872	2,458
Yes	2,931	623	208	84	31	247	244	1,087	13	12	38	24	46	274
Household tenure														
Own/buying	44,956	34,498	990	357	302	2,452	807	2,304	82	102	805	242	376	1,639
Rent	28,213	12,771	2,005	537	210	2,711	1,631	5,948	51	29	494	247	538	1,041
No cash rent	741	342	40	4	4	87	42	137	2	1	15	13	3	52

*Hispanics may be of any race.

Dash "—" represents or rounds to zero.

Note: Excludes children in group quarters, and those who are a family reference person or spouse.

SOURCE: Adapted from "C3. Living Arrangements of Children under 18 Years and Marital Status of Parents, by Age, Sex, Race, and Hispanic Origin and Selected Characteristics of the Child for All Children: 2013," in "America's Families and Living Arrangements: 2013: Children (C Table Series)," *Families and Living Arrangements*, U.S. Census Bureau, November 2013, http://www.census.gov/hhes/families/files/cps2013/tabC3-all .xls (accessed July 17, 2014)

TABLE 1.3

Economic circumstances of children under 18, by family structure, 2012

[Numbers in thousands]

| Characteristic | Total | Living with two parents | | Living with one parent | | Not living with any parent |
		Married	Unmarried	Mother only	Father only	
Number	**73,817**	**47,330**	**2,937**	**17,990**	**2,925**	**2,634**
Family income						
Under $15,000	9,746	1,824	997	5,638	397	893
$15,000 to $29,999	10,856	4,175	743	4,843	601	497
$30,000 to $49,999	13,083	7,531	609	3,708	715	520
$50,000 to $74,999	12,600	9,157	346	2,085	684	328
$75,000 to $99,999	9,145	7,807	111	780	246	202
$100,000 and over	18,387	16,836	134	938	286	193
Poverty status[a]						
Below 100 percent of poverty	16,397	5,155	1,344	8,152	586	1,160
100 to 199 percent of poverty	16,471	9,162	832	4,969	813	695
200 percent of poverty and above	40,949	33,012	761	4,869	1,527	780
Household receives public assistance						
Receives assistance	3,497	835	218	2,031	102	310
Does not receive assistance	70,321	46,495	2,720	15,960	2,821	2,325
Household receives food stamps						
Receives food stamps	15,673	5,230	1,016	8,037	633	759
Does not receive food stamps	58,144	42,100	1,921	9,954	2,292	1,876
Household tenure						
Owned home	45,134	34,431	1,055	6,408	1,608	1,630
Rented home[b]	28,683	12,899	1,882	11,581	1,317	1,004
Health insurance coverage						
Covered by health insurance	66,930	43,760	2,590	16,004	2,486	2,089
Not covered by health insurance	6,887	3,570	348	1,987	437	546
Parental employment status						
Father only in labor force	18,272	14,839	896	X	2,536	X
Mother only in labor force	15,778	2,141	171	13,465	X	X
Both father and mother in labor force	30,624	28,903	1,720	X	X	X
No coresident parent in labor force	6,510	1,446	150	4,525	389	X
No parents present	2,634	X	X	X	X	2,634
Percent	**100.0**	**100.0**	**100.0**	**100.0**	**100.0**	**100.0**
Family income						
Under $15,000	13.2	3.9	33.9	31.3	13.6	33.9
$15,000 to $29,999	14.7	8.8	25.3	26.9	20.5	18.9
$30,000 to $49,999	17.7	15.9	20.7	20.6	24.4	19.7
$50,000 to $74,999	17.1	19.3	11.8	11.6	23.4	12.5
$75,000 to $99,999	12.4	16.5	3.8	4.3	8.4	7.7
$100,000 and over	24.9	35.6	4.6	5.2	9.8	7.3
Poverty status[a]						
Below 100 percent of poverty	22.2	10.9	45.8	45.3	20.0	44.0
100 to 199 percent of poverty	22.3	19.4	28.3	27.6	27.8	26.4
200 percent of poverty and above	55.5	69.7	25.9	27.1	52.2	29.6
Household receives public assistance						
Receives assistance	4.7	1.8	7.4	11.3	3.5	11.8
Does not receive assistance	95.3	98.2	92.6	88.7	96.4	88.3
Household receives food stamps						
Receives food stamps	21.2	11.1	34.6	44.7	21.6	28.8
Does not receive food stamps	78.8	88.9	65.4	55.3	78.4	71.2
Household tenure						
Owned home	61.1	72.7	35.9	35.6	55.0	61.9
Rented home[b]	38.9	27.3	64.1	64.4	45.0	38.1

welfare.gov/systemwide/laws_policies/statutes/define.pdf) that the CAPTA Reauthorization Act of 2010 defines child abuse and neglect as "any recent act or failure to act on the part of a parent or caretaker, which results in death, serious physical or emotional harm, sexual abuse, or exploitation, or an act or failure to act which presents an imminent risk of serious harm."

STATE LEGISLATION. The Children's Bureau states in "Definitions of Child Abuse and Neglect in Federal Law" (2014, https://www.childwelfare.gov/can/defining/federal.cfm) that "while Federal legislation sets minimum standards for States that accept CAPTA funding, each State provides its own definitions of maltreatment within civil and criminal statutes."

TABLE 1.3

Economic circumstances of children under 18, by family structure, 2012 [CONTINUED]

[Numbers in thousands]

Characteristic	Total	Living with two parents		Living with one parent		Not living with any parent
		Married	Unmarried	Mother only	Father only	
Health insurance coverage						
Covered by health insurance	90.7	92.5	88.2	89.0	85.0	79.3
Not covered by health insurance	9.3	7.5	11.8	11.0	14.9	20.7
Parental employment status						
Father only in labor force	24.8	31.4	30.5	X	86.7	X
Mother only in labor force	21.4	4.5	5.8	74.8	X	X
Both father and mother in labor force	41.5	61.1	58.6	X	X	X
No coresident parent in labor force	8.8	3.1	5.1	25.2	13.3	X
No parents present	3.6	X	X	X	X	100.0

X Not applicable.
[a]For children in both primary families and subfamilies, poverty status of the primary family is shown.
[b]"No cash rent" is included with rented home.
Note: Data based on the Annual Social and Economic Supplement to the 2012 Current Population Survey. All people under age 18, excluding group quarters, householders, subfamily reference people, and their spouses or unmarried partners.

SOURCE: Jonathan Vespa, Jamie M. Lewis, and Rose M. Kreider, "Table 10. Children's Economic Situation by Family Structure: CPS 2012," in *America's Families and Living Arrangements: 2012*, U.S. Department of Commerce, Economics and Statistics Administration, U.S. Census Bureau, August 2013, http://www.census.gov/prod/2013pubs/p20-570.pdf (accessed July 17, 2014)

Local child protective services agencies operate under local or state jurisdiction. As is explained in Chapter 2, the agencies receive and investigate reports of child maltreatment and refer families for treatment services as appropriate. In some cases child maltreatment offenses rise to the level of criminal acts, and in these situations the agencies refer the cases to local law enforcement for prosecution. District attorneys (or prosecutors) prosecute people who are accused of committing criminal acts. The National District Attorneys Association oversees the National Center for Prosecution of Child Abuse. Among other things, the center operates the website "State Statutes" (http://www.ndaa.org/ncpca_state_statutes.html), which lists state statutes that deal with criminal child abuse offenses.

Under state civil laws, child protective services agencies coordinate with juvenile courts (or dependency or family courts, as they are known) in cases in which the state believes that children should be removed from their home and placed in temporary foster care. In addition, the state can pursue legal action to terminate the parental or custody rights of child abusers. The Children's Bureau maintains the website "State Statutes Search" (https://www.childwelfare.gov/systemwide/laws_policies/state), which lists state civil statutes that deal with child abuse and neglect, child welfare, and adoption.

In *Definitions of Child Abuse and Neglect*, the Children's Bureau notes that state civil laws typically cover four types of child abuse:

- Physical abuse—this is commonly described in state statues as "any nonaccidental physical injury to the child" and includes behaviors such as striking, kicking, burning, or biting the child or otherwise causing physical impairment. Many states also include "acts or circumstances that threaten the child with harm or create a substantial risk of harm to the child's health or welfare."

- Neglect—neglect is typically defined as "failure of a parent or other person with responsibility for the child to provide needed food, clothing, shelter, medical care, or supervision to the degree that the child's health, safety, and well-being are threatened with harm." Some states also include education neglect (failing to educate a child as required by law) and medical neglect (failing to provide needed medical treatment).

- Sexual abuse/exploitation—sexual abuse involves physically sexual acts that are conducted with children. These acts may be defined by law in general or specific terms. In addition, sexual exploitation involves using a child for the purposes of sexual gratification, for example, through prostitution or pornography.

- Emotional abuse—emotional abuse is commonly defined as "injury to the psychological capacity or emotional stability of the child as evidenced by an observable or substantial change in behavior, emotional response, or cognition." Evidence of injury from emotional abuse typically includes "anxiety, depression, withdrawal, or aggressive behavior."

Besides the four major types of abuse, the Children's Bureau notes that some state civil laws pertaining to child abuse also cover parental substance abuse and abandonment of a child.

Domestic Violence Legislation

FEDERAL LEGISLATION. The HHS indicates in "Information Memorandum" (March 28, 2011, http://www.acf.hhs.gov/sites/default/files/fysb/fvpsa_info_memo_2011_0.pdf) that via the Child Abuse Amendments of 1984 Congress enacted the Family Violence Prevention and Services Act (FVPSA), which provides federal funding to public and private entities that are devoted to domestic violence prevention and services. These entities include "States, Indian Tribes and Tribal organizations, local public agencies, nonprofit private organizations, and other persons seeking such assistance to implement programs to address the problem." The FVPSA has been amended and reauthorized over the years. As of November 2014, the most recent amendment occurred in December 2010 by way of passage of the CAPTA Reauthorization Act of 2010. The FVPSA (December 14, 2010, http://www.govtrack.us/congress/bills/111/s3817/text) provides funding for the following purposes:

- Assist States and Indian tribes in efforts to increase public awareness about, and primary and secondary prevention of, family violence, domestic violence, and dating violence

- Assist States and Indian tribes in efforts to provide immediate shelter and supportive services for victims of family violence, domestic violence, or dating violence, and their dependents

- Provide for a national domestic violence hotline

- Provide for technical assistance and training relating to family violence, domestic violence, and dating violence programs to States and Indian tribes, local public agencies (including law enforcement agencies, courts, and legal, social service, and health care professionals in public agencies), nonprofit private organizations (including faith-based and charitable organizations, community-based organizations, and voluntary associations), tribal organizations, and other persons seeking such assistance and training

In 1994 Congress passed the Violence against Women Act (VAWA) to enhance the investigation and prosecution of violent crimes against women, such as domestic violence, sexual assaults, and stalking. The following year the Office on Violence against Women (OVW) was created within the U.S. Department of Justice (DOJ). In "About the Office" (2014, http://www.ovw.usdoj.gov/overview.htm), the OVW explains that the VAWA "emerged from the efforts of a broad, grassroots coalition of advocates and survivors who informed the work of Congress." The agency administers financial and technical assistance to state and local programs that are devoted to the prevention of domestic violence, dating violence, sexual assault, and stalking.

The VAWA has been controversial since its passage. The original law granted female victims of violence, including battered women, federal civil rights protection. The civil rights section of the act was tested in 1996, when Christy Brzonkala filed a civil suit after allegedly being raped by two football players from Virginia Polytechnic Institute. In *United States v. Morrison et al.* (529 U.S. 598 [2000]), the U.S. Supreme Court ruled that Congress could not enact "a federal civil remedy for the victims of gender-motivated violence." Individuals who committed crimes motivated by a gender bias, the court stated, could not be held accountable at the federal level.

In 2000 Congress passed the Victims of Trafficking and Violence Protection Act (a revised VAWA), which included the sections Strengthening Law Enforcement to Reduce Violence against Women, Strengthening Services to Victims of Violence, Limiting the Effects of Violence on Children, and Strengthening Education and Training to Combat Violence against Women. As a result of the Supreme Court ruling, the new legislation made no mention of women's civil rights. The VAWA was renewed in 2005. The law was reauthorized again in March 2013 and included several new provisions aimed at extending protection to specific groups. As Julia Dahl reports in "President Obama Signs Violence against Women Act" (CBSNews.com, March 7, 2013), the reauthorized version of the law guaranteed Native American victims of domestic violence the right to pursue legal recourse against nonnative assailants. At the same time, the reauthorization of VAWA granted lesbian, gay, bisexual, and transgendered (LGBT) groups the right to apply for grants aimed at protecting LGBT individuals from acts of violence. The law also granted new protections to immigrant women, while providing housing assistance for women who no longer felt safe in their homes. Even after the passage of the VAWA reauthorization, lawmakers continued to craft additional legislation designed to establish further protections for victims of domestic violence. One notable effort was the Protecting Domestic Violence and Stalking Victims Act (https://www.congress.gov/bill/113th-congress/senate-bill/1290), which aimed to prevent perpetrators of domestic violence from acquiring firearms. As of November 2014, the proposed law was still in committee.

In "Grant Programs" (2014, http://www.ovw.usdoj.gov/ovwgrantprograms.htm), the OVW describes 24 grant programs that it operates. Some grants fund projects involving violence prevention and victim services provided in certain settings (e.g., college campuses) and for specific victim types (e.g., disabled women). In addition, grants provide funds to law enforcement agencies and courts to enhance their responses to domestic violence, dating violence, sexual assault, and stalking.

STATE LEGISLATION. State criminal laws specify the actions that are considered to be criminal offenses. All states further specify certain types of criminal offenses as domestic violence. The Justice Research and Statistics

Association (JRSA) is a nonprofit organization that compiles and publishes statistics related to issues of justice. Its Domestic Violence, Sexual Assault, and Stalking Data Resource Center (http://www.jrsa.org/dvsa-drc) lists the applicable statute for each state. The JRSA notes that state definitions of domestic violence vary widely but typically focus on violence between intimate partners. Some states exclude same-sex relationships and/or dating relationships, while others specify that intimate partners must be sexually involved for domestic violence statutes to apply.

For example, California's Domestic Violence Prevention Act is codified at Family Code Sections 6200 to 6219 (2014, http://www.leginfo.ca.gov/cgi-bin/display code?section=fam&group=06001-07000&file=6200-6219). It defines domestic abuse in terms of the offenses committed and the victim-offender relationship. The latter includes current and former spouses, cohabitants, people having "a dating or engagement relationship," and people who have had a child together. The law also includes certain children and any person "related by consanguinity or affinity within the second degree." *Consanguinity* and *affinity* are terms that often appear in legal definitions of domestic violence. Although they have specific meanings as set forth in state laws, in general *consanguinity* refers to biological relationships and *affinity* refers to relationships that are established through marriage. The degrees of consanguinity and affinity refer to the relative "closeness" of two parties. For example, a father and daughter have first-degree consanguinity, whereas a niece and uncle have second-degree consanguinity. Likewise, a husband and wife have first-degree affinity, whereas a woman and her husband's brother have second-degree affinity.

Domestic violence cases are also covered by civil laws, in that victims can sue their alleged attackers for monetary damages. Civil lawsuits can be brought even in cases in which criminal charges fail to achieve convictions. This gives victims another legal avenue against their abusers. In addition, victims can file civil lawsuits against third parties that are accused of helping in some way to facilitate domestic violence or for failing in legally required circumstances to interact on the victim's behalf. Chapter 9 describes major third-party lawsuits involving domestic violence that have shaped the legal system's responses to the problem.

Family Violence Reporting Requirements

One of the challenges of bringing family violence into the realm of the legal system is the secrecy that often surrounds such cases. In the past, authorities only became aware of problems if family members or perhaps concerned relatives or friends chose to notify the police or other public officials. To overcome this veil of secrecy, laws have been passed that require certain parties, such as teachers and doctors, to report to authorities any suspected or known cases of abuse that come to their attention.

In 1961 the pediatric radiologist C. Henry Kempe (1922–1984) and his associates proposed the term *battered-child syndrome* at a symposium on the problem of child abuse held under the auspices of the American Academy of Pediatrics. The term refers to the collection of injuries that are sustained by a child as a result of repeated mistreatment or beatings. The following year Kempe et al. published the landmark article "The Battered-Child Syndrome" (*Journal of the American Medical Association*, vol. 181, no. 1, July 7, 1962). The term *battered-child syndrome* eventually evolved into the word *maltreatment*, which encompasses not only physical assault but also other forms of abuse, such as malnourishment, failure to thrive, medical neglect, and sexual and emotional abuse.

Kempe et al. proposed that physicians be required to report child abuse. According to the National Association of Counsel for Children, by 1967, after Kempe et al.'s findings had gained general acceptance among health and welfare workers and the public, 44 states had passed legislation that required the reporting of child abuse to official agencies, and the remaining six states had voluntary reporting laws. Initially, only doctors were required to report and then only in cases of "serious physical injury" or "nonaccidental injury." In the 21st century all 50 states and the District of Columbia have laws that require not only doctors but also most professionals who serve children to report all forms of suspected abuse and either require or permit any citizen to report child abuse.

One of the reasons for the lack of prosecution of early child abuse cases was the difficulty in determining whether a physical injury was due to a deliberate assault or an accident. In the latter part of the 20th century, however, doctors of pediatric radiology were able to determine the incidence of repeated child abuse through sophisticated developments in x-ray technology. These advances allowed radiologists to see more clearly things such as subdural hematomas (blood clots around the brain resulting from blows to the head) and abnormal fractures. As a result, these advances brought about more recognition in the medical community of the widespread incidence of child abuse, along with growing public condemnation of abuse.

Reporting requirement laws have made a significant impact to the child protection system. The Children's Bureau indicates in *Child Maltreatment 2012* (December 17, 2013, http://www.acf.hhs.gov/sites/default/files/cb/cm2012.pdf) that professionals, such as educators and medical providers, were the sources for more than 1.2 million reports of suspected child abuse in 2012. As of

November 2014, the reporting requirements for child abuse were extensive and still growing. As is discussed further in Chapter 4, highly publicized cases of child abuse, particularly sexual abuse, during the early years of the 21st century have spurred legislators to expand the requirements to more professions and more settings.

Although some states have also implemented reporting requirements for domestic violence, the scope of this effort is not nearly as large as it is for child abuse cases. For example, according to the Kentucky Medical Association in *Reporting Requirements* (February 2012, https://www.kyma.org/uploads/file/Committee%20Meeting%20Documents/Domestic%20Violence/REPORTING%20REQUIREMENTS.pdf), "any" suspected or known abuse or neglect of a child must be reported to authorities. However, the state only requires reporting of cases involving adult victims when the abuse or neglect is believed to have been inflicted by the victim's spouse or in cases in which the adult has mental or physical disorders that render him or her particularly vulnerable to abuse.

SOCIAL AND PUBLIC HEALTH ISSUES

Society expects that biological ties or personal intimate relations between people will facilitate peaceful interactions (that is, interactions that are characterized by an interest in and a desire to maintain the other person's well-being). In child abuse and domestic violence cases such expectations are horribly dashed. The perpetrators of these crimes break the social code of conduct in which civilized people believe that parents will nurture and not harm their children and that adults in intimate relationships will not commit violence against each other. Therefore, child abuse and domestic violence are not just legal matters, they violate the social order of society.

In addition, child abuse and domestic violence have public health ramifications. As will be explained in subsequent chapters, victims of these traumatic events can suffer both short-term and long-term consequences to their physical and emotional well-being. In 2005 the U.S. surgeon general held a workshop on child abuse, "Making Prevention of Child Maltreatment a National Priority: Implementing Innovations of a Public Health Approach" (http://www.ncbi.nlm.nih.gov/books/NBK47486), at which Charles Wilson, the director of the San Diego Children's Hospital and Health Center, stated that child maltreatment was "a public health crisis, the full scale of which is masked by secrecy and denial." In 2010 the National Center for Injury Prevention and Control, a part of the Centers for Disease Control and Prevention (CDC), conducted the National Intimate Partner and Sexual Violence Survey, a comprehensive survey that collected information from adults about their experiences of sexual violence, stalking, and intimate partner violence. In *National Intimate Partner and Sexual Violence Survey: 2010 Summary Report* (November 2011, http://www.cdc.gov/violenceprevention/pdf/nisvs_report2010-a.pdf), Michele C. Black et al. describe the numerous health consequences that victims suffer and note that "sexual violence, stalking, and intimate partner violence are major public health problems in the United States."

The Status of U.S. Children

The Federal Interagency Forum on Child and Family Statistics (known simply as the Forum) regularly collects information about the well-being of U.S. children. Since 1997 the agency has published reports presenting its findings. In *America's Children in Brief: Key National Indicators of Well-Being, 2013*, the Forum reports on the status of U.S. children based on data compiled between 2011 and 2013. Table 1.4 summarizes selected data indicators. The child population in 2013 was 73.6 million, meaning that children made up nearly a quarter (23.3%) of the total U.S. population. More than half (52.4%) of children in 2013 were non-Hispanic white. As shown in Figure 1.3, this percentage has been dropping for decades and is expected to continue to decline through 2050, when non-Hispanic white children are projected to make up around 40% of the child population. By contrast, the Hispanic child population has been growing dramatically, and its share is expected to increase to about 40% by 2050.

In 2013 nearly two-thirds (64%) of U.S. children aged 17 years and younger lived with two married parents. (See Table 1.4.) Roughly half of children aged zero to four years received their primary child care from a relative (49%); among children aged three to six years, more than half (61%) were in center-based care arrangements. (Table 1.5 lists the various kinds of child care arrangements that are commonly used.) As shown in Table 1.4, in 2012 the birth rate among unmarried women aged 15 to 44 years was 45 births per 1,000 women; among females aged 15 to 17 years, the birth rate was 14 births per 1,000 women.

The socioeconomic status of children is of particular concern as a public health matter and has implications to child abuse prevalence rates. Chapter 3 examines the risk factors that are associated with child maltreatment and describes studies that find higher risks for children of lower socioeconomic status. As shown in Table 1.4, nearly a quarter (22%) of U.S. children were "in poverty" in 2012. Although there are differing federal definitions for poverty, the Forum based its data on poverty income thresholds, which are determined by the U.S. Census Bureau. The thresholds are minimum income levels for different family sizes and compositions. For example, the Forum notes that in 2011 the poverty

TABLE 1.4

TABLE 1.4

National indicators of children's well-being, 2011–13

National indicators of children's well-being, 2011–13 [CONTINUED]

	Most recent value (year)
Demographic background	
Child population[a]	
Children ages 0–17 in the United States	73.6 million (2013)
Children as a percentage of the population[a]	
Children ages 0–17 in the United States	23.3% (2013)
Racial and ethnic composition[a]	
Children ages 0–17 by race and Hispanic origin[b]	
White, non-Hispanic	52.4% (2013)
Black, non-Hispanic	13.8% (2013)
American Indian or Alaska Native, non-Hispanic	0.9% (2013)
Asian, non-Hispanic	4.6% (2013)
Native Hawaiian or other Pacific Islander, non-Hispanic	0.2% (2013)
Two or more races, non-Hispanic	4.0% (2013)
Hispanic	24.1% (2013)
Family and social environment	
Family structure and children's living arrangements	
Children ages 0–17 living with two married parents	64% (2013)
Births to unmarried women	
Births to unmarried women ages 15–44	45 per 1,000 (2012)
Births that are to unmarried women among all births	41% (2012)
Child care	
Children ages 0–4, with employed mothers, whose primary child care arrangement is with a relative	49% (2011)
Children ages 3–6, not yet in kindergarten, who were in center-based care arrangements	61% (2012)
Children of at least one foreign-born parent	
Children ages 0–17 living with at least one foreign-born parent	24% (2013)
Language spoken at home and difficulty speaking English	
Children ages 5–17 who speak a language other than English at home	22.3% (2012)
Children ages 5–17 who speak a language other than English at home and who have difficulty speaking English	5% (2012)
Adolescent births	
Births to females ages 15–17	14 per 1,000 (2012)
Child maltreatment[a]	
Substantiated reports of maltreatment of children ages 0–17	9.8 per 1,000 (2012)
Economic circumstances	
Child poverty and family income	
Children ages 0–17 in poverty	22% (2012)
Secure parental employment	
Children ages 0–17 living with at least one parent employed year round, full time	73% (2012)
Food insecurity	
Children ages 0–17 in households classified by USDA as "food insecure"	22% (2012)
Health	
Emotional and behavioral difficulties	
Children ages 4–17 reported by a parent to have serious difficulties with emotions, concentration, behavior, or getting along with other people	5% (2012)
Adolescent depression	
Youth ages 12–17 with past-year Major Depressive Episode	9% (2012)
Activity limitation	
Children ages 5–17 with activity limitation resulting from one or more chronic health conditions	9% (2012)

[a]Population estimates are not sample derived and thus not subject to statistical testing. Change between years identifies differences in the proportionate size of these estimates.
[b]Percentages may not sum to 100 due to rounding.

SOURCE: Adapted from "America's Children at a Glance," in *America's Children in Brief: Key National Indicators of Well-Being, 2014*, Federal Interagency Forum on Child and Family Statistics, 2014, http://www.childstats.gov/americaschildren/glance.asp (accessed July 16, 2014)

The Forum indicates that the percentage of children in poverty was 16% in 2000, crept up to 17% in 2006, and then increased each year through 2012. The rise in child poverty by this measure may be linked to the severe economic downturn in the United States that lasted from 2007 to 2009.

Figure 1.4 provides an overall child poverty breakdown by race, Hispanic origin, and family type between 1980 and 2011. Children living with married couples had, by far, the lowest poverty levels. In 2011 about 10% of these children were in poverty. By contrast, nearly 50% of the children living with female householders were in poverty. There were also striking differences by race and ethnic origin. Children in households headed by African American and Hispanic females had higher rates of poverty than did children in households headed by white females. Children of low socioeconomic status living with female householders face particular risks for family violence. One threat is the higher risk of child maltreatment due to low socioeconomic status. The Forum notes that the percentage of children living in families in severe poverty (below 50% of the poverty threshold for that family composition) was 10% in 2011.

Nearly three-quarters (73%) of U.S. children in 2012 lived with at least one parent who was employed full time year round. (See Table 1.4.) However, as the Forum reports in *America's Children in Brief*, there was a wide difference in terms of full-time, year-round parental employment between those children who lived with two married parents (85%) and children living in families maintained by single mothers (40%).

In 2012 nearly a quarter (22%) of U.S. children lived in households that were classified by the U.S. Department of Agriculture (USDA) as "food insecure." (See Table 1.4.) According to the Forum, food insecurity is assessed by the USDA through surveys that question parents and guardians about the adequacy of their household food supply. The Forum indicates that 1.1% of children lived in households that were deemed to have very low food security in 2011. This means that "at some time during the year one or more children were hungry, skipped a meal, or did not eat for a whole day because the household could not afford enough food."

threshold limit for a family of four including two adults and two children was $22,811 annually. Thus, any family matching that description and making an income of less than $22,811 annually was considered to be in poverty.

FIGURE 1.3

Percentage of children aged 0–17 years, by race and Hispanic origin, 1980–2012 and projected, 2013–50

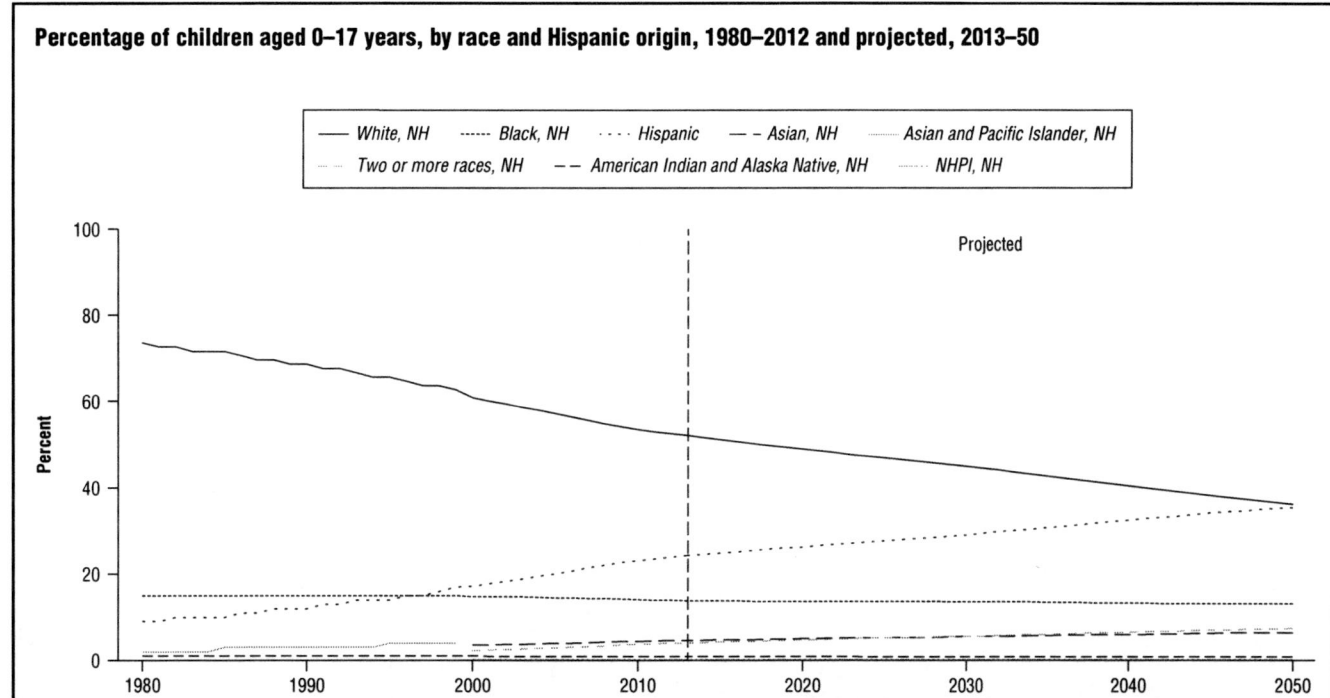

Note: The acronym NH refers to non-Hispanic origin. The acronym NHPI refers to the Native Hawaiian and other Pacific Islander population. Each group represents the non-Hispanic population, with the exception of the Hispanic category itself. Race data from 2000 onward are not directly comparable with data from earlier years. Data on race and Hispanic origin are collected separately. Persons of Hispanic origin may be of any race. Population projections are based on Census 2000 and may not be consistent with the 2010 Census results.

SOURCE: "Indicator POP3. Percentage of Children Ages 0–17 in the United States by Race and Hispanic Origin, 1980–2012 and Projected 2013–2050," in *America's Children: Key National Indicators of Well-Being, 2013*, Federal Interagency Forum on Child and Family Statistics, July 2013, http://www .childstats.gov/pdf/ac2013/ac_13.pdf (accessed July 16, 2014)

TABLE 1.5

Types of child care

Type	Description
In-home care	Care provided in the child's home
Relative care	Care provided by someone related to the child other than the parents in any setting, typically in the child's or relative's home
Family child care	An individual provider who provides child care services as the sole caregiver in a private residence other than the child's home
Group home care	Two or more providers who provide child care services in a private residence other than the child's home (this does not include 24-hour residential facilities)
Child care centers	Nonresidential facilities that provide care for children and include full-and part-time group programs, such as nursery and preschool programs. Child care centers can be commercial, work-site based, school-based (preschool or after school), or a recreational program (such as camps or parks), and care can also be run by a religious organization or by federal, state, or local governments

SOURCE: "Table 1. Types of Child Care," in *Child Care: Overview of Relevant Employment Laws and Cases of Sex Offenders at Child Care Facilities*, U.S. Government Accountability Office, August 2011, http://www.gao.gov/ assets/330/322722.pdf (accessed July 16, 2014)

The Forum notes that 90% of children had health insurance coverage at some point during 2011. This means that 10%, or roughly 7.4 million children, did not have health insurance coverage at any time during 2011. Chapter 2 describes the government programs that were in existence as of November 2014 to provide health insurance

to low-income children. The Forum finds that 4% of children in 2011 had "no usual source of health care," meaning that they did not have "a particular person or place" to visit for preventive and sick care. The percentage of children falling into this category was higher for those who were uninsured (28%) than for those who had health insurance (5%).

According to the Forum, "inadequate, crowded, or too costly housing can pose serious problems to children's physical, psychological, and material well-being." Nearly half (46%) of U.S. children in 2011 lived in households that reported "shelter cost burden, crowding, and/or physically inadequate housing." The agency explains that a shelter cost burden indicates that a household was paying housing costs in excess of 30% of its income.

As shown in Table 1.4, 5% of U.S. children aged four to 17 years in 2012 were reported by a parent to have "serious difficulties with emotions, concentration, behavior, or getting along with other people." In addition, 9% of children aged five to 17 years had an "activity limitation resulting from one or more chronic health conditions." Studies described in Chapter 3 indicate that children with physical, emotional, and/or behavioral problems are at higher risk for maltreatment than other children.

FIGURE 1.4

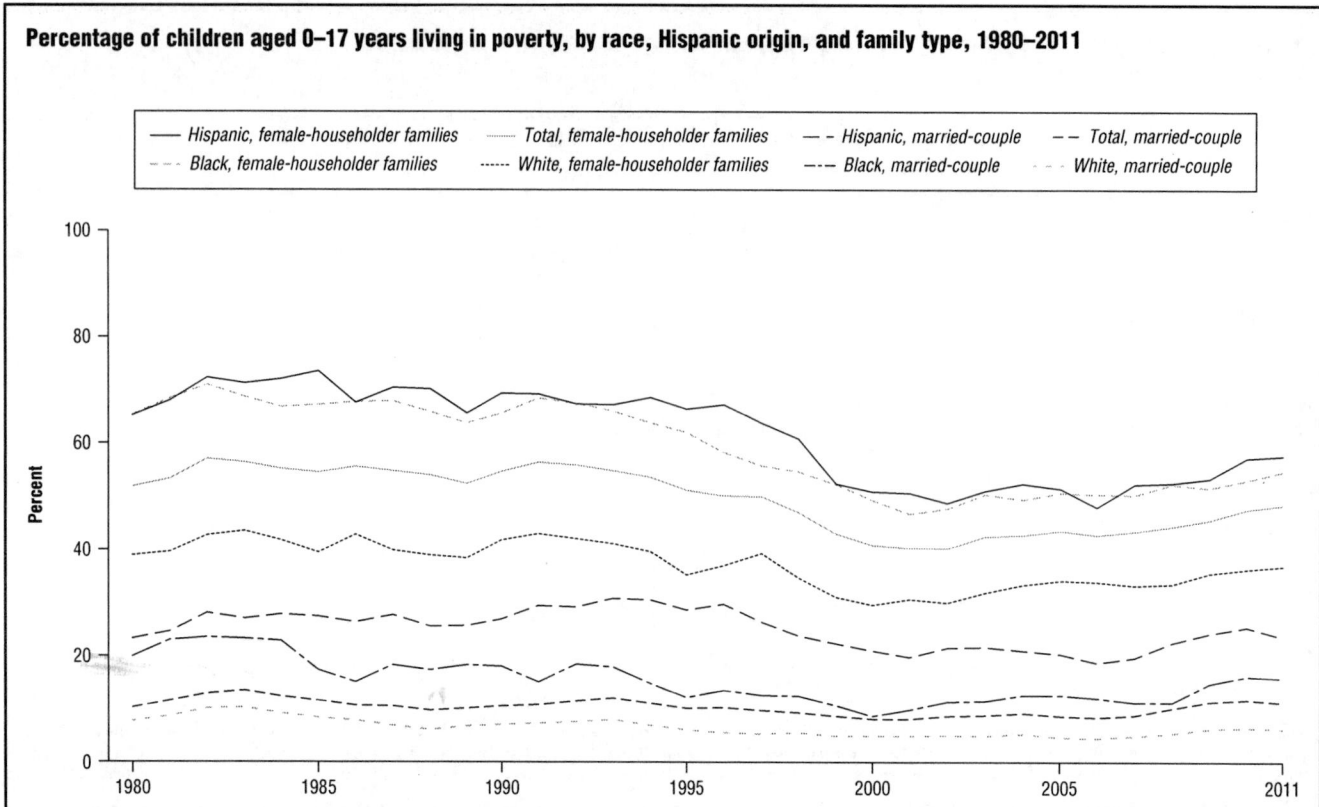

Percentage of children aged 0–17 years living in poverty, by race, Hispanic origin, and family type, 1980–2011

Note: In 2011, the poverty threshold for a two-parent, two-child family was $22,811. The proportion of children in male-householder families (no spouse present) historically has been small.

SOURCE: "Indicator ECON1.A. Percentage of Children Ages 0–17 Years Living in Poverty by Race, Hispanic Origin, and Family Structure, 1980–2011," in *America's Children: Key National Indicators of Well-Being, 2013*, Federal Interagency Forum on Child and Family Statistics, July 2013, http://www.childstats.gov/pdf/ac2013/ac_13.pdf (accessed July 16, 2014)

VIOLENT ENVIRONMENTS

Researchers are increasingly focusing on the environments in which family violence occurs. What they are finding is that some children experience a shocking amount of violence in their home and neighborhood. In addition, violence follows some people from childhood through adulthood in that child victims of violence tend to continue to be victimized by violence as adults. For example, Black et al. note that "violence often begins at an early age and commonly leads to negative health consequences across the lifespan."

The National Crime Victimization Survey

Since 1972 the Bureau of Justice Statistics (BJS), a part of the U.S. Department of Justice, has overseen an annual survey called the National Crime Victimization Survey (NCVS) in which the Census Bureau surveys a nationally representative sample of tens of thousands of households and asks people aged 12 years and older about their experiences of being victimized by certain crimes within the previous six months. The incidents include victimizations that were and were not reported to authorities. As is explained in Chapter 6, the NCVS is a major source of data regarding domestic violence in the United States. In addition, researchers use NCVS data to assess other areas of interest. For example, in *Nonfatal Domestic Violence, 2003–2012* (April 2014, http://www.bjs.gov/content/pub/pdf/ndv0312.pdf), Jennifer L. Truman and Rachel E. Morgan of the BJS examine NCVS data between 2003 and 2012 to determine what percentage of violent victimizations were perpetrated by intimate partners, immediate family members or other relatives, or friends/acquaintances. As Table 1.6 shows, more than half (53.1%) of all violent victimizations reported between 2003 and 2012 occurred between individuals who knew each other; 38.5% of violent victimizations were perpetrated by strangers, and in 8.5% of cases the identity of the assailant was unknown. Assaults perpetrated by well known or casual acquaintances accounted for 31.8% of all violent victimizations during this span, whereas 21.3% of incidents occurred between intimate partners or family members. Overall, the rate of violent victimizations that occurred between intimate partners fell dramatically between 1994 and 2012. (See Figure 1.5.)

Table 1.7 provides an overview of violent victimization rates between 2003 and 2012, by select demographic characteristics of the victims. During this period,

TABLE 1.6

Violent victimizations, by crime type and victim-offender relationship, 2003–12

Victim-offender relationship	All violent crime		Serious violent crime[a]		Simple assault	
	Average annual number	Percent	Average annual number	Percent	Average annual number	Percent
Total	**6,623,500**	**100%**	**2,194,070**	**100%**	**4,429,430**	**100%**
Known	3,514,570	53.1%	1,072,520	48.9%	2,442,050	55.1%
Domestic	1,411,330	21.3	501,220	22.8	910,110	20.5
Intimate partner[b]	967,710	14.6	343,760	15.7	623,950	14.1
Spouse	314,330	4.7	116,520	5.3	197,810	4.5
Ex-spouse	134,690	2.0	29,330	1.3	105,350	2.4
Boy/girlfriend	518,700	7.8	197,910	9.0	320,790	7.2
Immediate family	284,670	4.3	98,520	4.5	186,150	4.2
Parent	80,890	1.2	31,400	1.4	49,480	1.1
Child	97,490	1.5	32,820	1.5	64,680	1.5
Sibling	106,290	1.6	34,300	1.6	71,990	1.6
Other relative	158,950	2.4	58,940	2.7	100,010	2.3
Well-known/casual acquaintance	2,103,240	31.8	571,300	26.0	1,531,940	34.6
Stranger	2,548,860	38.5%	929,450	42.4%	1,619,410	36.6%
Unknown[c]	560,080	8.5%	192,100	8.8%	367,970	8.3%

[a]Includes rape or sexual assault, robbery, and aggravated assault.
[b]Includes current or former spouses, boyfriends, and girlfriends.
[c]Includes unknown victim-offender relationships and unknown number of offenders.
Note: Detail may not sum to total due to rounding.

SOURCE: Jennifer L. Truman and Rachel E. Morgan, "Table 1. Violent Victimization, by Type of Crime and Victim-Offender Relationship, 2003–2012," in *Nonfatal Domestic Violence, 2003–2012*, U.S. Department of Justice, Office of Justice Programs, Bureau of Justice Statistics, April 2014, http://www.bjs.gov/content/pub/pdf/ndv0312.pdf (accessed July 20, 2014)

FIGURE 1.5

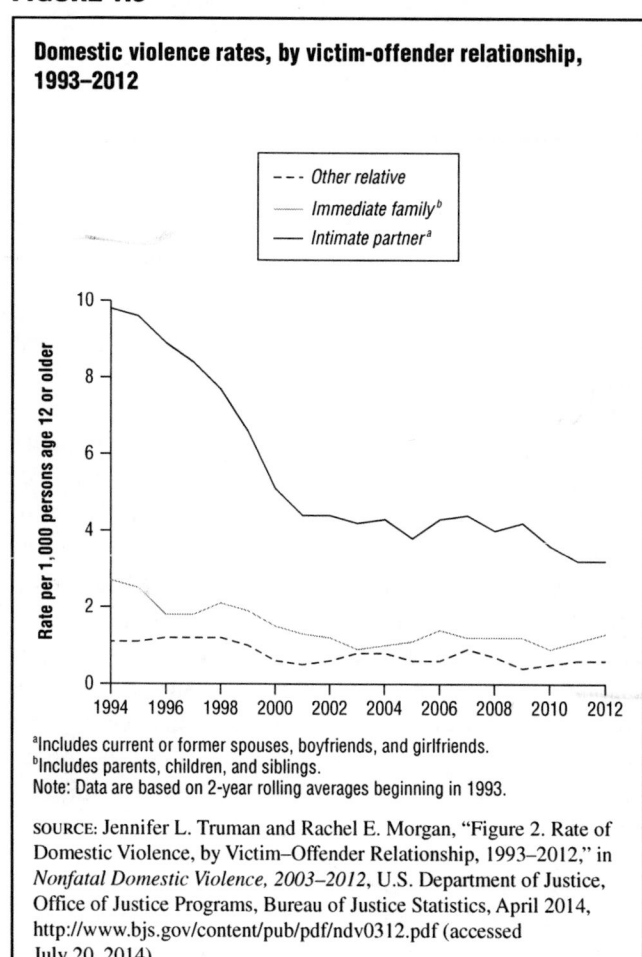

Domestic violence rates, by victim-offender relationship, 1993–2012

[a]Includes current or former spouses, boyfriends, and girlfriends.
[b]Includes parents, children, and siblings.
Note: Data are based on 2-year rolling averages beginning in 1993.

SOURCE: Jennifer L. Truman and Rachel E. Morgan, "Figure 2. Rate of Domestic Violence, by Victim–Offender Relationship, 1993–2012," in *Nonfatal Domestic Violence, 2003–2012*, U.S. Department of Justice, Office of Justice Programs, Bureau of Justice Statistics, April 2014, http://www.bjs.gov/content/pub/pdf/ndv0312.pdf (accessed July 20, 2014)

there were 5.6 domestic violence victims per 1,000 people aged 12 years and older. As Table 1.7 shows, women (8.4 per 1,000 individuals) were three times more likely than men (2.8 per 1,000) to be victims of domestic violence; women (6.2 per 1,000) were also considerably more likely than men (1.4 per 1,000) to be victimized by an intimate partner. Individuals between the ages of 18 and 24 (11.6 per 1,000 people) were more likely to be victims of domestic violence than those of any other age group. Among various racial categories, individuals who identified as belonging to two or more races (22.5 per 1,000) were considerably more likely than African Americans (6.7 per 1,000), whites (5.7 per 1,000), Hispanics/Latinos (4 per 1,000), or members of other races (3.7 per 1,000) to have been domestic violence victims between 2003 and 2012.

As Figure 1.6 shows, between 2003 and 2012 women were considerably more likely than men to be victims of domestic violence perpetrated by an intimate partner. Girlfriends who were victimized by their boyfriends accounted for 39% of all victimizations involving intimate partner violence during this span; female spouses accounted for one-quarter (25%) of all victimizations, and female ex-spouses accounted for 10% of victimizations. In domestic violence situations involving an immediate family member rather than an intimate partner males were more likely to be victims of abuse. As Truman and Morgan report, male victims of parental abuse accounted for 10.2% of violent victimizations involving

TABLE 1.7

Rates of violent victimization, by victim-offender relationship and select characteristics of victim, 2003–12

Demographic characteristic	Domestic violence				Well-known/casual acquaintance	Stranger
	Total	Intimate partner[a]	Immediate family[b]	Other relative		
Total	5.6	3.9	1.1	0.6	8.4	10.2
Sex						
Male	2.8	1.4	0.9	0.5	8.9	14.2
Female	8.4	6.2	1.4	0.8	7.9	6.4
Age						
12–17	5.0	1.1	2.6	1.2	26.9	15.2
18–24	11.6	8.7	1.8	1.2	14.0	19.9
25–34	8.7	7.3	0.7	0.7	7.5	14.5
35–49	6.4	4.7	1.2	0.5	6.4	9.7
50–64	2.9	1.5	1.0	0.5	4.8	5.9
65 or older	0.6	0.2	0.2	0.1	1.3	1.6
Race/Hispanic origin						
White[c]	5.7	3.9	1.2	0.6	8.6	9.7
Black[c]	6.7	4.7	0.7	1.2	10.1	12.3
Hispanic/Latino	4.0	2.8	0.6	0.6	6.3	10.4
Other race[c, d]	3.7	2.3	1.3	0.2	4.6	8.4
Two or more races[c]	22.5	16.5	4.4	1.6	24.6	26.7
Marital status						
Never married	7.0	4.4	1.7	0.9	15.6	17.1
Married	2.0	1.0	0.6	0.4	3.7	5.9
Widowed	2.3	0.6	1.5	0.2	2.2	2.3
Divorced	13.8	11.4	1.5	0.9	11.4	12.9
Separated	49.1	44.7	2.8	1.6	13.9	16.0

[a]Includes current or former spouses, boyfriends, and girlfriends.
[b]Includes parents, children, and siblings.
[c]Excludes persons of Hispanic or Latino origin.
[d]Includes American Indian, Alaska Native, Hawaiian, Asian, and other Pacific Islander.
Note: Victimization rates are per 1,000 persons age 12 or older. In a small percentage of victimizations, the victim-offender relationship was unknown or the number of offenders was unknown. These estimates are not shown.

SOURCE: Jennifer L. Truman and Rachel E. Morgan, "Table 11. Rate of Violent Victimization, by Victim Characteristics and Victim-Offender Relationship, 2003–2012," in *Nonfatal Domestic Violence, 2003–2012*, U.S. Department of Justice, Office of Justice Programs, Bureau of Justice Statistics, April 2014, http://www.bjs.gov/content/pub/pdf/ndv0312.pdf (accessed July 20, 2014)

an immediate family member; this rate was more than double that of female victims of parental abuse, who accounted for 4.3% of violent victimizations involving immediate family members. (See Figure 1.6.)

The National Survey of Children's Exposure to Violence

In 2008 the DOJ's Office of Juvenile Justice and Delinquency Prevention and the CDC oversaw a survey to measure lifetime and past-year exposure to violence for children. The National Survey of Children's Exposure to Violence (NatSCEV) was designed and conducted by the Crimes against Children Research Center at the University of New Hampshire.

In *Children's Exposure to Violence: A Comprehensive National Survey* (October 2009, https://www.ncjrs.gov/pdffiles1/ojjdp/227744.pdf), David Finkelhor et al. note that 10.2% of the children had been subjected to child maltreatment and that 9.8% had witnessed a family assault. Other types of violence exposure that children had experienced during the previous year were assault with no weapon or injury (36.7%), witnessing a community assault (19.2%), assault with a weapon and/or

injury (14.9%), sexual victimization (6.1%), and dating violence (1.4%).

David Finkelhor, Heather Turner, and Sherry Hamby explain in "Questions and Answers about the National Survey of Children's Exposure to Violence" (October 2011, https://www.ncjrs.gov/pdffiles1/ojjdp/235163.pdf) that the survey included a nationally representative sample of more than 4,500 children aged 17 years and younger. Children aged 10 years and older were questioned directly; the parents or other caregivers of younger children were questioned in place of the younger children. The survey participants were asked about past-year and lifetime exposures to violence, including direct exposure (through personal victimization) and indirect exposure (witnessing violent acts against others). In addition, the participants were asked about psychological and emotional victimizations, such as bullying, neglect by a parent/caregiver, and Internet victimization.

Finkelhor, Turner, and Hamby find that 61% of the children had been exposed to violence, crime, or abuse during the previous year. According to the survey, physical assault (including by siblings and other children) was

FIGURE 1.6

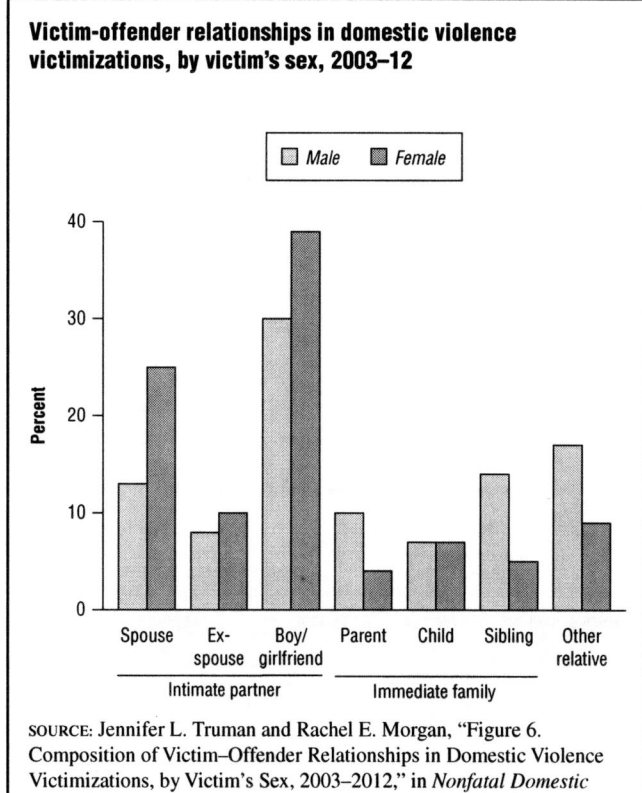

Victim-offender relationships in domestic violence victimizations, by victim's sex, 2003–12

Legend: ☐ Male ■ Female

Categories (x-axis): Spouse, Ex-spouse, Boy/girlfriend (Intimate partner); Parent, Child, Sibling, Other relative (Immediate family)

Y-axis: Percent, 0 to 40

SOURCE: Jennifer L. Truman and Rachel E. Morgan, "Figure 6. Composition of Victim–Offender Relationships in Domestic Violence Victimizations, by Victim's Sex, 2003–2012," in *Nonfatal Domestic Violence, 2003–2012*, U.S. Department of Justice, Office of Justice Programs, Bureau of Justice Statistics, April 2014, http://www.bjs.gov/content/pub/pdf/ndv0312.pdf (accessed July 20, 2014)

the most common type of victimization across almost all ages. It was slightly outranked among children aged 15 to 17 years by an experience of witnessing violence. The percentages of children experiencing past-year maltreatment and sexual victimizations were higher for older children than for younger children.

As Table 1.8 indicates, in 2010 there were 687,530 instances of violent victimization among children between the ages of 12 and 17. Of these victimizations, more than half (391,680, or 57%) were perpetrated by a friend or acquaintance. Between 2003 and 2012, friends or acquaintances perpetrated 38.8% of all violent victimizations against children aged 12 to 17 years. (See Table 1.9.)

POLYVICTIMS. One of the significant findings from the NatSCEV data was that some children had been exposed to multiple types of violence, and these experiences had greatly stressed them. David Finkelhor et al. note in *Polyvictimization: Children's Exposure to Multiple Types of Violence, Crime, and Abuse* (October 2011, https://www.ncjrs.gov/pdffiles1/ojjdp/235504.pdf), the most recent report on the subject as of November 2014, that 49% of the surveyed children reported two or more victimization types including direct and indirect victimizations during the previous year. The largest number of victimization types suffered was 18 victimizations. The

researchers decided to refer to the 8% of the children who had experienced seven or more victimizations during the previous year as "polyvictims" because these children showed significantly higher distress levels than did victims with less victimization types.

Finkelhor et al. assessed distress levels among all the surveyed children using standardized trauma checklists. As expected, nonvictims had the lowest trauma symptom scores. Distress levels were higher for victims classified as low chronic victims (those exposed to less than the average frequency of only one type of victimization) and high chronic victims (those exposed to more than the average frequency of only one type of victimization). Trauma symptom scores were the highest for the polyvictims. Finkelhor et al. theorize that these children scored so high because "there are relatively few areas of safety for them."

As Finkelhor et al. note, physical assault was the most common type of victimization with nearly all (98%) the victims having experienced a physical assault during the previous year. Other victimization types that were experienced by at least three-fourths of the polyvictims included any property crime (88%) and any exposure to community violence (84%). The researchers find that polyvictims suffered more injuries than nonpolyvictims and experienced "a disproportionate share of the most serious kinds of victimizations." For example, more than half (55%) of the polyvictims suffered an injury, compared with 12% of nonpolyvictims. In addition, the polyvictims had greater rates than did nonpolyvictims for the most serious types of victimizations: caregiver perpetration (53% versus 14%), weapons victimizations (42% versus 6%), and sexual victimizations (36% versus 6%).

Finkelhor et al. also observed the demographic characteristics of polyvictims. Overall, males had a higher rate (8.4%) than did females (7.5%), and older children aged 14 to 17 years were more likely to be polyvictims than younger children. Children in the middle socioeconomic category (8.8%) had a higher polyvictimization rate than children in the low (7.3%) or high (4.7%) economic groups. Non-Hispanic African American children (12.8%) suffered the highest rate among the racial and ethnic groups. Family structure also played a role. Children in two-parent families had a significantly lower rate at 5.2% than did children in other family structures (12.4% to 13.9%). Lastly, children living in cities with a population of 300,000 or more had a slightly higher rate (8.3%) than children in cities or towns with lower populations (7.8%).

Finkelhor et al. indicate that there are four pathways that children become polyvictims: dangerous families (i.e., families that experience "considerable violence and conflict"), family disruption and adversity (e.g., families that are beset with financial problems or substance abuse), dangerous neighborhoods, and emotional

TABLE 1.8

Violent victimizations among children aged 12–17, by victim-offender relationship, 2010

Age	Victimizations		Victims		Mean number of victimizations per victim
	Number	Rate[a]	Number	Rate[b]	
12–17	687,530	28.1	420,410	17.2	1.6
Intimate partner	/	/	/	/	/
Relative	35,900!	1.5!	27,060!	1.1!	1.3!
Friend/acquaintance	391,680	16.0	221,170	9.1	1.8
Stranger	199,920	8.2	141,950	5.8	1.4

/ Not reported.
!Interpret with caution; estimate based on 10 or fewer sample cases, or coefficient of variation is greater than 50%.
[a]Number of victimizations per 1,000 persons that occurred during the year.
[b]Number of persons per 1,000 who experienced at least one victimization during the year.
Note: Rates are based on a population ages 12–17 of 24,435,530.

SOURCE: Adapted from Janet L. Lauritsen and Maribeth L. Rezey, "Table 5. Violent Victimization, by Age and Victim-Offender Relationship, 2010," in *Measuring the Prevalence of Crime with the National Crime Victimization Survey*, U.S. Department of Justice, Office of Justice Programs, Bureau of Justice Statistics, September 2013, http://www.bjs.gov/content/pub/pdf/mpcncvs.pdf (accessed July 20, 2014)

TABLE 1.9

Percentage breakdown of violent victimizations, by victim-offender relationship and age of victim, 2003–12

Victim-offender releationship	Serious violent crime[a]				Simple assault			
	12–17	18–24	25–49	50 or older	12–17	18–24	25–49	50 or older
Total	**100%**	**100%**	**100%**	**100%**	**100%**	**100%**	**100%**	**100%**
Known	55.4%	46.9%	45.9%	47.3%	63.5%	54.8%	51.9%	53.5%
Domestic	16.7	22.3	25.2	17.2	6.8	24.2	25.6	20.0
Intimate partner[b]	4.7	17.2	21.0	9.2	1.1	17.7	20.1	9.5
Immediate family	7.0	2.8	2.3	4.9	4.3	4.0	3.2	7.3
Other relative	5.0	2.3	1.9	3.1	1.4	2.4	2.3	3.2
Well-known/casual acquaintance	38.8	24.7	20.7	30.1	56.7	30.7	26.3	33.4
Stranger	37.4%	43.5%	43.8%	41.6%	25.9%	37.9%	40.1%	39.4%

[a]Includes rape or sexual assault, robbery, and aggravated assault.
[b]Includes current or former spouses, boyfriends, and girlfriends.
Note: Detail may not sum to total due to rounding. In a small percentage of victimizations, the victim-offender relationship was unknown or the number of offenders was unknown. These estimates are not shown.

SOURCE: Jennifer L. Truman and Rachel E. Morgan, "Table 4. Percent of Violent Victimization, by Victim-Offender Relationship and Victim's Age, 2003–2012," in *Nonfatal Domestic Violence, 2003–2012*, U.S. Department of Justice, Office of Justice Programs, Bureau of Justice Statistics, April 2014, http://www.bjs.gov/content/pub/pdf/ndv0312.pdf (accessed July 20, 2014)

---

problems (i.e., children whose preexisting emotional problems cause them to engage in risky behavior, antagonize others, or limit their abilities to defend themselves). (See Figure 1.7.) Child maltreatment, domestic violence, and sexual victimization are factors that contribute to polyvictimization.

CORPORAL PUNISHMENT: CHILD ABUSE OR NOT?

Corporal punishment is physical punishment intended to inflict pain on the person being punished. Although the term is a catch-all for various physical punishments, it is widely used to refer to spanking and other physical methods of discipline used against children. In the United States all 50 states allow parents to use corporal punishment for purposes of disciplining their children. As long as the children do not suffer injury, parents may use their hand or even an object such as a belt. When states passed child abuse laws during the 1960s, provisions allowing parents

to use corporal punishment helped facilitate passage of the legislation. Despite its acceptance in the United States, corporal punishment against children is outlawed by some nations. The Global Initiative to End All Corporal Punishment of Children reports in "States with Full Abolition" (http://www.endcorporalpunishment.org/pages/progress/prohib_states.html) that as of November 2014 corporal punishment by parents, caretakers, and teachers was completely banned in 42 countries.

Studies on the Effects of Corporal Punishment

In "Parents' Discipline of Young Children: Results from the National Survey of Early Childhood Health" (*Pediatrics*, vol. 113, no. 6, June 2004), Michael Regalado et al. report on the parental use of corporal punishment for discipline in regard to the health and development of children under three years of age. Six percent of parents surveyed indicated they had spanked their children

FIGURE 1.7

Pathways by which children become polyvictims

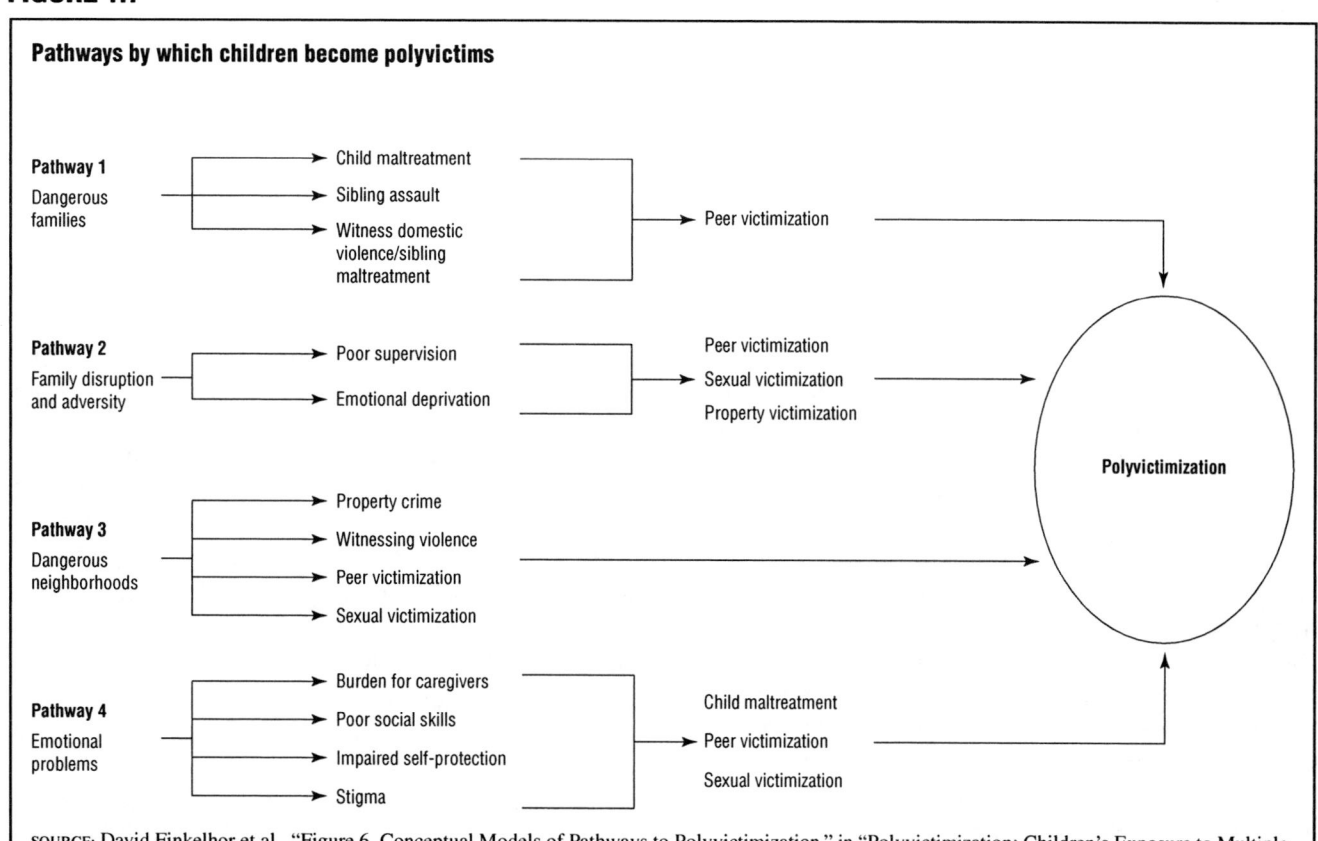

SOURCE: David Finkelhor et al., "Figure 6. Conceptual Models of Pathways to Polyvictimization," in "Polyvictimization: Children's Exposure to Multiple Types of Violence, Crime, and Abuse," *Juvenile Justice Bulletin*, U.S. Department of Justice, Office of Justice Programs, Office of Juvenile Justice and Delinquency Prevention, October 2011, https://www.ncjrs.gov/pdffiles1/ojjdp/235504.pdf (accessed July 16, 2014)

when they were four to nine months old, 29% spanked their children when they were 10 to 18 months old, and 64% spanked their children when they were 19 to 35 months old. Frequent spankings were also administered by some parents of children 10 to 18 months old (11%) and 19 to 35 months old (26%).

Studies on the spanking of children have mostly used sample populations of children aged two years and older. In "Spanking in Early Childhood and Later Behavior Problems: A Prospective Study of Infants and Young Toddlers" (*Pediatrics*, vol. 113, no. 5, May 2004), Eric P. Slade and Lawrence S. Wissow of Johns Hopkins Bloomberg School of Public Health conducted the first study of its kind in the United States by following a group of children younger than two years old to test "the hypothesis that spanking frequency before age 2 is positively associated with the probability of having significant behavior problems 4 years later."

Slade and Wissow collected data on 1,966 children and their mothers who participated in the National Longitudinal Survey of Mother-Child Sample, a large-scale national study of youth aged 14 to 21 years old. Some of these young people were mothers with children. Data were collected on the mother-children groups when the children were under two years of age. Four years later,

after the children had entered elementary school, Slade and Wissow interviewed the mothers to explore their hypothesis. Mothers were asked if they spanked their child the previous week and how frequently they spanked their children. They were also questioned about the child's temperament, mother-child interactions, and whether they had ever met with the child's teacher because of behavioral problems.

Slade and Wissow find that, when compared with children who were never spanked, non-Hispanic white children who were frequently spanked (five times per week) before age two were four times more likely to have behavioral problems by the time they started school. No connection was found between spanking and later behavioral problems among African American and Hispanic children. According to Slade and Wissow, the same results were found in studies involving children older than two years. The researchers surmise that the way non-Hispanic white families and other ethnic families view the spanking of children may influence the effects of spanking. For example, African American families typically do not consider spanking as "harsh or unfair."

Catherine A. Taylor et al. examine the relationship between the spanking of three-year-old children and later aggressive behavior in "Mothers' Spanking of 3-Year-

Old Children and Subsequent Risk of Children's Aggressive Behavior" (*Pediatrics*, vol. 125, no. 5, May 2010). The researchers find that frequent use of corporal punishment on three-year-olds (spanking more than twice over the course of a month) was associated with increased aggressive behavior at five years of age. The increased risk held true even when the researchers controlled for the level of aggression at age three as well as for key demographic features. Taylor et al. conclude that even "minor" forms of corporal punishment, including spanking, increase children's risk of aggressive behavior.

In "On Hitting Children: A Review of Corporal Punishment in the United States" (*Journal of Pediatric Health Care*, vol. 24, no. 2, March–April 2010), Michele Knox of the University of Toledo reviews the literature on corporal punishment and finds that in physical abuse cases corporal punishment was usually the precursor to physical abuse. She states, "Typically, someone in charge of caring for the child tries to discipline the child. The caregiver starts spanking to teach the child a lesson, but as the disciplinary incident progresses, the adult's anger becomes stronger, the hitting becomes harder, and the child ends up seriously hurt." As such, Knox concludes that the prevention of corporal punishment should be the primary target in the fight to end child maltreatment.

Matthew K. Mulvaney and Carolyn J. Mebert of the University of New Hampshire report in "Stress Appraisal and Attitudes towards Corporal Punishment as Intervening Processes between Corporal Punishment and Subsequent Mental Health" (*Journal of Family Violence*, vol. 25, no. 4, May 2010) that negative attitudes about corporal punishment affect its degree of harm. The researchers report that children's evaluations of corporal punishment as threatening were more significantly associated with the adverse mental health effects than with the actual frequency of the punishment. Mulvaney and Mebert also find that the mother-child relationship was more impacted by corporal punishment than was the father-child relationship.

In "Corporal Punishment and Child Behavioural and Cognitive Outcomes through 5 Years of Age: Evidence from a Contemporary Urban Birth Cohort Study" (*Infant & Child Development*, vol. 21, no. 1, January–February 2012), Michael J. McKenzie et al. report that corporal punishment can also exert a negative impact on a child's cognitive progress at a young age. McKenzie et al. find evidence that frequent spanking can inhibit the verbal development of children between the ages of three and five. According to McKenzie et al., children who experienced a high level of corporal punishment at the age of three tended to test lower on the Peabody Picture Vocabulary Test, a standard that measures vocabulary, academic aptitude, and other indicators of verbal intelligence.

In spite of studies demonstrating the negative impacts of corporal punishment on a child's well-being and development, spanking and other forms of physical discipline remain deeply ingrained within American culture. The notion that spanking or hitting is a traditional, and therefore normal, form of discipline is often used as a justification for corporal punishment. Indeed, as McKenzie et al. note, adults who were spanked during their own childhoods are more likely to use corporal punishment to discipline their own children.

The question of corporal punishment became the subject of intense national debate in September 2014, when Minnesota Vikings running back Adrian Peterson (1985–) was suspended by the National Football League after it was revealed that he had hit his four-year-old son with a switch. The incident had left the boy covered with cuts and bruises. Although Peterson subsequently expressed remorse for his actions on Twitter (September 15, 2014, https://twitter.com/AdrianPeterson/status/5115866003465 99424), he also attempted to justify his actions within the context of his own upbringing. "I have always believed that the way my parents disciplined me has a great deal to do with the success I have enjoyed as a man," Peterson stated. Despite facing felony charges of causing injury to a child, Peterson also insisted that he was "without a doubt, not a child abuser." Indeed, in 2014 a majority of Americans continued to believe that corporal punishment did not constitute actual abuse. As Tara Fowler writes in "Adrian Peterson Controversy: Is It OK to Spank Your Children?" (People.com, September 16, 2014), nearly three-quarters (74%) of mothers in the United States believed that spanking children between the ages of one and three was an acceptable form of discipline.

CHAPTER 2
DETECTING, MEASURING, AND PREVENTING CHILD ABUSE

CHILD ABUSE DATA SOURCES

Statistics on child abuse are difficult to interpret and compare because there is little consistency in how information is collected. The definitions of abuse vary from study to study, as do the methods of counting incidents of abuse. Some methods count only reported cases of abuse. Some statistics are based on estimates that are projected from a small study, whereas others are based on interviews.

As of November 2014, three federal government sources had published relatively recent comprehensive data on child abuse:

- *Child Maltreatment*—an annual report published by the Children's Bureau, an agency within the U.S. Department of Health and Human Services (HHS).

- The National Survey of Child and Adolescent Well-Being (NSCAW)—a research project of the Office of Planning, Research, and Evaluation (OPRE) within the Administration for Children and Families. Numerous reports have been published by the OPRE and private researchers based on NSCAW data.

- National Incidence Study of Child Abuse and Neglect (NIS)—as of November 2014, four NIS studies had been conducted by the private research company Westat under contract to the OPRE.

CHILD MALTREATMENT

The Child Abuse Prevention, Adoption, and Family Services Act of 1988 mandated that the HHS establish a national data collection program on child maltreatment. In 1990 the National Child Abuse and Neglect Data System (NCANDS) began operating. The database includes child maltreatment data from child protective services (CPS) agencies in the 50 states and the District of Columbia. The Children's Bureau publishes summary NCANDS data on an annual basis. As of November 2014, the most recent publication was *Child Maltreatment 2012* (December 2013, http://www.acf.hhs.gov/sites/default/files/cb/cm2012.pdf).

Referrals and Reports

Figure 2.1 indicates that in 2012 CPS agencies received an estimated 3.4 million referrals relating to 6.3 million children. Many referrals are made by phone, for example, to special hotlines that are maintained for the reporting of abuse allegations. The Children's Bureau notes that states differ in how they count the number of referrals they receive. For example, one state counted every call received via its hotline as a referral, even calls that were misdialed. About 2.1 million (62%) of the referrals received in 2012 were screened in, and nearly 1.3 million (38%) were screened out (not further acted on by CPS agencies). According to the Children's Bureau, screened-out referrals include calls that do not concern child abuse and neglect, calls that do not include enough information for the agency to act on, calls that are related to matters better handled by other agencies, and calls that concern children who are older than 18 years old.

Referrals that are screened in are called reports. As shown in Figure 2.1, more than half (58.7%) of the 2012 reports originated from professional sources. Another 18% were from nonprofessional sources, and 23.3% were unclassified, meaning the professional status of the caller was unknown. Table 2.1 provides detailed information about report sources between 2008 and 2012. Overall, education and legal and law enforcement personnel accounted for nearly one-third of all reports that were received in 2012. That year legal and law enforcement personnel (16.7%) accounted for most of the reports from professional sources, followed by

FIGURE 2.1

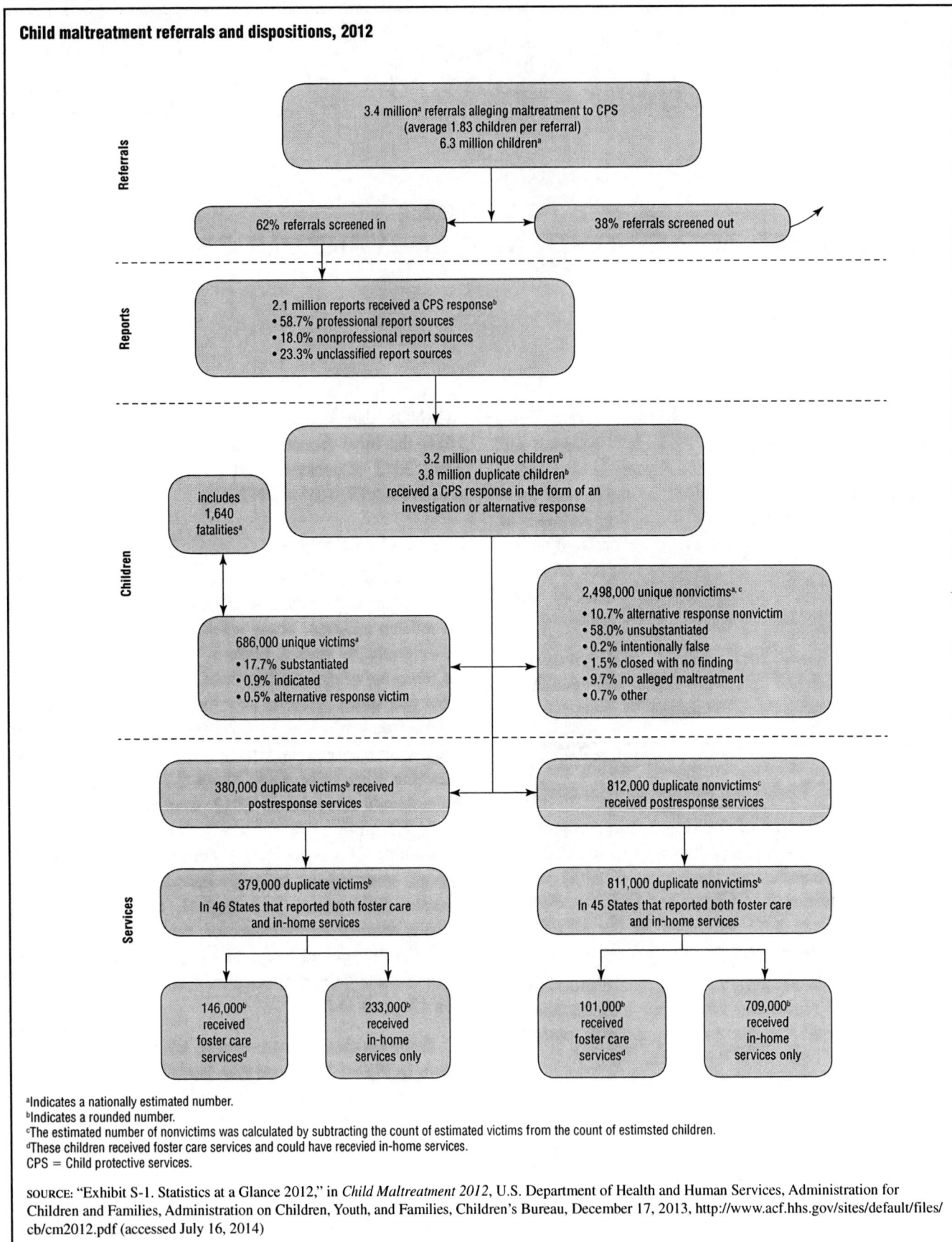

Child maltreatment referrals and dispositions, 2012

[a]Indicates a nationally estimated number.
[b]Indicates a rounded number.
[c]The estimated number of nonvictims was calculated by subtracting the count of estimated victims from the count of estimsted children.
[d]These children received foster care services and could have recevied in-home services.
CPS = Child protective services.

SOURCE: "Exhibit S-1. Statistics at a Glance 2012," in *Child Maltreatment 2012*, U.S. Department of Health and Human Services, Administration for Children and Families, Administration on Children, Youth, and Families, Children's Bureau, December 17, 2013, http://www.acf.hhs.gov/sites/default/files/cb/cm2012.pdf (accessed July 16, 2014)

education personnel (16.6%) and social services personnel (11.1%). Most reports from nonprofessional sources came from parents (6.5%) and other relatives (6.7%) of the children involved.

TABLE 2.1

Sources of reports of alleged child maltreatment, 2008–12

Report sources	Number				
	2008	2009	2010	2011	2012
Professional					
Child daycare providers	17,471	15,934	14,317	14,641	14,622
Education personnel	337,888	329,825	315,359	327,824	348,667
Foster care providers	11,420	11,727	10,129	9,387	9,170
Legal and law enforcement personnel	326,800	328,664	321,068	342,438	350,629
Medical personnel	165,404	163,080	158,194	171,067	178,898
Mental health personnel	85,273	87,880	89,342	95,878	97,951
Social services personnel	228,563	228,754	221,659	216,987	232,761
Total professionals	**1,172,819**	**1,165,864**	**1,130,068**	**1,178,222**	**1,232,698**
Nonprofessional					
Alleged perpetrators	1,150	1,124	879	734	707
Alleged victims	10,937	10,285	8,112	7,911	7,636
Friends and neighbors	101,229	97,508	85,046	90,659	93,569
Other relatives	146,250	141,037	133,975	138,149	139,990
Parents	133,526	135,375	131,386	134,381	136,101
Total nonprofessionals	**393,092**	**385,329**	**359,398**	**371,834**	**378,003**
Unclassified					
Anonymous sources	176,637	177,367	173,601	183,617	179,853
Other	161,660	157,857	151,874	168,573	156,336
Unknown	119,849	114,091	112,652	144,921	152,147
Total unclassified	**458,146**	**449,315**	**438,127**	**497,111**	**488,336**
Total	**2,024,057**	**2,000,508**	**1,927,593**	**2,047,167**	**2,099,037**
States reporting	**52**	**52**	**51**	**52**	**51**
Report sources	Percent				
Professional					
Child daycare providers	0.9	0.8	0.7	0.7	0.7
Education personnel	16.7	16.5	16.4	16.0	16.6
Foster care providers	0.6	0.6	0.5	0.5	0.4
Legal and law enforcement personnel	16.1	16.4	16.7	16.7	16.7
Medical personnel	8.2	8.2	8.2	8.4	8.5
Mental health personnel	4.2	4.4	4.6	4.7	4.7
Social services personnel	11.3	11.4	11.5	10.6	11.1
Total professionals	**57.9**	**58.3**	**58.6**	**57.6**	**58.7**
Nonprofessional					
Alleged perpetrators	0.1	0.1	0.0	0.0	0.0
Alleged victims	0.5	0.5	0.4	0.4	0.4
Friends and neighbors	5.0	4.9	4.4	4.4	4.5
Other relatives	7.2	7.1	7.0	6.7	6.7
Parents	6.6	6.8	6.8	6.6	6.5
Total nonprofessionals	**19.4**	**19.3**	**18.6**	**18.2**	**18.0**
Unclassified					
Anonymous sources	8.7	8.9	9.0	9.0	8.6
Other	8.0	7.9	7.9	8.2	7.4
Unknown	5.9	5.7	5.8	7.1	7.2
Total unclassified	**22.6**	**22.5**	**22.7**	**24.3**	**23.3**
Total	**100.0**	**100.0**	**100.0**	**100.0**	**100.0**
States reporting					

SOURCE: "Table 2-2. Report Sources, 2008–2012," in *Child Maltreatment 2012*, U.S. Department of Health and Human Services, Administration for Children and Families, Administration on Children, Youth, and Families, Children's Bureau, December 17, 2013, http://www.acf.hhs.gov/sites/default/files/cb/cm2012.pdf (accessed July 16, 2014)

Child Victims

The 2012 reports concerned 3.2 million unique children or 3.8 million duplicate children (children who were reported or counted more than once). (See Figure 2.1.) Nearly 2.5 million of the uniquely counted children were determined to be nonvictims. The remaining 686,000 were determined to be child maltreatment victims; this number included 1,640 children who died from maltreatment.

Many victims and nonvictims received in-home services and/or foster care services from CSA agencies in 2012.

Table 2.2 lists the child victimization rates for uniquely counted children between 2008 and 2012. These rates were calculated by dividing the estimated number of unique victims each year by the nation's child population for that year. A victimization rate of 9.2 victims per 1,000 child population was reported in 2012. This value was

TABLE 2.2

Child maltreatment rates, 2008–12

Year	States reporting	Child population of reporting states	Unique victims from reporting states	National victimization rate per 1,000 children	Child population of all 52 states	National estimate of unique victims
2008	50	74,398,024	704,714	9.5	75,411,627	716,000
2009	50	74,495,280	693,485	9.3	75,512,062	702,000
2010	51	74,151,984	688,157	9.3	75,017,513	698,000
2011	51	73,921,000	676,545	9.2	74,783,810	688,000
2012	51	74,150,798	678,810	9.2	74,577,451	686,000

Note: The national victimization rate was calculated by dividing the number of unique victims from reporting states by the child population of reporting states and multiplying by 1,000. Because fewer than 52 states reported data in a given year, the national estimate of victims was calculated by multiplying the national victimization rate by the child population of all 52 states and dividing by 1,000. The result was rounded to the nearest 1,000.

SOURCE: "Exhibit 3-C. Child Victimization Rates, 2008–2012," in *Child Maltreatment 2012*, U.S. Department of Health and Human Services, Administration for Children and Families, Administration on Children, Youth, and Families, Children's Bureau, December 17, 2013, http://www.acf.hhs.gov/sites/default/files/cb/cm2012.pdf (accessed July 16, 2014)

down slightly from 9.5 victims per 1,000 child population reported in 2008.

According to the Children's Bureau in *Child Maltreatment 2012*, 50.9% of the child maltreatment victims in 2012 were girls and 48.7% were boys. The sex of the remaining 0.4% of victims was unknown. Table 2.3 shows a victim breakdown by race and ethnicity for 2012, by state. White children (44%) accounted for the largest portion of the victims, followed by Hispanic children (21.8%) and African American children (21%). As shown in Figure 2.2, children younger than one year old accounted for the largest share of victims in 2012. More than one-fifth (21.9%) of the victims were in this age group. Table 2.4 categorizes victims in 2012 by age and maltreatment type. Children younger than two years old accounted for the largest percentages of victims of medical neglect (33.2%), neglect (29.7%), physical abuse (24.6%), and psychological maltreatment (21.4%). Children aged 12 to 14 years, however, made up the largest portion of sexual abuse victims, at 26.3%. (Child sexual abuse is examined in more detail in Chapter 4.)

FATALITIES. As noted earlier, an estimated 1,640 children died as a result of maltreatment in 2012. This equaled a national child fatality rate of 2.2 fatalities per 100,000 children. (See Table 2.5.) The fatality rate was down from values that were reported in 2008 and 2009, but represented a slight increase over figures from 2010 and 2011. Table 2.6 provides a detailed age breakdown of the fatalities in 2012. Children under the age of one year had, by far, the highest fatality rate at 18.8 fatalities per 100,000 population in that age group. Overall, fatality rates declined with increasing age, dropping to 6.5 fatalities per 100,000 population for children aged one year and 4.4 fatalities per 100,000 population for children aged two years. By comparison, the fatality rates for children aged 10 to 17 years ranged from 0.1 to 0.8 fatalities per 100,000 population in that age range.

The Children's Bureau notes in *Child Maltreatment 2012* that boys made up 57.6% of child fatalities due to maltreatment in 2012, whereas girls accounted for 42.1%. For 0.3% of the fatalities the sex of the children was unknown. White children (38.3%) made up the largest share of the fatalities, followed by African American children (31.9%) and Hispanic children (15.3%). However, the victimization rates were highest for Pacific Islander children (4.7 fatalities per 100,000 population of that race) and African American children (4.7 fatalities per 100,000 population of that race), followed by Native American or Alaskan Native children (2.2 fatalities per 100,000 population of that race), and Hispanics (1.7 fatalities per 100,000 population of that race). By comparison, white children had a fatality rate of 1.6 fatalities per 100,000 population of that race in 2012.

As reported by the Children's Bureau in *Child Maltreatment 2012*, the vast majority (69.9%) of child maltreatment fatalities in 2012 were due to neglect, either alone or combined with other maltreatment types. The second-largest cause was physical abuse (44.3%), again either alone or combined with other maltreatment types.

Perpetrators

According to the Children's Bureau, most (80.3%) of the child abuse victims in 2012 were maltreated by a parent. Biological parents (88.3%) accounted for the overwhelming majority of child maltreatment at the hands of parents; step-parents accounted for 3.9% of maltreatment, and adoptive parents accounted for 0.7% of maltreatment cases. In 7% of maltreatment cases involving a parent, the parental relationship was of an unknown type.

Figure 2.3 provides a breakdown by age of child maltreatment perpetrators in 2012. Nearly two-thirds (63%) were between the ages of 25 and 44. The largest component included perpetrators aged 25 to 34 years (39.6%), and the second-largest component consisted of

TABLE 2.3

Child maltreatment victims, by race and ethnicity and state, 2012

State	African-American	American Indian or Alaska Native	Asian	Hispanic	Multiple race	Pacific Islander	White	Unknown	Total unique victims
					Number				
Alabama	2,629	9	12	412	320	3	5,401	787	9,573
Alaska	75	1,481	19	82	202	37	643	389	2,928
Arizona	856	494	26	3,854	377	21	3,910	501	10,039
Arkansas	1,940	14	21	704	774	46	7,553	81	11,133
California	9,458	481	1,765	41,224	2,586	219	17,521	2,772	76,026
Colorado	884	66	70	3,852	356	41	4,961	252	10,482
Connecticut	1,776	17	61	2,535	402	1	3,122	237	8,151
Delaware	979		14	291	72	1	974	4	2,335
District of Columbia	1,106	2	2	230		1	10	790	2,141
Florida	15,667	90	208	9,165	1,932	26	25,187	1,066	53,341
Georgia	7,461	9	67	1,330	645	3	9,085	152	18,752
Hawaii	23	1	151	37	632	248	205	101	1,398
Idaho									
Illinois	8,856	19	183	3,871		18	13,969	581	27,497
Indiana	3,837	20	41	1,677	1,229	20	12,973	426	20,223
Iowa	1,193	90	92	986	442	28	7,548	372	10,751
Kansas	227	21	8	255	102	4	1,243	8	1,868
Kentucky	1,640	9	11	496	438	8	10,125	4,327	17,054
Louisiana	3,984	29	21	192	136	3	3,947	146	8,458
Maine	52	24	9	165	109	4	2,306	1,112	3,781
Maryland	5,720	10	137	895	252	1	4,559	1,505	13,079
Massachusetts	2,627	26	340	4,763	779	17	7,423	3,259	19,234
Michigan	7,821	172	88	1,594	2,596	5	20,622	536	33,434
Minnesota	777	351	114	472	563		1,913	48	4,238
Mississippi	3,238	18	10	206	122	1	3,756	248	7,599
Missouri	698	16	10	177	63	4	3,633	84	4,685
Montana	13	248	2	78	52	5	865	61	1,324
Nebraska	454	176	36	456	89	3	2,384	290	3,888
Nevada	1,103	40	62	1,486	400	67	2,173	105	5,436
New Hampshire	31		4	72	19	1	709	65	901
New Jersey	2,467	3	83	2,079	141	10	2,812	1,436	9,031
New Mexico	103	364	4	3,657	111	5	1,476	162	5,882
New York	19,620	253	1,157	17,148	1,469	25	22,296	6,407	68,375
North Carolina	6,980	696	64	2,218	1,097	28	11,865	202	23,150
North Dakota	45	290	5	107	91	8	813	43	1,402
Ohio	5,429	17	17	918	1,213	4	13,832	7,820	29,250
Oklahoma	955	574	26	1,437	2,484	6	4,145		9,627
Oregon	422	229	61	1,521	379	31	5,291	1,642	9,576
Pennsylvania									
Puerto Rico									
Rhode Island	390	21	23	818	199	2	1,527	238	3,218
South Carolina	4,055	15	30	464	581	11	5,962	321	11,439
South Dakota	39	568	3	74	94	1	418	27	1,224
Tennessee	1,019	5	8	273	181	5	4,101	4,477	10,069
Texas	10,066	49	237	29,118	1,974	54	19,499	1,554	62,551
Utah	255	162	68	1,957	135	102	6,686	54	9,419
Vermont	6		6	3	3		616	15	649
Virginia	1,583	2	41	615	319	21	3,081	164	5,826
Washington	449	375	97	982	589	51	3,651	352	6,546
West Virginia	121		2	63	254	2	3,961	188	4,591
Wisconsin	931	206	67	454	163	6	2,381	437	4,645
Wyoming	19	8	4	96	8		534	36	705
Total	**140,079**	**7,770**	**5,587**	**145,559**	**27,174**	**1,208**	**293,667**	**45,880**	**666,924**
Rate									
Percent	21.0	1.2	0.8	21.8	4.1	0.2	44.0	6.9	100.0
States reporting	49	45	49	49	47	46	49	48	49

perpetrators aged 35 to 44 years (23.4%). The Children's Bureau notes in *Child Maltreatment 2012* that 53.5% of the perpetrators in 2012 were women, and 45.3% were men. The sex of the remaining 1.3% was unknown. Figure 2.4 shows perpetrator race and ethnicity for 2012. The largest percentage was white (48.9%), followed by African American (19.9%) and Hispanic (18.9%).

As shown in Table 2.7, 60.2% of the perpetrators in 2012 committed neglect alone, which was, by far, the most prevalent single maltreatment type. Categories of child neglect are shown in Table 2.8. As Figure 2.5 indicates, chronic neglect can stem from a range of factors and can arise from external social circumstances (such as poverty), personal issues that impact the ability of parents to raise their children effectively, or specific childhood trauma.

TABLE 2.3

Child maltreatment victims, by race and ethnicity and state, 2012 [CONTINUED]

State	African-American	American Indian or Alaska Native	Asian	Hispanic	Multiple race	Pacific Islander	White
			Rate per 1,000 children				
Alabama	7.8	1.5	0.9	5.6	10.8	4.7	8.2
Alaska	12.4	44.7	1.9	5.3	8.7	12.3	6.7
Arizona	12.4	6.1	0.6	5.5	6.7	7.3	5.9
Arkansas	14.8	2.5	2.1	8.9	34.2	17.1	16.4
California	18.7	13.2	1.8	8.6	6.3	6.7	7.1
Colorado	17.6	9.0	2.0	10.1	7.2	24.5	7.0
Connecticut	20.2	9.0	1.7	15.3	14.4	3.1	6.6
Delaware	19.1		1.9	10.1	7.2	12.7	9.1
District of Columbia	16.7	10.2	0.9	15.3		13.3	0.5
Florida	19.2	8.9	2.0	8.0	14.8	9.4	14.0
Georgia	9.0	1.8	0.8	3.9	8.3	1.9	7.9
Hawaii	4.1	1.6	2.0	0.8	6.6	6.8	5.0
Idaho							
Illinois	18.2	4.2	1.3	5.3		25.5	8.7
Indiana	22.0	6.3	1.5	10.4	21.4	39.8	11.1
Iowa	38.9	35.5	6.3	14.8	17.6	39.3	13.0
Kansas	4.9	3.6	0.4	2.0	2.9	6.5	2.5
Kentucky	17.6	5.8	0.8	9.2	11.9	11.4	12.4
Louisiana	9.5	3.6	1.2	3.2	4.7	7.0	6.7
Maine	8.1	11.6	2.3	24.8	12.6	34.8	9.7
Maryland	13.4	3.3	1.8	5.5	4.0	1.7	7.4
Massachusetts	23.8	9.6	4.0	21.8	16.1	30.0	7.9
Michigan	21.3	12.3	1.4	9.2	26.6	9.6	13.3
Minnesota	7.9	20.2	1.6	4.5	9.5		2.1
Mississippi	10.0	4.1	1.5	7.3	8.0	4.6	10.2
Missouri	3.6	2.8	0.4	2.1	1.2	2.0	3.5
Montana	9.6	11.9	1.3	6.7	5.4	31.3	4.9
Nebraska	17.2	34.6	3.9	6.2	5.3	9.5	7.2
Nevada	19.6	7.1	1.6	5.6	10.6	15.6	8.5
New Hampshire	6.9		0.5	5.1	2.3	13.7	3.0
New Jersey	8.7	0.9	0.5	4.3	2.4	17.0	2.8
New Mexico	12.3	6.9	0.7	12.1	8.8	17.5	11.1
New York	28.8	17.1	3.8	17.3	11.3	13.8	10.4
North Carolina	13.0	24.0	1.1	6.7	12.8	16.4	9.5
North Dakota	14.1	22.5	3.5	16.6	15.8	86.0	6.5
Ohio	14.1	4.1	0.3	6.5	10.8	3.7	7.0
Oklahoma	12.5	5.9	1.6	10.2	28.6	3.9	8.0
Oregon	23.5	21.6	1.9	8.2	7.7	7.6	9.4
Pennsylvania							
Puerto Rico							
Rhode Island	25.6	18.7	3.3	17.4	21.8	13.2	11.2
South Carolina	11.9	3.8	2.0	5.3	16.3	18.8	10.0
South Dakota	9.7	21.1	1.3	7.4	11.0	11.8	2.7
Tennessee	3.4	1.6	0.3	2.3	3.8	5.8	4.1
Texas	12.3	2.6	0.9	8.5	12.8	9.9	8.4
Utah	25.2	19.0	4.8	13.0	4.7	10.8	10.0
Vermont	2.9		2.8	1.0	0.7		5.5
Virginia	4.1	0.4	0.4	2.8	3.4	16.9	3.0
Washington	7.2	15.9	0.9	3.1	4.9	4.1	3.9
West Virginia	8.4		0.7	8.0	18.9	21.1	11.5
Wisconsin	8.2	14.9	1.6	3.2	3.6	15.2	2.5
Wyoming	13.7	2.0	4.5	5.1	2.0		5.0
Total							
Rate	14.2	12.4	1.7	8.4	10.3	8.7	8.0
Percent							
States reporting							

SOURCE: "Table 3-7. Victims by Race and Ethnicity, 2012," in *Child Maltreatment 2012*, U.S. Department of Health and Human Services, Administration for Children and Families, Administration on Children, Youth, and Families, Children's Bureau, December 17, 2013, http://www.acf.hhs.gov/sites/default/files/cb/cm2012.pdf (accessed July 16, 2014)

FATALITIES. In *Child Maltreatment 2012*, the Children's Bureau reports that nearly four-fifths (80%) of the child abuse victims who died in 2012 were maltreated by a parent who either acted alone or with someone else. (See Table 2.9.) More than a quarter (27.1%) of the fatality victims were maltreated by their mother acting alone. The second-largest category was the mother and father together (21.2%). Overall, 14.3% of the fatalities were attributed to nonparents in 2012. Among specified nonparent perpetrators, female relatives (2.8%) of the parent and male partners (2.6%) made up the two largest groups of perpetrators.

FIGURE 2.2

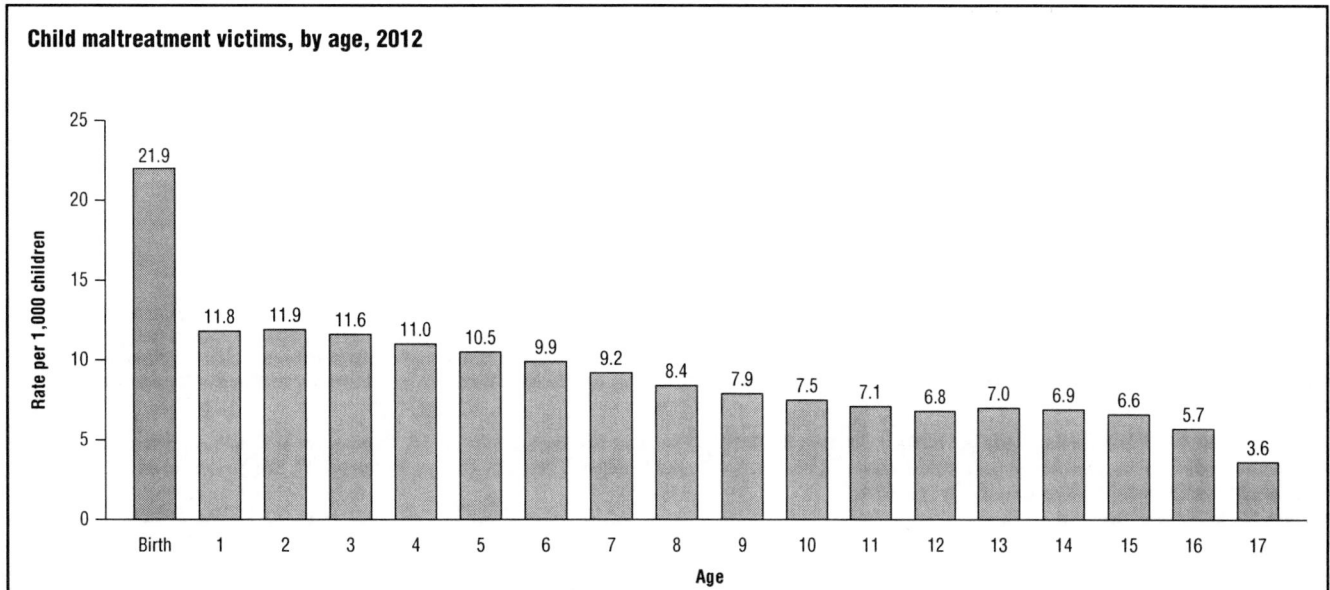

Child maltreatment victims, by age, 2012

Note: The calculation of percentages on this table do not include unborn, children with unknown age, and children with ages 18–21.

SOURCE: "Exhibit 3-D. Victims by Age, 2012," in *Child Maltreatment 2012*, U.S. Department of Health and Human Services, Administration for Children and Families, Administration on Children, Youth, and Families, Children's Bureau, December 17, 2013, http://www.acf.hhs.gov/sites/default/files/cb/cm2012.pdf (accessed July 16, 2014)

TABLE 2.4

Child maltreatment victims, by age and type of maltreatment, 2012

	Number					Percent				
Age	Medical neglect	Neglect	Physical abuse	Psychological maltreatment	Sexual abuse	Medical neglect	Neglect	Physical abuse	Psychological maltreatment	Sexual abuse
<1–2	5,212	157,713	30,689	12,371	1,660	33.2	29.7	24.6	21.4	2.6
3–5	2,456	111,770	21,327	11,518	8,802	15.6	21.0	17.1	19.9	14.0
6–8	2,157	88,314	20,883	10,331	10,827	13.7	16.6	16.8	17.8	17.2
9–11	1,925	68,383	17,619	9,280	11,600	12.3	12.9	14.1	16.0	18.4
12–14	2,097	58,491	18,308	8,229	16,560	13.4	11.0	14.7	14.2	26.3
15–17	1,806	44,800	14,887	5,936	13,133	11.5	8.4	12.0	10.3	20.9
Unborn, unknown, and 18–21	52	1,770	831	215	354	0.3	0.3	0.7	0.4	0.6
Total	15,705	531,241	124,544	57,880	62,936					
Percent						100.0	100.0	100.0	100.0	100.0

Notes: Based on data from 51 states. A child may have been the victim of more than one maltreatment type or the same maltreatment type reported several times and therefore, the maltreatment type count is a duplicate count. The categories of "other" and unknown maltreatment types were not included in this analysis. Alleged maltreatments are not and never have been included in this analysis during prior years.

SOURCE: "Exhibit 3-E. Selected Maltreatment Types of Victims by Age, 2012," in *Child Maltreatment 2012*, U.S. Department of Health and Human Services, Administration for Children and Families, Administration on Children, Youth, and Families, Children's Bureau, December 17, 2013, http://www.acf.hhs.gov/sites/default/files/cb/cm2012.pdf (accessed July 16, 2014)

NATIONAL SURVEY OF CHILD AND ADOLESCENT WELL-BEING

In *NSCAW II Baseline Report: Introduction to NSCAW II* (August 1, 2011, http://www.acf.hhs.gov/sites/default/files/opre/nscaw2_intro.pdf), Melissa Dolan et al. explain that the NSCAW studies were authorized under the Personal Responsibility and Work Opportunity Reconciliation Act of 1996. The studies are longitudinal studies, meaning that they involve research that was

conducted on the same test subjects over long periods, typically years. The first NSCAW study (now known as NSCAW I) tracked 5,501 children aged birth to 14 years between 1999 and 2007. The children were selected for the study because they were the subjects of maltreatment investigations by CPS agencies or because they were in foster care. NSCAW II began in 2008 and was ongoing as of November 2014. It was tracking 5,873 children for which maltreatment investigations were closed by CPS

TABLE 2.5

Child maltreatment fatality rates, 2008–12

Reporting year	States reporting	Child population of reporting states	Child fatalities from reporting states	National rate per 100,000 children	Child population of all 52 states	National estimate of child fatalities
2008	51	73,157,339	1,666	2.28	75,411,627	1,720
2009	51	73,234,095	1,685	2.30	75,512,062	1,740
2010	52	75,017,513	1,563	2.08	75,017,513	1,560
2011	51	73,373,783	1,545	2.11	74,783,810	1,580
2012	49	72,483,465	1,593	2.20	74,577,451	1,640

SDC = Summary Data Component.

Notes: Data are from the Child File and Agency File or the SDC. National fatality rates per 100,000 children were calculated by dividing the number of child fatalities by the population of reporting states and multiplying by 100,000. If fewer than 52 states reported data, the national estimate of child fatalities was calculated by multiplying the national fatality rate by the child population of all 52 states and dividing by 100,000. The estimate was rounded to the nearest 10. If 52 states reported data, the national estimate of child fatalities was calculated by taking the number of reported child fatalities and rounding to the nearest 10. Because of the rounding rule, the national estimate could have fewer fatalities than the actual reported number of fatalities.

SOURCE: "Exhibit 4-A. Child Fatality Rates per 100,000 Children, 2008–2012," in *Child Maltreatment 2012*, U.S. Department of Health and Human Services, Administration for Children and Families, Administration on Children, Youth, and Families, Children's Bureau, December 17, 2013, http://www.acf.hhs.gov/sites/default/files/cb/cm2012.pdf (accessed July 16, 2014)

TABLE 2.6

Child maltreatment fatalities, by age, 2012

		Child fatalities		
Age	Child population	Number	Percent	Rate per 100,000 children
<1	3,101,762	584	44.4	18.83
1	3,128,258	202	15.4	6.46
2	3,145,391	138	10.5	4.39
3	3,146,360	88	6.7	2.80
4	3,246,836	71	5.4	2.19
5	3,265,659	32	2.4	0.98
6	3,243,500	23	1.7	0.71
7	3,234,584	23	1.7	0.71
8	3,244,875	17	1.3	0.52
9	3,220,920	11	0.8	0.34
10	3,212,289	22	1.7	0.68
11	3,290,571	26	2.0	0.79
12	3,342,706	6	0.5	0.18
13	3,280,113	15	1.1	0.46
14	3,278,047	11	0.8	0.34
15	3,277,679	13	1.0	0.40
16	3,297,054	4	0.3	0.12
17	3,367,423	11	0.8	0.33
Unborn, unknown, and 18–21		18	1.4	
Total	**58,324,027**	**1,315**		
Percent			100.0	

Note: Based on data from 44 states.

SOURCE: "Table 4-3. Child Fatalities by Age, 2012," in *Child Maltreatment 2012*, U.S. Department of Health and Human Services, Administration for Children and Families, Administration on Children, Youth, and Families, Children's Bureau, December 17, 2013, http://www.acf.hhs.gov/sites/default/files/cb/cm2012.pdf (accessed July 16, 2014)

FIGURE 2.3

Child maltreatment perpetrators, by age, 2012

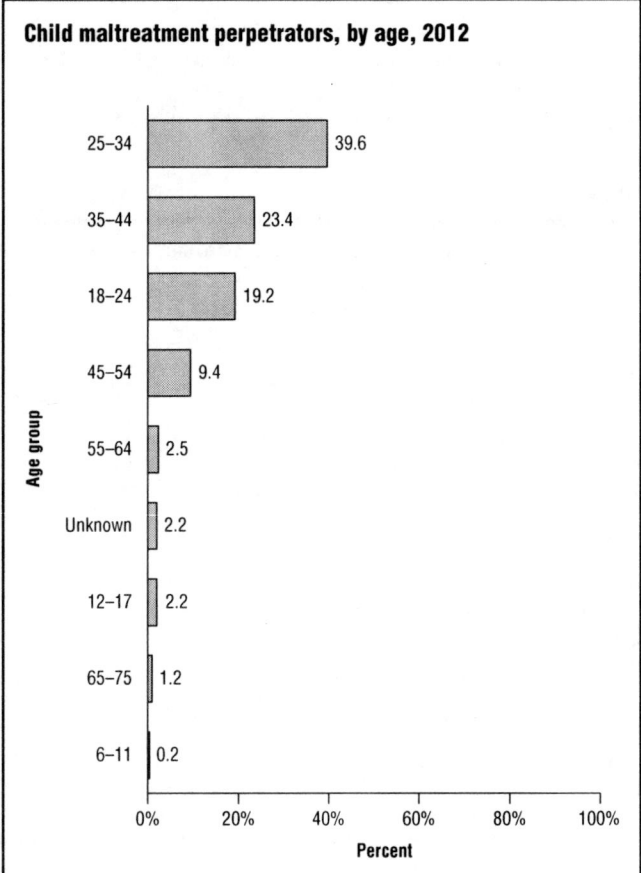

SOURCE: "Exhibit 5-A. Perpetrators by Age, 2012," in *Child Maltreatment 2012*, U.S. Department of Health and Human Services, Administration for Children and Families, Administration on Children, Youth, and Families, Children's Bureau, December 17, 2013, http://www.acf.hhs.gov/sites/default/files/cb/cm2012.pdf (accessed July 16, 2014)

---

agencies between February 2008 and April 2009. The children were in the age range of birth to 17.5 years at that time. As of January 2013, two NSCAW II data collections (or waves) had taken place. Baseline data were collected about the children between March 2008 and September 2009 during Wave 1. Wave 2 data collection for the same children occurred between October 2009 and January 2011, while Wave 3 data were compiled between June 2011 and December 2012.

The NSCAW studies are notable because they follow children as they progress through the child welfare system by monitoring their physical, mental, academic, health, social, and developmental well-being through

FIGURE 2.4

Child maltreatment perpetrators, by race and ethnicity, 2012

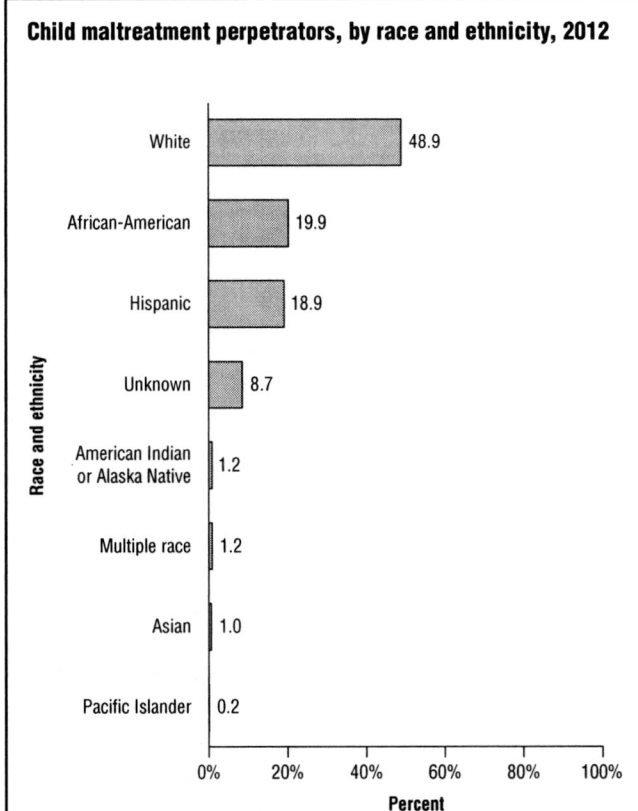

SOURCE: "Exhibit 5-B. Perpetrators by Race and Ethnicity, 2012," in *Child Maltreatment 2012*, U.S. Department of Health and Human Services, Administration for Children and Families, Administration on Children, Youth, and Families, Children's Bureau, December 17, 2013, http://www.acf.hhs.gov/sites/default/files/cb/cm2012.pdf (accessed July 16, 2014)

TABLE 2.7

Child maltreatment perpetrators, by type of maltreatment, 2012

	Duplicated perpetrators	
Maltreatment type	Number	Percent
Single maltreatment type		
Medical neglect	7,739	0.9
Neglect	537,649	60.2
Other	36,645	4.1
Physical abuse	91,288	10.2
Psychological abuse	26,227	2.9
Sexual abuse	56,514	6.3
Unknown	105	0.0
Multiple maltreatment types		
Two or more maltreatment types	137,492	15.4
Total	**893,659**	
Percent		**100.0**

Notes: Based on data from 50 states. The multiple maltreatment category includes any perpetrator who committed more than one type of maltreatment to a child in a specific record.

SOURCE: "Exhibit 5-C. Perpetrators by Maltreatment Type, 2012," in *Child Maltreatment 2012*, U.S. Department of Health and Human Services, Administration for Children and Families, Administration on Children, Youth, and Families, Children's Bureau, December 17, 2013, http://www.acf.hhs.gov/sites/default/files/cb/cm2012.pdf (accessed July 16, 2014)

interviews or assessments that are conducted with the children themselves, their parents, their caseworkers, and nonparent caregivers. Reports from caseworkers, teachers, and administrative records are also reviewed. The children's families and/or caregivers are assessed to determine their status in terms of physical and mental health, substance use, domestic violence and other criminal acts, and services received from welfare agencies. In addition, NSCAW data include information about the maltreatment investigations that were conducted and any interventions and services that resulted. Risk factors for maltreatment are also examined, as is explained in Chapter 3.

NSCAW II Data

Table 2.10 provides characteristics about the 4,972 children who were evaluated in NSCAW II, Wave 2. It should be noted that these data describe the children at the time the baseline data were collected, which was between October 2009 and January 2011. The OPRE explains that the children were selected to be as nationally representative as possible of children who come into contact with the child welfare system. However, extra

infants and children in out-of-home placement were added because the OPRE considers these to be "high-risk groups." In addition, the proportion of children receiving services to those not receiving services was adjusted to include more children receiving services.

Investigatory

Table 2.11 lists the types of maltreatment that the children were alleged to have received or the other reasons why the children were investigated by CPS agency caseworkers. It should be noted that children can fall under more than one category, for example, if they suffered from more than one type of maltreatment. Overall, neglect in the form of lack of supervision was the primary maltreatment type reported (980 incidences), followed by physical abuse (846 incidences) and failure to provide (446 incidences). Among problems other than maltreatment, a substance-abusing parent was by far the most common problem, with 605 incidences. Substance exposure (495 incidences) and domestic violence (466 incidences) were also notable factors.

Cecilia Casanueva et al. report in *NSCAW II Wave 2 Report: Child Safety* (August 2012, http://www.acf.hhs.gov/sites/default/files/opre/nscaw_child_safety.pdf) that, overall, when caseworkers were asked to name the "most serious" problem that spurred an investigation, the results were neglect in the form of lack of supervision (23.3%), physical abuse (21.9%), and substance-abusing parent (10.6%). Combined, these three problems accounted for more than half (55.8%) of the "most serious" problems cited.

TABLE 2.8

Types and examples of child neglect

Types of neglect	Examples
Abandonment	Abandonment by parents/caregivers
Physical	• Inadequate nutrition • Inadequate or unsuitable seasonal clothing • Unreasonably unclean clothing • Inadequate hygiene • Exposure to chronically unhygienic, unsafe, chaotic or cluttered environment
Medical	• Delays in medical/health care • Parental/caregiver failure to seek health care • Parental/caregiver failure to seek therapy for developmental delay
Psychological/emotional	• Deprivation of emotional nurturance • Emotional absence of parent/caregiver
Developmental	• Parental/caregiver failure to recognize developmental capacities/limits • Parent/caregiver failure to address developmental needs • Parent/caregiver failure to foster ordinary developmental milestones
Supervisory	• Being left alone for extended or prolonged periods given the child's age and capacities • Being left in a locked, closed vehicle • Parental/caregiver incapacitation
Guidance	• Exposure to antisocial/criminal behaviors by parents/caregivers • Exposure to illicit drug use by parents/caregivers • Parental/caregiver failure to prevent/discourage risk taking or criminal behavior
Educational	• Parental/caregiver failure to ensure school enrollment or other necessary educational institutions • Parent/caregiver failure to discourage frequent absenteeism

SOURCE: "Types of Neglect," in *Chronic Child Neglect*, U.S. Department for Health and Human Services, Administration for Children and Families, Administration on Children, Youth, and Families, Children's Bureau, January 2013, https://www.childwelfare.gov/pubs/chronic_neglect.pdf (accessed July 18, 2014)

FIGURE 2.5

Tiers of chronic child neglect

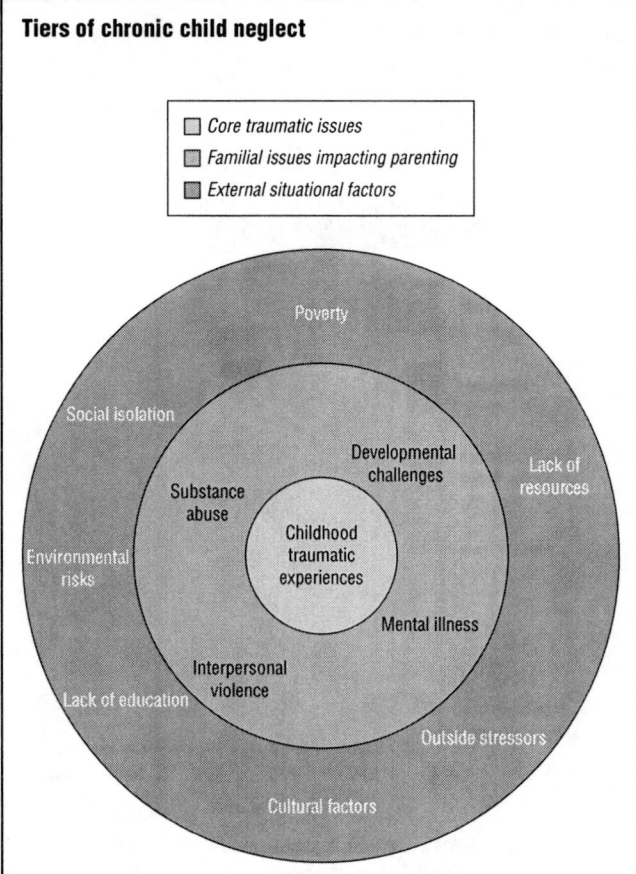

SOURCE: "Three Tiers of Chronic Neglect," in *Chronic Child Neglect*, U.S. Department for Health and Human Services, Administration for Children and Families, Administration on Children, Youth, and Families, Children's Bureau, January 2013, https://www.childwelfare.gov/pubs/chronic_neglect.pdf (accessed July 18, 2014)

CPS agency investigations of reports of child maltreatment result in a disposition, or finding, for each report. Although disposition terms differ from state to state, possible dispositions include:

• Substantiated or founded—sufficient evidence exists to support the allegation of maltreatment or risk of maltreatment

• Indicated or reason to suspect—the abuse and/or neglect cannot be confirmed, but there is reason to suspect that the child is maltreated or is at risk of maltreatment

• Unsubstantiated or unfounded—no maltreatment has occurred or sufficient evidence does not exist to conclude that the child is maltreated or is at risk of being maltreated

According to the OPRE, of 4,611 investigations analyzed in the NSCAW II Wave 2 report, less than one-quarter (22.1%) resulted in substantiated claims. Another 7.6% of investigations produced an indicated status, while 70.4% of investigations resulted in unsubstantiated claims. Children aged zero to two years had the highest percentage of substantiated claims (31.7%), followed by children aged 11 to 17 years (22.1%), children aged three to five years (21.3%), and children aged six to 10 years (15.6%).

Self-Reported Violence, Aggression, and Neglect

As noted earlier, the NSCAW studies include interviews with the children and their parents and/or caregivers. Table 2.12 shows child reports of violent acts that were committed by people who were living at home with the children. Only children aged eight to 17 years were questioned. Many of the children reported seeing acts that involved adults yelling and other children being spanked at home. Fewer percentages reported more serious acts, such as drug dealing, stabbings, and shootings. Overall, 11.1% of the children had seen a person arrested at their home, and 2.5% of the children had witnessed such an event within the previous month. When asked about violent acts that were committed against them personally by adults in the home, 42.3% said they had been yelled

TABLE 2.9

Perpetrators of child maltreatment fatalities, by relationship to victim, 2012

Perpetrator	Child fatalities Number	Child fatalities Percent
Parent		
Father	200	17.1
Father and other	25	2.1
Mother	318	27.1
Mother and other	147	12.5
Mother and father	248	21.2
Total parents	**938**	**80.0**
Nonparent		
Child daycare provider	14	1.2
Foster parent (female relative)		
Foster parent (male relative)	1	0.1
Foster parent (nonrelative)	2	0.2
Foster parent (unknown relationship)		
Friend or neighbor	2	0.2
Group home and residential facility staff	1	0.1
Legal guardian (female)	1	0.1
Legal guardian (male)		
More than one nonparental perpetrator	27	2.3
Other	33	2.8
Other professional		
Partner of parent (female)	1	0.1
Partner of parent (male)	30	2.6
Relative (female)	33	2.8
Relative (male)	23	2.0
Total nonparents	**168**	**14.3**
Unknown		
Unknown	66	5.6
Total unknown	**66**	**5.6**
Total	**1,172**	
Percent		100.0

Note: Based on data from 41 states.

SOURCE: "Table 4-4. Child Fatalities by Perpetrator Relationship, 2012," in *Child Maltreatment 2012*, U.S. Department of Health and Human Services, Administration for Children and Families, Administration on Children, Youth, and Families, Children's Bureau, December 17, 2013, http://www.acf.hhs.gov/sites/default/files/cb/cm2012.pdf (accessed July 16, 2014)

TABLE 2.10

Children represented in the National Survey of Child and Adolescent Well-Being II, Wave 2, 2009–11

	Population	Total %
Total	**4,972**	**100.0**
Gender		
Male	2,549	50.6
Female	2,423	49.4
Age (years)		
1–2	2,225	12.7
3–5	770	23.0
6–10	958	29.9
11–17	1,019	34.4
Race/ethnicity		
Black	1,569	22.4
White	1,675	41.4
Hispanic	1,379	28.9
Other	329	7.3
Setting		
In-home	3,420	86.2
Formal kin care	414	2.5
Informal kin care	419	7.8
Foster care	655	2.8
Group home or residential program	47	0.5
Other out of home	17	0.4
Insurance status		
Private	505	15.0
Public	4,141	75.0
Other	73	2.3
Uninsured	233	7.7

Note: All analyses were on weighted NSCAW II Wave 2 data; Populations are unweighted and, therefore, direct percentages cannot be calculated by hand. Reported *N*s vary slightly across analyses because of missing data in some variable categories.

SOURCE: Cecelia Casanueva et al., "Exhibit 1. Child Characteristics at Wave 2," in *NSCAW II Wave 2 Report: Child Safety*, U.S. Department of Health and Human Services, Administration for Children and Families, Office of Planning, Research, and Evaluation, August 2012, http://www.acf.hhs.gov/sites/default/files/opre/nscaw_child_safety.pdf (accessed July 16, 2014)

at, and 24.6% said they had been spanked. Smaller percentages said they had experienced an adult throwing something at them or shoving or slapping them "really hard." For the most violent acts, 3.2% of the children said an adult in the home had beat them up, and 0.3% said they had a gun or knife pointed at them by an adult.

Acts of caregiver aggression reported by children to have occurred within the previous year are shown in Table 2.13. Only children aged 11 to 17 years were questioned. Overall, 83.9% of the children reported experiencing nonviolent discipline by their caregivers (e.g., being told that a behavior was wrong). More than half (53.4%) reported psychological aggression (e.g., yelling or shouting), and 31% reported "minor" physical assault or corporal punishment (e.g., spanking on the bottom or slapping a hand). More than one in 10 (10.6%) of the children reported experiencing "severe physical assault" (e.g., hitting with a fist or knocking a child down), and 8.2% reported experiencing "very severe physical assault" (e.g., choking, burning, or threatening with a knife or gun) within the previous year from their caregivers.

Table 2.14 shows reports of in-home parental aggression against the children within the previous year as self-reported by the parents. Overall, 96.7% of the parents reported using nonviolent discipline on the children. More than three-quarters (75.4%) reported using psychological aggression, and 47.9% reported conducting "minor" physical assault or corporal punishment. Only 3.3% of the parents reported inflicting "severe physical assault" and 0.9% reported inflicting "very severe physical assault" within the previous year on the children. In addition, 21.1% of the parents admitted to neglect, while 1.2% admitted to committing sexual abuse of the children.

NATIONAL INCIDENCE STUDY OF CHILD ABUSE AND NEGLECT

As part of the 1974 Child Abuse Prevention and Treatment Act (CAPTA), Congress mandated the HHS

TABLE 2.11

Caseworker investigations in the National Survey of Child and Adolescent Well-Being II, Wave 2, 2009–11

Most serious type of child maltreatment or reason for investigation	Population	%
Total	**5,054**	**100.0**
Physical abuse	846	21.9
Sexual abuse	300	7.4
Failure to provide	446	9.2
Lack of supervision (neglect)	980	23.3
Emotional abuse	149	5.6
Abandonment	85	0.7
Moral/legal maltreatment	3	0.0
Educational maltreatment	39	0.7
Exploitation	4	0.2
Other	560	9.3
Prematurity or low birth weight	12	0.0
Substance exposure	495	2.5
Substance-abusing parent	605	10.6
Domestic violence	466	7.6
Voluntary relinquishment	13	0.1
Children in need of services	29	0.6
Investigation only way to get services	22	0.5

Note: All analyses were on weighted NSCAW II baseline data; Populations are unweighted and, therefore, direct percentages cannot be calculated by hand. Reported *N*s vary slightly across analyses because of missing data in some variable categories.

SOURCE: Cecelia Casanueva et al., "Exhibit 2. Most Serious Type of Child Maltreatment at Baseline and Other Reasons for Investigation by Caseworker Report," in *NSCAW II Wave 2 Report: Child Safety*, U.S. Department of Health and Human Services, Administration for Children and Families, Office of Planning, Research, and Evaluation, August 2012, http://www.acf.hhs.gov/sites/default/files/opre/nscaw_child_safety.pdf (accessed July 16, 2014)

to conduct a periodic National Incidence Study of Child Abuse and Neglect (NIS). As of November 2014, four NIS studies had been conducted by the private research company Westat under contract to the OPRE. The most recent report was *Fourth National Incidence Study of Child Abuse and Neglect (NIS-4) Report to Congress* (January 2010, http://www.acf.hhs.gov/sites/default/files/opre/nis4_report_congress_full_pdf_jan2010.pdf), written by Andrea J. Sedlak et al. and published jointly by the OPRE and the Children's Bureau.

During the NIS studies, data on maltreated children were collected not only from CPS agencies but also from professionals in community agencies, such as law enforcement, public health, juvenile probation, mental health, and voluntary social services, as well as from hospitals, schools, and day care centers. As such, the NIS reports are considered to be comprehensive sources of information about the incidence of child maltreatment in the United States.

Conducted during two three-month periods in 2005 and 2006, the studies described by Sedlak et al. constitute the most extensive report on child maltreatment in the United States as of November 2014. These studies were based on a nationally representative sample of 10,791 professionals in 1,094 agencies serving 122 counties. The study group included not only child victims investigated

TABLE 2.12

Home violence reported by children in the National Survey of Child and Adolescent Well-Being II, Wave 2, 2009–11

	VEX-R ever		VEX-R last month	
	Population	%	Population	%
VEX-R violence witnessing items				
Child saw adult yell at other	1,405	36.8	1,408	22.1
Child saw adult throw something at other	1,418	11.8	1,418	3.9
Child saw adult shove other	1,417	11.0	1,418	5.1
Child saw adult slap other	1,419	10.0	1,419	5.2
Child saw adult beat up other	1,421	4.6	1,421	1.3
Child saw adult steal at home	1,418	8.0	1,418	3.4
Child saw adult point knife or gun at other	1,414	2.1	1,418	1.0
Child saw adult stab other	1,423	1.2	1,423	0.6
Child saw adult shoot other	1,421	0.5	1,421	0.4
Child saw person arrested at home	1,416	11.1	1,417	2.5
Child saw person deal drugs at home	1,416	2.5	1,414	1.9
Child saw child being spanked	1,417	25.9	1,417	13.6
VEX-R violence victimization items				
Adult yelled at child	1,419	42.3	1,418	24.7
Adult threw something at child	1,420	8.6	1,421	3.9
Adult shoved child "really hard"	1,417	9.2	1,417	3.9
Adult slapped child "really hard"	1,418	10.8	1,418	4.2
Adult beat up child	1,392	3.2	1,393	1.2
Adult pointed a gun or knife at child	1,397	0.3	1,397	0.3
Adult spanked child	1,418	24.6	1,417	7.7

Note: All analyses were on weighted NSCAW II Wave 2 data; Populations are unweighted and, therefore, direct percentages cannot be calculated by hand. Reported Populations vary slightly across analyses because of missing data in some variable categories. Instrument used was the Violence Exposure Scale–Revised (VEX-R) (Fox & Leavitt, 1995). Only children 8 to 17 years old responded to the VEX-R. Results reported here are only for acts of violence committed by people living at home with the child.

SOURCE: Cecelia Casanueva et al., "Exhibit 7. Exposure to Violence among Children 8 to 17 Years Old by Child Report at Wave 2," in *NSCAW II Wave 2 Report: Child Safety*, U.S. Department of Health and Human Services, Administration for Children and Families, Office of Planning, Research, and Evaluation, August 2012, http://www.acf.hhs.gov/sites/default/files/opre/nscaw_child_safety.pdf (accessed July 16, 2014)

TABLE 2.13

Acts of discipline, aggression, and neglect reported by children in the National Survey of Child and Adolescent Well-Being II, Wave 2, 2009–11

	Population	CTS-PC nonviolent discipline %	CTS-PC psychological aggression %	CTS-PC minor physical assault (corporal punishment) %	CTS-PC severe physical assault %	CTS-PC very severe physical assault %
Total	927	83.9	53.4	31.0	10.6	8.2
Gender						
Male	413	80.0	46.0	29.4	10.8	5.8
Female	514	86.7	58.7	32.2	10.4	9.9
Age (years)						
11–12	279	84.2	50.4	33.5	9.4	5.0
13–14	267	82.9	52.4	29.3	9.4	9.3
15–17	376	84.4	56.8	30.6	12.4	10.0
Race/ethnicity						
Black	257	81.5	53.8	34.0	17.1	10.7
White	360	82.6	54.3	31.9	11.9	7.7
Hispanic	223	87.7	52.4	34.1	7.1	11.3
Other	58	83.3	51.8	10.9	4.9	0.9

CTS-PC = Conflict Tactics Scale Parent-Child.
Note: All analyses were on weighted NSCAW II Wave 2 data; Populations are unweighted and, therefore, direct percentages cannot be calculated by hand. Reported Populations vary slightly across analyses because of missing data in some variable categories. Instrument used was the Conflict Tactics Scale Parent-Child.

SOURCE: Cecelia Casanueva et al., "Exhibit 9. Caregiver Aggression and Neglect of Children 11 to 17 Years Old from a Caregiver in the Past Year by Child Report at Wave 2," in *NSCAW II Wave 2 Report: Child Safety*, U.S. Department of Health and Human Services, Administration for Children and Families, Office of Planning, Research, and Evaluation, August 2012, http://www.acf.hhs.gov/sites/default/files/opre/nscaw_child_safety.pdf (accessed July 16, 2014)

TABLE 2.14

Acts of discipline, aggression, and neglect of children reported by in-home parents in the National Survey of Child and Adolescent Well-Being II, Wave 2, 2009–11

	Population	CTS-PC nonviolent discipline %	CTS-PC psychological aggression %	CTS-PC minor physical assault (corporal punishment) %	CTS-PC severe physical assault %	CTS-PC very severe physical assault %	CTS-PC neglect %	CTS-PC sexual abuse %
Total	3,346	96.7	75.4	47.9	3.3	0.9	21.1	1.2
Gender								
Male	1,726	97.9	78.9	50.7	2.9	0.9	19.0	0.8
Female	1,620	95.4	71.8	45.0	3.7	0.9	23.2	1.7
Age (years)								
1–2	1,384	96.5	67.5	55.2	1.6	3.4	16.3	0.1
3–5	531	97.7	77.1	61.1	4.6	0.5	16.1	0.8
6–10	717	97.5	77.7	56.6	4.5	0.6	16.4	0.9
11–17	714	95.3	75.0	28.3	2.0	0.5	30.4	2.2
Race/ethnicity								
Black	326	97.0	73.6	44.6	6.3	1.1	26.0	1.1
White	582	98.2	83.0	42.7	1.6	0.7	24.7	2.5
Hispanic	160	91.2	66.9	28.1	1.3	0.0	26.4	0.6
Other	76	92.3	62.4	35.3	2.8	0.0	32.5	0.0

Note: All analyses were on weighted NSCAW II Wave 2 data; Populations are unweighted and, therefore, direct percentages cannot be calculated by hand. Reported Populations vary slightly across analyses because of missing data in some variable categories. The instrument used was the Conflict Tactics Scale Parent-Child Version (CTS-PC).

SOURCE: Cecelia Casanueva et al., "Exhibit 8. In-Home Parents' Aggression toward and Neglect of Children in the Previous Year by Self-Report at Wave 2," in *NSCAW II Wave 2 Report: Child Safety*, U.S. Department of Health and Human Services, Administration for Children and Families, Office of Planning, Research, and Evaluation, August 2012, http://www.acf.hhs.gov/sites/default/files/opre/nscaw_child_safety.pdf (accessed July 16, 2014)

by CPS agencies but also children seen by professionals in community institutions (such as day care centers, schools, homeless shelters, and hospitals) and in other investigating agencies (such as public health departments, police, and courts). In addition, victim counts were unduplicated, meaning that each child was counted only once.

Definition Standards

Sedlak et al. use two standardized definitions of abuse and neglect:

- Harm Standard—requires that an abusive act or incident of neglect result in demonstrable harm to be counted

- Endangerment Standard—allows children who had not yet demonstrated harm by maltreatment to be counted in the estimates of maltreated children if a non-CPS-agency professional considered them to be at risk of harm or if their maltreatment was substantiated or indicated in a CPS agency investigation

According to Sedlak et al., about 1.3 million children were victims of maltreatment in 2005–06, under the Harm Standard. This was a 19.1% decrease from the Third National Incidence Study of Child Abuse and Neglect (NIS-3; 1996) estimate of 1.6 million children in 1993. The rate of maltreatment per 1,000 children under the age of 18 years was 17.1 in 2005–06, which was not significantly different from the rate of maltreatment in 1986. Declines in the rates of all forms of abuse were at least marginally statistically significant between 1993 and 2005–06, although declines in rates of neglect were not.

Under the Endangerment Standard more than 2.9 million children experienced some type of maltreatment in 2005–06. This estimate was not significantly different from the 1993 estimate, but it was double the 1986 estimate of 1.4 million children. The rates of abuse under the Endangerment Standard declined from 18.2 per 1,000 children in 1993 to 11.3 per 1,000 children in 2005–06, whereas the rates of all forms of neglect remained about the same. The exception was emotional neglect, which rose significantly between 1993 and 2005–06.

NIS-4 data provide detailed information about maltreatment by child demographics, such as gender, age, and race and ethnicity. In addition, the data are broken down by family characteristics, including socioeconomic status.

Gender of Victims

NIS data allow comparisons of types of maltreatment suffered by boys and girls. Under both the Harm and Endangerment Standards of NIS-4, more girls were subjected to maltreatment than were boys. About 8.5 girls per 1,000 children and 6.5 boys per 1,000 children experienced Harm Standard abuse in 2005–06. Under the Harm Standard girls (3 per 1,000 children) were sexually abused about five times more often than were boys (0.6 per 1,000 children). Between 1993 and 2005–06 the rates of serious harm declined 33% for boys and 11% for girls. Although boys were more likely to suffer serious harm than were girls in 1993, Sedlak et al. indicate that by 2005–06 boys' and girls' rates of experiencing serious harm were approximately the same.

The girls' rate of Endangerment Standard abuse (12 per 1,000 children) was slightly higher than the boys' rate (10 per 1,000 children) in 2005–06. Under the Endangerment Standard girls (3.8 per 1,000 children) suffered sexual abuse at 3.8 times the rate of boys (1 per 1,000 children).

Age of Victims

Sedlak et al. find a low incidence of maltreatment in younger children, particularly among those under the age of five years. This may be because, before reaching school age, children are less observable to community professionals, especially educators (the group most likely to report suspected maltreatment). The researchers explain that there was a disproportionate increase in the incidence of maltreatment among children as they reached ages six to 14. Sedlak et al. note that the incidence of maltreatment among children older than the age of 14 years decreased. Older children are more likely to escape if the abuse becomes more prevalent or severe. They are also more able to defend themselves and/or fight back.

Under the Harm Standard only 8.5 per 1,000 children in the zero-to-two age group experienced overall maltreatment. The numbers were significantly higher for children aged six to 17 years. Under the Endangerment Standard 33.4 per 1,000 children aged zero to two years were subjected to overall maltreatment. The oldest age group (15- to 17-year-olds) had a lower rate of maltreatment under the Endangerment Standard, at 29 per 1,000 children. As with the Harm Standard, children between the ages of six and 14 years had a higher incidence of maltreatment.

Race and Ethnicity of Victims

Sedlak et al. find that African American children had a Harm Standard maltreatment rate of 24 per 1,000 children in 2005–06, which was nearly twice the maltreatment rate among white children, at 12.5 per 1,000 children. The Harm Standard maltreatment rate among Hispanic children was 14.2 per 1,000 children. The most significant differences between white and African American children were found for physical abuse; differences between white and African American children for neglect and sexual abuse were marginal. Findings for Endangerment Standard maltreatment revealed similar differences. These findings were different from those of previous years. NIS-3 and the Second National Incidence Study of Child Abuse and Neglect (1991) did not find any disproportionate differences in race in relation to maltreatment incidence.

NIS-4 was the first national survey of child maltreatment to include data on children with disabilities. According to Sedlak et al., in 2005–06 children with disabilities (3.1 per 1,000 children) had a significantly lower rate of maltreatment under the Harm Standard than did children without disabilities (4.2 per 1,000 children). However, children with disabilities (4.7 per 1,000 children) were at a significantly higher risk of emotional neglect under the Harm Standard than were children without disabilities (2.3 per 1,000 children). Under the Endangerment Standard, however, children with disabilities were less likely than children without disabilities to suffer physical abuse, sexual abuse, physical neglect, and emotional neglect. Even so, children with disabilities (9.1 per 1,000 children) had a much higher rate of serious harm resulting from maltreatment under the Endangerment Standard than did children without disabilities (6 per 1,000 children).

Family Characteristics of Victims

Under the Harm Standard children living with a single parent and an unmarried partner were most at risk for child maltreatment (57.2 per 1,000 children) in 2005–06, which was more than eight times the rate of children living with married biological parents (6.8 per 1,000 children). Children living with neither parent also had a high rate of maltreatment (33.2 per 1,000 children) as did children living with a single parent with no partner (28.4 per 1,000 children). These relative risks by family composition were similar for all types of abuse and neglect. According to Sedlak et al., children living with a single parent and an unmarried partner also had a much greater risk of suffering serious injury (20.8 per 1,000 children) than did children living with married biological parents (2.6 per 1,000 children).

Under the Endangerment Standard an estimated 136.1 per 1,000 children living with a single parent and an unmarried partner suffered some type of maltreatment in 2005–06, compared with 15.8 per 1,000 children living with married biological parents. In other words, nearly one out of every eight children living in a household with a single parent and an unmarried partner were maltreated under the Endangerment Standard. Children living with unmarried parents (88.9 per 1,000 children), single parents with no partner (66.3 per 1,000 children), neither parent (66 per 1,000 children), and other married parents (51.5 per 1,000 children) also had substantially higher rates of maltreatment than did children living with married biological parents (15.8 per 1,000 children) under the Endangerment Standard.

SOCIOECONOMIC STATUS. Sedlak et al. report that socioeconomic status (SES) was significantly related to the incidence rates of child maltreatment. A family was considered to have low SES if the household income was below $15,000 per year, if the parents had less than a high school education, or any household member participated in a poverty-related social program. Under the Harm Standard children in families with low SES (22.5 per 1,000 children) had much higher rates of maltreatment than did children not in low SES families (4.4 per 1,000 children) in 2005–06. Under the Endangerment Standard children in low SES families (55.1 per 1,000 children) were nearly six times more likely to experience maltreatment than children not in low SES families (9.5 per 1,000 children). Children in low SES families (10.3 per 1,000 children) also had higher rates of serious harm than children not in low SES families (1.8 per 1,000 children).

Perpetrators of Child Maltreatment

Sedlak et al. indicate that in 2005–06, 81% of child victims were maltreated by their biological parents. Biological parents perpetrated 72% of physical abuse and 73% of emotional abuse. However, 40% of sexually abused children were violated by someone other than a biological or nonbiological parent. Nearly two out of five (37%) children were sexually abused by a biological parent, and almost a quarter (23%) were sexually abused by a nonbiological parent or parent substitute, such as a stepparent or a mother's boyfriend.

Overall, children were somewhat more likely to be maltreated by female perpetrators (68%) than by male perpetrators (48%) in 2005–06. Among children maltreated by their biological parents, 75% were maltreated by their mother, and 43% were maltreated by their father (with some children being maltreated by both parents). Children who were maltreated by nonbiological parents or partners were more likely to be maltreated by male perpetrators (64%) than by female perpetrators (48%), as were children who were maltreated by other adults (75% were mistreated by male perpetrators and 20% by female perpetrators).

Neglected children differed from abused children with regard to the gender of the perpetrators in 2005–06. Because mothers or other females tended to be the primary caretakers, children were more likely to suffer all forms of neglect by female perpetrators (86%) than by male perpetrators (38%). In contrast, children were more often abused by male perpetrators (62%) than by female perpetrators (41%).

REPORTING CHILD ABUSE
Mandatory Reporting

In 1974 Congress enacted the first CAPTA, which set guidelines for the reporting, investigation, and treatment of child maltreatment. States had to meet these requirements to receive federal funding to assist child victims of abuse and neglect. Among its many provisions, CAPTA required the states to enact mandatory reporting laws and procedures so that CPS agencies could take action to protect children from further abuse. Each state now designates mandatory reporters, which typically include health care workers, mental health professionals, social workers, school personnel, child care providers, and law enforcement officers. Some states require all people to report suspected abuse or neglect, not just designated professionals. Most states do not recognize the right for communications between certain professionals and their clients to remain confidential (called "privileged communications") in the case of suspected child abuse. In addition, all states offer immunity to individuals who report incidents of child maltreatment "in good faith" or with sincerity. Besides physical injury and neglect, most states include mental injury, sexual abuse, and the sexual exploitation of minors as cases to be reported. Many states impose penalties, either a fine and/or imprisonment, for failure to report child maltreatment. A mandated reporter, such as a physician, may also be sued for negligence for failing to protect a child from harm.

It should be noted that state statutes regarding mandatory reporting differ significantly and are constantly changing. The National Conference of State Legislatures (NCSL) is a private organization that tracks state legislative action. In "Child Abuse and Neglect Reporting State Statute Overview" (December 2011, http://www .ncsl.org/issues-research/human-services/child-abuse-and-neglect-reporting-statutes.aspx), the NCSL lists state statutes that were enacted as of 2010 dealing with mandatory reporting. In addition, the organization tracks introduced legislation on the subject. According to the NCSL in "Mandatory Reporting of Child Abuse and Neglect 2013 Introduced State Legislation" (September 23, 2014, http://www.ncsl.org/research/human-services/ redirect-mandatory-rprtg-of-child-abuse-and-neglect-2013 .aspx), more than 300 mandatory reporting bills were introduced between 2012 and 2014 in 48 states and the District of Columbia, and 98 of the bills had been enacted.

CHILD ABUSE PREVENTION THROUGH INTERVENTION

One of the main functions of the nation's child welfare system is child abuse prevention. Most of the system's resources are geared toward intervention—that is, responding to reports of suspected child maltreatment and implementing measures to prevent these children (and any other children in the household) from suffering future maltreatment. Thus, the system is largely reactive in that it takes action after problems come to light.

Investigations and Assessments

As shown in Figure 2.6, screened-in maltreatment reports trigger CPS agency investigations or family assessments,

depending on the perceived safety concerns to the child and the future risk of maltreatment. Family assessments, which are also known as "alternative responses," are typically conducted in cases with lower safety concerns and risks. As Figure 2.6 shows, family assessments can result in child welfare or community-based services being offered to the child's family or a referral to other sources for assistance.

According to the Children's Bureau, 58% of the 3.2 million unique children maltreatment cases in 2012 were found to be unsubstantiated. (See Figure 2.1.) Another 17.7% were substantiated, and 0.9% were indicated. As shown in Figure 2.6, substantiated or founded cases are categorized by the level of harm to the child and the risk of future abuse. When a child is deemed to be at low or no risk, the case is typically closed, and the child's family may be referred for voluntary services. However, cases in which the child has been harmed and is at future risk of abuse or there are concerns about ongoing safety issues trigger more serious responses, including court action.

Judicial System Measures

State laws dictate the measures that authorities can take in dealing with children who are the subject of substantiated or founded maltreatment cases. These measures include two possible actions: protective custody and intervention by a state juvenile court.

PROTECTIVE CUSTODY. Protective custody is used when children are believed to be in such imminent danger that there is no time to obtain court approval before removing the children from their home. State laws prescribe who has the authority to place children in protective custody, notifications that must take place (e.g., to the children's parents, CPS agencies, and the court), how long a child can be held in protective custody, and the legal actions that are triggered. Protective custody is the means by which some children enter the child welfare system in the first place if, for example, they are found by police in a dangerous situation.

STATE JUVENILE COURT INTERVENTIONS. CPS agencies can petition state juvenile courts for intervention in child maltreatment cases. The juvenile court system handles legal matters that are related to minors (children under the age of 17 or 18 years, depending on state law). Offenses committed by minors are handled by the delinquency component of the court, while child maltreatment matters are handled by the dependency component of the court. In the fact sheet *How the Child Welfare System Works* (February 2013, https://www.childwelfare .gov/pubs/factsheets/cpswork.pdf), the Children's Bureau indicates that in substantiated or found cases in which families refuse voluntary in-home services offered by CPS agencies, the agencies can petition the juvenile

FIGURE 2.6

The child welfare system

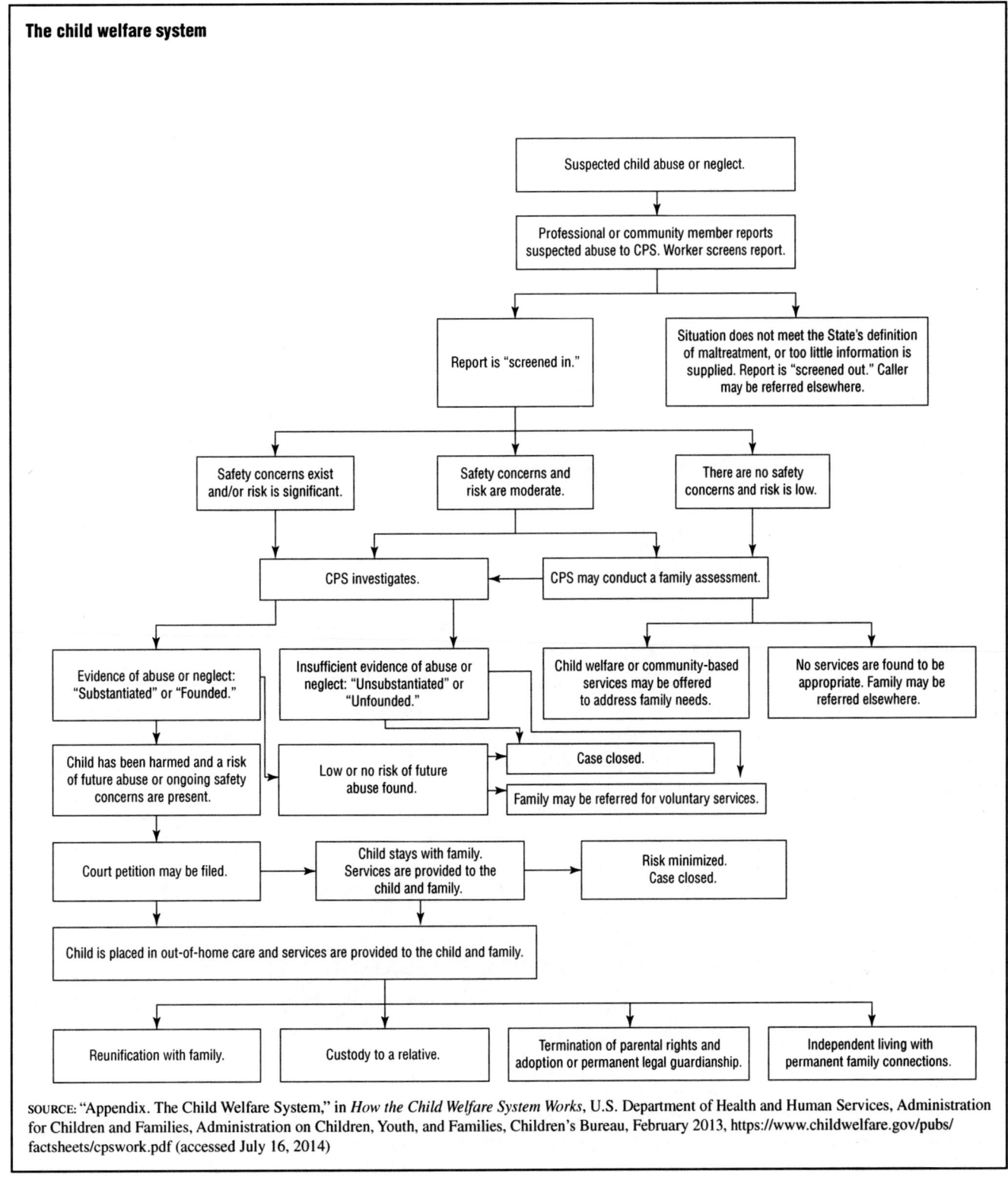

SOURCE: "Appendix. The Child Welfare System," in *How the Child Welfare System Works*, U.S. Department of Health and Human Services, Administration for Children and Families, Administration on Children, Youth, and Families, Children's Bureau, February 2013, https://www.childwelfare.gov/pubs/factsheets/cpswork.pdf (accessed July 16, 2014).

dependency court for "a judicial determination that abuse or neglect occurred." If granted, the court can require the family to participate in in-home services.

In addition, CPS agencies file juvenile court petitions in maltreatment cases in which they believe a child has been seriously harmed and is at high risk for further harm or in danger due to other safety threats. If the court agrees, it can authorize the removal of the child from the home. Removed children are often called wards or dependents of the state or court.

The juvenile court (or family court, depending on the state) also has the authority to terminate parental rights under certain circumstances. For example, the Sacramento County Public Law Library explains in "Termination of

TABLE 2.15

Foster care summary, 2008–12

	2008	2009	2010	2011	2012
Number in foster care on September 30 of the fiscal year	463,792	420,415	405,330	397,885	397,122
Number entered foster care during fiscal year	280,423	255,027	255,278	251,388	251,764
Number exited foster care during fiscal year	288,778	278,252	257,431	246,424	240,923
Number waiting to be adopted on September 30 of the fiscal year	125,712	114,711	109,544	106,350	101,666
Number waiting to be adopted whose parental rights (for all living parents) were terminated during fiscal year	79,392	71,429	65,753	62,769	58,625
Number adopted with public child welfare agency involvement during fiscal year	55,236	57,185	53,525	50,906	52,039

SOURCE: "Numbers at a Glance," in *The AFCARS Report: Preliminary FY 2012 Estimates as of November 2013*, no. 20, U.S. Department of Health and Human Services, Administration for Children and Families, Administration on Children, Youth, and Families, Children's Bureau, November 2013, http://www.acf.hhs.gov/sites/default/files/cb/afcarsreport20.pdf (accessed July 16, 2014)

Parental Rights" (April 2013, http://www.saclaw.org/pages/termination-parental-rights.aspx) that California law allows the juvenile dependency court to terminate the parental rights of the parents of wards of the court if the court finds "that the parent(s) have abused, neglected, or abandoned a child, and/or that the parents suffer from some mental or physical incapacity, including substance abuse, that prevents them from caring for the child." The court's order "permanently severs the legal parent-child relationship."

Foster Care

Children who are removed from their home under court order become part of the foster care system, which is administered at the state and local levels. As shown in Figure 2.6, foster children receive out-of-home care and services. Foster home choices include the homes of relatives, the homes of foster families, and group homes or institutions. Foster care is considered to be a temporary measure for child protection. In most cases, the ultimate goal is to reunite fostered children with their parents. In *How the Child Welfare System Works*, the Children's Bureau notes that administrators are supposed to develop a permanency plan for every child in foster care. These plans are typically based on input from the child's family. According to the Children's Bureau, federal law requires states to hold regular permanency hearings for every child who enters foster care. The first hearing must be held within 12 months from the time of entry into the system. Subsequent hearings must be held every 12 months thereafter. The agency states that "reunification with parents, except in unusual and extreme circumstances, is the permanency plan for most children."

Table 2.15 shows national foster care statistics for fiscal years (FYs) 2008 to 2012. (The federal fiscal year extends from October 1 through September 30.) As of November 2013, there were 397,122 children in foster care throughout the country. Approximately a quarter (101,666) of them were waiting to be adopted. In FY 2012, 52,039 foster care children were adopted through the involvement of public child welfare agencies.

Table 2.16 provides detailed data about the children who were in foster care as of September 30, 2012. There was a slightly higher percentage of boys (52%) than girls (48%) in foster care at that time, and the mean (average) age was 9.1 years. Nearly half of the children (47%) were aged seven years or younger. The largest single contingents were 16 and 17 year olds, each of which accounted for 7% of all children in foster care. There were also thousands of young adults aged 18 to 20 years in the system. Depending on state laws and policies, these are the ages at which children typically achieve emancipation (leave the foster care system) because they are legally considered to be adults.

In "The AFCARS Report: Preliminary FY 2012 Estimates as of November 2013" (November 2013, http://www.acf.hhs.gov/sites/default/files/cb/afcarsreport20.pdf), the Children's Bureau indicates that on a race and ethnicity basis, the largest shares of foster children were white (42%), African American (26%), and Hispanic (21%). (See Table 2.16.) The average time spent in foster care was 22.7 months. Overall, 47% of the children had been in foster care for less than a year, while 23% had spent at least a year, but less than two years, and 12% had spent at least two years, but less than three years. Another 9% of the children had been in foster care for three to four years, and 9% for five years or more. (It should be noted that the individual percentages do not sum to 100% due to rounding.)

As of September 30, 2012, nearly half (47%) of the children were living in the homes of foster families to whom they were not related, and 28% were living with relatives designated as foster parents. (See Table 2.16.) Smaller percentages were in institutions (9%) and group homes (6%). The permanency plan for just over half (53%) of all the children was to be reunited with their parent(s) or principal caretaker(s) at some point. Adoption was the goal for another 24% of the children.

More children entered the foster care system (251,764 entries) than exited it (240,923 exits) in FY

TABLE 2.16

Age as of September 30th		Years
Mean		9.1
Median		8.5

Age as of September 30th	Percent	Number
Less than 1 year	6%	24,977
1 year	8%	30,248
2 years	7%	27,405
3 years	6%	25,343
4 years	6%	23,569
5 years	5%	21,109
6 years	5%	19,322
7 years	4%	17,561
8 years	4%	16,018
9 years	4%	15,002
10 years	4%	14,239
11 years	4%	14,169
12 years	4%	14,770
13 years	4%	16,268
14 years	5%	19,450
15 years	6%	23,475
16 years	7%	27,300
17 years	7%	29,288
18 years	3%	11,280
19 years	1%	3,588
20 years	1%	2,448

Race/ethnicity		
American Indian/Alaskan Native	2%	8,266
Asian	1%	2,287
Black or African American	26%	101,915
Native Hawaiian/other Pacific Islander	0%	779
Hispanic (of any race)	21%	84,186
White	42%	164,990
Unknown/unable to determine	3%	11,155
Two or more races	6%	22,883

Sex		
Male	52%	207,947
Female	48%	189,113

Most recent placement setting		
Pre-adoptive home	4%	14,269
Foster family home (relative)	28%	108,841
Foster family home (non-relative)	47%	184,379
Group home	6%	23,822
Institution	9%	34,179
Supervised independent living	1%	4,114
Runaway	1%	4,969
Trial home visit	5%	21,261

Case plan goal		
Reunify with parent(s) or principal caretaker(s)	53%	202,894
Live with other relative(s)	3%	13,126
Adoption	24%	93,094
Long term foster care	5%	20,047
Emancipation	5%	20,305
Guardianship	4%	14,798
Case plan goal not yet established	5%	18,048

Time in care		Months
Mean		22.7
Median		13.1

Time in care (months)		Number
Less than 1 month	5%	20,308
1–5 months	22%	87,302
6–11 months	20%	78,599
12–17 months	14%	57,347
18–23 months	9%	37,247
24–29 months	7%	27,466
30–35 months	5%	17,897
3–4 years	9%	36,560
5 years or more	9%	34,389

2011. (See Table 2.15.) Table 2.17 provides detailed information about the children who exited the system.

TABLE 2.16

Children in foster care as of September 30, 2012 [CONTINUED]

Note: All races exclude children of Hispanic origin. Children of Hispanic ethnicity may be any race.

SOURCE: "Children in Foster Care on September 30, 2012," in *The AFCARS Report: Preliminary FY 2012 Estimates as of November 2013*, no. 20, U.S. Department of Health and Human Services, Administration for Children and Families, Administration on Children, Youth, and Families, Children's Bureau, November 2013, http://www.acf.hhs.gov/sites/default/files/cb/afcarsreport20.pdf (accessed July 16, 2014)

The mean age was 9.1 years. Half (50%) of those exiting were aged seven years or younger. Whites (44%) made up the largest contingent of the children who exited, followed by African Americans (25%) and Hispanics (20%). On average, a child who exited the system in FY 2012 had spent 20.4 months in foster care. Nearly three-quarters (74%) of the children who left had been in foster care for less than two years. Another 13% had spent at least two years, but less than three years in care, while 9% had been in care for three to four years and 6% had spent five years or more in foster care. (It should be noted that the individual percentages do not sum to 100% due to rounding.) Just over half (51%) of the children left the foster system to be reunited with their parent(s) or principal caretaker(s), while 22% were adopted, and 10% were emancipated.

The Debate about Family Preservation

The Adoption Assistance and Child Welfare Act of 1980 mandated: "In each case, reasonable efforts would be made (1) prior to the placement of a child in foster care, to prevent or eliminate the need for removal of the child from his home, and (2) to make it possible for the child to return to his home." However, because the law did not define the term *reasonable efforts*, states and courts interpreted the term in different ways. In many cases child welfare personnel took the "reasonable efforts" of providing family counseling, respite care, and substance abuse treatment, thus preventing the child from being removed from abusive parents.

The law was a reaction to what was seen as overzealousness during the 1960s and 1970s, when children, especially African American children, were taken from their homes because their parents were poor. In the 21st century, however, some believe that problems of drug or substance abuse can mean that returning the child to the home is likely a guarantee of further abuse. Others note that some situations exist where a parent's live-in partner, who sometimes has no emotional attachment to the child, may also present risks to the child.

Richard J. Gelles, a prominent family violence expert and once a vocal advocate of family preservation, had a change of heart after studying the case of 15-month-old

TABLE 2.17

Children exiting foster care during federal fiscal year (FY) 2012

Age at exit		Years
Mean		9.1
Median		8.2

Age at exit	Percent	Number
Less than 1 year	4%	10,380
1 year	8%	18,229
2 years	8%	19,167
3 years	7%	17,246
4 years	7%	15,590
5 years	6%	13,817
6 years	5%	12,101
7 years	5%	11,035
8 years	4%	9,972
9 years	4%	9,219
10 years	4%	8,487
11 years	3%	8,168
12 years	3%	7,693
13 years	3%	8,235
14 years	4%	8,967
15 years	5%	10,677
16 years	5%	12,437
17 years	5%	12,804
18 years	8%	20,208
19 years	2%	3,885
20 years	0%	928

Time in care		Months
Mean		20.4
Median		13.4

Time in care		Number
Less than 1 month	12%	27,712
1–5 months	15%	36,143
6–11 months	20%	47,059
12–17 months	16%	37,605
18–23 months	11%	26,804
24–29 months	8%	18,163
30–35 months	5%	11,789
3–4 years	9%	21,496
5 years or more	6%	13,997

Race/ethnicity		
American Indian/Alaskan Native	2%	4,800
Asian	1%	1,629
Black or African American	25%	59,253
Native Hawaiian/other Pacific Islander	0%	543
Hispanic (of any race)	20%	48,723
White	44%	106,515
Unknown/unable to determine	2%	5,549
Two or more races	6%	13,381

Reasons for discharge		
Reunification with parent(s) or primary caretaker(s)	51%	122,173
Living with other relative(s)	8%	19,663
Adoption	22%	51,225
Emancipation	10%	23,396
Guardianship	7%	16,418
Transfer to another agency	2%	4,229
Runaway	1%	1,209
Death of child	0%	327

Note: All races exclude children of Hispanic origin. Children of Hispanic ethnicity may be any race.

SOURCE: "Children Exiting Foster Care during FY 2012," in *The AFCARS Report: Preliminary FY 2012 Estimates as of November 2013*, no. 20, U.S. Department of Health and Human Services, Administration for Children and Families, Administration on Children, Youth, and Families, Children's Bureau, November 2013, http://www.acf.hhs.gov/sites/default/files/cb/afcarsreport20.pdf (accessed July 16, 2014)

David Edwards, who was suffocated by his mother after the child welfare system failed to come to his rescue. Although David's parents had lost custody of their first child because of abuse, and despite reports of David's abuse, the CPS agency made reasonable efforts to let the parents keep the child. In *The Book of David: How Preserving Families Can Cost Children's Lives* (1996), Gelles points out that CPS agencies need to abandon their blanket solution to child abuse in their attempt to use reasonable efforts to reunite the victims and their perpetrators. He contends that those parents who seriously abuse their children are incapable of changing their behavior.

By contrast, in "Foster Care vs. Family Preservation: The Track Record on Safety and Well-Being" (January 3, 2011, http://www.nccpr.org/reports/01SAFETY.pdf), the National Coalition for Child Protection Reform, a nonprofit organization of experts on child abuse and foster care who are committed to the reform of the child welfare system, contends that many allegedly maltreated children are unnecessarily removed from their home and that children are in more danger when placed in foster care than when given services to help preserve the family. The National Coalition for Child Protection Reform recognizes that although there are cases in which the only way to save a child is to remove him or her from an abusive home, in many cases providing support services to the family in crisis, while letting the child remain at home, helps ensure child safety.

How Successful Is Intervention?

The nation's child welfare system has achieved many successes. Thousands of maltreated children have been identified, many lives have been saved, and many more have been taken out of dangerous environments. It is impossible to tally the number of child abuse cases that might have ended in death; these children have been saved by changes in the laws, by awareness and reporting, and by the efforts of the professionals who intervened on their behalf. Mandatory reporting laws have certainly brought many maltreated children into the system who might have gone unnoticed otherwise.

Although many CPS agencies are conscientiously and effectively doing their job, they sometimes commit mistakes that result in great harm and even death to the children under their care. During the first decade of the 21st century there were several high-profile cases in which CPS agencies appear to have utterly failed the children they were supposed to be protecting.

For example, the Florida Department of Children and Families could not account for the disappearance of a five-year-old foster child, Rilya Wilson, who had been missing for more than a year before the agency noticed her absence in April 2002. At that time the agency had reportedly lost track of more than 530 children. Rilya's disappearance was only discovered after her caseworker was fired, and the new caseworker could not locate the child. The former caseworker had reported that Rilya was fine, although that caseworker had not visited the child at her foster home for months. The article "Trial in Rilya Wilson Case Continues" (FLCourier.com, December 20, 2012) notes that in 2005 Geralyn Graham, the live-in lover of Pamela Graham, who was Rilya's foster mother, was indicted for murdering the girl. During Geralyn's December 2012 trial, Pamela testified that Geralyn abused the girl by keeping her in a small room, tying her to her bed, and dipping her into "extremely hot bathtub water." Pamela claimed that her own fears of Geralyn and of being blamed by authorities prompted her to cover up Rilya's disappearance. She reportedly pleaded guilty to reduced charges in exchange for her testimony against Geralyn and was not expected to face jail time. Geralyn was facing a term of life in prison if convicted of murdering Rilya. In February 2013 Geralyn Graham was convicted on charges of kidnapping and child abuse, and sentenced to 55 years in prison. Rilya's body had not been found.

In *Child Maltreatment 2012*, the Children's Bureau provides limited data about children in the child welfare system who died due to maltreatment during 2012. The agency notes that 30 states specified how many of their total fatalities were of children whose families had received preservation services in the previous five years. Overall, 75 (8.5%) of the 887 fatalities fell into this category. It should be noted, however, that the 30 reporting states did not include some of the states with the largest numbers of maltreatment fatalities, specifically California and New York. According to the Children's Bureau, 35 states with a total of 1,009 maltreatment fatalities in 2012 reported that 22 of those fatalities were of children who had been reunited with their family within the previous five years. California and New York were not among the reporting states.

The Children's Bureau also provides data on the number of children under CPS agency protection who are found to have been maltreated by foster parents and other sanctioned caregivers. In 2012 there were 1,544 duplicate victims involving maltreatment by foster parents (both relatives and nonrelatives) and 759 involving maltreatment by group home and residential facility staff. These cases are particularly troubling because the victims were most likely in foster care after having already been maltreated by their parents or other caregivers. In addition, these cases raise questions about the CPS agencies' thoroughness in screening potential foster parents and the personnel who are employed to work at group homes and residential facilities.

Another area of interest regarding CPS agency performance is the appropriate response in cases where child maltreatment claims are not substantiated. As noted earlier, 17.7% of the 3.2 million unique children maltreatment claims investigated in 2012 were found to be substantiated or indicated. (See Figure 2.1.) Nearly three-fifths (58%) of the total claims were determined to be unsubstantiated. As part of the NSCAW II longitudinal study, researchers are following the well-being of children with substantiated and unsubstantiated cases of maltreatment.

Child Welfare Workforce

Child welfare caseworkers perform multiple tasks in the course of their jobs. Among other things, they investigate reports of child maltreatment, coordinate various services (mental health, substance abuse, and so on) to help keep families together, find foster care placements for children if needed, make regular visits to children and families, arrange placement of children in permanent homes when they cannot be safely returned to their parents or caretakers, and document all details pertaining to their cases. Caseworker supervisors monitor and support their caseworkers, sometimes taking on some of the cases when there is a staff shortage or heavy caseload. Child welfare caseworkers must typically earn at least a four-year bachelor's degree in social work to become a licensed bachelor's social worker, or LBSW. These degree paths typically include several hours of fieldwork as a prerequisite for graduating.

Workers in the child welfare system face particular emotional stresses in their job that can lead to burnout. The Children's Bureau notes in "Burnout/Secondary Trauma" (2014, https://www.childwelfare.gov/management/work force/retention/burnout.cfm) that workers can develop what is called vicarious trauma or secondary trauma from dealing with traumatized children and their families. As a result, workforce retention is a significant challenge for CPS agencies. According to the Children's Bureau in "Worker Turnover" (2014, https://www.childwelfare.gov/management/workforce/retention/turnover.cfm), in some jurisdictions worker turnover is as high as 90% per year.

MEASURING STATE PERFORMANCE. The Adoption and Safe Families Act of 1997 requires the HHS to submit an annual report to Congress regarding state performance in operating CPS and other child welfare programs. In *Child Welfare Outcomes 2008–2011 Report to Congress* (August 2013, https://www.acf.hhs.gov/sites/default/files/cb/cwo08_11.pdf), the Children's Bureau notes that the first report to Congress included child welfare data from 1998 and addressed seven national goals or desired outcomes:

- Outcome 1: Reduce recurrence of child abuse and/or neglect

- Outcome 2: Reduce the incidence of child abuse and/or neglect in foster care

- Outcome 3: Increase permanency for children in foster care

TABLE 2.18

State performance on original outcome measures of child welfare, 2008–11

Outcome measures	Median performance by year			
	2008	2009	2010	2011
*Measure 1.1: Of all children who were victims of substantiated or indicated child abuse and/or neglect during the first six months of the year, what percentage had another substantiated or indicated report within a six-month period? (Population = 52 states)	5.2%	5.6%	4.8%	5.2%
*Measure 2.1: Of all children who were in foster care during the year, what percentage were the subject of substantiated or indicated maltreatment by a foster parent or facility staff member? (Population = 47 states)	0.36	0.34	0.35	0.34
Measure 3.1: Of all children who exited foster care during the year, what percentage left to either reunification, adoption, or legal guardianship (i.e., were discharged to a permanent home)? (Population = 50 states)	87.7	87.3	86.7	87.3
Measure 3.2: Of all children who exited foster care during the year and were identified as having a diagnosed disability, what percentage left to either reunification, adoption, or legal guardianship (i.e., were discharged to a permanent home)? (Population = 42 states)	77.6	77.8	77.9	78.1
Measure 3.3: Of all children who exited foster care during the year and were older than age 12 at the time of their most recent entry into care, what percentage left either to reunification, adoption, or legal guardianship (i.e., were discharged to a permanent home)? (Population = 50 states)	67.6	66.6	65.6	66.0
*Measure 3.4: Of all children exiting foster care in the year to emancipation, what percentage were age 12 or younger at the time of entry into care? (Population = 50 states)	26.1	26.3	25.5	25.1
Measure 4.1: Of all children reunified with their parents or caretakers at the time of discharge from foster care during the year, what percentage were reunified in less than 12 months from the time of entry into foster care? (Population = 50 states)	67.2	67.2	68.4	68.0
Measure 5.1 a: Of all children discharged from care during the year to a finalized adoption, what percentage were discharged in less than 12 months from the date of the latest removal from home? (Population = 50 states)	3.0	3.4	3.6	3.7
Measure 6.1 a: Of all children served in foster care during the year who were in care for less than 12 months, what percentage had no more than two placement settings? (Population = 49 states)	85.3	85.3	85.3	85.9
Measure 6.1b: Of all children served in foster care during the year who were in foster care for at least 12 months but less than 24 months, what percentage had no more than two placement settings? (Population = 49 states)	61.8	60.6	61.6	63.4
Measure 6.1 c: Of all children served in foster care during the year who were in foster care for at least 24 months, what percentage had no more than two placement settings? (Population = 49 states)	31.9	30.5	33.0	32.8
*Measure 7.1: Of all children who entered foster care during the year and were age 12 or younger at the time of their most recent placement, what percentage were placed in a group home or institution? (Population = 50 states)	4.9	4.3	4.5	4.5

*For these measures, a lower number indicates better performance.
Note: Data for this table include all states for which adequate data are available.

SOURCE: "Table 1. Median State Performance, 2008–2011: Original Outcome Measures," in *Child Welfare Outcomes 2008–2011 Report to Congress*, U.S. Department of Health and Human Services, Administration for Children and Families, Administration on Children, Youth, and Families, Children's Bureau, August 16, 2013, http://www.acf.hhs.gov/sites/default/files/cb/cwo08_11.pdf (accessed July 16, 2014)

- Outcome 4: Reduce time in foster care to reunification without increasing reentry

- Outcome 5: Reduce time in foster care to adoption

- Outcome 6: Increase placement stability

- Outcome 7: Reduce placements of young children in group homes or institutions

Twelve measures, called the original outcome measures, were developed and are used to assess state performance in meeting these desired outcomes. The Children's Bureau notes that it includes 52 "states" in its assessment because it includes the District of Columbia and Puerto Rico.

Table 2.18 shows the original outcome measure performance between 2008 and 2011. It should be noted that the desirable trend over time for Measures 1.1, 2.1, 3.4, and 7.1 is for values to decrease, whereas the desirable trend for all other measures is for values to increase. In general, states improved their performance between 2008 and 2011 in nine of the measures, showed no improvement in one measure, and performed worse in two measures. The measure showing the greatest improvement, Measure 6.1b, assessed the states in terms of the percentage of children in foster care for a period of between 12

and 24 months who experienced no more than two placement settings over that span. As Table 2.18 indicates, the percentage of children in foster care for 12 to 24 months who experienced two or fewer placement settings actually fell from 61.8% in 2008 to 60.6% in 2009, before eventually rising to 63.4% in 2011.

Another area that showed strong improvement between 2008 and 2011 was Measure 3.4, which assessed states in terms of the number of children who achieved emancipation during the year and who were 12 years old or younger when they first entered foster care. As noted earlier, the age of emancipation is 18 to 21 years, depending on the state. A downward trend in Measure 3.4 indicates that, nationally, a lower percentage of children are aging out of the foster care system after having spent long periods (at least six to eight years) in the system. This indicates progress in achieving a more desirable outcome, such as family reunification or adoption, before the age of emancipation is reached. By contrast, Measure 3.3 assesses the performance of the states in discharging to permanent homes children who were aged 12 years or older at the time of their most recent entry into foster care. The downward trend in this measure indicates that states are doing less well at finding permanent homes for the relatively older children in their care.

TABLE 2.19

State performance on composite outcome measures of child welfare, 2008–11

Composite measures[a]	Median performance by year			
	2008	2009	2010	2011
Measure C1.1: Of all children discharged from foster care to reunification during the year who had been in care for eight days or longer, what percentage were reunified in less than 12 months from the date of the latest removal from home? (Includes trial home visit adjustment) (Population = 49 states)	68.4%	67.5%	67.5%	70.4%
*Measure C1.2: Of all children discharged from foster care to reunification during the year who had been in care for eight days or longer, what was the median length of stay (in months) from the date of the latest removal from home until the date of discharge to reunification? (Includes trial home visit adjustment) (Population = 49 states)	7.9 mos.	8.0 mos.	7.8 mos.	7.7 mos.
Measure C1.3: Of all children who entered foster care for the first time in the six-month period just prior to the year shown, and who remained in care for eight days or longer, what percentage were discharged from foster care to reunification in less than 12 months from the date of the latest removal from home? (Includes trial home visit adjustment) (Population = 48 states)	43.4	41.4	42.5	41.3
Measure C1.4: Of all children discharged from foster care to reunification in the 12-month period prior to the year shown, what percentage reentered care in less than 12 months from the date of discharge? (Population = 49 states)[b]	13.2	12.4	12.6	11.8
Measure C2.1: Of all children discharged from foster care to a finalized adoption during the year, what percentage were discharged in less than 24 months from the date of the latest removal from home? (Population = 50 states)	29.0	31.9	32.4	33.6
*Measure C2.2: Of all children discharged from foster care to a finalized adoption during the year, what was the median length of stay in care (in months) from the date of latest removal from home to the date of discharge to adoption? (Population = 50 states)	31.0 mos.	30.4 mos.	29.6 mos.	29.4 mos.
Measure C2.3: Of all children in foster care on the first day of the year who were in care for 17 continuous months or longer, what percentage was discharged from foster care to a finalized adoption by the last day of the year? (Population = 50 states)[c]	23.0	24.7	24.9	25.7
Measure C2.4: Of all children in foster care on the first day of the year who were in foster care for 17 continuous months or longer, and who were not legally free for adoption prior to that day, what percentage became legally free for adoption during the first six months of the year? (Population = 44 states)[d]	12.4	13.5	12.7	13.5
Measure C2.5: Of all children who became legally free for adoption in the 12-month period prior to the year shown, what percentage were discharged from foster care to a finalized adoption in less than 12 months from the date of becoming legally free? (Population = 44 states)	53.0	54.5	59.1	59.7
Measure C3.1: Of all children in foster care for 24 months or longer on the first day of the year, what percentage were discharged to a permanent home prior to their 18th birthday and by the end of the year? (Population = 50 states)	28.7	29.7	29.7	32.3
Measure C3.2: Of all children who were discharged from foster care during the year, and who were legally free for adoption at the time of discharge, what percentage were discharged to a permanent home prior to their 18th birthday? (Population = 44 states)[e]	93.3	93.8	94.9	95.0
*Measure C3.3: Of all children who, during the year shown, either (1) were discharged from foster care prior to age 18 with a discharge reason of emancipation, or (2) reached their 18th birthday while in foster care, what percentage were in foster care for three years or longer? (Population = 50 states)	46.1	45.8	44.4	43.6

[a]Data for this table include all states for which adequate data are available. Numbers are expressed as percentages except when measured by months, as noted. Individual measures developed for Composite 4: Placement stability are not shown in this table because the measures are nearly identical to the original measures of placement stability incorporated into measure 6.1.

[b]Although measure C2.1 is calculated exactly the same way as original measure 5.1b, the results can vary slightly because the source files are different for the composite measures. In the source files for measure C2.1, all children are excluded who were not age 17 for at least 1 day. No such exclusion exists for measure 5.1b. In addition, composites are calculated at the county level and then are aggregated to the state level, which also could influence slightly performance on C2.1 compared to 5.1b.

[c]The denominator for this measure excludes children who, by the last day of the year, were discharged from foster care with a discharge reason of reunification with parents or primary caretakers, living with relatives, or guardianship.

[d]A child is considered to be "legally free" for adoption if there is a date for parental rights termination reported to AFCARS for both mother and father. Also, the denominator for this measure excludes children who, during the first 6 months of the year, were discharged from foster care with a discharge reason of reunification with parents or primary caretakers, living with other relatives, or guardianship.

[e]A child is considered to be "legally free" for adoption if there is a date for the parental rights termination reported to AFCARS for both mother and father.

*For these composite measures, a lower number indicates better performance.

SOURCE: "Table 2. Median State Performance, 2008–2011: Composite Outcome Measures," in *Child Welfare Outcomes 2008–2011 Report to Congress*, U.S. Department of Health and Human Services, Administration for Children and Families, Administration on Children, Youth, and Families, Children's Bureau, August 16, 2013, http://www.acf.hhs.gov/sites/default/files/cb/cwo08_11.pdf (accessed July 16, 2014)

In 2005 the Children's Bureau developed an additional set of 12 outcome measures that it calls the composite measures. The agency indicates that the composite measures also address the seven national goals listed earlier, but provide more detailed information than do the original outcome measures. Table 2.19 shows the national results for the composite measures between 2008 and 2011. The desirable trend over time for Measures C1.2, C1.4, C2.2, and C3.3 is downward, whereas the desirable trend for all other measures is upward. Overall, there was improvement in all the composite measures between 2008 and 2011. The largest improvement was for Measure C2.5, which assesses the timeliness with which children were adopted once they were discharged from foster care. In 2011 nearly 60% of children who became legally free for adoption during the previous 12 months obtained a finalized adoption less than a year after being discharged from foster care. This percentage was up from 53% in 2008.

As shown in Table 2.18 and Table 2.19, not all 52 "states" (including the District of Columbia and Puerto Rico) reported data for every outcome measure. In addition, the Children's Bureau indicates that results differed significantly between states for some outcome measures. Thus, readers are advised to refer to *Child Welfare*

Outcomes 2008–2011 Report to Congress for a state-by-state breakdown of the performance data.

Funding the Child Welfare System

The nation's child welfare system is funded through federal, state, and local government budgets. Thus, determining total national spending is difficult. However, some private organizations publish spending estimates based on their own data collection efforts. Child Trends is a nonprofit research organization located in Washington, D.C. In *Federal, State, and Local Spending to Address Child Abuse and Neglect in SFYs 2008 and 2010* (December 2012, http://www.childtrends.org/wp-content/uploads/2013/03/Child_Trends-2012_06_20_FR_CaseyCWFinancing.pdf), the most recent report on child welfare system funding as of November 2014, Kerry DeVooght et al. of Child Trends present child welfare spending data for the 50 states, the District of Columbia, and Puerto Rico. As noted earlier, the federal government operates on a fiscal year that runs from October 1 to September 30. State fiscal years (SFYs) may or may not coincide with the federal fiscal year. According to DeVooght et al., national government spending for child welfare purposes was $29.4 billion in SFY 2010, broken down as follows:

- Federal government funds—$13.6 billion (or 46% of the total)

- State government funds—$12.5 billion (or 43% of the total)

- Local government funds—$3.3 billion (or 11% of the total)

Overall, total child welfare spending was up by 50% from 1996, when it was $19.6 billion. Funding increased by approximately 1% between SFY 2006 and SFY 2008 and by 2% between SFY 2008 and SFY 2010.

PROACTIVE CHILD ABUSE PREVENTION

Besides the interventional measures described earlier, the government also operates programs that function to proactively prevent child maltreatment from occurring in the first place. One component of this approach is public awareness. The HHS explains on the National Child Abuse Prevention Month website (2014, https://www.childwelfare.gov/preventing/preventionmonth/about) that in April 1983 the federal government held the first National Child Abuse Prevention Month. Since then the event has been held annually in April and has featured public awareness activities, proclamations from federal and state leaders, and conferences devoted to child well-being.

As is explained in Chapter 3, poverty is one of the primary risk factors associated with child maltreatment.

Major government programs that assist families and children in need include:

- The U.S. Department of Agriculture's (USDA) Women, Infants, and Children program (http://www.fns.usda.gov/wic/women-infants-and-children-wic) provides federal grants to states so that they can offer food assistance, nutrition education, and health care referrals to low-income pregnant women and women with infants and children up to age five who are at risk of poor nutrition.

- The USDA's Supplemental Nutrition Assistance Program (http://www.fns.usda.gov/snap/supplemental-nutrition-assistance-program-snap) is a federally administered program through which states provide financial assistance so that needy people can purchase food.

- The USDA's Child and Adult Care Food Program (http://www.fns.usda.gov/cacfp/child-and-adult-care-food-program) is a federally funded program through which states provide meals to low-income children and elderly adults. Children's programs include free and reduced-price breakfasts and lunches that are served at schools and day care facilities.

- The Office of Head Start (http://eclkc.ohs.acf.hhs.gov/hslc/hs) within the HHS's Administration for Children and Families provides federal grants to public and private agencies that operate programs for low-income preschoolers that enhance the children's school readiness and their cognitive, social, and emotional development.

- Medicaid (http://www.medicaid.gov/Medicaid-CHIP-Program-Information/By-Population/Children/Children.html) is a federal-state program that provides health coverage to individuals, including low-income children, who meet certain eligibility requirements.

- The Children's Health Insurance Program (http://www.medicaid.gov/CHIP/CHIP-Program-Information.html) is a federal-state program that provides free or low-cost health insurance to low-income children whose family income is too high to qualify for Medicaid.

- The Office of Family Assistance within the HHS operates Temporary Assistance for Needy Families (http://www.acf.hhs.gov/programs/ofa/programs/tanf), a federal grant program that provides funds to states to operate welfare programs for needy families.

- The Maternal, Infant, and Early Childhood Home Visiting Program (http://mchb.hrsa.gov/programs/homevisiting) is a federal grant program created by the Patient Protection and Affordable Care Act of 2010. Overseen by the HHS's Health Resources and Services Administration, the program facilitates home visits by experienced counselors to priority populations in local communities.

CHAPTER 3
CAUSES AND EFFECTS OF CHILD ABUSE

CAUSES OF CHILD ABUSE

Investigations into the possible causes of child abuse typically focus on examining the factors that characterize children who have been maltreated in the past. This includes data about the children themselves and their living circumstances, parents and other caregivers, families, and communities. Shared characteristics are seen as risk factors that indicate a higher likelihood that other children with the same characteristics may be subjected to maltreatment. The effects of child abuse can be devastating for many maltreated children. Emerging research is showing that the psychological consequences of maltreatment are particularly debilitating and long-lasting. As a result, child protective service (CPS) agencies are beginning to focus more resources on the emotional, social, and behavioral needs of children who come into contact with the child welfare system.

RISK FACTORS IDENTIFIED IN MAJOR MALTREATMENT STUDIES
National Incidence Studies

As explained in Chapter 2, the 1974 Child Abuse Prevention and Treatment Act mandated that the U.S. Department of Health and Human Services (HHS) conduct a periodic National Incidence Study of Child Abuse and Neglect (NIS). The findings from the first NIS study (NIS-1) were published in 1981 by the Children's Bureau (operated by the HHS) and included information that was gathered from CPS agencies between 1979 and 1980. Although the researchers' primary focus was determining the prevalence of child maltreatment, they correlated data on a handful of demographic characteristics between alleged maltreatment victims and children in the U.S. population as a whole. In *Study Findings: National Study of the Incidence and Severity of Child Abuse and Neglect* (September 1981), the Children's Bureau noted significantly higher representation of young children (aged five years and younger) and children in families with low

annual incomes (less than $15,000) among alleged maltreatment victims when compared with the total U.S. child population. No significant differences were found based on race.

NIS-2 studies were conducted during the 1980s; the original findings report was published in 1988, but technical errors prompted the Children's Bureau to publish a revised edition in 1991. In *National Incidence and Prevalence of Child Abuse and Neglect 1988, Revised Report* (September 1991), Andrea J. Sedlak began using the term *risk factors* to refer to shared characteristics of maltreated children and their families. Overall, Sedlak determined that low income was a "highly significant risk factor for child maltreatment." The significance of other characteristics, including child age, sex, and race/ethnicity; family size; and county type (e.g., metropolitan or rural) was less definitive. The NIS-2 data did indicate that incidences of abuse increased with child age, but that younger children were most at risk for serious injury and death. Sedlak noted, "Overall, it appeared that, while the youngest children were not as frequently maltreated as older ones, when they did experience maltreatment it tended to be more injurious, perhaps due to their greater physical frailty in comparison to older children." In addition, Sedlak reported that children living in families with four or more children had higher rates of maltreatment than did children living in smaller families.

Another report based on NIS-2 data was published in 1993 and specifically looked at risk factors that were associated with child maltreatment. The HHS's National Center on Child Abuse and Neglect (NCCAN) examined in *A Report to Congress: The National Center on Child Abuse and Neglect Study of High Risk Child Abuse and Neglect Groups, Appendix B: NIS-2 Reanalysis Report* (1993) seven key factors (family income, child's age, family structure, child's race/ethnicity, county metropolitan status, family size, and child's sex) and rated their strengths as predictors of risk for maltreatment. Overall, the NCCAN found family income to be the "most important predictor of risk for all maltreatment types" and indicated that children in low-income families were at "much higher risk in all categories of abuse and neglect." In addition, maltreatment risk "generally increased" with the child's age and was higher for females, only children, and children living in urban counties. The predictive nature of family structure as a risk factor varied across maltreatment types, and no single racial/ethnic group was found to be "consistently at higher risk."

NIS-3 studies were conducted throughout the early 1990s. The overall findings were reported by Andrea J. Sedlak and Diane D. Broadhurst in *Third National Incidence Study of Child Abuse and Neglect: Final Report* (September 1996). In regards to risk factors, Sedlak and Broadhurst reached the following conclusions:

- Girls were sexually abused three times more often than boys, but boys had a greater risk than girls of being subjected to emotional neglect and to physical abuse resulting in serious injury.

- There were no significant differences in maltreatment incidence by race.

- Compared with children living with both parents, children living with a single parent had a 77% greater risk of being harmed by physical abuse, an 80% greater risk of suffering serious injury or harm from abuse or neglect, and an 87% greater risk of being harmed by physical neglect.

- Compared with children in families with higher annual incomes, children in the lower income brackets were 22 times more likely to experience maltreatment fitting the Harm Standard and 25 times more likely to experience maltreatment fitting the Endangerment Standard. (See Chapter 2 for complete definitions of these standards; in brief, the Harm Standard requires that demonstrable harm to a child be present, whereas the Endangerment Standard requires only that a professional consider a child to be at risk of harm.) In addition, low-income children were 18 times more likely than higher-income children to be sexually abused and 56 times more likely to be educationally neglected.

As noted in Chapter 2, another round of NIS studies was conducted between 2005 and 2006, and the results were reported in *Fourth National Incidence Study of Child Abuse and Neglect (NIS-4) Report to Congress* (January 2010, http://www.acf.hhs.gov/sites/default/files/opre/nis4_report_congress_full_pdf_jan2010.pdf), which was authored by Andrea J. Sedlak et al. and published jointly by the HHS's Office of Planning, Research, and Evaluation (OPRE) and the Children's Bureau. Sedlak et al. assess various child, family, and community characteristics in terms of maltreatment incidence rates (the number of children maltreated per 1,000 children). The rates are calculated under both the Harm Standard and the Endangerment Standard and for different maltreatment types, depending on data availability. Sedlak et al. find that family structure, number of children in household, parental employment, and socioeconomic status are relevant factors to child abuse and neglect. In addition, the researchers provide data on the perceived role of perpetrator alcohol abuse, drug abuse, and mental illness in maltreatment cases.

As of November 2014, a release date for a fifth NIS study had not yet been announced.

Some Findings from NIS-4

FAMILY STRUCTURE. Single-parent families in which an unmarried partner was living in the household had the greatest risk of child maltreatment, whereas families headed by married biological parents had the lowest risk. In NIS-4 Sedlak et al. report the following incidence rates (number of children per 1,000 children) under the Harm Standard for maltreatment by family structure:

- All maltreatment—57.2 per 1,000 children for single parent with a cohabiting partner, compared with a range of 6.8 for married biological parents to 33.2 for neither parent living in household

- All abuse types—33.6 per 1,000 children for single parent with a cohabiting partner, compared with a range of 2.9 for married biological parents to 17.4 for other married parents living in household

- All neglect types—27 per 1,000 children for single parent with a cohabiting partner, compared with a range of 4.2 for married biological parents to 20.4 for neither parent living in household

NUMBER OF CHILDREN IN HOUSEHOLD. Sedlak et al. note that the number of children in a household is a risk factor in maltreatment rates. Under the Harm Standard for all maltreatment types the incidence rates by number of children in the household were 21.2 per 1,000 children (four or more children), 17.9 (one child), 15.7 (three children), and 11.9 (two children). Likewise, under the Endangerment Standard the rates were 62.9 per 1,000 children (four or more children), 38.2 (three children), 36.6 (one child), and 27.2 (two children). Under both standards, the presence of four or more children in the household was a significant risk factor for maltreatment.

PARENTAL EMPLOYMENT. According to Sedlak et al. in NIS-4, the incidence rates for all maltreatment types under the Harm Standard were 22.6 per 1,000 children for parent(s) not in the labor force, 15.9 for unemployed parent(s), and 7.6 for employed parent(s). Under the Endangerment Standard the rates were 57.7 per 1,000 children for parent(s) not in the labor force, 39.9 for unemployed parent(s), and 17.1 for employed parent(s). Thus, parental employment substantially lowered the risk for child maltreatment.

SOCIOECONOMIC STATUS. In their NIS-4 report, Sedlak et al. assess maltreatment incidence rates using a composite measure of socioeconomic status that incorporates household income, parental education level, and household member participation in a poverty-related program. The researchers designated children as having "low socioeconomic status" if their household income was less than $15,000 annually, their parents' highest education level was less than high school, or any household member participated in a poverty-related program. The incidence rate for all maltreatment types under the Harm Standard was 22.5 per 1,000 children for children of low socioeconomic status, compared with 4.4 for other children. Likewise, the incidence rate for all maltreatment types under the Endangerment Standard was 55.1 per 1,000 children for children of low socioeconomic status, compared with 9.5 for other children. Overall, children of low socioeconomic status were at "significantly" greater risk of maltreatment than other children.

PERPETRATOR PROBLEMS. As part of the NIS-4 data collection effort, researchers asked their sources (typically CPS agencies) if they believed that perpetrator alcohol use, drug use, and/or mental illness were factors in the specific child maltreatment cases they had investigated. Sedlak et al. note that under the Harm Standard for all maltreatment types the sources indicated they believed that 11.4% of the children they investigated had been maltreated by a perpetrator with an alcohol abuse problem. The percentages for drug abuse and mental illness were 10.8% and 7.2%, respectively.

National Survey of Child and Adolescent Well-Being

As explained in Chapter 2, the Personal Responsibility and Work Opportunity Reconciliation Act of 1996 authorized the performance of the National Survey of Child and Adolescent Well-Being (NSCAW) studies by the OPRE. The longitudinal studies (studies of the same group of people over time) began in 1997 with NSCAW I, which tracked 5,501 children aged birth to 14 years who had been the subjects of maltreatment investigations by CPS agencies or were in foster care. NSCAW I ran through 2007. NSCAW II began in 2008 and was ongoing as of November 2014. It was tracking 5,873 children aged birth to 17.5 years for which maltreatment investigations were closed by CPS agencies between February 2008 and April 2009. As of November 2014, three NSCAW II waves had taken place: Wave 1 (March 2008 to September 2009) featured baseline data collection; Wave 2 (October 2009 to January 2011) featured follow-up data collection on the same children; and Wave

3 (June 2011 to December 2012), which included further follow-up data relating to the children and their families.

From a risk factor standpoint, the NSCAW studies are informative because they include detailed characteristics about the children, their families, and/or their caregivers. NSCAW I data, in particular, provide insight into maltreatment risk factors that had not previously been comprehensively studied. These include child health problems, domestic violence in the household, and the parents' mental health status, substance abuse status, and own history of being abused. For example, the OPRE notes in *National Survey of Child and Adolescent Well-Being, Research Brief No. 7: Special Health Care Needs among Children in Child Welfare* (June 2007, http://www.acf.hhs.gov/sites/default/files/opre/special_health.pdf) that NSCAW I data indicate that 35% of the children who were the subjects of maltreatment investigations by CPS agencies had a chronic health problem or special need, such as emotional disturbance, speech impairment, and/or developmental delay, at the time of their baseline assessment (two to six months following the close of the maltreatment investigation).

In *NSCAW II Wave 3 Report: Wave 3 Tables* (June 2014, http://www.acf.hhs.gov/sites/default/files/opre/nscaw_wave_3_tables_june_2014_clean.pdf), Cecilia Casanueva et al. assess some of the lingering effects of maltreatment on NSCAW participants. As presented in Table 3.1, 37.4% of maltreated children between the ages of two and five showed signs of developmental difficulties at the time the Wave 3 data were compiled. In this age range, boys (42.3%) were considerably more likely than girls (30.8%) to show signs of developmental problems during the Wave 3 study. Among racial and ethnic groups, Hispanic children (40.9%) between the ages of two and five were the most likely to suffer from developmental issues, followed by whites (38.9%) and African Americans (32.8%).

Risks of behavioral, emotional, and other issues were also prevalent among NSCAW participants between the ages of 11 and 20. As Table 3.2 shows, more than one-third (37.6%) of participants in this age group demonstrated a risk of developing either behavioral or emotional problems, or a problem with substance abuse, at the time the Wave 3 data were compiled. This issue was most prevalent among children between the ages of 15 and 17, with nearly half (47.1%) of participants in this age group demonstrating a risk for behavioral, emotional, or substance abuse problems. When accounting for living arrangements, participants who lived in group homes or other residential programs demonstrated the highest level of risk, with more than three-quarters (77.2%) of individuals in this category in danger of developing behavioral, emotional, or substance abuse issues. At the same time, individuals in this category were also the most likely to

TABLE 3.1

Children with developmental problems reported in the National Survey of Child and Adolescent Well-Being II, Wave 3, by sex, age, race and ethnicity, home setting, and insurance status, 2011–12

	Developmental problems[a]
	%
Total	37.4
Gender	
Male	42.3
Female	30.8
Age (years)	
2	26.3
3–5	37.4
Race/ethnicity	
Black	32.8
White	38.9
Hispanic	40.9
Other	33.4
Setting	
In-home	38.7
Formal kin care	50.3
Informal kin care	19.5
Foster care	58.2
Insurance status	
Private	30.1
Public[b]	38.6
Other	21.0
Uninsured	42.5

[a]Developmental problem was defined based on young children having a diagnosed mental or medical condition that has a high probability of resulting in developmental delay (e.g., Down syndrome). Areas included cognitive development based on the Battelle Developmental Inventory (BDI) or Kaufman Brief Intelligence Test (K-BIT), communication development based on the Preschool Language Scale-3 (PLS-3), and adaptive development based on the Vineland Daily Living Skills.
[b]"Public" includes children who did not have private coverage at the time of interview, but who had Medicaid and/or a State Children's Health Insurance Program (SCHIP).
Note: All analyses were on weighted National Survey of Child and Adolescent Well-Being II, Wave 3 data.

SOURCE: Adapted from Cecelia Casanueva et al., "Exhibit 7. Developmental Problems among Children 2 to 5 Years Old at Wave 3," in *NSCAW II Wave 3 Report: Wave 3 Tables*, U.S. Department of Health and Human Services, Administration for Children and Families, Office of Planning, Research, and Evaluation, June 5, 2014, http://www.acf.hhs.gov/sites/default/files/opre/nscaw_wave_3_tables_june_2014_clean.pdf (accessed July 21, 2014)

have been arrested or picked up by the police. As Table 3.3 shows, 4.1% of participants between the ages of 11 and 20 who were living in group homes or residential programs at the time of the Wave 3 report had been arrested within the previous six months. By comparison, 2.6% of participants who were living at home had been arrested or picked up by police.

Casanueva et al. find that NSCAW participants also demonstrated a range of basic health needs at the time of the Wave 3 study. For example, about three-fifths (60.2%) of all participants needed a routine medical checkup or immunizations at the time the Wave 3 information was collected, while well over half (56.2%) needed basic dental care. (See Table 3.4.) As Table 3.4 shows, a high proportion of participants needing specific health services eventually received some form of care.

For example, 97.6% of children referred by caseworkers for medical checkups or immunizations went on to receive care, and 96.6% of children referred for dental care later visited a dentist.

A history of maltreatment can also impact future sexual behavior, particularly among girls. Table 3.5 offers an overview of sexual activities among female NSCAW participants between the ages of 11 and 20. Nearly half (46.1%) of all participants had had sex by the time of the Wave 3 report; 41.2% had had sex in the previous year. In addition, one out of five (20.5%) female NSCAW participants had experienced a pregnancy at some point in their lives. As Casanueva et al. report in *Child Well-Being Spotlight: Teenage Girls in the Child Welfare System Report High Rates of Risky Sexual Activity and Pregnancy* (July 8, 2014, http://www.acf.hhs.gov/sites/default/files/opre/sexual_outcomes_spotlight_13.pdf), female victims of maltreatment also experienced high incidences of forced sexual intercourse. Among female maltreatment victims between the ages of 14 and 17, 14.4% had been forced to have sex at some point in their lives; this figure more than doubled for female maltreatment victims between the ages of 18 and 20, with nearly one-third (29.1%) of young women in that age group having experienced forced sexual intercourse. (See Figure 3.1.)

As *NSCAW II Wave 3 Report: Wave 3 Tables* indicates, achieving stability can prove a significant challenge for child victims of maltreatment. Table 3.6 examines the living arrangements of NSCAW participants at the time of the Wave 3 report. As HHS explains on its Child Welfare Information website (2014, https://www.childwelfare.gov/permanency/overview), maltreated children achieve permanency when they have left foster care for a permanent legal living situation, whether they have reunited with their parents, gone to live with other relatives, or been adopted. As Table 3.6 shows, about half (49.9%) of NSCAW participants had achieved permanency by 2012. Even still, permanency did not necessarily indicate an improvement in the quality of care received by participants. Among children who had achieved permanency at the time of the Wave 3 report, a majority reported living with a primary caretaker who actively abused substances (53.2%), suffered from serious mental health issues (56.4%), or who exhibited poor parenting skills (52.6%). (See Table 3.6.)

Female caregivers (88.8%) outnumbered male caregivers (11.2%) at the time of the Wave 3 report, as shown in Table 3.7. Despite this wide discrepancy, male caregivers showed considerably greater likelihood of exhibiting behavioral problems or other issues that might negatively impact their ability to provide adequate care. For example, at the time of the Wave 3 report, fathers (30%) were considerably more likely than mothers (19.7%) to

TABLE 3.2

Children at risk of emotional/behavioral or substance abuse problems reported in the National Survey of Child and Adolescent Well-Being II, Wave 3, by sex, age, race and ethnicity, home setting, and insurance status, 2011–12

	Risk of a behavioral/ emotional problem[a]	Risk of a substance abuse problem[b]	Risk of a behavioral/ emotional or substance abuse problem
	%	%	%
Total	**32.9**	**14.4**	**37.6**
Gender			
Male	31.9	15.4	38.6
Female	33.7	13.6	36.8
Age (years)			
11–12	28.6	0.1	28.7
13–14	34.0	4.6	35.6
15–17	41.5	17.0	47.1
18–20	26.6	30.4	37.0
Race/ethnicity			
Black	33.0	7.3	36.0
White	33.1	15.6	38.7
Hispanic	29.5	13.2	33.3
Other	43.3	28.6	50.8
Setting			
In-home	33.6	8.2	36.3
Formal kin care	52.5	2.0	53.1
Informal kin care	35.3	6.4	37.2
Foster care	58.6	8.2	63.6
Group home or residential program	72.7	13.2	77.2
Insurance status			
Private	21.9	16.4	29.6
Public[c]	37.5	12.2	41.3
Other	31.0	12.4	36.3
Uninsured	26.2	21.9	31.4

[a]Risk of a behavioral/emotional problem was defined as scores in the clinical range on any of the following standardized measures among children 1.5 to 17 years old: Internalizing, Externalizing or Total Problems scales of the Child Behavior Checklist (CBCL: administered for children 1.5 to 18 years old), Youth Self Report (YSR; administered to children 11 years old and older), or the Teacher Report From (TRF; administered for children 6 to 18 years old); the Child Depression Inventory (CDI; administered to children 7 years old and older); or the PTSD section Intrusive Experiences and Dissociation subscales of the Trauma Symptoms Checklist (administered to children 8 years old and older). For young adults 18 to 20 years old, risk of a behavioral/emotional problem was defined as scores in the clinical range on the Internalizing, Externalizing or Total Problems scales of the Adult Self Report (ASF), the Composite International Diagnostic Interview Form, Short-Form Depression section (CIDI-SF), and the PTSD section of the Trauma Symptom Checklist for Adults (TSCA).
[b]Risk of a substance abuse problem was defined by a Total score of 2 or more on the CRAFFT (Car, Relax, Alone, Forget, Friends, Trouble) substance abuse screening test (CRAFFT). A CRAFFT total score of 2 or more is higahly correlated with having a substance-related diagnosis and the need for substance abuse treatment.
[c]"Public" includes children who did not have private coverage at the time of interview, but who had Medicaid and/or a State Children's Health Insurance Plan (SCHIP).
Note: All analyses were on weighted National Survey of Child and Adolescent Well-Being II Wave 3 data.

SOURCE: Adapted from Cecelia Casanueva et al., "Exhibit 14. Risk of a Behavioral/Emotional Problem or Substance Abuse Problem among Children 11 to 20 Years Old at Wave3," in *NSCAW II Wave 3 Report: Wave 3 Tables*, U.S. Department of Health and Human Services, Administration for Children and Families, Office of Planning, Research, and Evaluation, June 5, 2014, http://www.acf.hhs.gov/sites/default/files/opre/nscaw_wave_3_tables_june_2014_clean .pdf (accessed July 21, 2014)

demonstrate a need for alcohol or substance abuse treatment. (See Table 3.8.) Conversely, mothers (28.2%) were more than twice as likely as fathers to need mental health services (12.5%) at the time the Wave 3 data were compiled. (See Table 3.9.)

According to Casanueva et al., problems of maltreatment persisted well after the initial NSCAW baseline report was completed. At the time the Wave 3 information was collected in 2011 and 2012, nearly one-quarter (24.3%) of NSCAW participants were involved in a re-report of maltreatment; of these, nearly one-third (29.7%) were substantiated by a caseworker. (See Table 3.10.) Among maltreatment victims between the ages of 11 and 17, roughly half (49.9%) reported experiencing an incidence of psychological aggression (e.g., yelling or

shouting) in the 12 months prior to the Wave 3 study; more than one-quarter (28.8%) reported experiencing corporal punishment (e.g., being spanked on the bottom or slapped on the hand), while one in 10 (9.8%) were victims of serious physical assault (e.g., being punched with a fist or being knocked down). (See Table 3.11.)

Exposure to domestic violence is another serious issue confronting maltreatment victims. As Casanueva et al. report in "Domestic Violence (DV) among NSCAW Parents" (*Child Well-Being Spotlight: Parents Reported for Maltreatment Experience High Rates of Domestic Violence*, February 13, 2013, http://www.acf .hhs.gov/sites/default/files/opre/parentsinhome_v2.pdf), about one-quarter (24.7%) of parents involved in the NSCAW study reported being involved in a domestic

TABLE 3.3

Arrests in prior six months among adolescents reported in the National Survey of Child and Adolescent Well-Being II, Wave 3, by gender, age, race and ethnicity, and home setting, 2011–12

	Arrested or picked up by police in past 6 months
	%
Total	**3.4**
Gender	
Male	2.8
Female	3.8
Age (years)	
11–12	0.3
13–14	4.9
15–17	2.2
18–20	5.9
Race/ethnicity	
Black	3.9
White	1.8
Hispanic	4.1
Other	7.5
Setting	
In-home	2.6
Formal kin care	0.8
Informal kin care	1.2
Foster care	1.4
Group home or residential program	4.1

Note: All analyses were on weighted National Survey of Child and Adolescent Well-Being II Wave 3 data.

SOURCE: Adapted from Cecelia Casanueva et al., "Exhibit 16. Arrest in Past 6 Months of Adolescents 11 to 20 Years Old by Adolescent and Young Adult Report at Wave 3," in *NSCAW II Wave 3 Report: Wave 3 Tables*, U.S. Department of Health and Human Services, Administration for Children and Families, Office of Planning, Research, and Evaluation, June 5, 2014, http://www.acf.hhs.gov/sites/default/files/opre/nscaw_wave_3_tables_june_2014_clean.pdf (accessed July 21, 2014)

TABLE 3.4

Child service needs reported in the National Survey of Child and Adolescent Well-Being II, Wave 3, by referral status, 2011–12

Number of weeks	Needed service %	Referred to service %	Received service* %
Routine check-up/immunizations	60.2	62.1	97.6
Dental	56.2	48.7	96.6
Independent living training	32.9	28.2	75.6
Screening for learning or developmental disability	24.9	17.9	84.0
Emotional/behavioral/attention problem	45.0	34.8	94.3
Vision	22.5	12.1	98.7
Hearing	11.9	7.5	97.5
Health problem	13.4	9.0	98.1
Special education	23.1	9.7	96.9
Substance use	3.5	2.7	81.7
Delinquency	6.3	4.1	94.3

*Caseworkers are asked about service receipt only when a service referral is reported. The "Received" category represents the subset of children who were referred to a service and who received that service.
Note: All analyses were on weighted National Survey of Child and Adolescent Well-Being II, Wave 3 data.

SOURCE: Adapted from Cecelia Casanueva et al., "Exhibit 18. Child Service Need, Referral, and Receipt by Caseworker Report at Wave 3," in *NSCAW II Wave 3 Report: Wave 3 Tables*, U.S. Department of Health and Human Services, Administration for Children and Families, Office of Planning, Research, and Evaluation, June 5, 2014, http://www.acf.hhs.gov/sites/default/files/opre/nscaw_wave_3_tables_june_2014_clean.pdf (accessed July 21, 2014)

violence incident within the previous year. (See Figure 3.2.) Furthermore, as Carlos A. Cuevas et al. report in "Children's Exposure to Violence and the Intersection between Delinquency and Victimization" (*Juvenile Justice Bulletin: National Survey of Children's Exposure to Violence*, October 2013, http://www.ojjdp.gov/pubs/240555.pdf), exposure to violence at home can lead to future incidences of delinquency among children. As Figure 3.3 shows, more than one in five (20.8%) boys between the ages of 10 and 17 who had been exposed to violent behavior later engaged in some form of juvenile delinquency; another 17.9% reported being victims of delinquency, while 18.1% reported being both victims and perpetrators. By contrast, only 13% of girls in this age group who had encountered violent behavior later engaged in juvenile delinquency. (See Figure 3.3.) For boys, delinquency rates were highest among 16 year olds, with one-third (33.6%) of boys in that age group engaging in some form of delinquent behavior. (See Figure 3.4.) As Figure 3.5 shows, delinquency among adolescent girls also peaked at the age of 16, with 18.2% of girls in that age group engaging in delinquent behavior.

Child Maltreatment 2012

As noted in Chapter 2, the Children's Bureau publishes an annual summary report about maltreatment claims reported to CPS agencies in the 50 states, the District of Columbia, and Puerto Rico. As of November 2014, the most recent report was *Child Maltreatment 2012* (December 2013, http://www.acf.hhs.gov/sites/default/files/cb/cm2012.pdf). In 2012 CPS agencies handled maltreatment reports concerning 3.2 million unique children or 3.8 million duplicate children (i.e., children who were reported or counted more than once). Nearly 2.5 million of the uniquely counted children were found to be nonvictims of child maltreatment. This group includes children whose cases were investigated but not substantiated and those who received a response other than a formal CPS investigation, such as a caseworker working with a family to identify appropriate services. (Note that a child determined to be a nonvictim of maltreatment may still need and receive follow-up services.) The remaining 686,000 were determined to be victims; this number included 1,640 children who died from maltreatment.

The Children's Bureau does not provide a detailed analysis of risk factors, but it does present data regarding child and caregiver characteristics that include common risk factors. For example, 13.3% of child maltreatment victims in 2012 had one or more disabilities. (See Table 3.12.) The

TABLE 3.5

Rates of sexual experience and pregnancy among females aged 11 to 20 reported in the National Survey of Child and Adolescent Well-Being II, Wave 3, by age, race and ethnicity, home setting, type of sexual experience, and pregnancy status, 2011–12

	Ever had sex	Had sex in past 12 months	Ever had forced sex	Ever been pregnant
	%	%	%	%
Total	46.1	41.2	14.7	20.5
Age (years)				
11–12	1.5	0.1	0.5	0.0
13–14	11.9	10.9	2.9	0.8
15–17	51.3	45.9	16.7	21.2
18–20	92.5	83.4	29.1	45.1
Race/ethnicity				
Black	45.9	40.9	13.7	24.2
White	46.4	40.3	13.1	19.0
Hispanic	39.3	35.6	10.4	19.5
Other	61.3	58.7	32.6	21.9
Setting				
In-home	24.7	22.0	8.5	8.8
Formal kin care	35.2	29.1	5.4	14.4
Informal kin care	34.0	32.3	6.5	14.4
Foster care	21.8	17.5	2.8	3.5
Group home or residential program	27.4	11.0	17.9	3.4

Note: All analyses were on weighted National Survey of Child and Adolescnet Well-Being II Wave 3 data. "Sex" was defined as vaginal sex.

SOURCE: Adapted from Cecelia Casanueva et al., "Exhibit 15. Sexual Experience and Pregnancy by Female 11 to 20 Years Old by Adolescent and Young Adult Report at Wave 3," in *NSCAW II Wave 3 Report: Wave 3 Tables*, U.S. Department of Health and Human Services, Administration for Children and Families, Office of Planning, Research, and Evaluation, June 5, 2014, http://www.acf.hhs.gov/sites/default/files/opre/nscaw_wave_3_tables_june_2014_clean.pdf (accessed July 21, 2014)

FIGURE 3.1

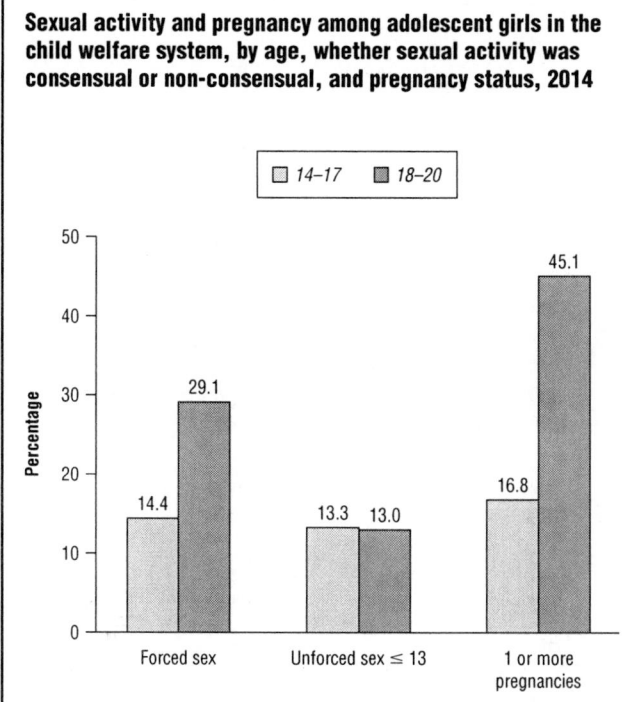

Sexual activity and pregnancy among adolescent girls in the child welfare system, by age, whether sexual activity was consensual or non-consensual, and pregnancy status, 2014

SOURCE: Cecelia Casanueva et al., "Sexual Activity and Pregnancy among Teenage Girls," in *Child Well-Being Spotlight: Teenage Girls in the Child Welfare System Report High Rates of Risky Sexual Activity and Pregnancy*, U.S. Department of Health and Human Services, Administration for Children and Families, Office of Planning, Research and Evaluation, June 12, 2014, http://www.acf.hhs.gov/sites/default/files/opre/sexual_outcomes_spotlight_13.pdf (accessed July 21, 2014)

disabilities included intellectual disabilities, emotional disturbance, visual or hearing impairment, learning or physical disabilities, behavioral problems, and other medical problems. It should be noted that not all 52 states (including the District of Columbia and Puerto Rico) reported child disability data for 2012. In addition, the Children's Bureau warns that not all disabilities may have been identified in the children and notes that some children had multiple disabilities.

Table 3.13 shows the numbers and percentages of unique victims by state whose caregivers had an alcohol abuse risk factor. For the 31 states that reported data for unique victims, 8.8% of the children had the risk factor. Twenty-one states reported data for unique nonvictims. Overall, 4.9% of the children had the alcohol abuse caregiver risk factor. A similar summary is presented in Table 3.14 for the drug abuse caregiver risk factor. The risk factor was present for 20% of the unique victims (with 34 states reporting data) and for 8.4% of the unique nonvictims (with 25 states reporting data). The Children's Bureau indicates that some states do not differentiate between alcohol abuse and drug abuse and report both risk factors for a child whose caregiver has any substance abuse problem.

More than a quarter (28.5%) of all unique maltreatment victims in 35 states in 2012 had a caregiver with a domestic violence risk factor. (See Table 3.15.)

TABLE 3.6

Risks in children's homes at time of maltreatment investigation as reported in the National Survey of Child and Adolescent Well-Being II, Wave 3, 2011–12

| | Total achieving permanency | | Type of permanency | | | |
| | | | Adoption | | Reunification | Discharged to relatives |
	Population	%	Population	%	%	%
Total	3,066	49.9	1,799	24.4	73.3	2.3
Gender						
Male	1,597	50.8	948	23.7	73.2	3.0
Female	1,469	48.9	851	25.2	73.3	1.4
Age (years) at baseline						
0–2	1,897	59.9	1,213	21.9	75.1	3
3–5	372	49.9	210	20.1	76.4	3.5
6–10	467	45.4	237	38.1	60.5	1.4
11–12	134	33.7	58	14.0	85.8	0.2
13–17	196	47.0	81	18.1	81.3	0.6
Race/ethnicity						
Black	1,057	41.2	515	29.4	69.6	0.9
White	946	52.3	580	25.1	71.9	3.1
Hispanic	845	51.9	569	21.8	75.5	2.7
Other	203	57.8	127	17.1	82.8	0.1
Setting at baseline						
In-home	969	57.5	630	18.4	79.2	2.4
Formal kin care	480	37.7	233	38.1	61.4	0.5
Informal kin care	506	29.2	255	20.4	75.8	3.7
Foster care	1,043	58.7	651	51.3	46.6	2.1
Group home or residential program	44	23.4	17	10.9	89.1	0
Developmental need at baseline (birth to 5 years old)*						
Yes	558	45.3	338	31.4	67.9	0.7
No	1,711	59.8	1,085	17.8	78.2	4.1
Risk of any behavioral/emotional or cognitive problems at baseline (children 6 to 17 years old)						
Yes	488	46.5	233	28.5	71.0	0.5
No	249	38.4	114	32.1	65.8	2.1
Caseworker risk assessment at baseline						
Active drug abuse by primary caregiver						
Yes	1,057	53.2	700	27.5	64.4	8
No	2,009	49.1	1,099	23.6	75.6	0.8
Primary caregiver had serious mental health problem						
Yes	965	56.4	610	25.0	73.9	1.1
No	2,101	48.0	1,189	24.2	73.1	2.7
Primary caregiver had poor parenting skills						
Yes	1,353	52.6	824	23.8	74.7	1.5
No	1,713	48.7	975	24.7	72.6	2.7
History of domestic violence against caregiver						
Yes	976	54.7	623	15.8	80.9	3.3
No	2,090	48.1	1,176	28.1	70.1	1.9
History of abuse or neglect of primary caregiver						
Yes	919	53.4	594	25.1	71.4	3.5
No	2,147	48.9	1,205	24.2	73.9	1.9
High stress on the family (e.g., unemployment, drug use, poverty, or neighborhood violence)						
Yes	1,840	54.8	1,124	19.8	78.1	2.1
No	1,226	44.3	675	30.8	66.6	2.6
Low social support						
Yes	1,120	54.9	701	26.3	70.2	3.5
No	1,946	48.0	1,098	23.6	74.6	1.8
Family have trouble paying basic necessities						
Yes	1,053	48.0	674	25.7	71.0	3.2
No	2,013	50.6	1,125	24.0	74.1	2.0

Only 8.6% of the unique nonvictims reported by 28 states had the risk factor. The Children's Bureau notes that the caregiver domestic violence risk factor is counted for homes in which the caregiver is either a victim of domestic violence or a perpetrator of domestic violence.

TABLE 3.6

Risks in children's homes at time of maltreatment investigation as reported in the National Survey of Child and Adolescent Well-Being II, Wave 3, 2011–12 [CONTINUED]

*Developmental need was defined based on young children having a diagnosed mental or medical condition that has a high probability of resulting in developmental delay (e.g., Down syndrome).

Areas included cognitive development based on the Battelle Developmental Inventory (BDI) or Kaufman Brief Intelligence Test (K-BIT), communication development based on the Preschool Language Scale-3 (PLS-3), and adaptive development based on the Vineland Daily Living Skills.

Note: Caseworkers were asked about reunification plans if the child was in out of home care at the time of the interview. Estimates of reunification may represent an underestimate of reunification attempts, as situations where the child was placed out of home and then reunified between interview waves would not be captured. All analyses were on weighted National Survey of Child and Adolescent Well-Being baseline, Adoption and Foster Care Analysis and Reporting System (AFCARS), Wave 2 and Wave 3 data; populations are unweighted and, therefore, direct percentages cannot be calculated by hand. Reported populations vary slightly across analyses because of missing data in some variable categories.

SOURCE: Cecelia Casanueva et al., "Exhibit 31. Permanency of Children Placed in Out-of-Home Care by Caseworker Report through Wave 3 and Adoption and Foster Care Analysis and Reporting System (AFCARS) Data," in *NSCAW II Wave 3 Report: Wave 3 Tables*, U.S. Department of Health and Human Services, Administration for Children and Families, Office of Planning, Research, and Evaluation, June 5, 2014, http://www.acf.hhs.gov/sites/default/files/opre/nscaw_wave_3_tables_june_2014_clean.pdf (accessed July 16, 2014)

Overall, 1,640 children died from maltreatment in 2012. Of these, nearly half (44.4%) were under the age of one year old. (See Figure 3.6.) Of all child fatalities that year, 69.9% were caused by neglect, and 44.3% were caused by physical abuse. (See Figure 3.7.) As shown in Table 3.16, the Children's Bureau assesses three specific caregiver risk factors for child maltreatment fatalities. However, data on caregiver risk factors were not available for all of these children because not all states reported the data. For the 27 to 31 states reporting caregiver risk factors, the data indicate that 6.3% of the child maltreatment fatalities were associated with a caregiver with alcohol abuse problems, 17.3% were associated with a caregiver with drug abuse problems, and 20.1% were associated with a caregiver involved in domestic violence. Again, the alcohol and drug abuse percentages include double-counted values for states that were not able to determine the specific type of substance being abused.

THE SOCIOECONOMIC EFFECT

As noted earlier, low socioeconomic status has long been considered a major risk factor for child maltreatment. The NIS studies, in particular, found a strong correlation between low family income and child maltreatment incidence rates. For example, using NIS-4 data from 2005–06, Sedlak et al. estimate that incidence rates for all maltreatment types were five to six times higher for children of low socioeconomic status than for other children. The researchers used household income data, parental education level, and household participation in poverty-related programs to assign families to socioeconomic brackets. As shown in Table 3.7 and described earlier, data collected for the NSCAW II Wave 3 assessment indicate that 52.7% of the families who came to the attention of CPS agencies in 2011–12 lived below the federal poverty level (16.8% of these families had incomes below 50% of the federal poverty level, and 35.9% had incomes in the range of 50% to 99% of the federal poverty level).

Because of the evidential link between low socioeconomic status and child maltreatment rates, it would be expected that child maltreatment rates would increase during times of national economic downturns. From late 2007 to mid-2009 the United States experienced an economic downturn of such historic proportions that it has been dubbed the Great Recession. Unemployment rates rose dramatically during this period, as did the number of homeowners who lost their homes because they could not afford to pay their mortgages. The latter phenomenon actually began several years earlier as the United States suffered from a housing industry slowdown and banking industry crisis that pushed many homeowners into financial difficulties. Rates increased dramatically for mortgage delinquencies (late mortgage payments) and foreclosures (seizures by banks and other mortgage holders of the homes of people who stop making mortgage payments). Although the national economy began to improve by mid-2009, the recovery was slow and halting. As a result, the negative effects of the Great Recession lingered into 2014.

Table 2.2 in Chapter 2 lists child maltreatment victimization rates between 2008 and 2012 as estimated by the Children's Bureau based on data reported by CPS agencies. The rates fell from 9.5 victims per 1,000 child population in 2008 to 9.2 victims per 1,000 child population in 2012. This is puzzling given the especially harsh economic conditions that prevailed during this period. As noted in Chapter 1, overall violent crime rates have been declining for several decades, and this trend continued in 2012. Some analysts believe the decreasing child maltreatment rates reflect the broader trend of less violence in American society. Others claim that tightened state budgets during and immediately after the Great Recession forced CPS agencies to reduce the number of cases they could investigate, which artificially lowered the child maltreatment victimization rates. This assertion is particularly controversial and is difficult to support evidentially given that the rates were already falling before the Great Recession began. For example, the Children's Bureau indicates in *Child Maltreatment 2005* (2007, http://archive.acf.hhs.gov/programs/cb/pubs/cm05/

TABLE 3.7

Caregivers represented in the National Survey of Child and Adolescent Well-Being II, Wave 3, 2011–12

Caregiver characteristics	Population	Total sample size = 3,893 %	In-home parents sample size = 3,145 %	Informal kin caregivers sample size = 342 %	Formal kin caregivers sample size = 193 %	Foster caregivers sample size = 213 %
Total	**3,893**	**100**	**86.6**	**8.8**	**2.0**	**2.6**
Gender						
Male	422	11.2	10.5	15.2	17.1	18.5
Female	3,471	88.8	89.6	84.8	83.0	81.5
Age (years)						
19 and under	24	0.2	0.2	0.0	3.0	0.0
20–29	1,043	24.2	27.4	4.5	3.1	0.7
30–49	2,138	61.9	66.8	30.2	18.9	38.1
50–59	479	10.3	4.9	47.5	41.1	40.4
60 and older	209	3.4	0.7	17.9	34.0	20.8
Race/ethnicity						
Black	1,037	22.2	21.6	20.9	36.2	37.3
White	1,670	48.1	47.8	54.8	45.2	36.8
Hispanic	950	24.9	25.7	18.1	17.1	24.9
Other	221	4.9	4.9	6.2	1.5	1.1
Education						
Less than high school	843	21.7	22.3	19.6	20.3	8.0
High school	1,648	43.2	43.9	38.5	51.0	31.6
More than high school	1,395	35.1	33.8	41.9	28.7	60.5
Percentage of federal poverty level						
<50	665	16.8	17.1	19.4	5.1	6.4
50–99	1,147	35.9	37.8	26.2	34.8	2.5
100–200	1,082	28.8	28.8	24.0	34.8	42.4
>200	811	18.5	16.3	30.4	25.3	48.8
Employment status						
Work, full time	1,225	34.0	33.5	37.5	33.8	37.6
Work, part time	592	15.6	16.4	10.1	8.7	13.7
Unemployed, looking for work	620	15.6	17.3	4.6	7.3	3.0
Does not work	1,367	32.6	30.7	46.4	49.9	34.5
Other	90	2.3	2.1	1.5	0.2	11.2
Marital status						
Married	1,332	34.8	33.8	34.4	43.1	65.2
Separated	375	10.1	10.2	13.2	6.3	1.9
Divorced	688	21.1	20.5	28.3	19.7	14.9
Widowed	121	3.0	1.5	11.9	15.7	12.3
Never married	1,377	31.0	34.0	12.2	15.3	5.6
Number of children in home						
1	970	22.5	20.5	42.9	27.2	17.7
2	1,016	26.6	27.3	18.6	23.8	36.1
3	841	24.6	24.4	29.6	19.2	17.3
4	539	14.6	15.8	1.5	18.1	15.9
5 or more	528	11.7	12.1	7.4	11.7	13.1
Number of adults in home						
1	1,205	31.0	31.4	27.9	28.6	28.9
2	1,875	47.8	48.0	45.5	54.8	43.8
3	540	14.9	14.3	19.1	13.5	23.0
4 or more	274	6.3	6.3	7.5	3.2	4.4

Note: All analyses were on weighted National Survey of Child and Adolescent Well-Being II, Wave 3 data; populations are unweighted and, therefore, direct percentages cannot be calculated by hand. Reported populations vary slightly across analyses because of missing data in some variable categories.

SOURCE: Cecelia Casanueva et al., "Exhibit 19. Caregiver and Household Characteristics at Wave 3," in *NSCAW II Wave 3 Report: Wave 3 Tables*, U.S. Department of Health and Human Services, Administration for Children and Families, Office of Planning, Research, and Evaluation, June 5, 2014, http://www.acf.hhs.gov/sites/default/files/opre/nscaw_wave_3_tables_june_2014_clean.pdf (accessed July 16, 2014)

cm05.pdf) that child maltreatment victimization rates declined from 12.5 victims per 1,000 child population in 2001 to 12.1 victims per 1,000 child population in 2005. Other data sources, including the NIS studies, show that the rates began declining during the 1990s.

CONSEQUENCES OF CHILDHOOD MALTREATMENT

The consequences of childhood maltreatment can be severe and long lasting. The immediate and most obvious consequences are from maltreatment incidents that cause

TABLE 3.8

Need for alcohol and substance abuse treatment among parents reported in the National Survey of Child and Adolescent Well-Being II, Wave 3, by type of service, 2011–12

	Need for substance abuse services[a]	Received inpatient alcohol or substance abuse service[b]	Received outpatient alcohol or substance abuse service[c]
	%	%	%
Total	20.8	0.3	0.9
Parent gender			
Male	30.0	0.0	0.5
Female	19.7	0.3	0.9
Parent age (years)			
Under 20	1.0	0.0	0.0
20–29	21.0	0.7	1.2
30–49	20.3	0.1	0.8
50–59	25.9	0.4	0.5
60 and older	25.4	0.0	0.0
Parent race/ethnicity			
Black	19.9	0.0	0.0
White	18.2	0.5	1.5
Hispanic	26.2	0.0	0.6
Other	20.9	0.0	0.3
Parent insurance status			
Public	23.0	0.3	1.2
Private	14.0	0.0	0.0
Uninsured	22.2	0.5	1.0

[a]Parents were determined to have a need for substance abuse services if they met any one of four criteria: (1) caseworker report of parent's need for services for a drug or alcohol problem at Wave 3, (2) AUDIT Total score ≥5, (3) DAST-20 Total score 2–4 or 5 or higher, or (4) the parent's self-reported need ("a lot" or "somewhat") for alcohol or substance abuse services in the past year, if she or he had not received a substance abuse service.
[b]Inpatient alcohol or substance abuse services include having been admitted overnight to hospital or medical facility for alcohol/drug problem in the last 12 months, having stayed overnight in a facility that provides alcohol or drug treatment in the last 12 months, or having used an emergency room for alcohol/drug abuse in past 12 months.
[c]Outpatient alcohol or substance abuse services include having been to a clinic or doctor regarding an alcohol or drug problem in the past 12 months.
Note: The term "in-home parents" refers to the parents of children living at home at Wave 3. Only permanent caregivers were asked about substance abuse service receipt; responses here reflect only those of in-home parents. Parents who indicated that they had not ever received substance abuse services were included as not having received these services in the past 12 months. All analyses were on weighted National Survey of Child and Adolescent Well-Being II Wave 3 data.

SOURCE: Adapted from Cecelia Casanueva et al., "Exhibit 23. In-Home Parents' Need for and Receipt of Alcohol or Substance Abuse Services in Past 12 Months (Wave 3)," in *NSCAW II Wave 3 Report: Wave 3 Tables*, U.S. Department of Health and Human Services, Administration for Children and Families, Office of Planning, Research, and Evaluation, June 5, 2014, http://www.acf.hhs.gov/sites/default/files/opre/nscaw_wave_3_tables_june_2014_clean.pdf (accessed July 21, 2014)

physical harm, such as injuries and even deaths. Neglect does not necessarily leave obvious physical marks like abuse does, and it often involves infants and young children who lack the language skills to describe their abuse. However, children subjected to neglect may show obvious signs of malnourishment or lack of proper medical care. Likewise, victims of sexual abuse may have telltale injuries or sexually transmitted diseases. These problems are readily evident and relatively easy to treat. More insidious and difficult to diagnose and treat are the long-term biological and psychological consequences of maltreatment. Exposure to severe and/or chronic trauma during childhood is blamed for what researchers call sequelae (diseases or disorders that emerge later in life, but are linked to previous experiences of disease, injury, or other trauma). Casanueva et al. list in *National Survey of Child and Adolescent Well-Being, Research Brief No. 18: Instability and Early Life Changes among Children in the Child Welfare System* (September 15, 2012, http://www.acf.hhs.gov/sites/default/files/opre/early_life.pdf) the following psychological sequelae that are associated with childhood traumas, such as maltreatment:

- Alcohol and drug abuse and dependence
- Depression
- Anxiety
- Conduct problems
- Schizophrenia
- Personality disorders
- Post-traumatic stress disorder
- Acute stress disorder
- Suicide
- Unfavorable psychological adjustment to subsequent traumatic events
- Difficulties with emotion regulation
- Greater vulnerability to developing traumatic symptoms when exposed to new traumatic events

It is important to note that the actions taken by CPS agencies after a maltreatment incident occurs, for example, removing a child from the home and putting him or

TABLE 3.9

Need for mental health services among parents reported in the National Survey of Child and Adolescent Well-Being II, Wave 3, by type of service, 2011–12

	Need for mental health services[a]	Received inpatient mental health service[b]	Received outpatient mental health service[c]	Used prescription medication for mental health problem[d]
	%	%	%	%
Total	**26.5**	**1.2**	**11.9**	**22.1**
Parent gender				
Male	12.5	0.2	4.7	13.6
Female	28.2	1.3	12.7	23.1
Parent age (years)				
Under 20	29.6	0.0	17.4	16.2
20–29	23.5	1.0	11.2	16.2
30–49	28.0	1.2	12.0	24.2
50–59	26.2	1.1	14.7	27.0
60 and older	11.9	0.0	3.4	4.7
Parent race/ethnicity				
Black	26.3	1.4	5.3	10.4
White	27.4	1.4	17.2	30.3
Hispanic	25.8	0.3	8.1	16.8
Other	26.9	2.0	10.7	25.2
Parent insurance status				
Public	33.6	1.6	15.7	29.3
Private	20.7	0.1	9.6	20.1
Uninsured	20.0	1.2	7.7	12.5

[a]Parents were determined to have a need for mental health services if they met any one of four criteria: (1) caseworker report of a parent's need for services for an emotional, psychological, or other mental health problem at Wave 3, (2) self-reported scores were within the clinical range on the major depression scale of the CIDI-SF, (3) a score exceeded 1.5 standard deviations below the norm (i.e., a score ≤35) on the Mental Health Component of the SF-12, or (4) the parent's self-reported need ("a lot" or "somewhat") for mental health services in the past year, if she or he had not received a mental health service.

[b]Inpatient mental health services include having been admitted overnight to hospital or medical facility for a mental health problem in the last 12 months or having used the emergency room for a mental health problem in past 12 months.

[c]Outpatient mental health services include having had one or more sessions of psychological counseling for emotional problems with any type of professional in the past 12 months or day treatment or partial hospitalization for mental health problem in past 12 months.

[d]This category includes the use of prescription medication for one's emotions, nerves, or mental health from any type of professional in past 12 months.

Note: The term "in-home parents" refers to the parents of children living at home at Wave 3. Only permanent caregivers were asked about mental health service receipt; responses here reflect only those of in-home parents. Parents who indicated that they had not ever received mental health services were included as not having received these services in the past 12 months. All analyses were on weighted National Survey of Child and Adolescent Well-Being II Wave 3 data.

SOURCE: Adapted from Cecelia Casanueva et al., "Exhibit 24. In-Home Parents' Need for and Receipt of Mental Health Services in Past 12 Months (Wave 3)," in *NSCAW II Wave 3 Report: Wave 3 Tables*, U.S. Department of Health and Human Services, Administration for Children and Families, Office of Planning, Research, and Evaluation, June 5, 2014, http://www.acf.hhs.gov/sites/default/files/opre/nscaw_wave_3_tables_june_2014_clean.pdf (accessed July 21, 2014)

her into the foster care system, are also traumatic events. Casanueva et al. indicate that the Child and Family Services Improvement and Innovation Act of 2011 includes "new language" that requires the states to develop plans to "monitor and treat emotional trauma associated with a child's maltreatment and removal."

The Administration on Children, Youth, and Families (ACYF) explains in the information memorandum "Promoting Social and Emotional Well-Being for Children and Youth Receiving Child Welfare Services" (April 17, 2012, http://www.acf.hhs.gov/sites/default/files/cb/im1204.pdf) that emerging scientific evidence has made it aware that its historical child welfare priorities of "ensuring safety and achieving permanency" are no longer sufficient. The agency notes that it intends to place much greater focus on the behavioral, social, and emotional domains, because recent research shows that most adverse effects of maltreatment are concentrated in these areas and cause problems "that ripple across the lifespan."

The ACYF states, "These effects can keep children from developing the skills and capacities they need to be successful in the classroom, in the workplace, in their communities, and in interpersonal relationships."

The agency examines six domains that are associated with childhood maltreatment: neurobiology, traumatic traits, behavioral problems, relational competence, mental health, and use of psychotropic medications. The domains are not stand-alone, but can have significant overlap. In other words, maltreated children can experience multiple problems across the domains. It is also important to understand that most problems are assessed in maltreated children months or even years after the maltreatment occurred. Thus, it is not entirely clear whether the problems existed beforehand or developed as a result of the maltreatment and/or subsequent interventions, such as removal from the home. In addition, there are few longitudinal studies that follow maltreated children into adulthood. Most studies that examine adults

TABLE 3.10

Re-reports of maltreatment among children reported in the National Survey of Child and Adolescent Well-Being II, Wave 3, by select characteristics and report status, 2011–12

	Re-reports sample size = 1,376	Substantiated sample size = 412	Indicated sample size = 75	Unsubstantiated sample size = 759
	%	%	%	%
Total	24.3	29.7	1.8	68.5
Gender				
Male	27.4	26.9	1.2	72.0
Female	21.1	33.7	2.5	63.8
Age (years) at baseline				
0–2	24.1	37.1	2.6	60.2
3–5	22.3	18.2	1.8	80.0
6–10	28.6	23.8	1.0	75.2
11–17	21.9	39.8	1.9	58.3
Race/ethnicity				
Black	21.7	28.8	1.4	69.8
White	27.5	29.6	1.9	68.5
Hispanic	22.9	29.2	1.6	69.2
Other	19.6	33.3	2.3	64.5
Setting at baseline*				
In-home bio and adoptive	24.0	29.7	1.6	68.7
Formal kin care	14.2	29.1	6.6	64.3
Informal kin care	28.5	23.6	1.2	75.3
Foster care	28.3	45.8	3.9	50.3
Group home or residential program	51.1	21.9	0.7	77.3

*During a period of reunification, children could have been reported again for maltreatment, and that could have prompted a return to an out-of-home placement. Thus, even if a child was at a foster care placement at the baseline and 18-month or 36-month follow-up, the re-report could have happened during a period of no foster home placement. Of the children who were at any point placed out of home, 54.4% were in-home with biological parents at baseline. Of those, 49.3% were reunified or had at least one reunification attempt across time. Of the children who were in out-of-home placement at baseline, at least one reunification attempt was made for 35.0% of those in formal kin care, 21.4% of those in informal kin care, 29.3% of those in foster care, and 35.8% of those in group home/residential treatment. Caseworkers were asked about reunification plans if the child was in out of home care at the time of the interview. Estimates may represent an underestimate of reunification attempts, as situations where the child was placed out of home and then reunified between interview waves would not be captured. Of those placed out of home at the time of interview, 39.2% had at least one attempt of reunification.

Note: All analyses were on weighted National Survey of Child and Adolescent Well-Being II baseline, National Child Abuse and Neglect System, Wave 2, and Wave 3 data.

SOURCE: Adapted from Cecelia Casanueva et al., "Exhibit 25. Re-reports of Maltreatment and Substantiation Status by Caseworker Report through Wave 3 and NCANDS," in *NSCAW II Wave 3 Report: Wave 3 Tables*, U.S. Department of Health and Human Services, Administration for Children and Families, Office of Planning, Research, and Evaluation, June 5, 2014, http://www.acf.hhs.gov/sites/default/files/opre/nscaw_wave_3_tables_june_2014_clean.pdf (accessed July 21, 2014)

rely on self-reports from the test subjects regarding their childhood experiences. This introduces a certain element of uncertainty to the adverse impact data that are reported by adults.

The following sections summarize the ACYF findings on domain effects and support them with separate, but relevant, published scientific studies.

Neurobiology

As the ACYF points out, early childhood is a key time for development of the neurological system, including the brain. Brain development, or learning, is the process of creating connections between neurons in the brain, called synapses. Neurons, or nerve cells, send signals to one another through synapses, which in turn form the neuronal pathways that enable the brain to respond to specific environments. An infant is born with very few formed synapses; however, sufficient numbers are present to accommodate breathing, eating, and sleeping. During the early years of life the brain develops synapses at a fast rate. Scientists find that repeated experiences strengthen

the neuronal pathways, making them sensitive to similar experiences that may occur later on in life. If these early life experiences are of a negative nature, the development of the brain may be impaired. For example, if an infant who cries for attention constantly gets ignored, his or her brain creates the neuronal pathways that enable him or her to cope with being ignored. If the infant continually fails to get the attention he or she craves, the brain strengthens those same neuronal pathways.

NSCAW II DATA. In *NSCAW II Baseline Report: Child Well-Being* (August 1, 2011, http://www.acf.hhs.gov/sites/default/files/opre/nscaw2_child.pdf), the OPRE reports scores on a neurodevelopment test for thousands of children who were assessed during the baseline assessment of the NSCAW II studies. As described earlier, NSCAW II baseline data collection was conducted between March 2008 and April 2009 on children for which maltreatment investigations were closed by CPS agencies between February 2008 and April 2009. According to the OPRE, 2,177 infants aged three months to 24 months were administered the Bayley Infant Neurodevelopmental

TABLE 3.11

Incidences of caretaker aggression and neglect experienced by children reported in the National Survey of Child and Adolescent Well-Being II, Wave 3, by select characteristics and type of maltreatment, 2011–12

	CTS-PC Nonviolent discipline	CTS-PC Psychological aggression	CTS-PC Minor physical assault (corporal punishment)	CTS-PC Severe physical assault	CTS-PC Very severe physical assault
	%	%	%	%	%
Total	**80.0**	**49.9**	**28.8**	**9.8**	**3.0**
Gender					
Male	76.5	41.2	26.9	7.0	3.2
Female	82.8	56.6	30.3	12.0	2.9
Age (years)					
11–12	71.1	43.9	32.5	10.1	3.3
13–14	86.1	55.2	37.8	12.0	3.3
15–17	81.7	49.6	19.8	8.0	2.6
Race/ethnicity					
Black	77.0	51.6	34.1	15.1	6.0
White	78.1	42.9	27.0	6.8	0.9
Hispanic	83.6	58.6	26.0	10.0	3.5
Other	85.1	46.3	36.6	10.0	5.2

Notes: CTS-PC = Conflict Tactics Scale Parent-Child. All analyses were on weighted National Survey of Child and Adolescent Well-Being II Wave 3 data.

SOURCE: Adapted from Cecelia Casanueva et al., "Exhibit 26. Caregiver Aggression and Neglect of Children 11 to 17 Years Old from a Caregiver in the Past Year by Child Report at Wave 3," in *NSCAW II Wave 3 Report: Wave 3 Tables*, U.S. Department of Health and Human Services, Administration for Children and Families, Office of Planning, Research, and Evaluation, June 5, 2014, http://www.acf.hhs.gov/sites/default/files/opre/nscaw_wave_3_tables_june_2014_clean.pdf (accessed July 21, 2014)

FIGURE 3.2

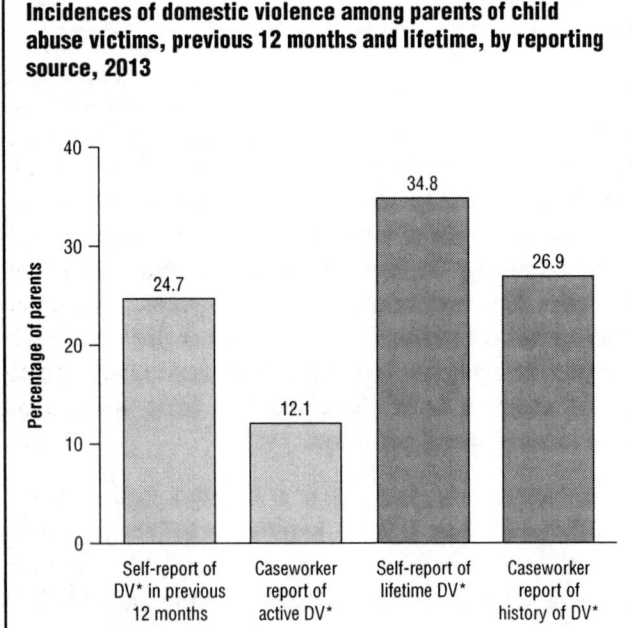

Incidences of domestic violence among parents of child abuse victims, previous 12 months and lifetime, by reporting source, 2013

*DV = Domestic violence.

SOURCE: Cecelia Casanueva et al., "Domestic Violence (DV) among NSCAW Parents," in *Child Well-Being Spotlight: Parents Reported for Maltreatment Experience High Rates of Domestic Violence*, U.S. Department of Health and Human Services, Administration for Children and Families, Office of Planning, Research and Evaluation, February 13, 2013, http://www.acf.hhs.gov/sites/default/files/opre/parentsinhome_v2.pdf (accessed July 20, 2014)

Screener (BINS), a test that was developed by Glen Aylward, a professor of pediatrics and psychiatry. The BINS test identifies infants with developmental delays and/or neurological impairments that need further diagnostic testing. The test assesses functions of the central nervous system, sensation and perception, motor skills, and cognitive processes, such as memory, learning, thinking, and reasoning. Overall, approximately half (50.8%) of the NSCAW II infants had scores indicating "high risk" for developmental delay or neurological impairment. This compares with 9% to 16% of the children in the general population with scores in this range. The latter cohort (group) does not include children with clinically diagnosed risk factors such as premature births, low birth weights, and respiratory distress syndrome. Overall, more than five times as many NSCAW II infants as infants in the general population (without clinically diagnosed risk factors) had "high risk" BINS scores.

The OPRE provides the results of five other tests of cognitive development and abilities in thousands of NSCAW II children and compares the scores with those of children in the general population or a comparable norm. In all cases five to eight times more of the NSCAW II children than general population or comparable norm children showed poor testing results.

A RETROSPECTIVE STUDY. Scientists find that childhood maltreatment has distinct negative effects on the

FIGURE 3.3

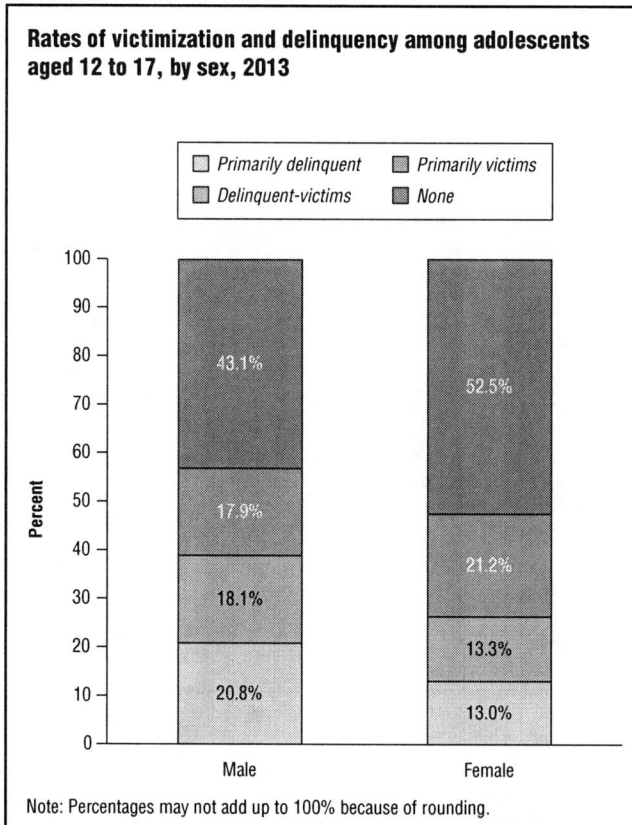

Rates of victimization and delinquency among adolescents aged 12 to 17, by sex, 2013

Note: Percentages may not add up to 100% because of rounding.

SOURCE: Carlos A. Cuevas et al., "Figure 1. Victimization-Delinquency Co-occurrence by Gender, Ages 10 to 17," in "Children's Exposure to Violence and the Intersection between Delinquency and Victimization," *Juvenile Justice Bulletin: National Survey of Children's Exposure to Violence*, U.S. Department of Justice, Office of Justice Programs, Office of Juvenile Justice and Delinquency Prevention, October 2013, http://www.ojjdp.gov/pubs/240555.pdf (accessed July 21, 2014)

biological development of the brain. For example, in "Childhood Maltreatment Is Associated with Reduced Volume in the Hippocampal Subfields CA3, Dentate Gyrus, and Subiculum" (*Proceedings of the National Academy of Sciences*, vol. 109, no. 9, February 28, 2012), a study that focuses on the hippocampus (a portion of the brain that plays a major role in memory and learning processes), Martin H. Teicher, Carl M. Anderson, and Ann Polcari of McLean Hospital in Belmont, Massachusetts, examine the brain scans of 193 young adults aged 18 to 25 years, who are described as "ethnically diverse" and "predominantly middle-class and well-educated." The childhood history of the subjects was determined using two surveys: the Adverse Childhood Experience Questionnaire and the Childhood Trauma Questionnaire. These are screening tools that are widely used by researchers to ascertain whether or not adults experienced traumatic events during childhood. As such, the surveys are known as retrospective (looking back) tests. Overall, 46% of the test group had no self-reported childhood exposure to maltreatment, while 16% reported exposure to three or more types of

maltreatment, mainly physical abuse and parental verbal abuse. Medicated subjects and subjects who had experienced nonmaltreatment-related childhood traumas (e.g., car wrecks) were not included in the study.

According to Teicher, Anderson, and Polcari, test subjects with high childhood maltreatment scores showed lower hippocampus volumes than did test subjects with low scores. Reduced hippocampal volume is associated with psychiatric disorders, such as depression, post-traumatic stress disorder, borderline personality disorder, and schizophrenia. The researchers note that their findings support other studies showing that early exposure to stress, particularly maltreatment between the ages of three and five years, negatively affects hippocampal development. These effects are not obvious until several years later. The researchers acknowledge that their test group of well-educated mostly middle-class adults is not representative of the overall maltreated population, which tends to be less educated and less privileged. However, Teicher, Anderson, and Polcari suspect that the latter population would show hippocampal reductions "to at least the same degree."

Indeed, other studies have seemed to corroborate Teicher, Anderson, and Polcari's findings. In "Childhood Maltreatment and Psychopathology Affect Brain Development during Adolescence" (*Journal of the American Academy of Child & Adolescent Psychiatry*, vol. 52, no. 9, September 2013), Sarah Whittle et al. conclude that experiences of childhood maltreatment can have a negative impact on brain development during early adolescence. As part of their study, Whittle et al. conducted magnetic resonance imaging (MRI) exams on adolescent boys aged 12 and 13 with follow-up testing at a later date. The results of the tests reveal diminished development in the left hippocampus of childhood trauma victims. At the same time, the MRIs revealed that victims of childhood trauma experienced increased growth of the left amygdala, the portion of the brain responsible for moderating emotions. As Christopher Bergland reports in "The Size and Connectivity of the Amygdala Predicts Anxiety" (PsychologyToday.com, November 20, 2013), an enlarged amygdala has been linked to higher incidences of chronic anxiety in children.

STRESS IMPAIRMENTS. Another neurobiological impact of childhood maltreatment is the occurrence of abnormally high levels of cortisol, a hormone that is released by the body during times of stress. The ACYF notes that scientific studies show that heightened stress impairs development of the prefrontal cortex, an area of the brain that engages in planning, decision-making, focusing, and self-regulation.

The National Scientific Council on the Developing Child is a project of the Center on the Developing Child at Harvard University. As of November 2014,

FIGURE 3.4

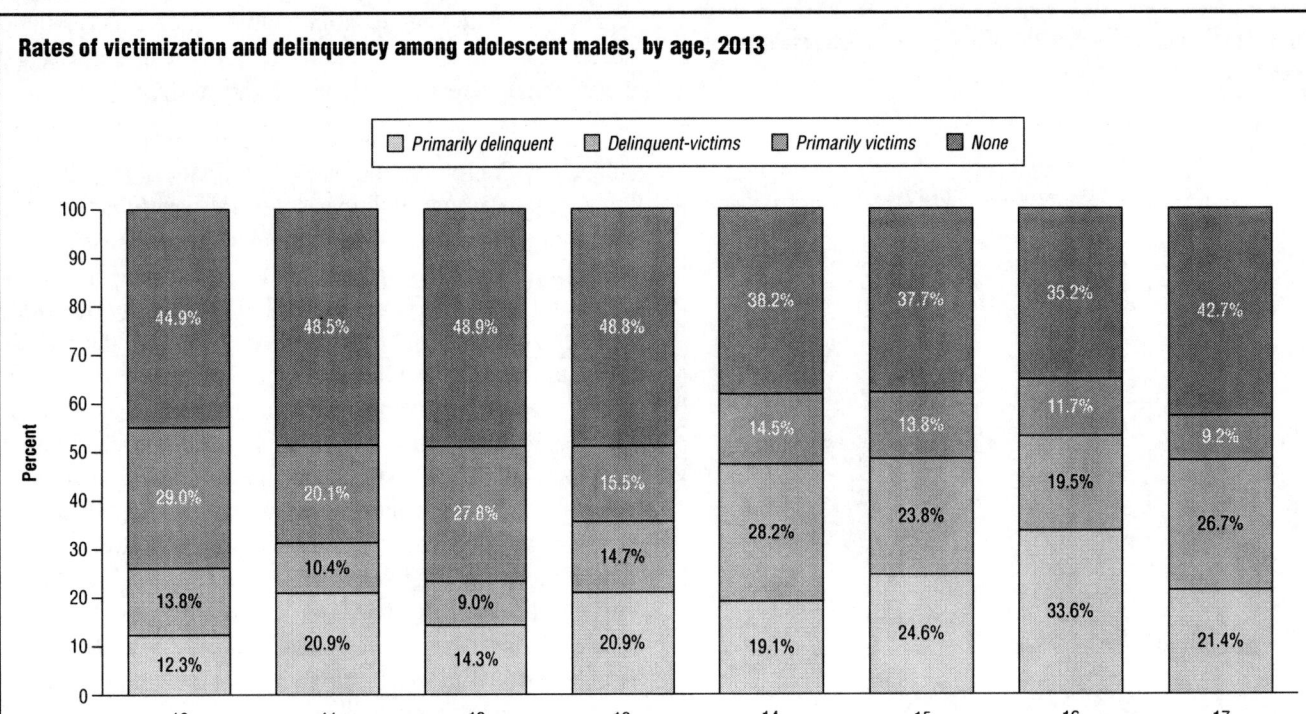

Rates of victimization and delinquency among adolescent males, by age, 2013

Note: Percentages may not add up to 100% because of rounding.

SOURCE: Carlos A. Cuevas et al., "Figure 2. Victimization-Delinquency Co-occurrence by Males Ages 10 to 17," in "Children's Exposure to Violence and the Intersection between Delinquency and Victimization," *Juvenile Justice Bulletin: National Survey of Children's Exposure to Violence*, U.S. Department of Justice, Office of Justice Programs, Office of Juvenile Justice and Delinquency Prevention, October 2013, http://www.ojjdp.gov/pubs/240555.pdf (accessed July 21, 2014)

FIGURE 3.5

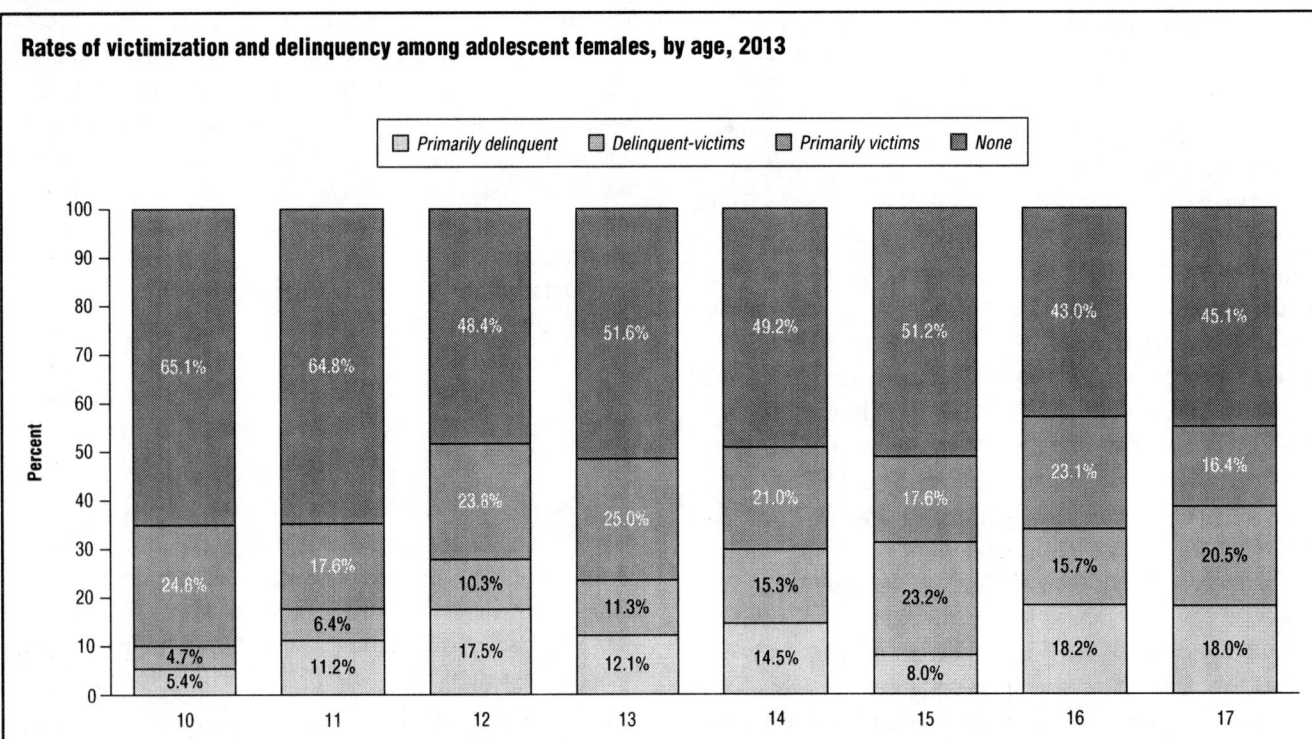

Rates of victimization and delinquency among adolescent females, by age, 2013

SOURCE: Carlos A. Cuevas et al., "Figure 3: Victimization-Delinquency Co-occurrence by Females Ages 10 to 17," in "Children's Exposure to Violence and the Intersection between Delinquency and Victimization," *Juvenile Justice Bulletin: National Survey of Children's Exposure to Violence*, U.S. Department of Justice, Office of Justice Programs, Office of Juvenile Justice and Delinquency Prevention, October 2013, http://www.ojjdp.gov/pubs/240555.pdf (accessed July 21, 2014)

TABLE 3.12

Child maltreatment victims with reported disabilities, by state, 2012

	Percent							
State	Behavior problem	Emotional disturbance	Learning disability	Intellectual disability	Other medical condition	Physically disabled	Visually or hearing impaired	Total reported disabilities
Alabama								
Alaska	1.6	0.7	1.2	0.1	0.6	0.1	0.1	4.4
Arizona	3.8	1.8	3.0	0.1	25.1	0.0	13.0	46.7
Arkansas	4.4	2.8	1.5	0.5	14.6	0.2	4.2	28.3
California	0.3	1.9	0.1	0.7	10.1	0.4	1.0	14.4
Colorado								
Connecticut	1.8	1.1	3.3	0.3	1.3	0.2	0.1	8.2
Delaware	4.2	13.3	3.2	1.3	10.4	0.2	0.3	32.9
District of Columbia		1.2			7.1			8.4
Florida	0.1	0.4	0.3	0.1	1.1	0.2	0.1	2.4
Georgia	5.3	9.3	1.5	0.5	3.7	0.5	0.5	21.2
Hawaii	5.7	3.1	0.3	0.4	6.4	0.4	0.7	17.0
Idaho								
Illinois		0.4	1.7	0.2	0.7	0.1	5.4	8.4
Indiana	11.8	4.7	2.2	1.0	1.3	0.9	0.2	22.1
Iowa								
Kansas		10.4	2.6	1.5	3.9	1.4	0.6	20.4
Kentucky	0.1	0.2	0.2	0.4	0.8	0.2	0.1	2.0
Louisiana								
Maine	0.1	15.0	0.0	0.0	0.1	0.0	0.0	15.4
Maryland	10.5	2.3	0.6	0.4	9.4	0.6	0.4	24.1
Massachusetts	0.1	0.5	0.6	0.2	1.9	0.1	0.1	3.5
Michigan								
Minnesota	14.6	8.9	1.4	2.6	5.8	0.8	0.4	34.5
Mississippi	4.5	0.3	1.2	0.4	5.9	0.1	0.2	12.7
Missouri	1.6	6.5	2.6	0.4	2.4	2.9	0.3	16.7
Montana	9.3	3.4	2.9	0.2	5.4	0.6	1.0	22.8
Nebraska	3.5	8.3	1.5	0.4	2.5	0.3	0.2	16.7
Nevada	7.0	6.2	0.2	0.8	0.6	0.7		15.5
New Hampshire	2.4	16.5	3.3	6.7	13.4	2.7	0.6	45.6
New Jersey	10.2	1.5	4.7	0.3	4.2	0.6	0.2	21.7
New Mexico	0.6	5.2	0.4	0.4	3.2	0.2	0.3	10.4
New York								
North Carolina								
North Dakota								
Ohio	4.3	3.8	0.9	1.3	2.6	0.3	0.4	13.7
Oklahoma	1.3	5.6	5.0	0.7	7.1	0.3	0.4	20.5
Oregon	1.4	2.3	0.6	0.6	1.7	0.2	0.2	7.0
Pennsylvania								
Puerto Rico	14.1	7.0	8.2	1.9	5.7	0.9	0.6	38.4
Rhode Island	2.5	4.5	0.6	0.7	4.2	0.4	0.2	13.1
South Carolina	16.4	2.6		0.9	8.0	16.4	0.7	44.9
South Dakota	8.7	3.3	4.1	0.7	5.2	0.8	1.1	23.9
Tennessee	1.5					0.0		1.6
Texas	0.6	0.0	0.2	0.1	0.8	0.1	0.2	2.0
Utah	12.2	4.0	1.4	2.5	2.0	0.3	0.6	23.0
Vermont		2.3	0.3		0.9	0.3	0.2	4.0
Virginia								
Washington	3.1	2.2	0.0	0.2	2.7	0.2	0.5	8.9
West Virginia	4.9	4.2	2.0	0.0				11.1
Wisconsin	1.0	5.3	3.1	0.6	3.1	0.6	0.5	14.1
Wyoming	5.1	1.8	2.8	2.0	2.6	0.3	0.3	14.9
Total								
Percent	3.2	2.5	1.1	0.5	4.3	0.7	1.0	13.3
States reporting								

SOURCE: Adapted from "Table 3–9. Victims with a Reported Disability, 2012," in *Child Maltreatment 2012*, U.S. Department of Health and Human Services, Administration for Children and Families, Administration on Children, Youth, and Families, Children's Bureau, December 17, 2013, http://www.acf.hhs.gov/sites/default/files/cb/cm2012.pdf (accessed July 16, 2014)

the council had published a series of 12 working papers (http://developingchild.harvard.edu/resources/reports_and_working_papers/working_papers) that summarize research on brain and neurological system development and the adverse effects of childhood traumas, such as abuse and neglect. In *Building the Brain's "Air Traffic Control" System: How Early Experiences Shape the Development of Executive Function* (2011, http://developingchild.harvard.edu/index.php/resources/reports_and_working_papers/working_papers/wp11), the council concludes that "adverse environments resulting from neglect, abuse, and/or exposure to violence can impair the development of executive function skills as a result of the disruptive effects of toxic stress on the developing

TABLE 3.13

Child maltreatment victims and nonvictims with alcohol abuse caregiver risk factors, by state, 2012

State	Unique victims	Unique victims with alcohol abuse caregiver risk factor		Unique nonvictims	Unique nonvictims with alcohol abuse caregiver risk factor	
		Number	Percent		Number	Percent
Alabama						
Alaska	2,928	323	11.0	6,866	340	5.0
Arizona						
Arkansas	11,133	175	1.6			
California						
Colorado						
Connecticut						
Delaware	2,335	253	10.8			
District of Columbia	2,141	709	33.1	11,671	1,414	12.1
Florida						
Georgia	18,752	598	3.2			
Hawaii	1,398	227	16.2	2,402	292	12.2
Idaho						
Illinois						
Indiana	20,223	1,006	5.0			
Iowa						
Kansas						
Kentucky						
Louisiana						
Maine	3,781	760	20.1	7,423	497	6.7
Maryland	13,079	192	1.5			
Massachusetts						
Michigan	33,434	2,747	8.2			
Minnesota	4,238	491	11.6	19,397	1,494	7.7
Mississippi	7,599	172	2.3			
Missouri	4,685	388	8.3	67,227	1,778	2.6
Montana	1,324	112	8.5	9,283	194	2.1
Nebraska						
Nevada	5,436	599	11.0	16,634	470	2.8
New Hampshire	901	128	14.2	10,549	469	4.4
New Jersey	9,031	1,428	15.8	67,133	3,226	4.8
New Mexico	5,882	2,305	39.2	16,017	3,749	23.4
New York						
North Carolina						
North Dakota	1,402	554	39.5	4,770	924	19.4
Ohio	29,250	379	1.3	73,484	862	1.2
Oklahoma	9,627	1,718	17.8	35,912	1,805	5.0
Oregon	9,576	447	4.7	23,597	328	1.4
Pennsylvania	3,416	378	11.1			
Puerto Rico	8,470	806	9.5			
Rhode Island	3,218	113	3.5	5,353	79	1.5
South Carolina						
South Dakota	1,224	579	47.3	4,492	626	13.9
Tennessee						
Texas	62,551	5,726	9.2	188,072	8,014	4.3
Utah	9,419	454	4.8			
Vermont						
Virginia						
Washington	6,546	1,984	30.3	37,184	3,916	10.5
West Virginia						
Wisconsin	4,645	160	3.4	28,998	643	2.2
Wyoming	705	200	28.4	4,923	57	1.2
Total	**298,349**	**26,111**		**641,387**	**31,177**	
Percent			8.8			4.9
States reporting	31	31		21	21	

SOURCE: "Table 3–11. Children with an Alcohol Abuse Caregiver Risk Factor, 2012," in *Child Maltreatment 2012*, U.S. Department of Health and Human Services, Administration for Children and Families, Administration on Children, Youth, and Families, Children's Bureau, December 17, 2013, http://www.acf.hhs.gov/sites/default/files/cb/cm2012.pdf (accessed July 16, 2014)

architecture of the brain." Likewise, in *The Science of Neglect: The Persistent Absence of Responsive Care Disrupts the Developing Brain* (2012, http://developingchild.harvard.edu/index.php/resources/reports_and_working_papers/working_papers/wp12), the council notes that "children who have experienced severe neglect are more likely to have cognitive problems, academic delays, deficits in executive function skills, and difficulties with attention regulation."

Traumatic Traits

The ACYF notes that traumatic events in childhood can cause children to develop chronic response tactics called hyperarousal and dissociation. During the state of

TABLE 3.14

Child maltreatment victims and nonvictims with drug abuse caregiver risk factors, by state, 2012

State	Unique victims	Unique victims with drug abuse caregiver risk factor		Unique nonvictims	Unique nonvictims with drug abuse caregiver risk factor	
		Number	Percent		Number	Percent
Alabama	9,573	402	4.2			
Alaska	2,928	167	5.7	6,866	159	2.3
Arizona						
Arkansas	11,133	339	3.0	50,996	609	1.2
California						
Colorado						
Connecticut						
Delaware	2,335	453	19.4			
District of Columbia	2,141	709	33.1	11,671	1,414	12.1
Florida						
Georgia	18,752	3,855	20.6	91,571	4,416	4.8
Hawaii	1,398	562	40.2	2,402	662	27.6
Idaho						
Illinois						
Indiana	20,223	3,683	18.2	72,252	2,044	2.8
Iowa						
Kansas						
Kentucky						
Louisiana						
Maine	3,781	1,134	30.0	7,423	995	13.4
Maryland	13,079	563	4.3			
Massachusetts						
Michigan	33,434	2,747	8.2			
Minnesota	4,238	710	16.8	19,397	1,404	7.2
Mississippi	7,599	438	5.8			
Missouri	4,685	1,018	21.7	67,227	3,048	4.5
Montana	1,324	188	14.2	9,283	224	2.4
Nebraska						
Nevada	5,436	599	11.0	16,634	470	2.8
New Hampshire	901	151	16.8	10,549	580	5.5
New Jersey	9,031	2,750	30.5	67,133	6,722	10.0
New Mexico	5,882	3,685	62.6	16,017	5,732	35.8
New York						
North Carolina						
North Dakota	1,402	486	34.7	4,770	524	11.0
Ohio	29,250	9,616	32.9	73,484	9,380	12.8
Oklahoma	9,627	3,711	38.5	35,912	3,736	10.4
Oregon	9,576	887	9.3	23,597	610	2.6
Pennsylvania	3,416	378	11.1			
Puerto Rico	8,470	780	9.2			
Rhode Island	3,218	311	9.7	5,353	225	4.2
South Carolina						
South Dakota	1,224	310	25.3	4,492	303	6.7
Tennessee	10,069	1,036	10.3	75,111	1,835	2.4
Texas	62,551	18,254	29.2	188,072	24,594	13.1
Utah	9,419	727	7.7			
Vermont						
Virginia						
Washington	6,546	2,967	45.3	37,184	7,465	20.1
West Virginia	4,591	388	8.5			
Wisconsin	4,645	245	5.3	28,998	756	2.6
Wyoming	705	235	33.3	4,923	64	1.3
Total	**322,582**	**64,484**		**931,317**	**77,971**	
Percent			**20.0**			**8.4**
States reporting	**34**	**34**		**25**	**25**	

SOURCE: "Table 3–12. Children with a Drug Abuse Caregiver Risk Factor, 2012," in *Child Maltreatment 2012*, U.S. Department of Health and Human Services, Administration for Children and Families, Administration on Children, Youth, and Families, Children's Bureau, December 17, 2013, http://www.acf.hhs.gov/sites/default/files/cb/cm2012.pdf (accessed July 16, 2014)

hyperarousal, the brain is always attuned to what it perceives as a threatening situation. The brain has "learned" that the world is a dangerous place and that it has to be constantly on the alert. The victim experiences extreme anxiety toward any perceived threat, or he or she may use aggression to control the situation. For example, children who have been physically abused may start a fight just so they can control the conflict and be able to choose their adversary. Males and older children are more likely to exhibit hyperarousal, whereas females and younger children are more likely to show dissociation. In the dissociative state, victims disconnect themselves from the negative experience. By "pretending" not to be there, their body and mind do not react to the abusive experience.

TABLE 3.15

Child maltreatment victims and nonvictims with domestic violence caregiver risk factors, by state, 2012

State	Unique victims	Unique victims with a domestic violence caregiver risk factor		Unique nonvictims	Unique nonvictims with domestic violence caregiver risk factor	
		Number	Percent		Number	Percent
Alabama	9,573	147	1.5			
Alaska	2,928	170	5.8	6,866	234	3.4
Arizona						
Arkansas	11,133	898	8.1	50,996	791	1.6
California						
Colorado						
Connecticut						
Delaware	2,335	1,131	48.4	12,472	370	3.0
District of Columbia	2,141	362	16.9	11,671	433	3.7
Florida	53,341	22,465	42.1	240,498	11,133	4.6
Georgia	18,752	6,814	36.3	91,571	6,419	7.0
Hawaii	1,398	386	27.6	2,402	534	22.2
Idaho						
Illinois	27,497	8,864	32.2	96,123	10,594	11.0
Indiana	20,223	3,277	16.2	72,252	2,624	3.6
Iowa						
Kansas						
Kentucky						
Louisiana						
Maine	3,781	1,229	32.5	7,423	950	12.8
Maryland	13,079	4,557	34.8			
Massachusetts	19,234	1,291	6.7	43,023	962	2.2
Michigan	33,434	17,531	52.4	138,174	19,361	14.0
Minnesota	4,238	1,197	28.2	19,397	3,486	18.0
Mississippi	7,599	176	2.3			
Missouri	4,685	794	16.9	67,227	4,802	7.1
Montana						
Nebraska						
Nevada	5,436	77	1.4			
New Hampshire	901	382	42.4	10,549	2,672	25.3
New Jersey	9,031	2,087	23.1	67,133	7,634	11.4
New Mexico	5,882	1,432	24.3	16,017	1,372	8.6
New York	68,375	14,587	21.3	149,288	6,556	4.4
North Carolina						
North Dakota	1,402	569	40.6	4,770	1,118	23.4
Ohio	29,250	6,437	22.0	73,484	7,517	10.2
Oklahoma	9,627	2,822	29.3	35,912	2,834	7.9
Oregon	9,576	3,503	36.6	23,597	4,478	19.0
Pennsylvania	3,416	165	4.8			
Puerto Rico	8,470	1,863	22.0			
Rhode Island	3,218	1,350	42.0	5,353	1,316	24.6
South Carolina						
South Dakota	1,224	361	29.5	4,492	778	17.3
Tennessee						
Texas	62,551	23,954	38.3	188,072	27,342	14.5
Utah	9,419	2,601	27.6	15,081	460	3.1
Vermont						
Virginia						
Washington	6,546	1,232	18.8	37,184	1,769	4.8
West Virginia						
Wisconsin	4,645	447	9.6	28,998	1,573	5.4
Wyoming	705	132	18.7			
Total	**475,045**	**135,290**		**1,520,025**	**130,112**	
Percent			**28.5**			**8.6**
States reporting	**35**	**35**		**28**	**28**	

SOURCE: "Table 3–10. Children with a Domestic Violence Caregiver Risk Factor, 2012," in *Child Maltreatment 2012*, U.S. Department of Health and Human Services, Administration for Children and Families, Administration on Children, Youth, and Families, Children's Bureau, December 17, 2013, http://www.acf.hhs.gov/sites/default/files/cb/cm2012.pdf (accessed July 16, 2014)

According to the ACYF, if maltreated children do not receive treatment to overcome these learned traits, the traits can become their standard responses to everyday experiences that are not threatening. As a result, the children have trouble forming interpersonal relationships and experience other difficulties, including managing intense emotions, such as anger and anxiety. In addition, they are prone to forming incorrect perceptions of themselves and others and interpreting communications from others inaccurately.

Behavioral Problems

The ACYF indicates that the prevalence of behavioral problems is high among maltreated children. Researchers

FIGURE 3.6

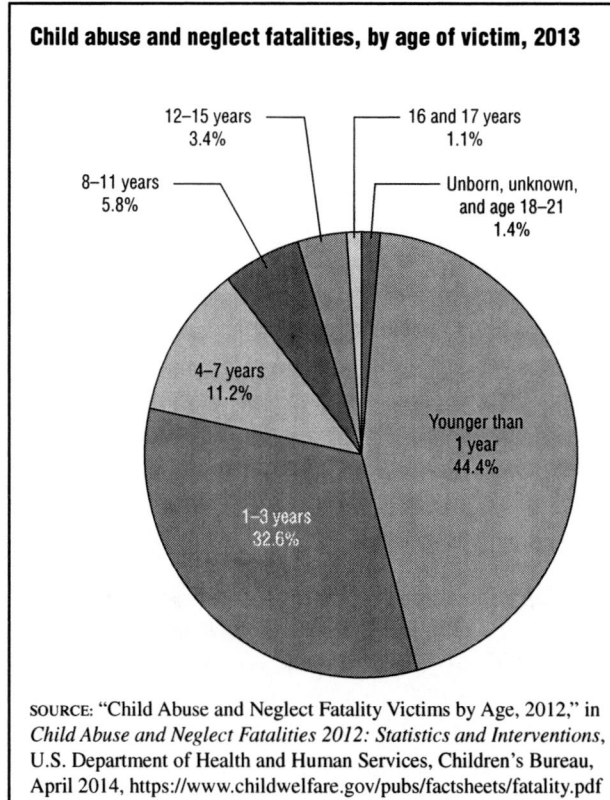

Child abuse and neglect fatalities, by age of victim, 2013

SOURCE: "Child Abuse and Neglect Fatality Victims by Age, 2012," in *Child Abuse and Neglect Fatalities 2012: Statistics and Interventions*, U.S. Department of Health and Human Services, Children's Bureau, April 2014, https://www.childwelfare.gov/pubs/factsheets/fatality.pdf (accessed July 20, 2014)

FIGURE 3.7

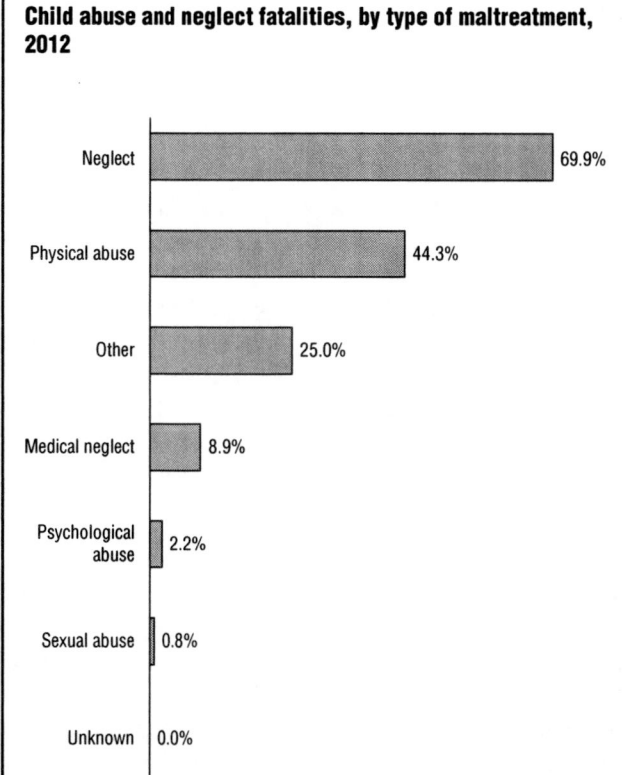

Child abuse and neglect fatalities, by type of maltreatment, 2012

SOURCE: "Child Abuse and Neglect Fatalities by Reported Maltreatment Type, 2012," in *Child Abuse and Neglect Fatalities 2012: Statistics and Interventions*, U.S. Department of Health and Human Services, Children's Bureau, April 2014, https://www.childwelfare.gov/pubs/factsheets/fatality.pdf (accessed July 20, 2014)

commonly assess behavioral problems using standardized surveys for which behaviors are reported by the children themselves or by parents, caregivers, or schoolteachers. One example is the Child Behavior Checklist, which was developed by Thomas Achenbach of the University of Vermont. The Child Behavior Checklist assesses internalizing behaviors (e.g., withdrawal and anxiety) and externalizing behaviors (e.g., acting up and aggression) based on parent and caregiver information.

In *NSCAW II Baseline Report: Child Well-Being*, the OPRE reports scores on behavioral tests for thousands of children who were assessed during the NSCAW II baseline assessment studies, which were conducted between March 2008 and April 2009. According to the OPRE, 3,417 children aged 1.5 to 17 years were administered the Child Behavior Checklist. The results show that 22.9% of them had a standardized score of 64 or more, indicating "clinical range" behavioral problems. For comparison, the OPRE notes that 8% of children in the general population or a comparable norm would be expected to have a Child Behavior Checklist score in the clinical range. Thus, the percentage of children with clinical-level behavioral problems was nearly three times higher among the NSCAW II children than among children in the general population or a comparable norm.

The percentage of NSCAW II children with scores in the clinical range was slightly higher for boys (24.5%)

TABLE 3.16

Child fatalities due to mistreatment, by selected caregiver risk factors, 2012

Caregiver risk factor	States reporting	Child fatalities from reporting states	Child fatalities with a caregiver risk factor	
			Number	Percent
Alcohol abuse	27	697	44	6.3
Domestic violence	31	1,096	220	20.1
Drug abuse	30	753	130	17.3

Note: For each caregiver risk factor, the analysis includes only those states that reported at least 1 percent of child victims' caregiver with the risk factor.

SOURCE: "Exhibit 4-E. Child Fatalities with Selected Caregiver Risk Factors, 2012," in *Child Maltreatment 2012*, U.S. Department of Health and Human Services, Administration for Children and Families, Administration on Children, Youth, and Families, Children's Bureau, December 17, 2013, http://www.acf.hhs.gov/sites/default/files/cb/cm2012.pdf (accessed July 16, 2014)

than for girls (21.2%). The percentages by child age were: aged 11 to 17 years (30.4%), aged six to 10 years (25.8%), aged three to five years (15.7%), and aged 1.5 to two years (9.7%). There were small to negligible differences in the percentages based on race and ethnicity. However, children in different settings showed decidedly different scores. Children who stayed in their home or lived with relatives had the lowest percentage (22.4%) of clinical range scores, compared with children in foster care (32.2%) and children in group homes or other residential programs (47.3%).

Overall, the NSCAW II data indicate that 57.6% of the children aged 11 to 14 years and 56.9% of the children aged 15 to 17 years had emotional and/or behavioral problems. More than a quarter of the children aged 11 to 14 years old had poor social skills (28.2%) or had ever repeated a grade (25.5%). Smaller percentages had run away during the previous six months (12.6%), had a substance use disorder (12.3%), had made a court appearance during the previous year (8.2%), or had ever been pregnant (1.9% of girls).

Although the percentage of older youths exhibiting poor social skills (27.2%) was similar to that seen in younger youths (28.2%), on all other well-being indicators higher percentages of older youths than younger youths showed problem behaviors. Among youths aged 15 to 17 years the percentages experiencing problems were 42.5% for repeating a grade, 33.2% for a substance use disorder, 20.7% for having made a court appearance during the previous year, and 18.4% for running away during the previous six months. In addition, 10.5% of the girls in this age group had ever been pregnant. Furthermore, Casaneuva et al. note in *Child Well-Being Spotlight: Teenage Girls in the Child Welfare System Report High Rates of Risky Sexual Activity and Pregnancy* that, three years after the baseline report of maltreatment, 16.8% of NSCAW participants between the ages of 14 and 17, and 45.1% of participants between the ages of 18 and 20, had experienced at least one pregnancy.

A DECADES-LONG STUDY. During the 1980s Cathy S. Widom of the State University of New York, Albany, led a study in which researchers tracked down and interviewed hundreds of young adults who were known through court records to have been maltreated as children. Widom is widely known for her work on the cycle of violence theory. This theory suggests that childhood physical abuse increases the likelihood that the child victim will later be arrested or commit a violent crime as a teen or adult. Widom's study is considered to be one of the most detailed longitudinal studies of the consequences of childhood maltreatment.

Widom explains in "Childhood Victimization: Early Adversity, Later Psychopathology" (*National Institute of Justice Journal*, January 2000) that she began the study in 1986 by tracking down 908 children in a midwestern metropolitan region who were six to 11 years old when they were maltreated (between 1967 and 1971). A control group of 667 children with no history of childhood maltreatment was used for comparison. Each group contained about two-thirds whites and one-third African Americans and about an equal number of males and females. Widom examined the long-term consequences of childhood maltreatment on the subjects' intellectual, behavioral, social, and psychological development. When the two groups were first interviewed for the study, they had a median age (half were older, half were younger) of about 29 years.

Widom finds that although a large proportion of maltreated children did not become juvenile delinquents or criminals, those who suffered childhood abuse or neglect were more likely than those with no reported maltreatment to be arrested as juveniles (31.2% versus 19%) and as adults (48.4% versus 36.2%) when surveyed in 1986. The maltreated victims (21%) were also more likely than those with no reported childhood maltreatment history (15.6%) to be arrested for a violent crime during their teen years or adulthood.

Widom notes that the victims' later psychopathology (psychological disorders that result from maltreatment during childhood) manifested itself in suicide attempts, antisocial personality, and alcohol abuse and/or dependence. When surveyed in 1989, victims of maltreatment were more likely than individuals in the control group to report having attempted suicide (18.8% versus 7.7%) and having manifested antisocial personality disorder (18.4% versus 11.2%). Both groups, however, did not differ much in the rates of alcohol abuse and/or dependence.

Widom finds that gender plays a role in the development of psychological disorders in adolescence and adulthood. In 1989 females (24.3%) with a history of childhood maltreatment reported being more likely to attempt suicide, compared with their male counterparts (13.4%). In contrast, a significantly larger percentage of male victims (27%) than female victims (9.8%) developed an antisocial personality disorder. Although mistreated males (64.4%) and control subjects (67%) had similar proportions of alcohol abuse or dependence, females who experienced abuse or neglect were more likely than the control group to have alcohol problems (43.8% versus 32.8%).

Another phase of Widom's cycle of violence research was conducted when the maltreated and control groups had a median age of 32.5 years. Aside from collecting arrest records from federal, state, and local law enforcement agencies, Widom and Michael G. Maxfield also conducted interviews in 1994 with the subjects and reported their findings in *An Update on the "Cycle of Violence"* (February 2001, http://www.ncjrs.gov/pdffiles1/nij/184894.pdf). Overall, Widom and Maxfield find that childhood abuse or neglect increased the likelihood of arrest in adolescence by 59% and in adulthood by 28%. Childhood maltreatment also increased the likelihood of committing a violent crime by 30%.

Although earlier analysis of the maltreated group found that most of the victims did not become offenders, Widom and Maxfield's study shows that nearly half (49%) of the victims had experienced a nontraffic offense as teenagers or adults. Comparison by race shows that although both white and African American maltreated children had more arrests than the control group, there was no significant difference among whites in the maltreated and control groups. Among African American children, however, the maltreated group had higher rates of arrests. Maltreated African Americans were nearly twice as likely as their counterparts in the control group to be arrested as juveniles (40.6% versus 20.9%).

Widom and Maxfield also examined the type of childhood maltreatment that might lead to violence later in life. They find that physically abused children (21.1%) were the most likely to commit a violent crime in their teen or adult years and were closely followed by those who experienced neglect (20.2%). Although their study shows that just 8.8% of children who had been sexually abused were arrested for violence, Widom and Maxfield note that the victims were mostly females and that "females less often had a record of violent offenses."

In 2008 Widom reported on yet another phase of her longitudinal study. In "Childhood Victimization and Lifetime Revictimization" (Child Abuse and Neglect, vol. 32, no 8, August 2008), Widom, Sally J. Czaja, and Mary Ann Dutton describe the results of interviews that were conducted between 2000 and 2002 with members of the two original cohorts. At the time of the interviews the average age of the participants was 39.5 years. The researchers note that 896 of the original participants were interviewed again for the study. Some of the original participants could not be located, had died, were incapacitated, or refused to participate. However, the subjects interviewed between 2000 and 2002 were similar in demographics and maltreatment history to the original participants. Widom, Czaja, and Dutton find that higher percentages of the abused/neglected group had suffered violent victimizations than did the control group. For example, 54% of the abused/neglected group reported having been threatened with a weapon, compared with 45% of the control group. Other significant differences were seen when the participants reported having been physically harmed (76% of abused/neglected group, compared with 60% of control group), been coerced into unwanted sex (36% of abused/neglected group, compared with 18% of control group), and been the victim of a mugging (16% of abused/neglected group, compared with 11% of control group). The researchers conclude that the childhood victims of maltreatment, regardless of the type of maltreatment, had a greater risk than did the control group members of lifetime revictimization.

Helen W. Wilson and Cathy S. Widom report in "Pathways from Childhood Abuse and Neglect to HIV-Risk Sexual Behavior in Middle Adulthood" (Journal of Consulting and Clinical Psychology, vol. 79, no. 2, April 2011) on interviews that were conducted between 2003 and 2004 with 800 of the original survey participants. At that time the average age of the participants was 41 years. The researchers find that the subjects who were abused/neglected as children self-reported riskier sexual behavior than did members of the control group. In particular, the abused/neglected individuals reported sexual behavior that was more likely to expose them to the human immunodeficiency virus (HIV), a virus that causes the acquired immunodeficiency syndrome (AIDS).

A number of scholars have also identified a link between childhood abuse or neglect and intimate partner violence during adulthood. In "Exposure to Family Violence and Attachment Styles as Predictors of Dating Violence Perpetration among Men and Women: A Mediational Model" (Journal of Interpersonal Violence, vol. 29, no. 1, January 2014), Mary Lee, Marla Reese-Weber, and Jeffrey H. Kahn find that individuals who were abused as children have a higher likelihood of perpetrating acts of violence against their partners while dating as adults. As Lee, Reese-Weber, and Kahn note, this higher tendency toward dating violence was prevalent in both male and female victims of child abuse and neglect. Furthermore, intimate partner violence, particularly when it occurs during adolescence, can lead to a range of health and behavioral issues in adulthood. As Deinera Exner-Cortens, John Eckenrode, and Emily Rothman write in "Longitudinal Associations between Teen Dating Violence Victimization and Adverse Health Outcomes" (Pediatrics, vol. 131, no. 1, January 2013), teenage victims of dating violence, whether physical or psychological, demonstrate a higher tendency to struggle with substance abuse problems, antisocial attitudes, and intimate partner violence as adults.

Relational Competence

Relational competence is the competence with which people enter into relationships and socially interact with each other. These interactions begin at birth and are particularly important for infants, who must form strong bonds with their caregivers to thrive. Such relationships form the basis for future emotional connections. Childhood maltreatment and subsequent interventions by the child welfare system can disrupt the attachment process, resulting in severe consequences for the child's healthy emotional development.

In NSCAW II Wave 3 Report: Wave 3 Tables, Casanueva et al. report on the prevalence of placement instability (changes in caregiver and household) among NSCAW participants. As Casanueva et al. note, among children who were under the age of two at the time of the

NSCAW baseline report, nearly one-third (30.4%) had experienced two placements at the time Wave 3 data were compiled; another 5.2% had experienced three placements during this period, and 3% had experienced four or more placements.

Placement instability is a serious problem for very young children. As Casanueva et al. note in *National Survey of Child and Adolescent Well-Being, Research Brief No. 18: Instability and Early Life Changes among Children in the Child Welfare System*, infants are "hard-wired" to form emotional attachments to their primary caregivers. Scientists find that attachment disruptions can cause children to suffer emotional problems, internalized and externalized behavior problems, and subsequent psychopathology. Infants who are removed from their home and placed into foster care are at substantial risk for these poor outcomes because they face significant challenges in forming healthy attachments to new caregivers. This is particularly true if the infants "experienced difficult and harsh rearing conditions" before they left their home. Casanueva et al. indicate that maltreated infants who enter foster care "exhibit behaviors like avoidance, rejection, and opposition to care by new caregivers, pushing away foster parents even when they are distressed." Foster parents who are unable to overcome these difficulties are likely to return the children to the child welfare system, thus, increasing the placement instability in the children's lives. According to Casanueva et al., young children who have been adopted after multiple foster home placements exhibit more emotional and behavioral problems than do children who had never been placed in foster care or those who had only one "stable" placement following removal from their original home.

In *NSCAW II Baseline Report: Child Well-Being*, the OPRE reports scores on social skills tests for thousands of children who were part of the studies. According to the OPRE, 618 children aged 12 months to 18 months were assessed using the Brief Infant Toddler Social and Emotional Assessment (BITSEA), a test that was developed by the psychologists Margaret Briggs-Gowan and Alice Carter. The test has two subscales that score children on social-emotional problems and social-emotional competence. The OPRE indicates that 34.6% of the NSCAW II infants who were administered the BITSEA problem test had scores in the "possible problem" range. For comparison, 25% of the infants in the general population or a comparable norm would be expected to have a score in this range. On the BITSEA competence subscale, 21.2% of the NSCAW II infants had scores in the "possible deficit/delay" range, indicating that they may not have acquired the social and emotional skills that are expected for children of their age and sex. This percentage was higher than the 15% of the infants in the general population or a comparable norm that would be expected to

score in this range. Overall, NSCAW II infants living in their own home with their parents had higher scores on the BITSEA competence subscale than did NSCAW II infants living in foster care.

NSCAW II children aged three years to 17 years were assessed using the Social Skills Rating System (SSRS), which was developed by the psychologists Frank Gresham and Stephen Elliot. SSRS results were based on caregiver reports and divided the children into three broad groups: fewer skills, average skills, and more skills. Overall, 34.3% of the NSCAW II children were rated as having fewer skills. This compares with 15% of the children in the general population or a comparable norm who would be expected to fall into this category. The percentages of NSCAW II children rated as having fewer skills by placement setting were: kin care (32.5%), in-home (34.1%), foster care (43.3%), and group home or residential program (43.8%). Thus, children in group homes or residential programs were more likely than children in other settings to rate poorly in social skills.

Mental Health

The ACYF notes that scientific studies show high rates of mental illness among older children in foster care. In the United States mental illnesses are typically classified in accordance with the definitions and criteria outlined in the *Diagnostic and Statistical Manual of Mental Disorders* (*DSM*), which is published by the American Psychiatric Association. Other less stringent screening tools are also used by researchers, particularly to assess children.

NSCAW II DATA. In *NSCAW II Baseline Report: Child Well-Being*, the OPRE reports the results obtained during the NSCAW II baseline assessment studies, which were conducted between March 2008 and April 2009. Researchers assessed depression symptoms in 1,720 children aged seven to 17 years using the Children's Depression Inventory, a screening tool that was developed by the psychologist Maria Kovacs. The results show that 11.4% of the children had a score within the clinical range for depression based on self-reported results for the previous two weeks. The percentages within the clinical range varied strongly by placement setting: kin care (8.5%), in-home care (11.6%), foster care (13.2%), and group home or residential program (20.1%). For comparison, the OPRE notes that an estimated 6.7% of children aged seven to 17 years in the general population or a comparable norm would be expected to have a score within the clinical range for depression.

OLDER YOUTHS IN FOSTER CARE. J. Curtis McMillen et al. report in "Prevalence of Psychiatric Disorders among Older Youths in the Foster Care System" (*Journal of the American Academy of Child and Adolescent Psychology*, vol. 44, no. 1, January 2005) their findings from interviews that were conducted between December 2001 and June 2003 with 373 youths aged 17 years old in the foster care system of eight Missouri counties. The researchers used the diagnostic interview procedures from the fourth edition of the *DSM* (*DSM-IV*) to estimate the previous-year and lifetime prevalence of psychiatric disorders in the youths. Overall, 62% of the youths were assessed as having had at least one psychiatric disorder during their lifetime. More than one-third (37%) of the youths met the criteria for having had a psychiatric disorder in the previous year.

McMillen et al. indicate that nearly half (47%) of the youths met the lifetime prevalence criteria for conduct disorder. In "Conduct Disorder" (March 4, 2013, http://www.ncbi.nlm.nih.gov/pubmedhealth/PMH0001917), the U.S. National Library of Medicine indicates that conduct disorder is "a set of ongoing emotional and behavioral problems that occurs in children and teens. Problems may involve defiant or impulsive behavior, drug use, or criminal activity." According to McMillen et al., the percentages of youths who met the lifetime prevalence criteria for other psychiatric disorders were: major depression (27%), attention deficit/hyperactivity disorder (ADHD; 20%), and post-traumatic stress disorder (PTSD; 14%). The Cochrane Database of Systematic Reviews in "Parent Training for Attention Deficit Hyperactivity Disorder (ADHD) in Children Aged 5 to 18 Years" (2012, http://www.ncbi.nlm.nih.gov/pubmedhealth/PMH0032947) defines ADHD as "a neurodevelopmental disorder characterized by high levels of inattention, hyperactivity and impulsivity that are present before the age of seven years, seen in a range of situations, inconsistent with the child's developmental level and causing social or academic impairment." PTSD is an anxiety disorder that can develop in people who experience or witness a traumatic event involving actual or threatened injury or death. People with PTSD may experience flashbacks (reexperience the trauma), sleep disturbances, emotional numbness, depression, rage, memory loss, concentration problems, anxiety, and physical symptoms.

In "Prevalence and Timing of Diagnosable Mental Health, Alcohol, and Substance Use Problems among Older Adolescents in the Child Welfare System" (*Children and Youth Services Review*, vol. 32, no. 4, April 1, 2010), Thomas E. Keller et al. report the results of interviews that were conducted in 2002 with 732 youths aged 17 to 18 years in the foster care systems of Illinois, Iowa, or Wisconsin. The researchers used an interview technique that was designed to provide diagnoses in accordance with the *DSM-IV*. The results indicate that 15.1% of the youths met the lifetime prevalence criteria for PTSD. The percentages for other disorders were 14.1% for alcohol abuse or dependence, 8.2% for major depression, and 6.3% for substance abuse or dependence.

Use of Psychotropic Medications

Psychotropic medications are drugs that affect psychological functions, such as moods and emotions. In "Promoting Social and Emotional Well-Being for Children and Youth Receiving Child Welfare Services," the ACYF indicates that a study published in 2010 by Rutgers University found that among children covered by Medicare (a federal health insurance program), children in foster care were prescribed psychotropic medications at a much higher rate than were children not in foster care. The ACYF admits that "numerous studies" show that psychotropic medication rates are "comparatively high" for foster children; however, the agency notes that this discrepancy is due in part to the high rates of emotional and behavioral disorders among foster care children.

Leyla F. Stambaugh et al. examine in *National Survey of Child and Adolescent Well-Being, Child Well-Being Spotlight: Children in Out-of-Home Placements Receive More Psychotropic Medications and Other Mental Health Services than Children Who Remain In-Home following a Maltreatment Investigation* (August 15, 2012, http://www.acf.hhs.gov/sites/default/files/opre/nscaw2_child_out.pdf) NSCAW II Wave 2 data that were collected between 2008 and 2010 for 1,371 children aged 16 months to 19 years. The vast majority (1,057) of the children were living in-home, while 314 were living out of the home. More than half (58.2%) of the in-home children were receiving no mental health services or psychotropic medications. The remainder of the in-home children were receiving specialty mental health services and medications (21.5%), specialty mental health services only (18.5%), or medications only (1.8%). Only 30% of the out-of-home children were receiving no services. Of the remainder, about one-third (33.1%) were receiving specialty mental health services and medications, 27.5% were receiving specialty mental health services only, and 9.4% were receiving medications only. Overall, the percentages of children receiving psychotropic medications and/or specialty mental health services were higher among the out-of-home children than among the in-home children.

CHAPTER 4
CHILD SEXUAL ABUSE

Child sexual abuse is a horrendous misuse of an adult's trust and power over a child. When the abuser is particularly close to the victim, the child feels betrayed and trapped in a situation in which an adult who claims to care for the child is assaulting him or her. Many experts believe sexual abuse is the most underreported type of child maltreatment. A victim, especially a young child, may not know what he or she is experiencing. In many cases, the child is threatened to keep the abuse secret or feels embarrassed or guilty about it. Adults who may be aware of the abuse sometimes get involved in a conspiracy of silence. The effects of childhood sexual abuse can be severe and long-lasting by contributing to behavioral, mental, and physical problems years after the abuse occurs.

WHAT IS CHILD SEXUAL ABUSE?

It is important to understand that there are two types of laws in the United States that deal with the sexual abuse of children. Criminal laws define the types of sexual conduct for which offenders can be prosecuted in criminal court. Sexual acts committed against children by family members (interfamilial sexual abuse) and by non-family members may rise to the legal definition of criminal behavior. Because children (up to a certain age) are deemed incapable of voluntarily consenting to sexual activity, all sexual acts perpetrated on children are considered to be coercive. This distinction protects children, particularly older children, against claims from adult perpetrators that the sexual activity was voluntary on the part of the child. In addition, criminal laws generally forbid certain types of sexual conduct no matter the age of those involved. One example is incest, which is sexual activity between closely related family members.

Civil laws typically focus on interfamilial child sexual abuse. Under civil law, the parents (and other caretakers with custody rights) of children who are sexually abused can be investigated by child protective services (CPS) agencies and have their parental or custody rights terminated if they played a role in the abuse. In addition, civil laws include reporting requirements, as described in Chapter 2, that require certain professionals (such as educators) to report all forms of suspected child abuse to authorities.

Civil law definitions of child sexual abuse differ by jurisdiction. At the federal level, the Child Abuse Prevention and Treatment Act of 2010 defines sexual abuse at 42 USC Section 5106g (2014, http://www.law.cornell.edu/uscode/text/42/5106g) as follows:

> The term "sexual abuse" includes—
>
> (A) the employment, use, persuasion, inducement, enticement, or coercion of any child to engage in, or assist any other person to engage in, any sexually explicit conduct or simulation of such conduct for the purpose of producing a visual depiction of such conduct; or
>
> (B) the rape, and in cases of caretaker or inter-familial relationships, statutory rape, molestation, prostitution, or other form of sexual exploitation of children, or incest with children.

In *Definitions of Child Abuse and Neglect* (February 2011, https://www.childwelfare.gov/systemwide/laws_policies/statutes/define.pdf), the Children's Bureau within the U.S. Department of Health and Human Services (HHS) indicates that nearly all 50 U.S. states, the District of Columbia, Puerto Rico, and U.S. territories include civil definitions of child sexual abuse in their laws; however, these definitions vary. The agency provides a summary of the laws by jurisdiction. For example, Texas defines child sexual abuse as including the following acts:

- Sexual conduct harmful to a child's mental, emotional, or physical welfare, including conduct that constitutes the offense of indecency with a child, sexual assault, or aggravated sexual assault

- Failure to make a reasonable effort to prevent sexual conduct harmful to a child

- Compelling or encouraging a child to engage in sexual conduct

- Causing, permitting, encouraging, engaging in, or allowing the photographing, filming, or depicting of a child if the person knew or should have known that the resulting photograph, film, or depiction of the child is obscene or pornographic

- Causing, permitting, encouraging, engaging in, or allowing a sexual performance by a child

Under both criminal and civil laws child sexual abuse encompasses activities that fall into two broad categories. Physical contact acts involve intercourse or other penetrating and invasive sexual actions. Fondling and other inappropriate touching also fall into this category. Nonphysical contact acts include exposure (i.e., indecently exposing oneself to a child), voyeurism (spying on or secretly videotaping a child for the purposes of sexual gratification), allowing a child to be sexually abused by someone else (e.g., through prostitution), and using a child for pornographic purposes (e.g., in the production of sexually explicit photographs or videos).

CHILD SEXUAL ABUSE DATA

Data about child sexual abuse are available from two primary types of sources. First are CPS agencies and other social service agencies or institutions that compile data about child abuse cases as they are reported and investigated. Second are surveys or interviews in which adults or children (typically youths) are asked about childhood sexual abuse. Survey-based studies are known as retrospective studies because they rely on subjects "looking back" at past events. Each type of data source has its drawbacks and limitations. For example, CPS agencies may only be aware of a fraction of the child sexual abuse cases occurring in their communities because it is likely that not all cases are reported to the authorities. Surveys and other retrospective studies depend on the accurate memories of the subjects who are questioned. In addition, these studies typically feature small and geographically limited populations. Nevertheless, both types of sources provide clues about the prevalence of child sexual abuse and the victims, perpetrators, and risk factors that are involved.

NATIONAL INCIDENCE STUDIES

As explained in Chapter 2, there have been four comprehensive studies conducted as part of the National Incidence Study of Child Abuse and Neglect (NIS):

- NIS-1—data collection between 1979 and 1980

- NIS-2—data collection in 1986

- NIS-3—data collection in 1993

- NIS-4—data collection between 2005 and 2006

Child Sex Abuse Prevalence

The Children's Bureau notes in *Study Findings: National Study of the Incidence and Severity of Child Abuse and Neglect* (September 1981) that in regards to sexual abuse, NIS-1 researchers only counted cases in which an in-home parent or other adult caretaker was implicated. The Children's Bureau provides an estimated incidence rate for sexual exploitation (i.e., child sexual abuse) of 0.7 per 1,000 children in the U.S. population in 1979–80.

For the NIS-2, NIS-3, and NIS-4 studies researchers used two standards to assess abuse and neglect: the Harm Standard and the Endangerment Standard. (See Chapter 2 for a detailed explanation of these standards, but, in general, the Harm Standard requires that demonstrable harm to a child be present, whereas the Endangerment Standard requires only that a professional consider a child to be at risk of harm.) In addition, the criteria for child sexual abuse cases were expanded to include more types of perpetrators. In *National Incidence and Prevalence of Child Abuse and Neglect: 1988, Revised Report* (September 5, 1991), Andrea J. Sedlak notes that during NIS-2 researchers began including cases in which adult caretakers other than parents or parent substitutes (e.g., foster parents and stepparents) "permitted" sexual abuse to happen. The researchers also counted cases in which "nonparental teenage caretakers had perpetrated or permitted the abuse." The NIS-1 through NIS-3 studies generally divided child sexual abuse acts into broad categories based on whether or not penetration or genital contact occurred. For example, in *Third National Incidence Study of Child Abuse and Neglect: Final Report* (September 1996), Andrea J. Sedlak and Diane D. Broadhurst divide sexual actions against children into three categories:

- Intrusion—oral, anal, or genital penile penetration or anal or genital digital or other penetration

- Molestation with genital contact—acts in which some form of actual genital contact occurred, but intrusion did not occur

- Other or unknown sexual abuse—unspecified acts not known to have involved intrusion or actual genital contact

By the time the NIS-4 studies were conducted in 2005–06, a more refined list had been developed for classifying various types of child sexual abuse. Andrea J. Sedlak et al. provide in *Fourth National Incidence Study of Child Abuse and Neglect (NIS-4) Report to Congress* (January 2010, http://www.acf.hhs.gov/sites/default/files/opre/nis4_report_congress_full_pdf_jan2010.pdf) a list of the types of sexual abuse that were cataloged by NIS-4 researchers:

- Intrusion sex without force
- Intrusion sex involving use of force
- Child's prostitution or involvement in pornography with intrusion
- Molestation with genital contact
- Providing sexually explicit materials
- Child's involvement in pornography without intrusion
- Failure to supervise child's voluntary sexual activity
- Attempted/threatened sexual abuse with physical contact
- Other/unknown sexual abuse

Because of the criteria and standard differences between NIS-1 and the succeeding NIS studies, the prevalence rates from NIS-2, NIS-3, and NIS-4 are not directly comparable to the rate of 0.7 per 1,000 children in population that was calculated in NIS-1. Sedlak et al. report the following incidence rates for child sexual abuse based on NIS-4 data:

Under the Harm Standard:

- NIS-2 (1986)—1.9 per 1,000 child population
- NIS-3 (1993)—3.2 per 1,000 child population
- NIS-4 (2005–06)—1.8 per 1,000 child population

Under the Endangerment Standard:

- NIS-2 (1986)—2.1 per 1,000 child population
- NIS-3 (1993)—4.5 per 1,000 child population
- NIS-4 (2005–06)—2.4 per 1,000 child population

Child Sex Abuse Victims, Perpetrators, and Risk Factors

According to the Children's Bureau, the NIS-1 data indicate that girls made up 83% of the victims, whereas boys accounted for 17% of the victims. The vast majority (88%) of the victims were white. Older children accounted for more than half of the victims, with the largest percentages for children aged 15 to 17 years (32%), 12 to 14 years (28%), and nine to 11 years (21%). Fathers and father substitutes acting alone accounted for 36% of the perpetrators, followed by both mothers/substitutes and fathers/substitutes at 21%. In regards to household characteristics, the Children's Bureau reports that nearly half (46%) of the households involved in child sexual abuse cases were in rural counties. Most (80%) of the households were in the two lowest annual family income brackets, which included incomes up to $15,000 per year.

Sedlak et al. note that the NIS-2 data indicated a higher prevalence rate for child sexual abuse among females (3.3 per 1,000 child population) than among males (1 per 1,000 child population). In addition, the abuse was six times more frequent among children in low-income families than among children in high-income families. In *A Report to Congress: The National Center on Child Abuse and Neglect, Study of High Risk Child Abuse and Neglect Groups, Appendix B: NIS-2 Reanalysis Report* (1993), the HHS's National Center on Child Abuse and Neglect (NCCAN) examines risk factors for the occurrence of various types of child maltreatment, including sexual abuse. According to NCCAN, in addition to females and children in lower income families, the children at the greatest risk include older children in white, African American, and Hispanic families and older children in father-only households. No relationship was found between risk and county metropolitan status or between risk and number of children in household.

Sedlak and Broadhurst note the following findings regarding child sexual abuse:

- Girls were sexually abused about three times more often than boys under both the Harm Standard and the Endangerment Standard.
- Children were "consistently vulnerable" to sexual abuse from the age of three years upward.
- Low-income children were 18 times more likely than high-income children to be sexually abused under both the Harm Standard and the Endangerment Standard.

For nearly half (46%) of the sexually abused children, the perpetrators were people other than a parent or parent figure. Another 29% of the victims were sexually abused by a birth parent and 25% by other parent or parent-substitute (e.g., stepparent or father's girlfriend). The incidence rates under the Harm Standard for children living with both parents or a single parent of either sex were 2.5 to 2.6 per 1,000 child population. The comparable rate for children living with neither parent was much higher, at 6.3 per 1,000 child population.

The NIS-4 studies were conducted between 2005 and 2006. As described in Chapter 3, Sedlak et al. assess various child and household characteristics in terms of incidence rates for maltreatment overall and for specific types of maltreatment. The rates for sexually abused children were calculated for many, but not all, of the characteristics based on data availability. According to Sedlak et al.:

- The incidence rates for sexual abuse under the Harm Standard were 3 per 1,000 child population for girls and 0.6 per 1,000 child population for boys. Under the Endangerment Standard the rates were 3.8 per 1,000 child population for girls and 1 per 1,000 child population for boys.

- Most (87%) of the sexually abused children were abused by a male, compared with only 11% who were abused by a female.

- The perpetrators in child sexual abuse cases were much more likely to be male when they were the child's nonbiological parent. However, children who were sexually abused by their biological parents had the highest percentage of female perpetrators (22% versus 6% or less in other relationship categories).

- The incidence rates under the Harm Standard by race/ethnicity were: African American (2.6 per 1,000 African American child population), Hispanic (1.8 per 1,000 Hispanic child population), and white (1.4 per 1,000 white child population).

- For 42% of the sexually abused children, the perpetrators were people other than a parent (whether biological or nonbiological) or a parent's partner; 36% of the victims were sexually abused by a biological parent.

- The incidence rates under the Harm Standard by parental employment status were: parents not in the labor force (3.7 per 1,000 child population), parents steadily employed (1.1 per 1,000 child population), and parents unemployed (0.9 per 1,000 child population).

- The incidence rates under the Harm Standard by socioeconomic status were: families with low socioeconomic status (1.7 per 1,000 child population) and families without low socioeconomic status (0.6 per 1,000 child population). Under the Endangerment Standard the rates were: families with low socioeconomic status (2.4 per 1,000 child population) and families without low socioeconomic status (0.7 per 1,000 child population). (For a description of how Sedlak et al. categorize families via socioeconomic status, see Chapter 3.)

Unlike in previous NIS studies, NIS-4 researchers compiled detailed information about the family structures and living arrangements of the children. Sedlak et al. report the following incidence rates in descending order for child sexual abuse.

Under the Harm Standard:

- Single parent with partner (9.9 per 1,000 child population)

- Neither parent (5.3 per 1,000 child population)

- Other married parents (4.3 per 1,000 child population)

- Single parent with no partner (2.4 per 1,000 child population)

- Unmarried parents (2.4 per 1,000 child population)

- Married biological parents (0.5 per 1,000 child population)

Under the Endangerment Standard:

- Single parent with partner (12.1 per 1,000 child population)

- Neither parent (6.3 per 1,000 child population)

- Other married parents (5.5 per 1,000 child population)

- Single parent with no partner (3.4 per 1,000 child population)

- Unmarried parents (3.2 per 1,000 child population)

- Married biological parents (0.7 per 1,000 child population)

NATIONAL SURVEY OF CHILD AND ADOLESCENT WELL-BEING

Chapter 2 describes the National Survey of Child and Adolescent Well-Being (NSCAW) studies, which are longitudinal studies that cover thousands of children. NSCAW I ran from 1997 to 2007; and NSCAW II began in 2008 and was ongoing as of November 2014. NSCAW II has included three data collections or waves: Wave 1 (March 2008 to September 2009) featured baseline data collection, while Wave 2 (October 2009 through January 2011) and Wave 3 (June 2011 through December 2012) featured follow-up data collection on the same children. Although NSCAW researchers did not specifically focus on sexual abuse, they did collect some data regarding this maltreatment type.

As shown in Table 2.11 in Chapter 2, the types of maltreatment and other reasons for investigation by CSA agency caseworkers were known in 5,054 NSCAW II baseline cases. Overall, 7.4% of the cases had a report that included sexual abuse.

The NSCAW studies include interviews by researchers with the children and their parents and/or caregivers. Table 2.14 in Chapter 2 shows reports of in-home parental aggression against the children within the previous year as self-reported by the parents and/or caregivers. In *NSCAW II Baseline Report: Maltreatment* (August 1, 2011, http://www.acf.hhs.gov/sites/default/files/opre/nscaw2_maltreatment.pdf), Cecilia Casanueva et al. indicate that 4.2% of the in-home parents/caregivers reported that their child "was touched in a sexual way or was forced to have sex by an adult or older child, including a member of the family or anyone outside the family." As shown in Table 2.14, in-home parents and caregivers of children aged 11 to 17 years old (2.2%) were more likely to report sexual abuse than those of children aged three to five years old (0.8%).

CHILD MALTREATMENT

Each year the HHS's National Child Abuse and Neglect Data System collects child maltreatment data from CPS agencies in the 50 states and the District of Columbia and Puerto Rico (which are collectively known as the 52 states). Summaries of the compiled information are

TABLE 4.1

Abused children, by type of maltreatment and state, 2012

State	Medical neglect	Neglect	Other	Physical abuse	Psychological maltreatment	Sexual abuse	Unknown	Total maltreatments
								Percent
Alabama	0.8	38.2		49.6	0.3	21.9		110.7
Alaska	2.7	95.8		15.3	17.9	5.8		137.6
Arizona		96.9		10.4	0.3	3.7		111.3
Arkansas	8.0	69.0	0.0	18.5	1.3	20.8		117.7
California		86.7	0.1	9.8	18.3	5.6		120.5
Colorado	1.7	82.6		12.3	3.2	9.9	0.6	110.4
Connecticut	2.6	86.2		6.2	33.4	5.6		134.0
Delaware	0.9	34.5	10.2	14.9	44.9	6.5		111.9
District of Columbia	6.0	63.7	39.2	14.8	1.5	2.6		127.9
Florida	2.3	56.9	50.0	10.5	1.4	4.7		125.8
Georgia	4.5	68.3		13.6	23.3	5.0		114.6
Hawaii	1.1	14.9	80.4	13.9	0.6	5.9		116.8
Idaho								
Illinois	2.3	70.4		25.3	0.2	18.1		116.3
Indiana	2.0	86.3		10.6	0.2	15.1		114.2
Iowa	1.0	93.5	8.8	12.7	0.5	5.0		121.5
Kansas	1.6	18.4	21.8	22.3	12.6	33.3		110.0
Kentucky	0.0	97.4		8.9	0.3	4.0		110.7
Louisiana	0.0	81.2	0.7	28.2	0.9	8.9		120.0
Maine	0.0	77.0		19.3	37.6	6.8		140.7
Maryland	0.0	73.4		23.4	0.2	13.8		110.8
Massachusetts	0.0	98.3	0.0	14.9	0.2	4.2		117.6
Michigan	3.2	93.1	41.1	25.4	43.6	3.8		210.2
Minnesota	1.2	72.4		19.2	0.7	20.2		113.7
Mississippi	3.8	72.9	0.3	19.2	13.6	14.3		124.2
Missouri	3.5	60.4	0.1	29.8	4.5	24.3		122.6
Montana	0.8	91.2	0.4	14.6	7.4	5.0		119.3
Nebraska	0.0	93.6		13.1	1.2	8.0		115.9
Nevada	2.5	75.7		34.7	1.7	4.9		119.5
New Hampshire	2.4	84.4		7.4	2.7	13.5		110.4
New Jersey	2.4	84.8		12.4	0.8	10.5		110.9
New Mexico	2.7	86.6	0.1	13.6	22.0	3.6		128.5
New York	6.0	108.3	30.4	10.7	0.8	3.3		159.5
North Carolina	2.2	87.0	0.6	9.4	0.5	8.2	0.8	108.6
North Dakota	2.3	70.8		14.3	36.7	4.3		128.4
Ohio	1.9	48.5		42.2	6.7	18.8		118.1
Oklahoma	2.0	54.6		58.1	22.4	6.3		143.4
Oregon	1.6	49.9	55.9	9.4	2.0	7.9	0.1	126.8
Pennsylvania	3.2	3.3		32.1	0.5	66.2		105.3
Puerto Rico	6.4	63.5	1.1	22.9	44.4	2.6	12.6	153.4
Rhode Island	2.5	91.4	1.6	13.4	0.2	5.2		114.2
South Carolina	3.8	68.6	0.4	40.2	1.4	6.0		120.3
South Dakota	0.0	94.8		10.9	1.4	4.3		111.4
Tennessee	1.9	63.2		13.6	2.9	29.7		111.4
Texas	2.6	83.2		19.0	0.8	9.5	0.0	115.1
Utah	0.2	26.8	7.3	41.7	28.4	21.3		125.7
Vermont	2.5	3.1		44.4	0.9	62.6		113.4
Virginia	1.6	64.9		28.5	1.1	15.2		111.3
Washington	0.0	87.6		21.3		6.4		115.3
West Virginia	1.4	54.1	11.9	34.1	28.8	5.4		135.7
Wisconsin	0.0	58.9		21.6	1.1	28.0		109.6
Wyoming	0.6	73.3	1.6	2.6	21.4	10.4		109.8
Total								
Percent	2.3	78.3	10.6	18.3	8.5	9.3	0.2	127.5
States reporting								

SOURCE: Adapted from "Table 3-8. Maltreatment Types of Victims, 2012," in *Child Maltreatment 2012*, U.S. Department of Health and Human Services, Administration for Children and Families, Administration on Children, Youth, and Families, Children's Bureau, December 17, 2013, http://www.acf.hhs.gov/sites/default/files/cb/cm2012.pdf (accessed July 16, 2014)

published annually by the Children's Bureau in the report *Child Maltreatment*. As of November 2014, the most recent report was *Child Maltreatment 2012* (December 2013, http://www.acf.hhs.gov/sites/default/files/cb/cm2012.pdf).

According to the Children's Bureau, the maltreatment types by uniquely counted victims were neglect (78.3%), physical abuse (18.3%), and sexual abuse (9.3%). It should be noted that these percentages add up to more than 100% because some victims experienced more than one type of maltreatment. As shown in Table 2.4 in Chapter 2, 62,936 uniquely counted children were sexual abuse victims in 2012. Table 4.1 provides a state-by-state breakdown for the victims in 2012 based on reporting data from 49 states, the District of Columbia, and Puerto Rico (no data were available from Idaho). The proportion of sexual abuse victims as a percentage of all maltreatment victims was highest in Pennsylvania (66.2%) and Vermont (62.6%) in 2012, whereas Puerto Rico (2.6%) and the District of Columbia (2.6%) reported the lowest proportion of sexual abuse victims.

RETROSPECTIVE SURVEYS ABOUT CHILD SEXUAL ABUSE

As noted earlier, retrospective surveys are another major source of data on child sexual abuse prevalence. Survey-based studies rely on the truthfulness and accurate recollections of the test subjects. In rare cases, the researchers may have access to external evidence, such as childhood medical reports, that can lend credence to claims from adults that they suffered sexual abuse as children. However, most surveys depend solely on memories, as no collaborating evidence is available. As a result, survey methodologies are very important. Considerations include the number and types of questions that are asked, how they are asked, and by whom. The population size and demographics of the survey subjects are also key variables that affect results. Subject age is particularly relevant because older memories may be less reliable than those formed more recently. As noted earlier, there is no single legal definition of what constitutes sexual abuse. Thus, researchers conducting retrospective surveys about childhood sexual abuse may question subjects about certain sexual activities and not others. In addition, some subjects may not consider sexual events to rise to the level of "abuse," thus, the choice of terminology can influence survey results.

Another confounding factor is the stigma that is associated with certain sexual activities. As such, survey participants may be reluctant to admit to events about which they feel embarrassed or ashamed. Furthermore, the subjects may not remember childhood sexual abuse. Some researchers believe that memory repression (repression by the mind of painful or unpleasant memories) causes some people to be unable to remember childhood traumas. Overall, there are numerous factors that affect the reliability of retrospective survey data and the relevance of the data to the population at large.

Adult Surveys Reveal High Prevalence Rates

Numerous retrospective surveys related to childhood sexual abuse have been conducted since the 1970s, and they consistently show much higher rates of child sexual abuse than the rates indicated by agency reports, such as *Child Maltreatment*. This discrepancy underlies the oft-stated claim that child sexual abuse cases are vastly underreported to authorities.

One of the early landmark retrospective studies of child sexual abuse was conducted in 1978 by the sociologist Diana E. H. Russell of Mills College. Russell surveyed 930 adult women in San Francisco, California, about their early sexual experiences and reported her findings in *The Secret Trauma: Incest in the Lives of Girls and Women* (1986). Russell noted that 38% of the women had suffered sexual abuse before their 18th birthday. About 16% had been abused by a family member. Russell's study is one of many cited by people who believe that much more child sexual abuse occurs than is officially reported by government studies. They suggest the high results recorded in her study reflect the thoroughness of her preparation and the fact that she asked the participants 14 different questions, any one of which might have set off a memory of sexual abuse.

In *The Epidemic of Rape and Child Sexual Abuse in the United States* (2000), Diana E. H. Russell and Rebecca M. Bolen revisit the prevalence rates reported in Russell's 1978 survey. Russell and Bolen believe those rates are underestimated. The 1978 survey subjects did not include two groups that are regarded to be highly probable victims of child sexual abuse: females in institutions and those not living at home. Russell and Bolen also find that some women were reluctant to reveal experiences of abuse to survey interviewers, whereas others did not recall these experiences.

David Finkelhor is a national authority on child sexual abuse and is the director of the Crimes against Children Research Center at the University of New Hampshire. In "Current Information on the Scope and Nature of Child Sexual Abuse" (*Future of Children: Sexual Abuse of Children*, vol. 4, no. 2, Summer–Fall 1994), Finkelhor states his opinion that surveys of adults regarding their childhood experiences probably give the most complete estimates of the actual extent of child sexual abuse. He reviews 19 adult retrospective surveys and finds that the proportion of adults who indicated sexual abuse during childhood ranged widely, from 2% to 62% for females and from 3% to 16% for males. Finkelhor observes that the surveys that reported higher levels of abuse were those that asked multiple questions about the possibility of abuse. Multiple questions are more effective because they provide respondents various cues about the different kinds of experiences the researchers are asking about in their surveys. Multiple questions also give the respondents ample time to overcome their embarrassment. In his 2009 study "The Prevention of Childhood Sexual Abuse" (*Future of Children*, vol. 19, no. 2, Fall 2009), Finkelhor offers different estimates concerning percentages of adult victims of childhood sexual abuse, with the proportion of female victims falling somewhere between 25% and 40%, and male victims between 8% and 13%. As Finkelhor et al. report in

"Child Maltreatment Rates Assessed in a National Household Survey of Caregivers and Youth" (*Child Abuse & Neglect*, vol. 39, no. 9, September 2014), a 2011 survey based on interviews with caregivers of children under the age of nine, as well as with children between the ages of 10 and 17, found that 2.2% of children had suffered sexual abuse within the past year.

Between 1995 and 1997 the Centers for Disease Control and Prevention (CDC) collaborated with the insurance company Kaiser Permanente to survey more than 17,000 adults regarding their childhood experiences. The CDC states in "ACE Study" (May 13, 2014, http://www.cdc.gov/violenceprevention/acestudy) that the Adverse Childhood Experiences (ACE) Study "is one of the largest investigations ever conducted to assess associations between childhood maltreatment and later-life health and well-being." The survey subjects were all members of a Kaiser Permanente health maintenance organization and were questioned during their physical examinations at a clinic in San Diego, California. The CDC indicates in "Prevalence of Individual Adverse Childhood Experiences" (May 13, 2014, http://www.cdc.gov/violenceprevention/acestudy/prevalence.html) that 20.7% of the 17,337 subjects said they had experienced sexual abuse in childhood. The rates by sex were 24.7% for women and 16% for men. The agency explains that childhood sexual abuse was defined as: "An adult or person at least 5 years older ever touched or fondled you in a sexual way, or had you touch their body in a sexual way, or attempted oral, anal, or vaginal intercourse with you or actually had oral, anal, or vaginal intercourse with you." As of November 2014, researchers continued to track the medical status of the survey subjects. According to the CDC in "ACE Study," more than 50 academic papers and 100 conferences and presentations have used data from the ACE Study.

In "Childhood Sexual Abuse among Black Women and White Women from Two-Parent Families" (*Child Maltreatment*, vol. 11, no. 3, August 2006), a retrospective study, Maryann Amodeo et al. of Boston University examined 290 African American and white women to determine differences in prevalence of child sexual abuse. The researchers used questionnaires and face-to-face interviews, as well as interviews with siblings, to determine whether child sexual abuse had occurred. The results indicated prevalence rates of 34.1% for African American women and 22.8% for white women.

As retrospective studies of childhood sexual abuse gain in popularity, some standardized surveying tools are being developed. For example, David DiLillo et al. compare in "Retrospective Assessment of Childhood Sexual and Physical Abuse: A Comparison of Scaled and Behaviorally Specific Approaches" (*Assessment*, vol. 13, no. 3, September 2006) two of the most common screening tools: the Childhood Trauma Questionnaire (CTQ) and the Computer Assisted Maltreatment Inventory (CAMI). The researchers used both scales to assess 1,195 undergraduate students at the University of Nebraska, Lincoln; Miami University; and the University of Southern California. The sample population included 863 women and 332 men, and the average age was 20.3 years. Overall, the CTQ and the CAMI provided consistent agreement in that 92% of the subjects were classified equivalently by both tools in terms of sexual abuse victimization. The results indicate that 7% of the subjects were deemed by both tools to be childhood victims of sexual abuse.

In "Potential Impact of Childhood Sexual Abuse among Males, by Whether It Occurred at or after Sexual Debut" (*Journal of Interpersonal Violence*, vol. 25, no. 1, January 2010), William C. Holmes of the University of Pennsylvania School of Medicine surveyed 197 men by telephone in the Philadelphia, Pennsylvania, area. More than two out of 10 (22%) participants disclosed child sexual abuse histories.

The willingness to disclose a history of sexual abuse is crucial to treating psychological problems suffered by adult victims of child sexual abuse. Over the years, psychologists and other counseling professionals have developed a range of methods aimed at combating the lingering negative effects of sexual abuse in adult patients. As Michael D. Earley et al. report in "Mindfulness Intervention for Child Abuse Survivors: A 2.5-Year Follow-Up" (*Journal of Clinical Psychology*, vol. 70, no. 10, October 2014), one approach that has shown positive results is mindfulness-based treatment. Mindfulness is a form of cognitive therapy that helps patients attain emotional awareness through education, meditation, and other methods. As Earley et al. note, mindfulness has been shown to be effective in treating disorders caused by sexual abuse, including anxiety, depression, and post-traumatic stress disorder (PTSD).

Youth and Children Surveys

Some retrospective studies target youths and children for their recollections of previous sexual abuse. The surveys may focus on the lifetime prevalence of such victimizations or the incidences during a particular period, typically the previous year.

NATIONAL SURVEY OF ADOLESCENTS (1995). Rochelle F. Hanson et al. report in "Correlates of Adolescent Reports of Sexual Assault: Findings from the National Survey of Adolescents" (*Child Maltreatment*, vol. 8, no. 4, November 2003) the results from the National Survey of Adolescents, which was conducted in 1995. A random sample of 4,023 U.S. adolescents aged 12 to 17 years included 51.3% males and 48.7% females. A majority (70.2%) were non-Hispanic whites. The children were grouped into several age cohorts (groups). Interviews were conducted by telephone, with the consent of the parent or guardian.

A total of 326 (8.1%) adolescents indicated that they had experienced child sexual abuse. Approximately four out of five (78.1%) of those reporting child sexual abuse were female, and one out of five (21.9%) were male. Most (58.2%) were white, 23.6% were African American, and 9.4% were Hispanic. Other ethnic groups made up the remaining 8.8% of child sexual abuse victims.

Of the 326 victims, 30.7% had been raped, 26.8% reported fearing for their life during the assault, and 10% had suffered physical injuries. Alcohol or drugs were involved in 6.7% of the incidents. Single incidents were reported by about two-thirds (64.1%) of the victims. Three-quarters (76.4%) knew the perpetrator. Specifically, 4.3% identified their father or stepfather as the abuser, 17.5% named another relative, 52.8% reported an unrelated acquaintance, and 1.8% knew the perpetrator but did not identify the person. Nearly a quarter (23%) said the perpetrator was a stranger, and two victims did not identify the perpetrator.

DEVELOPMENTAL VICTIMIZATION SURVEY (2002–03). In "The Victimization of Children and Youth: A Comprehensive, National Survey" (*Child Maltreatment*, vol. 10, no. 1, February 2005), David Finkelhor et al. describe the Developmental Victimization Survey, which was conducted in 2002–03 using a nationally representative sample of 2,030 children and youth aged two to 17 years. The purpose of the study was to ascertain any violent victimizations of the children during the previous year. Researchers directly interviewed older children (those aged 10 years and older) and interviewed the caretakers of younger children.

Finkelhor et al. find that more than half of the children had been victimized during the previous year, either by a physical assault, a property offense, a form of child maltreatment, a form of sexual victimization, or a form of indirect victimization, such as witnessing an act of violence. One youth out of 12 had been sexually victimized during the study year. This provided an incidence rate of 82 sexual victimizations per 1,000 child population. The rate for girls was 96 per 1,000 girls, and the rate for boys was 67 per 1,000 boys. The incidence rates by victim age were: youths aged 13 to 17 years (168 per 1,000 child population), children aged six to 12 years (53 per 1,000 child population), and children aged two to five years (15 per 1,000 child population). The vast majority (86%) of the sexual perpetrators were juveniles. In addition, 91% of the perpetrators were acquaintances of the victims, 7% were strangers, and 2% were family members.

The overall rates for particular types of sexual victimization were sexual assault (32 per 1,000 child population),

completed rape (4 per 1,000 child population), and flashing or sexual exposure by an adult perpetrator (4 per 1,000 child population). For sexual assaults, the breakdown by perpetrator type was 21 per 1,000 child population for a peer (i.e., another youth), 6 per 1,000 child population for a known adult, and 4 per 1,000 child population for an adult stranger.

NATIONAL SURVEY OF CHILDREN'S EXPOSURE TO VIOLENCE (2008). The National Survey of Children's Exposure to Violence (NatSCEV; http://www.unh.edu/ccrc/jvq-new/NatSCEV%20overview%20for%20toolkit.pdf) is a project of the University of New Hampshire's Crimes against Children Research Center. NatSCEV was conducted in 2008 using a nationally representative sample of 4,549 children aged zero to 17 years who were assessed for their one-year and lifetime experiences of violence.

In "Violence, Abuse, and Crime Exposure in a National Sample of Children and Youth" (*Pediatrics*, vol. 124, no. 5, November 2009), David Finkelhor et al. report on the results of the NatSCEV study, a survey that repeated many of the elements used in the Developmental Victimization Survey in 2002–03. According to the researchers, NatSCEV data indicate an overall previous-year sexual victimization rate of 6.1% (7.4% among females and 4.8% among males). The highest percentages were for youths aged 14 to 17 years (16.3%) and those aged 10 to 13 years (7.7%). In regards to lifetime victimization, the overall prevalence rate was 9.8% (12.2% among females and 7.5% among males). Again, the highest percentages were for youths aged 14 to 17 years (27.8%) and those aged 10 to 13 years (9.4%).

The NatSCEV results for particular types of sexual victimization were sexual assault (1.8% previous year and 3.9% lifetime), completed rape (0.2% previous year and 0.7% lifetime), and flashing or sexual exposure by an adult perpetrator (0.4% previous year and 0.6% lifetime). For sexual assaults, the breakdown by perpetrator type for previous year victimizations was 1.3% for a peer (i.e., another youth), 0.3% for a known adult, and 0.3% for an adult stranger. The percentages for lifetime sexual assaults by perpetrator type were 2.7% for a peer, 1.2% for a known adult, and 0.5% for an adult stranger.

NATIONAL CRIME VICTIMIZATION SURVEYS (1994–2010). Since 1972 the Bureau of Justice Statistics (BJS), an agency within the U.S. Department of Justice, has conducted an annual survey called the National Crime Victimization Survey (NCVS). The BJS surveys tens of thousands of households and compiles data from subjects aged 12 years and older regarding crime victimizations, both reported and not reported to authorities. Only certain crimes, including rape and sexual assault, are included in the survey questions.

Nicole White and Janet L. Lauritsen of the University of Missouri, St. Louis, describe in *Violent Crime against Youth, 1994–2010* (December 2012, http://www.bjs.gov/content/pub/pdf/vcay9410.pdf) trends in violent crimes that were committed against youths between 1994 and 2010 based on NCVS data. Approximately 41,000 households and 73,300 individual subjects were interviewed as part of the 2010 NCVS. According to White and Lauritsen, the rate of rape or sexual assault against youths aged 12 to 17 years declined from 7 victimizations per 1,000 youths in 1994 to 2.2 victimizations per 1,000 youths in 2010, a decrease of 68%.

MINNESOTA STUDENT SURVEYS (1998–2010). The Minnesota Student Survey is administered by the Minnesota Center for Health Statistics (MCHS) within the Minnesota Department of Health. Every three years the MCHS surveys approximately 100,000 students in the sixth, ninth, and 12th grades on a variety of topics. Not all questions are given to students in all grade levels.

In "Minnesota Student Survey: Selected Single Year Results by State, County and CHB [Community Health Board], 1998–2010" (2014, http://www.health.state.mn.us/divs/chs/mss/singleyr/mss_singleyr.xlsx), the MCHS reports selected results from the five student surveys that were conducted between 1998 and 2010. Students in all three grades were asked if someone inside or outside their family had ever "touched them sexually." The results indicate that 5% to 6% of the sixth graders, 7% to 9% of the ninth graders, and 7% to 8% of the 12th graders indicated that this had happened to them. Between 2007 and 2010 the ninth and 12th graders were also asked about sexual behaviors they had experienced while on school property during the previous year (specifically if another student had "touched, grabbed or pinched them in a sexual way"). Overall, 21% to 23% of the ninth graders and 18% to 20% of the 12th graders had experienced such an event. In addition, 28% to 29% of the ninth graders and 23% of the 12th graders said they had experienced "unwanted sexual comments, jokes, gestures or looks."

NATIONAL SURVEY OF CHILDREN'S EXPOSURE TO VIOLENCE (2009–13). Since 2009 the Office of Juvenile Justice and Delinquency Prevention (OJJDP), a division of the U.S. Department of Justice, has published the *Juvenile Justice Bulletin: National Survey of Children's Exposure to Violence* (2014, http://www.ojjdp.gov/publications/pubresults.asp?sei=94#2009), a periodic report covering various issues relating to child victimization. The OJJDP had published six bulletins as of November 2014. In "Children's Exposure to Violence and the Intersection between Delinquency and Victimization" (October 2013, http://www.ojjdp.gov/pubs/240555.pdf), Carlos A. Cuevas et al. examine rates of sexual victimization among both perpetrators and victims

of juvenile delinquency between the ages of 10 and 17. As Cuevas et al. note, children who have been both perpetrators and victims of delinquent acts are considerably more likely to report being sexually victimized than children who have solely been victims of juvenile delinquency. For example, two in five (40%) boys who were both perpetrators and victims of juvenile delinquency experienced some form of sexual victimization, compared with 13% of boys who were only victims of juvenile delinquency. These rates are even higher among female perpetrators and victims. According to Cuevas et al., more than half (58%) of girls who were both perpetrators and victims of delinquency reported experiencing sexual victimization; by comparison, one-quarter (27%) of girls who were only victims reported being sexually victimized.

What Makes Victims Disclose?

Hanson et al. report on the factors that contribute to the likelihood that an adolescent will disclose sexual abuse. The researchers also examine whether, among the different ethnic and racial groups, adolescents differ in the rates of disclosure and in the factors contributing to that disclosure. About two-thirds (68.1%) of the victims told interviewers they disclosed their sexual abuse to someone. Just 4.5% of those who disclosed first told a police officer or social worker. One-third (34.3%) told their mother or stepmother and nearly four out of 10 (39.3%) told a close friend. The other victims told another relative (6.1%), a teacher (1.8%), a father or stepfather (1.7%), or a doctor or other health professional (1.3%). About 3.4% indicated they disclosed the abuse to someone but did not say who it was. Another 3.9% would not say whom they told of the abuse or could not remember whom they first told. Overall, just 33.6% indicated they ever reported the abuse to police or other authorities.

According to Hanson et al., more females (74%) than males (46.5%) disclosed to someone that they had been sexually abused. White victims (75.1%) were more likely than Hispanics (67.7%) and African Americans (55.8%) to tell someone of their abuse. Those who feared for their life during the assault (80.7%) were especially likely to disclose the abuse. Other factors that were related to high levels of disclosure were having experienced a penetration assault (72%), having suffered physical injury (70.6%), having used substances (68.2%), or having been assaulted once (67.9%). The likelihood of telling someone of the abuse was also influenced by the relationship between the victim and the perpetrator. Hanson et al. grouped perpetrators into four categories: father/stepfather, another relative (e.g., uncle or grandparent), unrelated acquaintance, and stranger. Those who were abused by a relative other than a father/stepfather (87.7%) and those who were abused by a stranger (70.7%) were more likely to report the abuse than those who were sexually abused by an unrelated acquaintance (62.2%) or by a father/stepfather (57.1%).

In "Children's Disclosures of Sexual Abuse: Learning from Direct Inquiry" (*Child Abuse and Neglect*, vol. 35, no. 5, May 2011), Paula Schaeffer, John M. Leventhal, and Andrea Gottsegen Asnes report on the results of 191 interviews of child sexual abuse victims aged three to 18 years. The researchers note three primary reasons that children disclosed the abuse: internal incentives (e.g., nightmares), external prompts (e.g., someone questioned the child about whether abuse occurred), and direct evidence (e.g., someone witnessed the abuse). In addition, Schaeffer, Leventhal, and Asnes find five major factors that influenced children to delay disclosure: perpetrator threats (e.g., that the child would get into trouble for disclosing), internal fears (e.g., that disclosure would have bad consequences), lack of opportunity to disclose the abuse, lack of understanding that the abuse constituted unacceptable behavior, and relationship factors (e.g., the victim considered the perpetrator to be a friend). In "To Tell or Not to Tell? Factors Influencing Young People's Informal Disclosures of Child Sexual Abuse" (*Journal of Interpersonal Violence*, vol. 29, no. 5, March 2014), Rosaleen McElvaney, Sheila Greene, and Diane Hogan identify other psychological factors that influence a child's decision to disclose incidents of sexual abuse. These factors include shame, apprehension about being believed, concern about the consequences of disclosure, and peer pressure. As McElvaney, Greene, and Hogan note, engaging a child directly about their emotional well-being remains vital to helping urge them to disclose incidences of sexual victimization.

NONFAMILY PERPETRATORS IN POSITIONS OF TRUST

As described earlier, agency reports and retrospective studies dealing with child sexual abuse tend to categorize perpetrators into broad groups, such as parents, other relatives, acquaintances, peers, and strangers. Sexual attacks on children by strangers, although much less common than other types of attacks, capture national attention and tend to dominate media reports on the subject. Another category of perpetrators that attracts intense public scrutiny consists of nonfamily members who hold positions of trust in the community and interact with children regularly. Examples include teachers, coaches, religious leaders, pediatricians, and employees and volunteers who are affiliated with child organizations and clubs. Child sex scandals involving perpetrators in these positions make headlines and cause widespread outrage. These cases are particularly upsetting because the perpetrators are considered by other community members to be respectable, trustworthy, and commendable for their work with children.

Depending on the circumstances, the sexual misdeeds may be viewed by the public as individual failings or as institutional failings. For example, a case in which a perpetrator worked for an organization that took swift action to notify authorities once allegations came to light is likely to be seen as an instance of deviant behavior by the individual. However, if there is any evidence that others in an organization suspected or knew of the abuse and failed to take appropriate action, the case is seen as proof of gross institutional misconduct by the organization involved. In 2012 media reports surfaced that the Boy Scouts of America (BSA) kept secret for decades allegations of sexual abuse by troop leaders. The article "Report Dredges Up Boy Scouts Sex Abuse Scandal" (AP.org, September 16, 2012) notes that the *Los Angeles Times* gained access to some of the BSA's "perversion" files dating from 1970 to 1991. In hundreds of cases the files reveal that leaders within the organization did not report sexual abuse allegations to authorities. However, the article indicates that a BSA spokesperson released a statement ensuring the public that this practice no longer occurs in the organization and that all abuse suspicions are reported to local authorities.

Educators

Child sexual abuse by educators began attracting widespread public attention during the 1990s. At that time it was common for teachers accused of sexual misconduct with students to be allowed by school administrators to quietly resign. Because of lax screening procedures, these teachers could then move to another school district or state and obtain a new teaching position. In "Dirty Secrets: Why Sexually Abusive Teachers Aren't Stopped" (Post-Gazette.com, October 31, 1999), Jane Elizabeth Zemel and Steve Twedt summarize more than a dozen cases of teachers who were accused, and sometimes convicted, of sexually abusing students. Many of the teachers were so-called mobile molesters because they were able to move from school to school after being quietly fired or allowed to resign after allegations surfaced about their misconduct. Besides describing these egregious examples, the authors note that they uncovered 727 cases between 1994 and 1999 across the United States in which educators lost their teaching licenses for "sex offenses." Zemel and Twedt complain that some of the offending teachers were caught "only after they had been molesting students for many years."

Since the late 1990s, greater public awareness, tighter screening, and stricter laws have helped alleviate some of the worst problems described by Zemel and Twedt. Nevertheless, child sexual abuse cases involving teachers continue to occur. Because there is no central clearinghouse that tracks and reports the cases, it is difficult to know the prevalence of sexual misconduct by teachers with children. In *Educator Sexual Misconduct: A Synthesis of Existing Literature* (June 2004, http://www2.ed.gov/rschstat/research/pubs/misconductreview/report.pdf), a study commissioned by the U.S. Department of Education, Charol Shakeshaft of Hofstra University notes that her literature review revealed few empirical studies (studies based on observational data and statistical analyses) related to educator sexual misconduct. As a result, she relied on two Hostile Hallways surveys that she had overseen for the American Association of University Women. The surveys were conducted in 1993 and 2001 and involved 3,695 public school students in grades eight to 11. Shakeshaft projects the numbers in her surveys to the whole public school system. She estimates that 9.6% of public school children (or around 4.5 million students at that time), had experienced sexual misconduct by educators ranging from being told sexual jokes, to being shown pictures of a sexual nature, to sexual intercourse. Educators included teachers and other school officials, such as principals, coaches, counselors, substitute teachers, teacher's aides, security guards, bus drivers, custodians, and other employees.

Creating Safer Havens is a nonprofit organization in California devoted to child welfare issues. It operates the website "Child Sexual Abuse Cases: Teachers" (http://www.creatingsaferhavens.com/child-sexual-abuse-teachers-cases.html), which presents brief summaries of news stories collected from around the country that relate to cases of educator sexual misconduct with children. As of November 2014, more than 80 cases were listed since 2012 (note that some stories concern the same cases). The cases cover a broad range of activities, including rape and sexual assault, fondling, soliciting children online for sexual purposes, producing child pornography, and failing to report suspected sexual abuse.

Priests

Public concern about sexual abuse by priests skyrocketed during the first decade of the 21st century as a result of a scandal surrounding abuse and cover-ups within the Catholic Church. Thomas F. Reilly (1942–), the former attorney general of Massachusetts, explains in *The Sexual Abuse of Children in the Roman Catholic Archdiocese of Boston* (July 23, 2003, http://www.bishop-accountability.org/resources/resource-files/reports/ReillyReport.pdf) the culture of secrecy involving the sexual abuse of an estimated 1,000 minors in the archdiocese of Boston since 1940. Reilly's 18-month-long investigation finds that "there is overwhelming evidence that for many years Cardinal [Bernard] Law and his senior managers had direct, actual knowledge that substantial numbers of children in the Archdiocese had been sexually abused by substantial numbers of its priests."

Reilly started the investigation in March 2002, shortly after John J. Geoghan (1935–2003), a former priest in the archdiocese of Boston, was sentenced to nine

to 10 years in prison for sexually abusing a 10-year-old boy. Reilly's investigators found that starting in 1979 the archdiocese had received complaints of child sexual abuse against Geoghan. Church documents, which had previously been sealed, revealed that the church had not only moved Geoghan from parish to parish but had also paid settlements amounting to $15 million to the victims' families. Reilly notes that the archdiocese's own files showed that 789 people had brought sexual complaints against the Boston clergy. However, Reilly believes the actual number of victims is higher. There were 237 priests and 13 church workers who had been accused of rape and sexual assault.

EXTENT OF CHILD SEXUAL ABUSE BY PRIESTS. Responding to emerging allegations of sexual abuse by priests, in June 2002 the U.S. Conference of Catholic Bishops commissioned a study of the nature and scope of the problem of child sexual abuse in the Catholic Church in the United States. The John Jay College of Criminal Justice of the City University of New York conducted the study based on information provided by 195 dioceses, which represented 98% of all diocesan priests in the United States. The researchers also collected data from 140 religious communities, which accounted for approximately 60% of religious communities and 80% of all priests in the religious communities.

The Nature and Scope of the Problem of Sexual Abuse of Minors by Catholic Priests and Deacons in the United States 1950–2002 (February 2004, http://www.usccb.org) indicates that of the 109,694 priests and deacons (collectively referred to as priests) who served between 1950 and 2002, 4,392 (4%) allegedly abused children under the age of 18 years. Most (55.7%) of these priests had a single allegation of abuse. Another 26.9% had two to three allegations, 13.9% had four to nine allegations, and 3.5% had 10 or more allegations.

The report shows that 10,667 individuals made allegations of child sexual abuse by priests between 1950 and 2002. About 81% of the victims were male, and 19% were female. Approximately half (50.7%) were between the ages of 11 and 14. More than a quarter (26.7%) were aged 15 to 17 years, 16.5% were aged eight to 10 years, and 6.1% were aged seven years or younger. The number of allegations rose steadily between 1950 and 1980 before dropping off sharply.

At the time of the allegations, most of the priests were serving in the capacity of associate pastor (42.3%) or pastor (25.1%). One out of 10 (10.4%) were serving as resident priests. Most of the abuse occurred in the priest's home or parish residence (40.9%), in church (16.3%), and in the victim's home (12.4%). Nearly half (49.6%) of the priests socialized with the alleged victim's family, mostly (79.6%) in the family's home.

In "Child Sexual Abuse in the Catholic Church: How Situational Crime Prevention Strategies Can Help Create Safe Environments" (*Criminal Justice and Behavior*, vol. 35, no. 5, May 2008), a follow-up study, Karen J. Terry and Alissa Ackerman find that many victims of abuse by priests were groomed for the abuse: 7.8% of children were given gifts, and 17% of children were given other enticements, such as alcohol, drugs, money, or trips. Only 7.8% of victims were threatened, usually psychologically rather than physically.

In 2010 allegations surfaced that Pope Benedict XVI (1927–) had acted to shield the Catholic Church from scandal rather than protect hundreds of children from the priests who abused them when he served as an archbishop in Germany and as the Vatican's chief doctrinal enforcer. Laurie Goodstein reports in "Vatican Declined to Defrock U.S. Priest Who Abused Boys" (NYTimes.com, March 24, 2010) that "top Vatican officials—including the future Pope Benedict XVI—did not defrock a priest who molested as many as 200 deaf boys" between 1950 and 1974. According to Goodstein, this case was only one of thousands that were forwarded to the Congregation for the Doctrine of the Faith, the Vatican office that decides whether accused priests should be brought to trial. The Vatican, she reports, continues to fight to keep the documents secret, noting that "the Vatican has tended to view the matter in terms of sin and repentance more than crime and punishment." Richard Owen notes in "Sins in the Church to Blame for Child Abuse Scandal, Admits Pope" (SundayTimes.co.uk, May 12, 2010) that Pope Benedict issued a statement in May 2010 indicating that the Catholic Church took responsibility for the child abuse that occurred within the church.

In 2013 Pope Benedict was succeeded by Pope Francis (1936–). Pope Francis took an active stance in contending with the issue of child sexual abuse in the Catholic Church. Catherine Hornby writes in "Pope Francis Targets Child Abuse, Leaks in Vatican Legal Reform" (Reuters.com, July 11, 2013) that in July 2013 Pope Francis revised a law prohibiting crimes against children in Vatican City to cite a range of sex-related crimes, including sexual abuse, child prostitution, and child pornography. In "What's the State of the Church's Child Abuse Crisis?" (PBS.org, February 24, 2014), Sarah Childress reports that in December 2013 the pope also established a special Vatican committee aimed at combating child sexual abuse and providing assistance for its victims.

Notorious Predators in Positions of Trust

Two other cases involving child sexual predators in positions of trust are noteworthy because of the circumstances involved.

In 2010 Earl B. Bradley (1953–), a pediatrician in Delaware, was indicted on hundreds of counts of sexually abusing child patients. In "Delaware Crime: Dr. Earl Bradley Sex Case Ignites Outrage" (DelawareOnline.com, February 24, 2010), Cris Barrish reports that Bradley was accused of raping or sexually assaulting more than 100 children. Much of the evidence against Bradley was obtained from videos that he made of the attacks, which date back to 1998. According to Barrish, all but one of the victims were girls. In August 2011 Bradley was found guilty of 24 counts and sentenced to 14 life terms plus 164 years in prison with no possibility of parole.

Another case of note is that of Jerry Sandusky (1944–), a former assistant football coach at Pennsylvania State University (Penn State). In "Timeline of Jerry Sandusky Sex Abuse Case; State Files Suit over Related NCAA Sanctions" (PennLive.com, January 2, 2013), Penn Live indicates that in 1977 Sandusky founded a charity called the Second Mile that was "dedicated to helping children with absent or dysfunctional families." In this capacity Sandusky interacted with boys who were typically aged seven to 13 years and sexually victimized at least eight of them. Some of the incidents took place in the locker and shower rooms that were used by the football team on the Penn State campus. In addition, he took some of the victims on trips to bowl games in which the Penn State football team competed. On two occasions fellow employees at the university reportedly witnessed Sandusky having sexual relations with boys in the shower room. The first witness told coworkers, but failed to notify authorities. The second witness notified Joe Paterno (1926–2012), the head coach of the Penn State football team, the day after he witnessed the sex act. Although Paterno alerted university officials to the allegations, neither the campus police nor city police were notified. In 2011 Sandusky was arrested after one of his victims told authorities about being sexually abused. The resulting scandal and apparent cover-up by Penn State officials cost Paterno and other top university officials their jobs. In addition, three of the officials were criminally charged for their roles in the cover-up. In June 2012 Sandusky was found guilty of 45 abuse counts; months later he was sentenced to 30 to 60 years in prison. As of November 2014, the trials for the charged university officials had still not taken place.

The Bradley and Sandusky cases both triggered the passage of new legislation designed to prevent such events from happening again. In the press release "Nine Bills Stemming from Earl Bradley Case Become Law" (June 30, 2010, http://governor.delaware.gov/news/2010/1006june/20100630-legislation.shtml), the state of Delaware indicates that its legislature passed nine bills in June 2010 that, among other things, strengthened the state's mandatory reporting system, provided new measures for screening doctors, and required another adult to be present when doctors examine children aged 15 years or younger who are undressed or undergoing specific physical examinations. According to the article "Jerry Sandusky Sex Abuse Case Has States Re-examining Mandatory Reporter Laws" (Associated Press, June 9, 2012), by June 2012 six states had expanded their mandatory reporting requirements and/or developed new policies and reporting procedures in response to the Sandusky case. Florida passed a particularly strict law that makes it a felony for mandated reporters to fail to report suspected child abuse. In addition, Florida institutions, such as universities, can face hefty fines and be denied state funding for failing to comply with the new law. The Sandusky case also prompted some lawmakers to seek tougher mandatory reporting laws on the national level. Beth Brelje notes in "Sandusky Case Leads to Tougher Stand on Reporting Child Abuse" (Pocono Record.com, May 17, 2014) that in May 2014 Senator Bob Casey (1960–; D-PA) proposed a new federal statute that would legally require members of certain professions, including doctors, school employees, and camp counselors, among others, to report any incidences of child abuse to law enforcement.

SEXUAL PREDATORS ON THE INTERNET

The Internet presents an attractive venue to child predators because they can act anonymously. Internet chat rooms, social networking sites, e-mail, and other computer-mediated communication methods provide adults with opportunities to form online relationships with children, engage in sexual banter with them, solicit or provide sexually explicit photographs or videos, and even arrange for personal meetings. Older children, particularly preteens and teenagers, tend to be highly active on the Internet. Adults who are sexually interested in youths can pose online as youths themselves in an effort to appear less threatening to children who might spurn sexually charged conversations with adults.

In 2000, 2005, and 2010 Finkelhor and his colleagues at the University of New Hampshire's Crimes against Children Research Center spearheaded national telephone surveys of thousands of youths across the country to determine to what extent the children had experienced unwanted online sexual communications. Lisa M. Jones, Kimberly J. Mitchell, and David Finkelhor discuss in "Trends in Youth Internet Victimization: Findings from Three Youth Internet Safety Surveys 2000–2010" (*Journal of Adolescent Health*, vol. 50, no. 2, February 2012) the results from the three surveys. Each survey included approximately 1,500 children aged 10 to 17 years who were Internet users. The youths were asked if they had ever experienced any of three types of online communications:

unwanted sexual solicitations, harassment, or exposure to pornography. Overall, 9% of the youths who participated in the 2010 survey reported experiencing unwanted sexual solicitations, down from 13% in the 2005 survey and 19% in the 2000 survey. As Mitchell, Jones, Finkelhor, and Janis Wolak report in "Understanding the Decline in Unwanted Online Sexual Solicitations for U.S. Youth 2000–2010: Findings from Three Youth Internet Safety Surveys" (*Child Abuse & Neglect*, vol. 37, no. 12, December 2013), the decline in online sexual solicitations between 2000 and 2010 was primarily among preteens between the ages of 10 and 12.

In "The Internet and Family and Acquaintance Sexual Abuse" (*Child Maltreatment*, vol. 10, no. 1, February 2005), Kimberly J. Mitchell, David Finkelhor, and Janis Wolak find that although the percentage of youth who used the Internet rose between 2000 and 2005, the percentage of youth who communicated with people they knew only online dropped from 40% to 34%. This decline might be due to a heightened awareness of pedophiles (adults who have a sexual interest in prepubescent children) on the Internet. In fact, the researchers find that when youth were sexually solicited online, most were able to deal with the problem by blocking solicitors or leaving sites. Most did not report feeling distressed by the experience, but about 4% of youth did report feeling upset or distressed as a result of the online solicitation. Other studies have attempted to identify the personality traits of adolescents who develop online friendships. As Wendy A. Walsh, Wolak, and Mitchell report in "Close Relationships with People Met Online in a National U.S. Sample of Adolescents" (*Cyberpsychology*, vol. 7, no. 3, 2013), in 2013 one in 10 teenage Internet users reported having formed a close relationship with someone they met over the Internet. According to Walsh, Wolak, and Mitchell, adolescents who were frequent Internet users, who suffered from depression, who engaged in delinquent activities, who searched for online pornography, and/or who had experienced harassment or sexual solicitations over the Internet were twice as likely as teens who did not belong in any of these categories to form close online relationships.

EFFECTS OF CHILD SEXUAL ABUSE

As described in Chapter 2, all types of child abuse have negative consequences over the short term and long term to the mental and physical health of the victims. Table 4.2 is a list compiled by the Children's Bureau of typical symptoms seen in the victims of childhood sexual abuse. In *Trauma-Focused Cognitive Behavioral Therapy for Children Affected by Sexual Abuse or Trauma* (August 2012, http://www.childwelfare.gov/pubs/trauma/trauma.pdf), the agency notes that the symptoms shown in Table 4.2 "can impact the child's daily life and affect behavior, school performance, attention, self-perception, and emotional regulation." A type of therapy called trauma-focused

TABLE 4.2

Negative effects often seen in victims of child sexual abuse

- Maladaptive or unhelpful beliefs and attributions related to the abusive events, including:
  - A sense of guilt for their role in the abuse
  - Anger at parents for not knowing about the abuse
  - Feelings of powerlessness
  - A sense that they are in some way "damaged goods"
  - A fear that people will treat them differently because of the abuse
- Acting out behaviors, such as engaging in age-inappropriate sexual behaviors
- Mental health disorders, including major depression
- Posttraumatic stress disorder (PTSD) symptoms, which are characterized by:
- Intrusive and reoccurring thoughts of the traumatic experience
  - Avoidance of reminders of the trauma (often places, people, sounds, smells, and other sensory triggers)
  - Emotional numbing
  - Irritability
  - Trouble sleeping or concentrating
  - Physical and emotional hyperarousal (often characterized by emotional swings or rapidly accelerating anger or crying that is out of proportion to the apparent stimulus)

SOURCE: Adapted from "TF-CBT Addresses the Effects of Sexual Abuse and Trauma," in *Trauma-Focused Cognitive Behavioral Therapy for Children Affected by Sexual Abuse or Trauma*, U.S. Department of Health and Human Services, Administration for Children and Families, Administration on Children, Youth and Families, Children's Bureau, August 2012, http://www.childwelfare.gov/pubs/trauma/trauma.pdf (accessed July 16, 2014)

cognitive behavioral therapy (TF-CBT) has been clinically proven to help children, adolescents, and their parents and caregivers in dealing with the trauma inflicted by childhood sexual victimization. The Children's Bureau explains that TF-CBT combines elements of cognitive therapy, behavioral therapy, and family therapy to "reduce negative emotional and behavioral responses following child sexual abuse."

High-Risk Behaviors in Female Child Sexual Abuse Victims

In "Sexual At-Risk Behaviors of Sexually Abused Adolescent Girls" (*Journal of Child Sexual Abuse*, vol. 12, no. 2, 2003), a study of sexual at-risk behaviors of 125 female adolescents aged 12 to 17 years who had experienced sexual abuse, Caroline Cinq-Mars et al. administered a self-report questionnaire that asked about the subjects' sexual activities, not including sexual abuse experiences. Afterward, the subjects were interviewed regarding their sexual abuse experiences, including information about the perpetrator (both family and nonfamily members), the frequency and duration of the abuse, the severity of the abuse, and whether or not they told someone about the abuse.

Among offending family members, fathers were the perpetrators in 30.4% of incidents. Stepfathers and extended family members each were responsible for 28.8% of the sexual abuse, and brothers accounted for another 9.6% of abuse. The victims experienced more than one incident of sexual abuse, with the mean (average) number of incidents per victim being 1.8. The mean age for the start of abuse was 9.3 years. More than one-third (36.8%) of the victims experienced sexual abuse before the age of 11 years.

Over half (55.3%) of the subjects reported being sexually active. More than half (54.5%) had their first consensual intercourse before the age of 15 years. The rate of pregnancy was 15%. Cinq-Mars et al. find three sexual abuse characteristics that were associated with the adolescents' sexual at-risk behavior. Adolescents who experienced abuse involving penetration were 13 times as likely to have been pregnant and twice as likely to have more than one consensual partner in the 12 months preceding the study. Having been abused by more than one perpetrator (in one or more incidents) was also closely associated with at-risk behaviors: pregnancy (eight times as likely), having more than one consensual sexual partner (four times as likely), and irregular condom use (three times as likely). Finally, physical coercion during abuse increased the odds of pregnancy (four times as likely), having more than one consensual sexual partner (five times as likely), and irregular condom use (three times as likely).

As Brigitte Leeners et al. report in "Risk Factors for Unfavorable Pregnancy Outcome in Women with Adverse Childhood Experiences" (*Journal of Perinatal Medicine*, vol. 42, no. 2, March 2014), female victims of sexual abuse are also more likely than nonvictims to engage in risky behavior during pregnancy. Leeners et al. report that roughly one-third (31.7%) of child sexual abuse victims later smoked during pregnancy, a rate more than three times higher than that of pregnant women who were not victims of childhood sexual abuse (9.4%). At the same time, victims of childhood sexual abuse experienced high likelihoods of experiencing emotional abuse (44.7%), physical abuse (16.5%), and sexual abuse (12.9%) while they were pregnant.

In addition, Leeners et al. found that victims of child sexual abuse are susceptible to certain "triggers" that make them recall memories of their abuse during pregnancy. Nearly one in five pregnant women (19.2%) in the study reported that the experience of having a vaginal examination triggered memories of the sexual abuse they endured as a child.

Substance Abuse

A number of studies, such as Christiane Brems et al.'s "Childhood Abuse History and Substance Use among Men and Women Receiving Detoxification Services" (*American Journal of Drug and Alcohol Abuse*, vol. 30, no. 4, November 2004), Patricia B. Moran, Sam Vuchinich, and Nancy K. Hall's "Associations between Types of Maltreatment and Substance Use during Adolescence" (*Child Abuse and Neglect: The International Journal*, vol. 28, no. 5, May 2004), and Cathy S. Widom et al.'s "Long-Term Effects of Child Abuse and Neglect on Alcohol Use and Excessive Drinking in Middle Adulthood" (*Journal of Studies on Alcohol and Drugs*, vol. 68, no. 3, May 2007) show that child sexual abuse increases the risk for substance abuse later in life. In "Abnormal T2 Relaxation Time in the Cerebellar Vermis of Adults Sexually Abused in Childhood: Potential Role of the Vermis in Stress-Enhanced Risk for Drug Abuse" (*Psychoneuroendocrinology*, vol. 27, nos. 1–2, January–February 2002), Carl M. Anderson et al. of Harvard Medical School uncover how this occurs. They find that the vermis, the region that is flanked by the cerebellar hemispheres of the brain, may play a key role in the risk for substance abuse among adults who have experienced child abuse. The vermis develops gradually and continues to produce neurons, or nerve cells, after birth. It is known to be sensitive to stress; as a result, stress can influence its development.

Anderson et al. compared young adults aged 18 to 22 years, including eight with a history of repeated sexual abuse in childhood and 16 others as the control group. Using functional magnetic resonance imaging technology, the researchers measured the resting blood flow in the vermis. They find that the subjects who had been victims of sexual abuse had diminished blood flow. Anderson et al. suggest the stress experienced with repeated sexual abuse may have caused damage to the vermis, which in turn could not perform its job of controlling irritability in the limbic system (a collection of connected clusters of nerve cells). Located in the center of the brain, the limbic system is responsible for, among other things, regulating emotions and memory. Therefore, the damaged vermis induces a person to use drugs or alcohol to suppress the irritability.

Because the subjects who had been sexually abused as children had no history of alcohol or substance abuse, Anderson et al. wanted to confirm their findings, which linked an impaired cerebellar vermis and the potential for substance abuse in sexual abuse survivors. After analyzing test data collected from the 537 college students recruited for the study, they find that students who reported frequent substance abuse showed higher irritability in the limbic system. They also exhibited symptoms usually associated with drug use, including depression and anger.

In "Childhood Sexual Abuse and Adolescent Substance Use: A Latent Class Analysis" (*Drug and Alcohol Dependence*, vol. 109, nos. 1–3, June 1, 2010), Sunny Hyucksun Shin, Hyokyoung Grace Hong, and Andrea L. Hazen analyze data on 1,019 adolescents followed in the Patterns of Youth Mental Health Care Public Service Systems Study. The researchers find that not only is child sexual abuse associated with drug and alcohol use during adolescence but also that sexual abuse shapes the patterns of substance use of teen girls. Female adolescent victims of child sexual abuse were five times more likely than nonvictims to heavily use multiple kinds of drugs. These findings held true even when Shin, Hong, and Hazen controlled for peer substance use, family influences, mental disorders, and other types of child maltreatment. The researchers also note that male sexual abuse survivors were not more likely to use drugs and alcohol during adolescence than were nonvictims. As Carolyn E. Sartor et al. report in "Childhood Sexual Abuse and Early Substance Use in Adolescent Girls: The Role of Familial Influences" (*Addiction*, vol. 108, no. 5, May 2013), roughly one-third (32.7%) of female victims of child sexual abuse used alcohol for the first time when they were 14 years old or younger, compared with 20% of girls in that age group who had never experienced child sexual abuse. (See Table 4.3.) At the same time, nearly a third (29.7%) of female sexual abuse victims had tried marijuana by the time they were 15 years old, compared with 12.9% of nonvictims who had tried marijuana by that age.

Sexual Revictimization and Self-Harming Behaviors

In "Revictimization and Self-Harm in Females Who Experienced Childhood Sexual Abuse: Results from a Prospective Study" (*Journal of Interpersonal Violence*, vol. 18, no. 12, December 2003), Jennie G. Noll et al. report on a longitudinal study (a study of the same group of people over time) that examines the effects of child

TABLE 4.3

Age of first use of alcohol, cigarettes, and marijuana among adolescent girls, by child sexual abuse status, 2013

	Alcohol			Cigarettes			Cannabis		
		Prevalence (%)			Prevalence (%)			Prevalence (%)	
	Age range (years)	CSA[a]	No CSA[b]	Age range	CSA[a]	No CSA[b]	Age range (years)	CSA[a]	No CSA[b]
Early	≤14	32.7	20.0	≤12	35.5	19.0	≤15	29.6	12.9
Average	15–17	41.3	44.5	13–16	39.6	36.0	16–18	30.6	26.3
Late	≥18	20.9	28.6	≥17	12.6	18.0	≥19	8.4	11.7
Never		5.1	6.9		12.3	27.0		31.4	49.1

[a]Child sexual abuse (CSA), sample size = 487.
[b]No child sexual abuse (CSA), sample size = 3,274.

SOURCE: Carolyn E. Sartor et al., "Table 2. Age at First Use of Alcohol, Cigarettes, and Cannabis by Childhood Sexual Abuse (CSA) Status," in "Childhood Sexual Abuse and Early Substance Use in Adolescent Girls: The Role of Familial Influences," *Addiction*, vol. 108, no. 5, May 2013, pp. 993–1000.

sexual abuse on female development. This was the first prospective study that followed children from the time sexual abuse was reported through adolescence and into early adulthood. Referred by CPS agencies, the participants had experienced sexual abuse by a family member before the age of 14 years. The median age (half were younger and half were older) at the start of sexual abuse was seven to eight years, and the median duration of abuse was two years. The study consisted of 84 abused children and a comparison group of 82 nonabused children. Two yearly interviews followed the first assessment of the group and two more interviews were conducted within five years of the sexual abuse report.

Noll et al. note that this study was the first to provide information about the revictimization of child sexual abuse survivors not long after their abuse (seven years after the abuse, when the participants were in their adolescence and early adulthood). The researchers find that participants who had been sexually abused during childhood were twice as likely as the comparison group to have experienced sexual revictimization, such as rape or sexual assault, and almost four times as likely to harm themselves through suicide attempts or self-mutilation. They also suffered 1.6 times more physical victimization, such as domestic violence. Compared with the nonabused group, the abused group reported 20% more significant lifetime traumas subsequent to being sexually abused. Significant lifetime traumas reported by the participants included separation and losses (e.g., having family or friends move away or die), emotional abuse and/or rejection by family, natural disasters, and witnessing violence.

In "Substance Use and PTSD Symptoms Impact the Likelihood of Rape and Revictimization in College Women" (*Journal of Interpersonal Violence*, vol. 24, no. 3, March 2009), Terri L. Messman-Moore, Rose Marie Ward, and Amy L. Brown find that substance use and PTSD increase the likelihood that college women will be raped or otherwise revictimized. They argue that PTSD sufferers use drugs and alcohol or maladaptive sexual behavior to cope with PTSD symptoms and that these coping behaviors increase their risk of further victimization.

Noll et al. observe that child sexual abuse is the "strongest predictor of self-harm," even when other types of abuse are present. They surmise that the victims may have negative feelings toward their own body and want to hurt it. Noll et al. indicate that some researchers believe victims may want to reveal internal pains through the outward manifestation of self-harm. Others wish to re-experience feelings of shame in an attempt to resolve it.

However, Jennifer J. Muehlenkamp et al. find a stronger correlation between physical abuse and self-injury than between sexual abuse and self-injury. In "Abuse Subtypes and Nonsuicidal Self-Injury: Preliminary Evidence of

Complex Emotion Regulation Patterns" (*Journal of Nervous and Mental Disease*, vol. 198, no. 4, April 2010), the researchers report that a relatively weak association exists between child sexual abuse and later nonsuicidal self-injury. They theorize that people with a history of sexual abuse may be more likely to engage in other self-destructive behaviors such as eating disorders and substance abuse than in externalizing self-injury. Muehlenkamp et al. suggest that more research is needed into the emotional difficulties that are experienced by child sexual abuse survivors and their association with self-harming behavior.

Effects on Boys

MALE VICTIMS' PERCEPTION OF CHILD SEXUAL ABUSE AND CLINICAL FINDINGS. Sharon M. Valente of the Research and Education Department of Veteran Affairs in Los Angeles, California, notes in "Sexual Abuse of Boys" (*Journal of Child and Adolescent Psychiatric Nursing*, vol. 18, no. 1, January 2005) that boys who have been sexually abused display a range of psychological consequences to the traumatic experience. She finds that common responses include anxiety, denial, dissociation, and self-mutilation. Valente also indicates that boys who have been sexually abused are at risk for running away. According to Susan Rick of Louisiana State University Health Science Center in "Sexually Abused Boys: A Vulnerable Population" (*Journal of Multicultural Nursing and Health*, Winter 2003), sexually abused boys have "prominent symptoms such as fear, depression, guilt, self destructive behavior and hypersexuality." Lynn Sorsoli, Maryam Kia-Keating, and Frances K. Grossman suggest in "'I Keep That Hush-Hush': Male Survivors of Sexual Abuse and the Challenges of Disclosure" (*Journal of Counseling Psychology*, vol. 55, no. 3, July 2008) that feelings of shame surrounding sexual abuse may be even more intense for male survivors than for female survivors. As a result, this shame makes it even less likely for male survivors than female survivors to disclose their abuse histories.

A Longitudinal Study of the Effects of Child Sexual Abuse

In "The Effects of Child Sexual Abuse in Later Family Life: Mental Health, Parenting, and Adjustment of Offspring" (*Child Abuse and Neglect: The International Journal*, vol. 28, no. 5, May 2004), Ron Roberts et al. seek to determine the effects of child sexual abuse on adult mental health, parenting relationships, and the adjustment of the children of mothers who had been victims of child sexual abuse. The researchers investigated 8,292 families, a subsample of the Avon Longitudinal Study of Parents and Children, which is a continuing study of women and their families in Avon, England. The participating women had self-reported experiences of sexual assault before adolescence. Four family groups were included:

- Single-mother families (9% of the study sample)— consist of a nonmarried woman with no partner and her children
- Biological families (79.5%)—consist of two parents and their biological children with no other children from previous relationships
- Stepmother/complex stepfamilies (4.6%)—consist of a father with at least one biological child (living in the household or visiting regularly) who is not the biological offspring of the mother
- Stepfather families (6.9%)—consist of a mother and at least one biological child (living in the household or visiting regularly) who is not the biological offspring of the father

The researchers report that 26% of survivors of child sexual abuse had teen pregnancies. These women were disproportionately likely to be currently living in a nontraditional family—single-mother families (3%) and stepfather families (2.9%)—than in a biological family (1.3%).

Roberts et al. did not have a similar finding when it came to stepmother/complex stepfamilies. In this group just 0.8% reported child sexual abuse. The researchers surmise that a woman who has experienced child sexual abuse tends to choose a partner without children because she might feel inadequate to take care of more children.

Child sexual abuse also has consequences on the adult survivors' mental health. Mothers who reported child sexual abuse were likely to report more depression and anxiety and lower self-esteem. These mental problems in turn affect the mothers' relationships with their children and the children's adjustment. Mothers with a history of child sexual abuse reported less self-confidence and less positive relationships with their children. The children were hyperactive and had emotional, peer, and conduct problems. As D. R. Wilson et al. report in "Overcoming Sequelae of Childhood Sexual Abuse with Stress Management" (*Journal of Psychiatric & Mental Health Nursing*, vol. 19, no. 7, September 2012), emotional issues stemming from childhood sexual abuse can lead victims to adopt poor coping skills when confronting stressful situations as adults, which can result in a range of both psychological and physiological health issues.

CHAPTER 5
CHILD ABUSE AND THE LAW

As explained in earlier chapters, child abuse cases can fall under the jurisdiction of civil or criminal courts, depending on the circumstances. Chapter 2 describes the civil court proceedings that child protective services (CPS) agencies undertake in cases in which they remove a child from the home, provide in-home protective services, or require the abuser to get treatment. These cases are handled in juvenile or family courts and are broadly known as child abuse, child protection, dependency, or child welfare cases. Civil laws also allow adults who suffered abuse as children to file lawsuits seeking monetary damages from their alleged abusers and/or from third parties that played a role in the abuse. Criminal proceedings are initiated by a government prosecutor if an alleged abuser is charged with a crime, such as sexual abuse. These cases are handled in criminal courts.

CHILDREN'S LEGAL RIGHTS
IN CHILD PROTECTION CASES

Historically, children who appeared in dependency court were not subject to constitutional due process rights or legal representation. This changed in 1972, when the U.S. Supreme Court ruled in *In re Gault* (387 U.S. 1) that children, whether they have committed a crime or are the victims of a crime, are entitled to due process and legal representation. The original case involved delinquency (i.e., criminal offenses committed by juveniles). However, the protections afforded by the Supreme Court's decision were soon applied to the civil court proceedings used in dependency cases.

In "Session 3: Children's Rights in the Context of Welfare, Dependency, and the Juvenile Court" (*UC Davis Journal of Juvenile Law and Policy*, vol. 8, no. 2, 2004), John E. B. Myers of the University of the Pacific notes, "Prior to *Gault*, lawyers were uncommon in abuse and neglect cases. The child protection agency was represented by a social worker, who presented the agency's

position to the judge. Parents, most of whom were poor, seldom had legal representation. Rules of evidence and procedure were downplayed or ignored, and informality was the order of the day." Ever since the Supreme Court's ruling in *Gault*, attorneys have played a much larger role in dependency court hearings. Judges in these hearings can appoint temporary guardians called guardians ad litem (guardians at law) to represent the children's interests during dependency hearings. The guardians may be attorneys working pro bono (without compensation) or specially trained volunteers. For example, in "Frequently Asked Questions" (2014, http://www.guardianadlitem.org/vol_faq.asp), the Florida Guardian ad Litem Program notes that "anyone with common sense, compassion and dedication to children can be a Guardian ad Litem."

Another program devoted to advocating for children involved in dependency hearings is the court-appointed special advocate (CASA) program. The National CASA Association indicates in *Toward a Breakthrough Year: Annual Report 2013* (2014, http://nc.casaforchildren.org/apps/annualreport2013/index.html) that in 2013 nearly 75,000 CASA and guardian ad litem volunteers helped more than 238,000 abused and neglected children.

Guardians ad litem and CASA volunteers try to ensure that the legal system serves the best interests of the child. A volunteer reviews all records pertaining to the maltreated child, including CPS reports and medical and school records. The volunteer also meets with the child, parents and family members, social workers, health care providers, school officials, and other people who may know of the child's history. The research compiled by the volunteer helps the child's lawyer (if one is involved) and the court in deciding what is best for the child.

Table 5.1 shows a state-by-state count of the number of duplicate victims and the number who experienced court actions in 2012. (A "duplicate" count tallies a child

TABLE 5.1

Child maltreatment victims with court action, 2012

State	Duplicate victims	Duplicate victims with court action	
		Number	Percent
Alabama	9,824	640	6.5
Alaska	3,417	746	21.8
Arizona	10,665	5,951	55.8
Arkansas	12,012	2,454	20.4
California	81,740	26,089	31.9
Colorado	10,953	2,146	19.6
Connecticut	8,735	1,840	21.1
Delaware	2,409	402	16.7
District of Columbia	2,236	381	17.0
Florida	57,263	3,011	5.3
Georgia	19,462	2,370	12.2
Hawaii	1,432	757	52.9
Idaho			
Illinois	29,854	3,519	11.8
Indiana	21,754	10,354	47.6
Iowa	12,264	3,796	31.0
Kansas	1,922	776	40.4
Kentucky	18,487	4,742	25.7
Louisiana	8,964	2,416	27.0
Maine	4,000	169	4.2
Maryland	14,196	1,812	12.8
Massachusetts	21,008	4,550	21.7
Michigan	37,110	8,149	22.0
Minnesota	4,421	1,508	34.1
Mississippi	8,188	265	3.2
Missouri	4,834	1,622	33.6
Montana	1,379	770	55.8
Nebraska	4,300	1,391	32.3
Nevada	5,724	2,694	47.1
New Hampshire	943	528	56.0
New Jersey	9,592	2,465	25.7
New Mexico	6,517	1,156	17.7
New York			
North Carolina			
North Dakota	1,442	397	27.5
Ohio	31,982	5,647	17.7
Oklahoma	10,331	1,950	18.9
Oregon	10,468	3,698	35.3
Pennsylvania			
Puerto Rico	9,223	305	3.3
Rhode Island	3,456	1,076	31.1
South Carolina	11,827	2,073	17.5
South Dakota			
Tennessee	10,421	1,148	11.0
Texas	64,689	10,762	16.6
Utah	9,982	1,860	18.6
Vermont	715	168	23.5
Virginia	5,959	682	11.4
Washington	7,159	2,332	32.6
West Virginia	4,716	779	16.5
Wisconsin	4,902	534	10.9
Wyoming	719	345	48.0
Total	**623,596**	**133,225**	
Percent			21.4
States reporting	47	47	

SOURCE: "Table 6-6. Victims with Court Action, 2012," in *Child Maltreatment 2012*, U.S. Department of Health and Human Services, Administration for Children and Families, Administration on Children, Youth, and Families, Children's Bureau, December 17, 2013, http://www.acf.hhs.gov/sites/default/files/cb/cm2012.pdf (accessed July 16, 2014)

TABLE 5.2

Child maltreatment victims with court-appointed representatives, 2012

State	Duplicate victims	Duplicate victims with court-appointed representatives	
		Number	Percent
Alabama	9,824	582	5.9
Alaska	3,417	446	13.1
Arizona	10,665	7,438	69.7
Arkansas	12,012	81	0.7
California	81,740	30,855	37.7
Colorado			
Connecticut			
Delaware	2,409	402	16.7
District of Columbia	2,236	103	4.6
Florida	57,263	369	0.6
Georgia	19,462	3,306	17.0
Hawaii	1,432	707	49.4
Idaho			
Illinois			
Indiana	21,754	1,864	8.6
Iowa	12,264	3,691	30.1
Kansas			
Kentucky	18,487	4,295	23.2
Louisiana			
Maine	4,000	885	22.1
Maryland	14,196	58	0.4
Massachusetts	21,008	4,068	19.4
Michigan			
Minnesota	4,421	1,330	30.1
Mississippi	8,188	2,644	32.3
Missouri			
Montana	1,379	380	27.6
Nebraska	4,300	1,405	32.7
Nevada	5,724	458	8.0
New Hampshire			
New Jersey	9,592	503	5.2
New Mexico	6,517	1,156	17.7
New York			
North Carolina			
North Dakota	1,442	273	18.9
Ohio	31,982	1,233	3.9
Oklahoma	10,331	1,950	18.9
Oregon			
Pennsylvania			
Puerto Rico	9,223	1	0.0
Rhode Island	3,456	1,048	30.3
South Carolina	11,827	165	1.4
South Dakota			
Tennessee	10,421	103	1.0
Texas			
Utah	9,982	1,860	18.6
Vermont	715	168	23.5
Virginia	5,959	41	0.7
Washington			
West Virginia	4,716	55	1.2
Wisconsin			
Wyoming	719	49	6.8
Total	**433,063**	**73,972**	
Percent			17.1
States reporting	35	35	

SOURCE: "Table 6-7. Victims with Court-Appointed Representatives, 2012," in *Child Maltreatment 2012*, U.S. Department of Health and Human Services, Administration for Children and Families, Administration on Children, Youth, and Families, Children's Bureau, December 17, 2013, http://www.acf.hhs.gov/sites/default/files/cb/cm2012.pdf (accessed July 16, 2014)

for each reported incidence of abuse, so a victim may be counted more than once.) It should be noted that data were not available from five states: Idaho, New York, North Carolina, Pennsylvania, and South Dakota. Of the 623,596 duplicate victims reported, 133,225 (21.4%) had court actions in 2012. Table 5.2 shows the number of

duplicate victims who had court-appointed representatives in 2012. Data from 33 states, Washington, D.C., and Puerto Rico are presented. Of the 433,063 duplicate victims shown in Table 5.2, 73,972 (17.1%) victims had court-appointed representatives.

DIFFICULTIES IN PROSECUTING CHILD ABUSERS

Abusive acts that are defined as criminal offenses are prosecuted in criminal court. In many cases the victim, a child, may be the key witness. This can present challenges for prosecutors, particularly when the victim is a young child (for example, age six or younger) because the question of competency arises. Several studies have examined children's reliability in recalling and retelling past events. Researchers find that different settings and interview techniques may result in children remembering different details at different times.

Prosecutors also worry about the possible harm the child may suffer in having to relive the abuse and in being interrogated by adversarial defense attorneys. For instance, if the child is an adolescent making accusations of sexual abuse, the defendant's attorney may accuse the teenage victim of seducing the defendant or having willingly taken part in the acts. Other factors that prosecutors must consider include the slowness of the court process and the possibility that the case may be delayed, not just once, but several times. This is hard enough for adults to tolerate, but it is particularly difficult for children because the delay prolongs their pain. Children may become more reluctant to testify or may no longer be able to retell their stories accurately. There is a far greater difference between an 11-year-old retelling an event that happened at six years of age than a 31-year-old testifying about something that happened when he or she was 26 years old.

In "Child Maltreatment and the Justice System: Predictors of Court Involvement" (*Research on Social Work Practice*, vol. 15, no. 5, September 2005), Andrea J. Sedlak et al. indicate that several factors make it more likely that child maltreatment cases reported to CPS, the sheriff's office, the prosecutor's office, or dependency court are prosecuted. The researchers note that cases involving a male perpetrator and a female victim or victims are the most likely to be prosecuted, with sexual abuse being the type of maltreatment with the highest likelihood of prosecution. Abuse cases with multiple victims, especially when a parent abuses his or her own child as well as another child, are also likely to be prosecuted. By contrast, cases with a disabled victim are less likely than other cases to be prosecuted.

CONSIDERATIONS IN CHILD SEXUAL ABUSE PROSECUTIONS

Sedlak et al. note that child sexual abuse cases have the highest likelihood among maltreatment cases of being tried in criminal court. William G. Jones explains in *Working with the Courts in Child Protection* (2006) that the types of maltreatment cases that are typically prosecuted are those that include sex offenses and those that cause serious injury or death.

Still, a number of obstacles confront the prosecution of child sexual assault cases. Indeed, a high percentage of rape and sexual assault cases ultimately go unreported to the authorities. Table 5.3 provides a breakdown of rape and sexual assault cases of minors aged 12 to 17 years between 2008 and 2012. Of the 26,606 rape and sexual assault cases involving children between the ages of 12 and 14 that were documented in 2012, roughly half (13,528, or 51%) were reported to the police; another 10,924 (41%) went unreported, and the reporting status of 2,154 (8%) cases was unknown. As Table 5.4 shows, a comparable number of rape and sexual assault victims between the ages of 12 and 14 (13,596, or 51%) received victim services following their attacks that year. Older victims were far less likely to report sexual crimes than younger victims. Of the 12,060 known cases of rape and sexual assault involving children aged 15 to 17 years in 2012, 4,904 (41%) were reported to the police, and 7,156 (59%) went unreported. (See Table 5.3.)

TABLE 5.3

Victims of child sexual assault, by age and reporting to police, 2008–12

Crime type	2008	2009	2010	2011	2012
Rape/sexual assault					
12 to 14	20,770	35,538	32,781	3,961	26,606
Yes, reported to the police	4,488	—	14,618	—	13,528
No, did not report to the police	16,282	35,538	18,163	3,961	10,924
Do not know	—	—	—	—	2,154
15 to 17	35,633	19,692	20,531	20,995	12,060
Yes, reported to the police	9,433	15,691	14,344	7,202	4,904
No, did not report to the police	26,200	4,000	6,187	13,792	7,156

*Special tabulations from the NCVS Victimization Analysis Tool (NVAT).
*Detail may not sum to total due to rounding and/or missing data.
—Estimate is equal to 0 sample cases.

SOURCE: Adapted from "Number of Rape/Sexual Assaults by Age and Reporting to the Police, 2008–2012," in *NCVS Victimization Analysis Tool (NVAT)*, U.S. Department of Justice, Office of Justice Programs, Bureau of Justice Statistics, July 22, 2014, http://www.bjs.gov/index.cfm?ty=nvat (accessed July 22, 2014)

TABLE 5.4

Victims of child sexual assault, by age and victim services status, 2012

Crime type	2012
Rape/sexual assault	346,830
12 to 14	26,606
Services received from victim service agencies	13,596
No services received from victim service agencies	9,232
15 to 17	12,060
No services received from victim service agencies	12,060

*Special tabulations from the NCVS Victimization Analysis Tool (NVAT).
*Detail may not sum to total due to rounding and/or missing data.

SOURCE: Adapted from "Number of Rape/Sexual Assaults by Age and Victim Services, 2012," in *NCVS Victimization Analysis Tool (NVAT)*, U.S. Department of Justice, Office of Justice Programs, Bureau of Justice Statistics, July 22, 2014, http://www.bjs.gov/index.cfm?ty=nvat (accessed July 22, 2014)

In "Child Sexual Abuse: Can Anatomy Explain the Presentation?" (*Clinical Pediatrics*, vol. 47, no. 1, January 2008), Dena Nazer and Vincent J. Palusci of the Children's Hospital of Michigan in Detroit, Michigan, note that prosecuting a child sexual abuse case is particularly challenging. A child who is physically abused will often display unmistakable signs of the abuse, such as bruises and broken bones. Sexual abuse does not necessarily leave such visible marks. Therefore, the abuse is less likely to be noticed by others and is more difficult to verify once an accusation is made.

In "How Long to Prosecute Child Sexual Abuse for a Community Using a Children's Advocacy Center and Two Comparison Communities?" (*Child Maltreatment*, vol. 13, no. 1, February 2008), Wendy A. Walsh et al. examine the effect of the particular difficulties encountered in child sexual abuse cases on the length of time it took to resolve them. The researchers find that less than half (44%) of child sexual abuse cases in the legal system were resolved within one year, and nearly one-third (30%) remained unresolved at the two-year mark. Only one out of five was resolved within six months, which is the American Bar Association standard for felony cases.

According to Wendy A. Walsh et al. in "Prosecuting Child Sexual Abuse: The Importance of Evidence Type" (*Crime and Delinquency*, vol. 56, no. 3, July 2010), the sexual abuse cases that were the most likely to have charges filed had at least some of these types of evidence: a child disclosure, a corroborating witness, an offender confession, or an additional report against the alleged perpetrator. Cases lacking physical evidence were twice as likely to be filed if there was a corroborating witness. Regardless of whether a child disclosed the abuse or not, a case was much more likely to be filed if there were at least two types of evidence present.

Tisha R. Wiley of the Juvenile Protective Association finds in "Legal and Social Service Responses to Child Sexual Abuse: A Primer and Discussion of Relevant Research" (*Journal of Child Sexual Abuse*, vol. 18, no. 3, May–June 2009) that only a small proportion of child sexual abuse cases are ever prosecuted. Cases involving female victims and older victims are more likely to be prosecuted than those involving male victims or younger victims. The more severe the abuse, the more likely it will be prosecuted. If a child is inconsistent in his or her story or if the child's family is against the prosecution, the case is unlikely to be brought to court. Children must also be willing and able to testify in court.

The Question of Competency

Traditionally, judges protected juries from incompetent witnesses, which during the early years of the United States were considered to include women, slaves, and children. Children in particular were believed to live in a fantasy world, and their inability to understand terms such as *oath*, *testify*, and *solemnly swear* denied them the right to appear in court. In 1895 the U.S. Supreme Court established in *Wheeler v. United States* (159 U.S. 523) the status of child witnesses. The court explained:

> There is no precise age which determines the question of competency. This depends on the capacity and intelligence of the child, his appreciation of the difference between truth and falsehood, as well as of his duty to tell the former. The decision of this question rests primarily with the trial judge, who sees the proposed witness, notices his manner, his apparent possession or lack of intelligence, and may resort to any examination which will tend to disclose his capacity and intelligence, as well as his understanding of the obligations of an oath.... To exclude [a child] from the witness stand ... would sometimes result in staying the hand of justice.

As a result of this ruling, the courts formalized the *Wheeler* decision by requiring judges to interview all children to determine their competency. The Federal Rules of Evidence (http://www.law.cornell.edu/rules/fre) are rules that have been codified into law by Congress and dictate certain evidentiary practices and procedures that most federal courts have to follow. In general, the state courts also abide by the Federal Rules of Evidence, which were codified in 1975. Rule 601, Competency to Testify in General (http://www.law.cornell.edu/rules/fre/rule_601), states: "Every person is competent to be a witness unless these rules provide otherwise." Under U.S. Code Section 3509, Child Victims' and Child Witnesses' Rights (http://www.gpo.gov/fdsys/pkg/USCODE-2011-title18/pdf/USCODE-2011-title18-partII-chap223-sec3509.pdf), a child is presumed to be competent, and a competency examination is only required upon written motion and an "offer of proof of incompetency."

Is a Child's Account Reliable?

Some experts believe children do not lie about sexual abuse. They point out that children cannot describe events unfamiliar to them. For example, the average six-year-old has no concept of how forced penetration feels or what semen tastes like. Experts also note that children lie to get themselves out of trouble, not into trouble, and reporting sexual abuse is definitely trouble. Children sometimes recant or deny that any abuse has happened, after they disclosed it. Perhaps the reaction to the disclosure is unfavorable, or the pain of talking about the experience is too great. The child's recanting under interrogation in a court of law may prove damaging to the case and may encourage claims that the child has made false accusations.

Kenneth V. Lanning surmises in "Criminal Investigation of Sexual Victimization of Children" (John E. B. Myers et al., eds., *The APSAC Handbook on Child Maltreatment*, 2002) that children rarely lie about sexual abuse. Some children, however, may recount what they believe in their mind to be the truth, although their account may turn out to be inaccurate. Lanning gives the following explanations for these inaccuracies:

- The child may be experiencing distorted memory because of trauma

- The child's story might be a reflection of normal childhood fears and fantasy

- The child may have been confused by the abuser's use of trickery or drugs

- The child's testimony may be influenced by the suggestive questions of investigators

- The child's account might reflect urban legends and cultural mythology

Nazer and Palusci point out that children's accounts of sexual abuse sometimes do contain bizarre or impossible events. This does not mean that the child was not sexually abused; instead, understanding sexual abuse may be beyond a child's ability at his or her developmental stage. For example, if a child is penetrated in the course of sexual abuse, the child may perceive the painful object to be a knife. In addition, when faced with sexual abuse and the emotional pain that surrounds the trauma of the abuse, children may have distorted memories of exactly what occurred.

CHILDREN CAN BE UNRELIABLE WITNESSES IF SUBJECTED TO SUGGESTED EVENTS. In "Children's Eyewitness Reports after Exposure to Misinformation from Parents" (*Journal of Experimental Psychology: Applied*, vol. 7, no. 1, March 2001), Debra Ann Poole and D. Stephen Lindsay examine children's eyewitness reports after the children were given misinformation by their parents and show that children may not be able to distinguish fact from fiction when subjected to suggested events before formal interviews.

A total of 114 children aged three to eight years participated (on a one-to-one basis) in four science activities with a man called "Mr. Science." Three interviews were conducted afterward. The first interview occurred right after the science activities in which an interviewer asked each child nonsuggestive questions about the activities. About three and a half months later the children's parents read them a story about their science experience. The story included two science activities they had experienced and two others that they had not experienced. The story also included an event in which the child experienced unpleasant touching by Mr. Science. In reality this event did not happen. The children were then interviewed. The final step in the interview consisted of a source-monitoring procedure, in which the children were reminded of their actual experiences, as well as the story, to help them distinguish fact from fiction. A final interview was conducted one month later. This time the children were not given any misinformation.

The interview conducted right after the science activities showed that the children recalled their experiences, with the amount of events reported increasing with the age of the child. When prompted for more information, the amount of new information reported also increased with age. The reports resulting from the promptings remained accurate. In the interview that occurred soon after the children were read the story with misleading suggestions, 35% (40) of the children reported 58 suggested events in free recall (without prompting from the interviewer), including 17 events about unpleasant touching by Mr. Science. In the last interview, with no additional misinformation given the children, 21% (24) of the children reported 27 suggested events, including nine suggested events that involved unpleasant touching by Mr. Science. Even when the children were prompted to provide more information about their experiences, they continued to report false events. Poole and Lindsay conclude that because children's credibility as eyewitnesses depends on their ability to distinguish their memories from other sources, interviewers will have to develop better procedures to help them do so.

BEST INTERVIEWING TECHNIQUES. In "Toward a Better Way to Interview Child Victims of Sexual Abuse" (*NIJ Journal*, no. 267, Winter 2010), Sara Harris of Palladian Partners, Inc., notes that "in many child sexual abuse cases, there is no witness other than the child and no corroborating evidence—the entire case can hang on a child's recollection of the alleged abuse." The importance of obtaining reliable information from sexually abused children has prompted the development and testing of various interview protocols. Harris describes a protocol that was developed during the 1990s by the

Eunice Kennedy Shriver National Institute of Child Health and Human Development (NICHD). Evidence shows that when compared with other protocols, the NICHD protocol elicits more information and information of greater detail and accuracy. The U.S. Department of Justice's National Institute of Justice funded a study to assess the protocol's usefulness in a real-life situation. Researchers examined 1,280 child sexual abuse cases that were handled by the Salt Lake County, Utah, sheriff's office between 1994 and 2000. According to Harris, 551 of the interviews were conducted before the detectives were trained in the NICHD protocol, and 729 interviews were conducted using the protocol. The results indicate that more cases were accepted for prosecution after the protocol was implemented. In addition, prosecutors obtained a higher percentage of guilty verdicts in cases in which the protocol was used.

Tisha R. Wiley reviews the "best practices" for interviewing child victims of sexual abuse. According to Wiley, a single interview, rather than multiple interviews, is considered best for the child. Research also suggests that open-ended questions should be used as much as possible, to be followed up with specific questions when needed. Leading questions, complex questions, and intimidating techniques should be avoided. On the other hand, other studies have concluded that multiple conversations with child sexual abuse victims can be more effective in helping interviewers create a more accurate and complete report. As Carmit Katz and Irit Hershkowitz note in "Repeated Interviews with Children Who Are the Alleged Victims of Sexual Abuse" (*Research on Social Work Practice*, vol. 23, no. 2, March 2013), research shows that repeated, open-ending questioning can provide investigators with evidence that would otherwise be unattainable in a single interview.

ANATOMICALLY DETAILED DOLLS. Many legal professionals use dolls with sexual organs that are made to represent the human anatomy to help sexually abused children explain what has happened to them in court. Advocates of the use of dolls report that they make it easier to get a child to talk about things that can be difficult to discuss. Lori S. Holmes of CornerHouse in Minneapolis, Minnesota, notes in "Using Anatomical Dolls in Child Sexual Abuse Forensic Interviews" (*American Prosecutors Research Institute Update*, vol. 13, no. 8, 2000) that the use of anatomical dolls helps the child demonstrate internal consistency. A child who has made allegations of abuse can show the interviewer exactly what happened to him or her, thus confirming the oral disclosure. In "Anatomical Dolls: Their Use in Assessment of Children Who May Have Been Sexually Abused" (*Journal of Child Sexual Abuse*, vol. 14, no. 3, 2005), Kathleen Coulborn Faller of the University of Michigan also finds that selective use of the dolls to help children who have trouble speaking about sexual abuse is warranted.

However, potential problems exist in using dolls. According to the affordance phenomenon, children will experiment with any opportunities provided by a new experience. Some experts believe that what might appear to be sexual behavior, such as putting a finger in a hole in the doll, may have no more significance than a child putting a finger through the hole in a doughnut. In addition, some researchers, such as Karen L. Thierry et al. in "Developmental Differences in the Function and Use of Anatomical Dolls during Interviews with Alleged Sexual Abuse Victims" (*Journal of Consulting and Clinical Psychology*, vol. 73, no. 6, December 2005), compare children's verbal details of sexual abuse with their enactments with anatomical dolls and find that children under age six using the dolls often contradict the verbal details provided without the dolls. They also find that children from three to 12 years old produce more fantastic details with the dolls than without them.

THE CONFRONTATION CLAUSE AND HEARSAY

The Sixth Amendment to the U.S. Constitution lays out the rights of people who are accused of crimes: "In all criminal prosecutions, the accused shall enjoy the right to a speedy and public trial, by an impartial jury of the state and district wherein the crime shall have been committed, which district shall have been previously ascertained by law, and to be informed of the nature and cause of the accusation; to be confronted with the witnesses against him; to have compulsory process for obtaining witnesses in his favor, and to have the assistance of counsel for his defense."

The so-called confrontation clause ("to be confronted with the witnesses against him") is a key consideration in the criminal prosecution of child abuse cases. It is particularly difficult for children to deal with the fear and intimidation of testifying in open court with their alleged abuser sitting in the room with them. In the past, live testimony of children in the courtroom was the only choice. However, video technologies developed during the 20th century have introduced new testimony options. They have also raised issues of constitutionality that have been debated by the highest courts in the country.

Testimony by Closed-Circuit Television

Closed-circuit television (CCTV) is a system in which video is transmitted only to specific television monitors. Hence, the system is "closed" or limited to only certain participants. During trials, the use of CCTV allows witnesses to testify live from locations other than the courtroom. One-way CCTV systems only include television monitors in the courtroom, whereas two-way systems also include a television monitor at the witness's location. In other words, in a two-way CCTV setup the witness can see live what is happening in the courtroom.

In 1990 the U.S. Supreme Court upheld in *Maryland v. Craig* (497 U.S. 836) the use of one-way CCTV in a case where a six-year-old child had to testify against her prekindergarten teacher, Sandra Craig, who had been charged with sexual assault and battery. Justice Sandra Day O'Connor (1930–) noted in the majority opinion that the Sixth Amendment confrontation clause does not guarantee an "absolute" right to a face-to-face meeting with the witness. A CCTV system does permit cross-examination and observation of the witness's demeanor by those in the courtroom, including the defendant. Justice O'Connor declared, "We are therefore confident that use of the one-way closed-circuit television procedure, where necessary to further an important state interest, does not impinge upon the truth-seeking or symbolic purposes of the Confrontation Clause."

The National Center for Prosecution of Child Abuse (NCPCA) is a project of the National District Attorneys Association. District attorneys (or prosecutors as they are commonly called) prosecute cases on behalf of the government against defendants who are accused of criminal offenses. The NCPCA summarizes in *Closed-Circuit Televisions Statutes* (August 2012, http://www.ndaa.org/pdf/CCTV%20(2012).pdf) state statutes that deal with the use of CCTV testimony instead of in-court testimony for children. The conditions under which children testify and the age under which they are allowed vary considerably. In some states the jury stays in the courtroom while the child, the judge, the prosecutor, the defendant, and the defense attorney are in a different room, whereas in other states the child is alone in a room separate from the jury and other participants. Some states only allow the youngest children to testify via CCTV.

Hearsay

Another component of the confrontation clause is the issue of hearsay. In legal terminology, hearsay evidence is evidence other than the live testimony in the courtroom of a witness who is swearing to the truth of what he or she saw, heard, or otherwise experienced. As noted earlier, CCTV testimony is not considered hearsay evidence because of the U.S. Supreme Court's decision in *Maryland v. Craig*. However, there are many other kinds of evidence that may be considered hearsay. For example, a statement that a victim made to police, doctors, or other people after being victimized could be considered hearsay evidence if the original recipient of that statement cannot testify in court. Issues related to the admissibility of hearsay evidence are very controversial and have been the subject of many court cases.

Article VIII, Hearsay, of the Federal Rules of Evidence (2014, http://www.law.cornell.edu/rules/fre/rule_802) defines what constitutes hearsay evidence and includes the Rule against Hearsay (i.e., the Hearsay Rule),

which simply states: "Hearsay is not admissible unless any of the following provides otherwise: a federal statute; these rules; or other rules prescribed by the Supreme Court." Hearsay law is constantly evolving and has elicited some confusing opinions from the courts, including the U.S. Supreme Court.

The Hearsay Rule is intended to prevent the conviction of defendants by reports of evidence offered by someone other than a witness. With a few exceptions, hearsay is inadmissible as testimony because the actual witness cannot be cross-examined and his or her demeanor cannot be assessed for credibility of testimony. Some courts consider spontaneous declarations or excited utterances made by a person right after a stressful experience as reliable hearsay. Courts also typically allow statements that individuals have made to physicians and other medical personnel for purposes of medical treatment or diagnosis. In this case it is generally assumed that people who consult with a physician are seeking treatment and, therefore, tell the physician the truth about their illness.

Hearsay Issues in Child Sexual Abuse Cases

Hearsay evidence is especially important in cases of child sexual abuse because these cases may rely on evidence such as videotaped out-of-court testimony and statements by child victims to physicians, parents, counselors, and other adults in the aftermath of an assault. In addition, cases can take years to come to trial, by which time a child may have forgotten the details of the abuse.

Videotaping children's statements is widely practiced in child abuse cases for several reasons. It limits the number of interviews the child must undergo. This is important because recounting abusive events can be highly traumatic. Also, a videotaped statement can be a powerful tool to deal with the problem of a child who recants his or her testimony when put on the witness stand. The case can still be prosecuted, with the jury witnessing the child's opposing statements. Some experts believe that a videotaped statement containing sufficient details from the child and elicited through nonleading questions makes for compelling evidence.

Whether to accept the hearsay evidence from a child's reports of abuse to a parent or other person has been frequently debated as has the constitutionality of videotaped statements by children alleging abuse.

OHIO V. ROBERTS. In *Ohio v. Roberts* (448 U.S. 56 [1980]), a case that was not about child abuse, the U.S. Supreme Court established the basis for permitting hearsay evidence: the actual witness has to be unavailable and his or her statement has to be reliable enough to permit another person to repeat it to the jury. Many judges have chosen to interpret unavailability on physical standards rather than on the emotional unavailability that children who are afraid to testify may exhibit. Furthermore, legal experts insist that the reliability of a statement does not refer to whether the statement appears to be truthful, but only that it has sufficient reliability for the jury to decide whether it is true.

After *Ohio v. Roberts*, many courts decided that spontaneous statements by child abuse victims, especially victims of sexual assault, fulfilled the hearsay requirements. In *White v. Illinois* (502 U.S. 346 [1992]), the Supreme Court found that a four-year-old girl's statements to her babysitter, her mother, a police officer, an emergency department nurse, and a doctor fulfilled the hearsay requirements because they were all either spontaneous declarations or made for medical treatment. In *Bugh v. Mitchell* (329 F.3d 496 [2003]), the U.S. Court of Appeals for the Sixth Circuit ruled that a child's statements to her mother, a counselor, a county social services supervisor, and a doctor about sexual abuse by her father were admissible as hearsay evidence because a three-year-old would have limited ability to lie about the circumstances of an attack. However, in *Carpenter v. State* (786 N.E.2d 696 [2003]) the Indiana Supreme Court decided that out-of-court statements made by a three-year-old who had been sexually assaulted by her father to her mother and grandfather were inadmissible because the state could not establish the precise time of alleged molestation or whether the child's statements occurred immediately after the alleged molestation.

CRAWFORD V. WASHINGTON OVERRULES *OHIO V. ROBERTS*. In *Crawford v. Washington* (541 U.S. 36 [2004]), the U.S. Supreme Court overturned its ruling in *Ohio v. Roberts*. *Crawford v. Washington* concerned an out-of-court tape-recorded statement that a woman had made to police that seemed to implicate her husband in an assault of another man. Prosecutors could not force the woman to testify in court about the statement because most state laws prohibit one spouse from testifying against the other without the other's consent. The trial court found the wife's statement to be reliable and trustworthy and accepted it as evidence. Her husband was subsequently convicted of the crime. During the appeals process the U.S. Supreme Court agreed to hear the case to determine whether the state's use of the wife's statement violated the confrontation clause of the Sixth Amendment.

The U.S. Supreme Court held that when a hearsay statement is "testimonial," the confrontation clause bars the state from using that statement against a criminal defendant unless the person who made the statement is available to testify at trial or the defendant had a previous opportunity to cross-examine that person. The court did not, however, define what it meant by a "testimonial" statement, which precipitated more legal wrangling. In addition, some convictions that had been obtained based on hearsay evidence were overturned, including several

child sexual abuse cases. According to Erin Thompson in "Child Sex Abuse Victims: How Will Their Stories Be Heard after *Crawford v. Washington*?" (*Campbell Law Review*, vol. 27, no. 2, Spring 2005), convictions in *People v. Espinoza* (No. H026266, 204 WL 1560376, at 1 [Cal. App. 6 July 13, 2004]), *People v. Vigil* (104 P.3d 258, 261 [Colo. Ct. App. 2004]), *In the Interest of R.A.S.* (No. 03CA12092004 WL 1351383, at 1 [Colo. App. June 17, 2004]), and *Snowden v. State* (156 Md. App. 139; 846 A.2d 36, 42 [Md. Ct. App. 2004]) were all overturned because the perpetrators had been convicted based on videotaped testimony, with no opportunity for cross-examination of the child witnesses.

In 2006 the U.S. Supreme Court provided some guidance on what does and does not constitute "testimonial" evidence in its decisions in two cases: *Davis v. Washington* (Nos. 05-5224 and 05-5705) and *Hammon v. Indiana* (No. 05-5705). The court refused to provide an exhaustive list of testimonial and nontestimonial statements, but it did note in *Davis v. Washington* that "statements are nontestimonial when made in the course of police interrogation under circumstances objectively indicating that the primary purpose of interrogation is to enable police assistance to meet an ongoing emergency. They are testimonial when the circumstances objectively indicate that there is no such ongoing emergency, and that the primary purpose of the interrogation is to establish or prove past events potentially relevant to later criminal prosecution."

With this guidance, prosecutors have been left with the challenge of trying to ensure that any videotaped victim or witness statements introduced in child sexual abuse trials are either nontestimonial in nature or otherwise exempt from the Hearsay Rule.

STATUTE OF LIMITATIONS AND RECOVERED MEMORY

A statute of limitations is a law that sets the time within which criminal charges or civil claims can be filed and after which a victim loses the right to do so. State laws differ dramatically in their time limits regarding child sexual abuse claims and differentiate between criminal and civil claims. Most states allow delayed commencement dates for the time window during which cases of child sexual abuse can be prosecuted. In these cases, the clock for the statute of limitations does not begin ticking until the child reaches a prescribed age, such as 18 years. This distinction is important because it allows adults who were abused as children to bring cases against their alleged abusers years later.

In "Statutes of Limitation for Prosecution of Offenses against Children" (August 2012, http://www.ndaa.org/pdf/Statute%20of%20Limitations%20for%20Prosecution%20of%20Offenses%20Against%20Children%202012.pdf), the NCPCA summarizes state criminal statutes that deal with statutes of limitation in crimes involving child victims. The provisions can be quite complex and depend on various factors, including the severity of the crime. For example, Maryland has no statute of limitations for felonies, a category into which most sexual offenses would fall. Thus, sexual abuse cases alleged to have occurred many decades ago can still be prosecuted in criminal court.

The National Conference of State Legislatures provides in "State Civil Statutes of Limitations in Child Sexual Abuse Cases" (July 2012, http://www.ncsl.org/issues-research/human-services/state-civil-statutes-of-limitations-in-child-sexua.aspx) a state-by-state listing of civil statutes of limitations that are relevant to child sexual abuse.

Repressed Memory Controversy

States delay the start of their statute of limitations window for cases involving child abuse because the thinking is that adults may have lacked the will to act when they were minors, perhaps out of fear of their abusers or because they did not understand the seriousness and criminal nature of what was being done to them. Increasingly, the courts are being asked to grant exceptions to statute of limitations time ranges by people who claim they were abused as children and then repressed the memories for many years before recovering them. This contention is extremely controversial both within the field of psychology and in the courts.

RESEARCHERS DISAGREE. During the late 1800s the Austrian psychoanalyst Sigmund Freud (1856–1939) first proposed the theory of repression, which hypothesizes that the mind can reject unpleasant ideas, desires, and memories by banishing them into the unconscious. Some clinicians believe that dissociative amnesia, as it is called, can occur through memory repression, thus allowing a victim of a traumatic experience, such as childhood sexual abuse, to forget the horrible incident. Some also believe that forgotten traumatic experiences can be eventually recovered.

Other memory researchers do not agree, explaining that children who have suffered serious psychological trauma do not repress the memory; rather, they can never forget it. They cite examples of survivors of World War II (1939–1945) concentration camps or children who have witnessed the murder of a parent who never forget. Their explanation for recovered memories is that the memories are inaccurate. These researchers point to studies that demonstrate that memory is unreliable and that it can be manipulated to "remember" events that never happened.

In the middle of this controversy are clinicians and memory researchers who believe that the workings of the mind have yet to be fully understood. They agree that, while it is possible for a trauma victim to forget and then remember a horrible experience, it is also possible for a person to have false memories.

COURT FINDINGS. From a legal standpoint, the scientific validity of repressed memory is important because recovered memories may serve as the impetus for an alleged victim's pursuit of criminal and/or civil charges against an accused abuser.

According to Anita Lipton in "Recovered Memories in the Courts" (Sheila Taub, ed., *Recovered Memories of Child Sexual Abuse: Psychological, Social, and Legal Perspectives on a Contemporary Mental Health Controversy*, 1999), between 1983 and 1998 many individuals who had recovered memories of childhood sexual abuse sued their alleged abusers. During those years a total of 589 lawsuits based on repressed memory were filed, of which 506 were civil and 83 were criminal.

In 1991 Paula Hearndon sued her stepfather, Kenneth Graham, for sexually abusing her from 1968 to 1975 (when she was between the ages of eight and 15). According to Hearndon, the "traumatic amnesia" she experienced because of the abuse lasted until 1988. Because of Florida's four-year statute of limitations on felonies, the lawsuit did not proceed. However, in *Hearndon v. Graham* (767 So. 2d 1179, 1184 [2000]), the Florida Supreme Court ruled 5–2 that memory loss resulting from the trauma of childhood sexual abuse should be considered an exception to the statute of limitations. The court, while observing that disagreements about recovered memory exist, stated, "It is widely recognized that the shock and confusion resultant from childhood molestation, often coupled with authoritative adult demands and threats for secrecy, may lead a child to deny or suppress such abuse from his or her consciousness."

The admissibility of child sexual abuse claims based on recovered memories varies by state. For example, the NCPCA cites in "Statutes of Limitation for Prosecution of Offenses against Children" the following statement from the Delaware criminal code: "No prosecution under this subsection shall be based upon the memory of the victim that has been recovered through psychotherapy unless there is some evidence of the corpus delicti [essence of the crime] independent of such repressed memory." By contrast, the NCPCA notes that Kansas law allows extension of its statute of limitations in cases of repressed memory, but only under certain conditions and when "there is substantially competent expert testimony indicating the victim psychologically repressed such witness' memory of the fact of the crime, and in the expert's professional opinion the recall of such memory is accurate and free of undue manipulation, and substantial corroborating evidence can be produced in support of the allegations contained in the complaint or information."

In "Repressed Memories in a Controversial Conviction" (*Journal of the American Academy of Psychiatry and the Law*, vol. 38, no. 4, December 2010), Anthony J. Wolf and Melvin J. Guyer relate a case brought to trial in 2005 in Massachusetts that centered around the recovered memories of a young adult, who testified that he was sexually abused as a boy during the late 1980s by a priest at his church school. The victim said he recovered memories of the abuse after learning that the priest had been accused of sexually abusing children. The victim was part of a successful civil lawsuit against the archdiocese of Boston over the alleged abuse and obtained $500,000 in the settlement. He then pursued criminal charges against the priest, who was convicted in 2005 of two counts of sexual abuse of a child. The defense appealed the case to the Massachusetts Supreme Court, which upheld the conviction in 2010 in *Commonwealth v. Shanley* (455 Mass. 752).

In 2012 the Minnesota Supreme Court sided with a lower court in ruling that a man who claimed to have recovered memories of being abused as a child could not get an extension of the state's statute of limitations. The article "Minnesota Supreme Court Rejects Church Abuse Case Based on Repressed Memories" (Associated Press, July 26, 2012) indicates the plaintiff filed his original claim in 2006, but it was rejected because it was "well outside the state's six-year statute of limitations." According to the article, the higher court agreed with the lower court's finding that "studies claiming to have proven the existence of repressed memory 'lacked foundational reliability.'"

LEGAL PROTECTIONS FOR CHILDREN
Child Pornography

Although the First Amendment protects pornography as an expression of free speech, it does not protect child pornography. Child pornography has been banned since 1982, when the U.S. Supreme Court ruled in *New York v. Ferber* (458 U.S. 747) that pornography depicting children engaged in sexually explicit acts can be banned, whether or not it is obscene, because of the state's interest in protecting children from sexual exploitation. In other words, such images are not protected by the First Amendment.

Since the Supreme Court's decision, federal and state legislators have strived to pass child pornography laws that can withstand constitutional challenges. As of November 2014, several federal laws applied, including 18 USC Chapter 110, Sexual Exploitation and Other Abuse of Children (http://www.law.cornell.edu/uscode/text/18/part-I/chapter-110), and 18 USC Chapter 71, Obscenity, particularly Section 1466A, Obscene Visual Representations of the Sexual Abuse of Children (http://www.law.cornell.edu/uscode/text/18/1466A). Child pornography laws specifically targeting online activities include 47 USC Section 231, Restriction of Access by Minors to Materials Commercially Distributed by Means of World Wide Web That Are Harmful to Minors (http://www.law.cornell.edu/uscode/text/47/231), and 47 USC Section 254, Universal Service (http://www.law.cornell.edu/uscode/text/47/254).

Federal agencies regularly conduct widespread sting operations in which dozens of people are arrested for child pornography offenses. In late 2012 U.S. Immigration and Customs Enforcement led Operation Sunflower, which netted more than 240 alleged perpetrators. Carol Cratty reports in "245 Arrested in U.S.-Led Child Sex Abuse Operation" (CNN.com, January 4, 2013) that authorities identified 123 victims and removed 44 children who were living with accused abusers. Most of the victims (110) lived in the United States, and the vast majority (222) of the people arrested were apprehended in the United States.

Ending the "Incest Exception"

As described in Chapter 4, incest is a crime involving sexual activities between close relatives. Critics claim that in some states people who sexually abuse children receive penalties that are too light because they are prosecuted under incest laws rather than under child sexual abuse laws. Andrew Vachss is an advisory board member of the National Association to Protect Children, a nonprofit organization devoted to child protection issues. In the editorial "The Incest Loophole" (NYTimes.com, November 20, 2005), Vachss notes that incest laws were "founded on biblical prohibitions and intended to prevent the conception of genetically impaired children." In other words, the laws were intended to keep adult close relatives (such as first cousins) from procreating.

Many of these laws have been on the books for more than a century and feature relatively lenient penalties for violations. A problem arises when people accused of sexually abusing biological relatives (such as their own children) are prosecuted under incest laws rather than under much tougher sexual abuse laws. According to the National Association to Protect Children (PROTECT) in "PROTECT Legislative Victories" (2014, http://www.protect.org/victories), the organization has helped eliminate the incest loophole in Arkansas, California, Illinois, North Carolina, and New York. North Carolina's incest law had been on the books since 1879. Under the law, a father who raped his child was found guilty of a minor felony, which was punishable by probation, and an uncle who raped his niece was required to perform 45 days of community service for the misdemeanor offense of incest. Under Arkansas's old incest laws, an adult who raped a child in his or her own family was considered guilty of incest and was either fined or given probation. In Illinois the laws had been deliberately revised in 1981 with a view to keeping families together by imposing a punishment of probation or two years of counseling rather than jail time for incestuous offenders. In 2006 California repealed its incest exception law of 1981, which had allowed judges to grant a sentence of probation to men and women convicted of sexually abusing family members.

Prenatal Drug Exposure

In 1997 the South Carolina Supreme Court held in *Whitner v. South Carolina* (328 S.C. 1, 492 S.E.2d 777) that pregnant women who use drugs can be criminally prosecuted for child maltreatment. The court found that a viable fetus (potentially capable of surviving outside the womb) is a person covered by the state's child abuse and neglect laws. Cornelia Whitner's newborn tested positive for cocaine. She was prosecuted, pled guilty to child neglect, and was sentenced to eight years in prison in 1992. The ruling was appealed to the South Carolina Supreme Court by Whitner. The South Carolina Supreme Court upheld the conviction, which was the first time the highest court of any state upheld the criminal conviction of a woman charged with such an offense.

Whitner's lawyer had argued that if a woman could be prosecuted for child abuse for having used drugs while pregnant, what was to keep the law from prosecuting her for smoking or drinking alcohol or even for failing to obtain prenatal care? Other critics of the law argued that women who are substance abusers and who fear prosecution might not seek prenatal care and counseling for their drug problems, which would further endanger the child.

In another South Carolina case Regina McKnight, a crack cocaine addict, was arrested in 1999 after giving birth to a stillborn infant (dead at birth). In 2001 she was convicted of homicide by child abuse and was sentenced to 12 years in prison. The jury found her guilty of killing a viable fetus, which is considered to be a child under South Carolina law. In January 2003 the South Carolina Supreme Court ruled in *State v. McKnight* (No. 25585)

against McKnight. The court pointed out that the state legislature amended the homicide by child abuse statute in 2000, about three years after the court held in *Whitner v. South Carolina* that the term *child* includes a viable fetus. The court added, "The fact that the legislature was well aware of this Court's opinion in *Whitner*, yet failed to omit 'viable fetus' from the statute's applicability, is persuasive evidence that the legislature did not intend to exempt fetuses from the statute's operation." In October 2003 the U.S. Supreme Court refused to hear McKnight's case.

According to the Children's Bureau in "Parental Drug Use as Child Abuse" (July 2012, https://www .childwelfare.gov/systemwide/laws_policies/statutes/ drugexposed.pdf), the Child Abuse Prevention and Treatment Act of 2010 requires that all states have policies and procedures that ensure that CPS agencies are notified of substance-exposed newborns. In addition, the law requires that all states establish "a plan of safe care" for substance-exposed newborns. The Children's Bureau notes that as of July 2012 at least 19 states and the District of Columbia had substance-exposed-newborns reporting procedures in place. Furthermore, 12 states and the District of Columbia included prenatal substance exposure in their definitions of child abuse and neglect.

Critics complain that subjecting the mothers of newborns to civil and criminal penalties discourages them from seeking treatment for drug and alcohol problems during pregnancy. Jeanne Flavin and Lynn M. Paltrow highlight in "Punishing Pregnant Drug-Using Women: Defying Law, Medicine, and Common Sense" (*Journal of Addictive Diseases*, vol. 29, no. 2, April 2010) the "inherent unfairness of a system that expects low-income and drug-dependent pregnant women to provide their fetuses with the health care and safety that these women themselves are not provided and have not been guaranteed." The researchers surmise that "the arrests, detentions, prosecutions, and other legal actions taken against drug-dependent pregnant women distract attention from significant social problems, such as our lack of universal health care, the dearth of policies to support pregnant and parenting women, the absence of social supports for children, and the overall failure of the drug war."

CHAPTER 6

THE PREVALENCE OF DOMESTIC VIOLENCE

As described in Chapter 1, there is no single legal definition of domestic violence. One factor is the scope of victim-offender relationships that are included in varying definitions. Some analysts count only cases that involve current and former intimate partners (i.e., spouses, girlfriends, and boyfriends), whereas other analysts also include cases that involve violence between relatives (other than spouses) and cases between nonintimate and nonfamily household cohabitants (e.g., roommates). This makes it difficult to compare domestic violence prevalence data that are collected from different studies. Another complication is the definition of violence itself. Some analysts consider only physical acts, such as assaults, as domestic violence incidents, whereas others also count threats. Thus, readers of publications that present domestic violence prevalence data should take note of the definitions and terms that are used by the authors.

Because many domestic violence cases may go unreported, it is impossible to be certain exactly how many cases occur each year. Variations in definitions, the types of questions posed by researchers, and the context in which they are asked compound the difficulty. For example, when victims are questioned in the presence of their abuser or other family members, they may be more reluctant to report instances of violence. Thus, studies on the prevalence of domestic violence can present statistics that differ widely. Many researchers fear that available data represent only a fraction of a problem of much larger proportions.

NATIONAL CRIME VICTIMIZATION SURVEY

The Bureau of Justice Statistics (BJS) is an agency within the U.S. Department of Justice. Since 1972 the BJS has overseen an annual survey called the National Crime Victimization Survey (NCVS), in which the U.S. Census Bureau surveys a nationally representative sample of tens of thousands of households and asks people aged 12 years and older about their experiences within the previous six months of being victimized by certain crimes. The participants are asked both about victimizations they reported and those they did not report to authorities. Only incidents that occurred within the United States are counted. The sample values are used to calculate national victimization estimates using U.S. population data. The survey participants are asked to provide demographic information about themselves, such as their age, sex, race and ethnicity, education level, marital status, and income. The participants reporting victimization incidents are asked for certain details about the events, including information about the offenders.

Each year the BJS publishes the report *Criminal Victimization*, which summarizes the collected data. Other summary reports are occasionally released that examine victimization trends over time for specific types of crimes. In addition, the agency maintains a searchable database of historical NCVS results that can be accessed online using the NCVS Victimization Analysis Tool (NVAT; http://www.bjs.gov/index.cfm?ty=nvat).

Terms and Definitions

Because the NCVS only covers victimizations in which the victims can be interviewed, murders are not included in the data set. In "NCVS Victimization Analysis Tool (NVAT): Definitions" (2014, http://www.bjs.gov/index.cfm?ty=nvat), the BJS notes that violent victimizations include rapes, sexual assaults, personal robberies, and assaults. Specific crimes in these categories are defined by the agency as follows:

- Aggravated assault—an attack or attempted attack with a weapon, regardless of whether the victim is injured, or an attack without a weapon when serious injury results.

- Rape—unlawful penetration of a person against the will of the victim, with use or threatened use of force, or attempting such an act. Includes psychological coercion and physical force. Forced sexual intercourse means vaginal, anal, or oral penetration by the offender. Also includes incidents where penetration is from a foreign object, such as a bottle. Includes male and female victims, and both heterosexual and homosexual rape. Attempted rape includes verbal threats of rape.

- Robbery—the unlawful taking or attempted taking of property that is in the immediate possession of another, by force or threat of force, with or without a weapon, and with or without injury.

- Sexual assault—a wide range of victimizations, separate from rape or attempted rape. These crimes include attacks or attempted attacks generally involving unwanted sexual contact between the victim and the offender. Sexual assaults may or may not involve force and include grabbing or fondling. Sexual assault also includes verbal threats.

- Simple assault—an attack or attempted attack without a weapon that results in either no injury, minor injury (e.g., bruises, black eyes, cuts, scratches, or swelling) or an undetermined injury requiring less than two days of hospitalization.

According to the BJS, neither interviewers nor victims classify victimizations as specific crimes during the interviews. However, the interviewers do ask detailed questions about the nature of each event. A computer program uses the victims' answers to classify the victimizations as particular crimes. For incidents that include more than one crime (e.g., robbery and rape), only the most serious crime is counted using the following hierarchy: rape, sexual assault, robbery, and assault.

The BJS considers domestic violence as violence involving intimate partners or family members. Concerning victim-offender relationships, the following specific terms are used:

- Intimate partners—spouses or ex-spouses, boyfriends or ex-boyfriends, and girlfriends or ex-girlfriends

- Other relatives—parents or stepparents, children or stepchildren, brothers or sisters, and other relatives

Violent Victimizations

In *Criminal Victimization, 2013* (September 2014, http://www.bjs.gov/content/pub/pdf/cv13.pdf), Jennifer Truman and Lynn Langton of the BJS summarize NCVS data for 2013. They note that approximately 160,040 people aged 12 years and older from 90,630 households across the country were interviewed during the survey.

Table 6.1 shows the number of total violent victimizations calculated for 2013 and for 2004 and 2012 based on separate surveys that were conducted in those years.

Overall, Truman and Langton estimate that 6.1 million total violent victimizations occurred in 2013. Of these, 1.1 million (18%) were considered to be domestic violence. Violent intimate partner victimizations numbered 748,800 and accounted for 67% of the domestic violence victimizations and 12% of the total violent victimizations.

The BJS considers rape, sexual assault, robbery, and aggravated assault to be serious violent crimes. In 2012 there were nearly 2.1 million total victimizations involving serious violent crimes; in 2013 the number of victimizations involving serious violent crimes declined to 1.9 million. (See Table 6.1.) However, among serious violent crimes, the number of those victimized by serious domestic violence increased to 464,730 in 2013 from 411,080 in 2012, and serious intimate partner violence victimizations rose to 360,820 in 2013 from 270,240 in 2012. In 2013 nearly four out of five (77%) of the serious domestic violence victimizations were between intimate partners.

Table 6.2 provides a breakdown of victim-offender relationships for NCVS data between 2008 and 2012. Strangers committed the largest number (2.7 million) of violent victimizations in 2012 and made up nearly 40% of the total. Well-known and casual acquaintances followed, with 2.3 million victimizations, or 34% of the total. Overall, the statistics presented in Table 6.2 indicate the following percentages between 2008 and 2012:

- 19% to 24% of total violent victimizations were domestic violence

- 12% to 18% of total violent victimizations involved intimate partners

- 63% to 74% of domestic violence victimizations involved intimate partners

Table 6.3 shows domestic violence rates between 2003 and 2012. During this span, 5.6 out of 1,000 male and female individuals aged 12 years and older were victims of some form of domestic violence. Of these, 3.9 out of 1,000 individuals were involved in a domestic violence incident with an intimate partner; 1.1 out of 1,000 involved an immediate family member, and 0.6 out of 1,000 involved another relative. (See Table 6.3.) Among victims of intimate partner violence, 2.1 out of 1,000 individuals were victimized by a boyfriend or girlfriend, 1.3 out of 1,000 were victimized by a spouse, and 0.5 out of 1,000 were victimized by an ex-spouse.

As presented in Table 6.4, female victims of serious violence are far more likely to be victimized by people they know than by strangers. Between 2003 and 2012, more than one-third (37%) of serious violent crimes involving female victims were domestic violence incidents; more than one-quarter (26.6%) involved an intimate partner. (See Table 6.4.) Overall, nearly two-thirds

TABLE 6.1

Violent victimizations, by crime type, 2004, 2012, and 2013

Type of violent crime	Number			Rate[a]		
	2004	2012	2013	2004	2012	2013
Violent crime[b]	6,726,060	6,842,590	6,126,420	27.8	26.1	23.2‡
Rape/sexual assault	255,770	346,830	300,170	1.1	1.3	1.1
Robbery	616,420	741,760	645,650	2.6	2.8	2.4
Assault	5,853,870	5,754,010	5,180,610	24.2	22.0	19.6
Aggravated assault	1,418,660	996,110	994,220	5.9	3.8	3.8
Simple assault	4,435,220	4,757,900	4,186,390	18.3	18.2	15.8‡
Domestic violence[c]	1,434,190	1,259,390	1,116,090	5.9	4.8	4.2
Intimate partner violence[d]	1,031,720	810,790	748,800	4.3	3.1	2.8
Stranger violence	2,672,240	2,710,110	2,098,170†	11.1	10.3	7.9†
Violent crime involving injury	1,984,920	1,573,460	1,603,960	8.2	6.0	6.1
Serious violent crime[e]	2,290,850	2,084,690	1,940,030	9.5	8.0	7.3
Serious domestic violence[c]	467,240	411,080	464,730	1.9	1.6	1.8
Serious intimate partner violence[d]	334,620	270,240	360,820	1.4	1.0	1.4
Serious stranger violence	966,390	1,020,400	737,940‡	4.0	3.9	2.8‡
Serious violent crime involving weapons	1,650,430	1,415,120	1,174,370	6.8	5.4	4.4
Serious violent crime involving injury	828,620	762,170	739,210	3.4	2.9	2.8

Note: Detail may not sum to total due to rounding. Total population age 12 or older was 241,703,710 in 2004; 261,996,320 in 2012; and 264,411,700 in 2013.
†Significant change from 2012 to 2013 at the 95% confidence level.
‡Significant change from 2012 to 2013 at the 90% confidence level.
[a]Per 1,000 persons age 12 or older.
[b]Excludes homicide because the NCVS is based on interviews with victims and therefore cannot measure murder.
[c]Includes victimization committed by intimate partners and family members.
[d]Includes victimization committed by current or former spouses, boyfriends, or girlfriends.
[e]Includes rape or sexual assault, robbery, and aggravated assault.

SOURCE: Jennifer L. Truman and Lynn Langton, "Table 1. Violent Victimization, by Type of Violent Crime, 2004, 2012, and 2013," in *Criminal Victimization, 2013*, U.S. Department of Justice, Office of Justice Programs, Bureau of Justice Statistics, September 2014, http://www.bjs.gov/content/pub/pdf/cv13.pdf (accessed November 14, 2014)

TABLE 6.2

Violent victimization, by victim-offender relationship, 2008–12

Crime type	2008	2009	2010	2011	2012
Violent victimization	6,393,471	5,669,237	4,935,983	5,812,523	6,842,593
Intimates	1,103,392	1,039,650	773,434	850,772	810,794
Other relatives	454,603	343,020	356,129	504,135	448,598
Well-known/casual acquaintances	1,781,331	1,756,014	1,573,294	1,779,618	2,263,252
Stranger	2,154,770	2,165,849	1,812,303	2,146,307	2,710,114
Do not know relationship	486,084	217,989	288,667	240,956	371,910
Do not know number of offenders	413,292	139,707	132,156	290,736	228,660

Note: Detail may not sum to total due to rounding and/or missing data.

SOURCE: "Number of Violent Victimizations by Victim-Offender Relationship, 2008–2012," in *NCVS Victimization Analysis Tool (NVAT)*, U.S. Department of Justice, Office of Justice Programs, Bureau of Justice Statistics, July 16, 2014, http://www.bjs.gov/index.cfm?ty=nvat (accessed July 16, 2014)

(65%) of female victims of serious violent crimes knew their assailants. By contrast, just over one-third (34.3%) of male victims were attacked by someone they knew.

Between 2003 and 2012, fewer than half (44.6%) of domestic violence victims were injured during a domestic dispute. (See Table 6.5.) This rate was slightly higher among victims of intimate partner violence. As Table 6.5 shows, 48.1% of intimate partner violence victims during this period sustained injuries. Of all domestic violence victims who suffered injuries between 2003 and 2012, more than one-third (36.6%) received medical treatment. (See Table 6.5.)

Of domestic violence incidents that occurred between 2003 and 2012, more than three-quarters (77%) took place at or near the victim's home; another 10.7% occurred at or near the home of a friend, neighbor, or relative, and 12.3% took place at some other location, such as a business, parking lot, school, or open area. (See Table 6.6.) By comparison, only about one out of five (19.7%) violent incidents involving strangers took place at or near the victim's home, and 75% took place at another location. Urban (6.9 per 1,000 population) and rural (6.7 per 1,000) individuals were more likely than those living in the suburbs (4.5 per 1,000) to have been a victim of domestic violence between 2003 and 2012, as shown in Table 6.7, and were more likely for that violence to have been perpetrated by an intimate partner, immediate family member, or acquaintance.

TABLE 6.3

Rates of violent victimization, by degree of violence and victim-offender relationship, 2003–12

Victim-offender relationship	Total violent crime	Serious violent crime[a]	Simple assault
Domestic	5.6	2.0	3.6
Intimate partner[b]	3.9	1.4	2.5
Spouse	1.3	0.5	0.8
Ex-spouse	0.5	0.1	0.4
Boy/girlfriend	2.1	0.8	1.3
Immediate family	1.1	0.4	0.7
Parent	0.3	0.1	0.2
Child	0.4	0.1	0.3
Sibling	0.4	0.1	0.3
Other relative	0.6	0.2	0.4
Well-known/casual acquaintance	8.4	2.3	6.1
Stranger	10.2	3.7	6.5

[a]Includes rape or sexual assault, robbery, and aggravated assault.
[b]Includes current or former spouses, boyfriends, and girlfriends.
Note: Victimization rates are per 1,000 persons age 12 or older. In a small percentage of victimizations, the victim-offender relationship was unknown or the number of offenders was unknown. These estimates are not shown.

SOURCE: Jennifer L. Truman and Rachel E. Morgan, "Table 2. Rate of Violent Victimization, by Victim–Offender Relationship, 2003–2012," in *Nonfatal Domestic Violence, 2003–2012*, U.S. Department of Justice, Office of Justice Programs, Bureau of Justice Statistics, April 2014, http://www.bjs.gov/content/pub/pdf/ndv0312.pdf (accessed July 20, 2014)

TABLE 6.4

Percentage breakdown of violent victimizations, by degree of violence, victim's sex, and victim-offender relationship, 2003–12

Victim-offender relationship	Serious violent crime[a]		Simple assault	
	Male	Female	Male	Female
Total	100%	100%	100%	100%
Known	34.3%	65.0%	43.5%	68.7%
Domestic	10.0	37.0	9.4	33.6
Intimate partner[b]	5.8	26.6	4.5	25.3
Immediate family	2.7	6.5	3.2	5.4
Other relative	1.5	4.0	1.7	3.0
Well-known/casual acquaintance	24.3	28.0	34.1	35.1
Stranger	54.8%	28.6%	46.1%	25.4%
Average annual violent victimizations	1,151,980	1,042,090	2,382,070	2,047,370

[a]Includes rape or sexual assault, robbery, and aggravated assault.
[b]Includes current or former spouses, boyfriends, and girlfriends.
Note: Detail may not sum to total due to rounding. In a small percentage of victimizations, the victim-offender relationship was unknown or the number of offenders was unknown. These estimates are not shown.

SOURCE: Jennifer L. Truman and Rachel E. Morgan, "Table 3. Percent of Violent Victimization, by Victim-Offender Relationship and Victim's Sex, 2003–2012," in *Nonfatal Domestic Violence, 2003–2012*, U.S. Department of Justice, Office of Justice Programs, Bureau of Justice Statistics, April 2014, http://www.bjs.gov/content/pub/pdf/ndv0312.pdf (accessed July 20, 2014)

TABLE 6.5

Violent victimizations resulting in injury and medical treatment, by victim-offender relationship, types of injury, and treatment status, 2003–12

Type of injury and treatment	Domestic violence				Well-known/casual acquaintance	Stranger
	Total	Intimate partner[a]	Immediate family[b]	Other relative		
Injury	100%	100%	100%	100%	100%	100%
Not injured	55.4	51.9	62.6	63.5	78.3	78.7
Injured	44.6	48.1	37.4	36.5	21.7	21.3
Serious injuries[c]	8.9	11.1	4.1	4.2	3.8	4.4
Bruises or cuts	39.6	43.2	32.1	31.3	17.3	17.7
Other injuries	4.1	3.3	7.3	3.1	3.1	2.5
Treatment for injury[d]	100%	100%	100%	100%	100%	100%
No treatment	63.4	66.1	59.1	49.5	63.0	52.6
Any treatment	36.6	33.9	40.6	50.5	37.0	47.4
Treatment setting[e]	100%	100%	100%	100%	100%	100%
At the scene/home of victim, neighbor, or friend/other location	47.0	51.4	46.2	24.3	38.5	39.1
In doctor's office/hospital emergency room/overnight at hospital	53.0	48.6	53.8	75.7	61.5	60.9
Average annual violent victimizations	1,411,330	967,710	284,670	158,950	2,103,240	2,548,860

[a]Includes current or former spouses, boyfriends, and girlfriends.
[b]Includes parents, children, and siblings.
[c]Includes sexual violence injuries, gunshot wounds, knife wounds, internal injuries, unconsciousness, and broken bones.
[d]Includes only victims who were injured.
[e]Includes only victims who were injured and received treatment.
Note: Detail may not sum to total due to rounding. In a small percentage of victimizations, the victim-offender relationship was unknown or the number of offenders was unknown. These estimates are not shown.

SOURCE: Jennifer L. Truman and Rachel E. Morgan, "Table 6. Violent Victimization Resulting in Injury and Medical Treatment, by Victim-Offender Relationship, 2003–2012," in *Nonfatal Domestic Violence, 2003–2012*, U.S. Department of Justice, Office of Justice Programs, Bureau of Justice Statistics, April 2014, http://www.bjs.gov/content/pub/pdf/ndv0312.pdf (accessed July 20, 2014)

WEAPON USE. Table 6.8 provides a breakdown of weapon use during violent victimizations by intimate partners and other relatives between 2008 and 2012. In 2012 no weapon was used in 670,452 violent victimizations by intimate partners. This was 83% of the total 810,794 violent victimizations by intimate partners that

TABLE 6.6

Locations of violent victimizations, by victim-offender relationship, 2003–12

Location of crime	Domestic violence				Well-known/casual acquaintance	Stranger
	Total	Intimate partner[a]	Immediate family[b]	Other relative		
Total	100%	100%	100%	100%	100%	100%
At or near victim's home	77.0	78.6	77.7	66.0	29.5	19.7
At or near friend, neighbor, or relative's home	10.7	8.3	16.2	15.4	9.5	5.3
Other location[c]	12.3	13.1	6.2	18.6	61.0	75.0
Average annual violent victimizations	1,411,330	967,710	284,670	158,950	2,103,240	2,548,860

[a]Includes current or former spouses, boyfriends, and girlfriends.
[b]Includes parents, children, and siblings.
[c]Includes commercial places, parking lots or garages, schools, open areas, public transportation, and other locations.
Note: Detail may not sum to total due to rounding. In a small percentage of victimizations, the victim-offender relationship was unknown or the number of offenders was unknown. These estimates are not shown.

SOURCE: Jennifer L. Truman and Rachel E. Morgan, "Table 10. Location of Violent Victimization, by Victim-Offender Relationship, 2003–2012," in *Nonfatal Domestic Violence, 2003–2012*, U.S. Department of Justice, Office of Justice Programs, Bureau of Justice Statistics, April 2014, http://www.bjs.gov/content/pub/pdf/ndv0312.pdf (accessed July 20, 2014)

TABLE 6.7

Rates of violent victimizations, by setting and victim-offender relationship, 2003–12

Location of residence	Domestic violence				Well-known/casual acquaintance	Stranger
	Total	Intimate partner[a]	Immediate family[b]	Other relative		
Urban	6.9	5.1	1.2	0.6	8.8	14.2
Suburban	4.5	3.0	1.0	0.6	7.8	8.8
Rural	6.7	4.3	1.6	0.8	9.5	7.2

[a]Includes current or former spouses, boyfriends, and girlfriends.
[b]Includes parents, children, and siblings.
Note: Victimization rates are per 1,000 persons age 12 or older. In a small percentage of victimizations the victim-offender relationship was unknown or the number of offenders was unknown. These estimates are not shown.

SOURCE: Jennifer L. Truman and Rachel E. Morgan, "Table 12. Rate of Violent Victimization, by Household Location and Victim-Offender Relationship, 2003–2012," in *Nonfatal Domestic Violence, 2003–2012*, U.S. Department of Justice, Office of Justice Programs, Bureau of Justice Statistics, April 2014, http://www.bjs.gov/content/pub/pdf/ndv0312.pdf (accessed July 20, 2014)

year. A firearm was used in 38,232 of the victimizations, a knife in 34,039 of the victimizations, and another type of weapon in 48,857 of the victimizations. Overall, an identified weapon was used in 121,128 of the victimizations, or 15% of the total victimizations by intimate partners.

Trends in Intimate Partner Violence

As noted earlier, NCVS data indicate that between 2008 and 2012 the majority (63% to 74%) of domestic violence victimizations involved intimate partners. In *Intimate Partner Violence: Attributes of Victimization, 1993–2011* (November 2013, http://www.bjs.gov/content/pub/pdf/ipvav9311.pdf), Shannan Catalano of the BJS uses NCVS data to describe trends between 1993 and 2011 in intimate partner victimizations via rape, sexual assault, robbery, aggravated assault, and simple assault.

Figure 6.1 shows an overall decrease in intimate partner violence between 1994 and 2011. Incidences of simple assault against female victims registered the biggest decline during this span, followed by incidences of

serious violence against female victims. Table 6.9 offers a detailed breakdown of intimate partner violence between 1994 and 2011, by severity of the crime and sex of the victim; the data shown are for victims aged 12 years and older. As Table 6.9 shows, there were nearly 1.8 million female victims of intimate partner violence in 1994, out of a total female population of 109.4 million in that age group. In other words, there were 16.1 female victims of intimate partner violence per 1,000 members of the population that year. By 2011 the number of female victims of intimate partner violence had fallen to 620,850 out of a total population of 131.2 million, or 4.7 out of 1,000 females 12 years of age or older. Although far fewer males become victims of intimate partner violence, the rate of male intimate partner violence victims also fell significantly between 1994 and 2011. Whereas three out of every 1,000 males aged 12 years and older were victims of intimate partner violence in 1994, by 2011 this proportion had fallen to 1.5 out of 1,000. (See Table 6.9.)

Table 6.9 also breaks down intimate partner violence into two categories: serious violence and simple assault, with serious violence includes such crimes as rape or

TABLE 6.8

Violent victimization, by type of violence, weapon use, and victim-offender relationship, 2008–12

Crime type	2008	2009	2010	2011	2012
Violent victimization	**6,393,471**	**5,669,237**	**4,935,983**	**5,812,523**	**6,842,593**
Intimates	**1,103,392**	**1,039,650**	**773,434**	**850,772**	**810,794**
No weapon	721,187	864,594	623,137	680,010	670,452
Firearm	41,643	13,630	75,669	46,837	38,232
Knife	59,099	28,096	48,742	41,367	34,039
Other type weapon	141,428	26,100	9,393	39,969	48,857
Type weapon unknown	5,688	51,658	10,802	13,221	11,468
Do not know if offender had weapon	134,346	55,572	5,691	29,368	7,745
Other relatives	**454,603**	**343,020**	**356,129**	**504,135**	**448,598**
No weapon	391,753	294,983	297,562	438,520	360,261
Firearm	—	3,452	9,709	10,159	—
Knife	24,799	—	15,399	21,521	57,474
Other type weapon	10,906	20,648	20,015	9,918	26,513
Type weapon unknown	19,022	8,207	—	16,248	—
Do not know if offender had weapon	8,123	15,729	13,444	7,768	4,349
Well-known/casual acquaintances	**1,781,331**	**1,756,014**	**1,573,294**	**1,779,618**	**2,263,252**
No weapon	1,438,113	1,263,312	1,273,099	1,465,315	1,842,368
Firearm	52,723	65,562	84,430	95,493	70,810
Knife	102,200	120,132	72,817	85,920	83,082
Other type weapon	101,933	175,022	78,700	75,000	111,054
Type weapon unknown	13,718	26,516	16,866	9,654	35,538
Do not know if offender had weapon	72,643	105,470	47,382	48,236	120,400
Stranger	**2,154,770**	**2,165,849**	**1,812,303**	**2,146,307**	**2,710,114**
No weapon	1,477,892	1,418,400	1,069,015	1,319,518	1,608,556
Firearm	209,133	271,417	203,448	255,404	299,141
Knife	126,299	111,973	105,910	137,625	159,533
Other type weapon	87,179	165,410	180,725	152,224	232,515
Type weapon unknown	22,219	18,570	40,638	26,797	64,764
Do not know if offender had weapon	232,049	180,079	212,565	254,739	345,604
Do not know relationship	**486,084**	**217,989**	**288,667**	**240,956**	**371,910**
No weapon	373,776	118,043	201,207	157,474	282,846
Firearm	38,985	31,407	30,806	44,784	33,875
Knife	17,735	23,631	20,090	6,762	6,424
Other type weapon	31,615	18,497	11,955	9,731	21,316
Type weapon unknown	6,663	10,098	6,084	12,631	6,637
Do not know if offender had weapon	17,311	16,313	18,526	9,575	20,811
Do not know number of offenders	**413,292**	**139,707**	**132,156**	**290,736**	**228,660**
No weapon	353,698	96,317	83,131	176,355	140,186
Firearm	28,805	24,641	10,941	15,250	18,659
Knife	5,608	3,732	—	46,594	—
Other type weapon	3,236	—	11,462	11,143	13,888
Type weapon unknown	6,001	—	2,931	10,168	41,301
Do not know if offender had weapon	15,944	15,017	23,690	31,225	14,626
Rape/sexual assault	**349,691**	**305,574**	**268,574**	**244,188**	**346,830**
Intimates	**103,675**	**43,198**	**109,205**	**44,155**	**64,412**
No weapon	100,299	39,815	63,818	32,818	64,412
Firearm	—	—	43,747	—	—
Knife	—	3,383	1,640	—	—
Other type weapon	—	—	—	2,925	—
Do not know if offender had weapon	3,376	—	—	8,412	—
Other relatives	**24,670**	**34,779**	**12,921**	**1,721**	**3,458**
No weapon	24,670	34,779	12,921	1,721	3,458
Well-known/casual acquaintances	**90,611**	**187,848**	**97,817**	**117,760**	**162,288**
No weapon	75,693	142,724	83,889	104,002	103,856
Firearm	—	—	7,328	—	2,508
Knife	2,732	42,636	2,895	—	12,297
Other type weapon	—	2,488	—	2,891	38,761
Do not know if offender had weapon	12,186	—	3,705	10,866	4,866
Stranger	**76,907**	**36,586**	**43,167**	**72,807**	**59,126**
No weapon	54,279	30,302	25,566	61,719	42,687
Firearm	—	—	3,224	2,609	—
Type weapon unknown	—	—	2,044	—	—
Do not know if offender had weapon	22,628	6,284	12,333	8,478	16,439

sexual assault, aggravated assault, and robbery. As Table 6.9 shows, rates of serious violence among female victims of intimate partner violence fell steadily between 1994, when there were 5.9 victims per 1,000 females 12 years old or older, and 2011, when there were 1.6 victims per 1,000 members of that population. Overall, this figure

TABLE 6.8

Violent victimization, by type of violence, weapon use, and victim-offender relationship, 2008–12 [CONTINUED]

Crime type	2008	2009	2010	2011	2012
Do not know relationship	**9,346**	**3,163**	**5,464**	**4,835**	**17,174**
No weapon	9,346	3,163	—	4,835	11,028
Firearm	—	—	2,073	—	—
Knife	—	—	—	—	3,317
Type weapon unknown	—	—	3,391	—	—
Do not know if offender had weapon	—	—	—	—	2,829
Do not know number of offenders	**44,483**	**—**	**—**	**2,911**	**40,372**
No weapon	44,483	—	—	2,911	2,154
Type weapon unknown	—	—	—	—	38,218
Robbery	**679,789**	**635,073**	**568,510**	**557,258**	**741,756**
Intimates	**66,750**	**49,507**	**58,642**	**56,876**	**80,712**
No weapon	29,558	43,055	43,983	37,128	58,621
Firearm	—	—	4,366	3,657	15,106
Knife	37,193	—	2,584	6,781	6,985
Other type weapon	—	3,104	2,113	—	—
Type weapon unknown	—	3,347	2,710	1,482	—
Do not know if offender had weapon	—	—	2,886	7,829	—
Other relatives	**107,356**	**40,128**	**42,107**	**57,801**	**44,386**
No weapon	104,178	24,561	37,028	40,351	44,386
Firearm	—	3,452	1,900	—	—
Other type weapon	—	8,672	—	—	—
Type weapon unknown	3,178	3,443	—	14,836	—
Do not know if offender had weapon	—	—	3,179	2,615	—
Well-known/casual acquaintances	**100,330**	**130,447**	**117,023**	**105,243**	**94,606**
No weapon	58,259	88,150	75,593	61,082	30,824
Firearm	6,518	30,668	2,874	5,666	25,954
Knife	11,288	3,765	38,555	23,617	4,720
Other type weapon	12,695	7,864	—	4,169	21,147
Do not know if offender had weapon	11,570	—	—	10,708	11,961
Stranger	**321,487**	**328,691**	**310,096**	**266,911**	**451,631**
No weapon	126,369	155,822	82,824	79,642	118,461
Firearm	102,497	101,212	117,978	91,629	145,598
Knife	39,960	34,822	35,199	24,693	76,111
Other type weapon	7,189	17,614	8,088	11,914	26,637
Type weapon unknown	4,066	4,677	10,583	3,656	14,683
Do not know if offender had weapon	41,407	14,545	55,424	55,377	70,141
Do not know relationship	**62,085**	**58,587**	**40,642**	**58,156**	**47,842**
No weapon	34,158	15,980	6,622	16,042	13,440
Firearm	17,749	17,456	13,521	32,832	22,158
Knife	6,513	8,477	10,477	2,098	—
Other type weapon	—	4,144	—	—	5,079
Type weapon unknown	—	—	—	2,165	—
Do not know if offender had weapon	3,665	12,530	10,021	5,019	7,166
Do not know number of offenders	**21,780**	**27,714**	**—**	**12,271**	**22,578**
No weapon	15,269	2,978	—	—	10,902
Firearm	6,511	18,804	—	9,335	9,273
Knife	—	3,732	—	2,935	—
Other type weapon	—	—	—	—	2,403
Do not know if offender had weapon	—	2,199	—	—	—
Aggravated assault	**969,216**	**1,029,273**	**857,751**	**1,053,391**	**996,106**
Intimates	**227,880**	**157,771**	**100,933**	**161,627**	**125,115**
No weapon	17,215	48,120	13,488	35,078	14,610
Firearm	41,643	13,630	27,555	43,180	23,126
Knife	21,906	24,713	44,518	34,586	27,054
Other type weapon	141,428	22,996	7,281	37,044	48,857
Type weapon unknown	5,688	48,311	8,091	11,739	11,468
Other relatives	**53,715**	**19,853**	**56,223**	**46,858**	**92,992**
No weapon	2,166	3,112	13,000	3,847	9,005
Firearm	—	—	7,809	10,159	—
Knife	24,799	—	15,399	21,521	57,474
Other type weapon	10,906	11,976	20,015	9,918	26,513
Type weapon unknown	15,844	4,764	—	1,412	—

represents a decrease of nearly 370% over an 18-year period. For male intimate partner violence victims aged 12 years and older, the rate of serious violence also fell, from 1.1 per 1,000 individuals to 0.4 per 1,000. Among victims of both sexes, the rate of serious violence among victims of intimate partner violence aged 12 years and older fell from 3.6 per 1,000 individuals in 1993 to one per 1,000 in 2012. (See Figure 6.2.) Rates of simple

TABLE 6.8

Violent victimization, by type of violence, weapon use, and victim-offender relationship, 2008–12 [CONTINUED]

Crime type	2008	2009	2010	2011	2012
Well-known/casual acquaintances	**254,071**	**329,992**	**247,312**	**260,667**	**203,087**
No weapon	16,730	30,181	42,396	30,943	7,990
Firearm	46,205	34,894	74,229	89,827	42,348
Knife	88,179	73,732	31,367	62,303	66,064
Other type weapon	89,239	164,669	78,700	67,940	51,146
Type weapon unknown	13,718	26,516	16,866	9,654	35,538
Do not know if offender had weapon	—	—	3,755		
Stranger	**310,708**	**456,257**	**368,408**	**464,043**	**509,640**
No weapon	11,367	39,310	10,919	22,056	16,716
Firearm	106,637	170,205	82,246	161,165	153,543
Knife	86,339	77,151	70,712	112,932	83,422
Other type weapon	79,990	147,796	172,637	140,310	205,878
Type weapon unknown	18,152	13,893	28,011	23,141	50,081
Do not know if offender had weapon	8,223	7,902	3,883	4,439	—
Do not know relationship	**85,704**	**59,565**	**47,670**	**49,311**	**41,317**
No weapon	14,969	6,009	4,418	12,499	3,618
Firearm	21,236	13,951	15,211	11,952	11,717
Knife	11,222	15,154	9,612	4,664	3,107
No weapon	31,615	14,353	11,955	9,731	16,238
Type weapon unknown	6,663	10,098	2,693	10,466	6,637
Do not know if offender had weapon	—	—	3,781	—	
Do not know number of offenders	**37,138**	**5,836**	**37,205**	**70,886**	**23,954**
No weapon	—	—	3,166	—	—
Firearm	22,294	5,836	10,941	5,915	9,387
Knife	5,608	—	—	43,659	—
Other type weapon	3,236		11,462	11,143	11,485
Type weapon unknown	6,001	—	2,931	10,168	3,083
Do not know if offender had weapon	—	—	8,704	—	—
Simple assault	**4,394,774**	**3,699,316**	**3,241,148**	**3,957,686**	**4,757,902**
Intimates	**705,086**	**789,175**	**504,654**	**588,113**	**540,555**
No weapon	574,115	733,603	501,848	574,986	532,809
Do not know if offender had weapon	130,970	55,572	2,805	13,127	7,745
Other relatives	**268,862**	**248,260**	**244,878**	**397,755**	**307,761**
No weapon	260,739	232,531	234,613	392,602	303,412
Do not know if offender had weapon	8,123	15,729	10,265	5,154	4,349
Well-known/casual acquaintances	**1,336,318**	**1,107,727**	**1,111,143**	**1,295,949**	**1,803,271**
No weapon	1,287,430	1,002,257	1,071,221	1,269,288	1,699,697
Do not know if offender had weapon	48,888	105,470	39,922	26,661	103,573
Stranger	**1,445,668**	**1,344,315**	**1,090,632**	**1,342,546**	**1,689,717**
No weapon	1,285,877	1,192,967	949,707	1,156,100	1,430,693
Do not know if offender had weapon	159,791	151,348	140,925	186,445	259,024
Do not know relationship	**328,949**	**96,674**	**194,890**	**128,654**	**265,577**
No weapon	315,304	92,891	190,167	124,099	254,761
Do not know if offender had weapon	13,646	3,783	4,724	4,556	10,817
Do not know number of offenders	**309,891**	**106,156**	**94,952**	**204,669**	**141,756**
No weapon	293,947	93,338	79,965	173,444	127,130
Do not know if offender had weapon	15,944	12,818	14,986	31,225	14,626

—Estimate is equal to 0 sample cases.
Note: Detail may not sum to total due to rounding and/or missing data.

SOURCE: "Number of Violent Victimizations, Rape/Sexual Assaults, Robberies, Aggravated Assaults, and Simple Assaults by Victim-Offender Relationship and Weapon Category, 2008–2012," in *NCVS Victimization Analysis Tool (NVAT)*, U.S. Department of Justice, Office of Justice Programs, Bureau of Justice Statistics, July 16, 2014, http://www.bjs.gov/index.cfm?ty=nvat (accessed July 16, 2014).

assault among victims of intimate partner violence also fell during this span, from 6.2 per 1,000 individuals in 1993 to 2.2 per 1,000 in 2012. (See Figure 6.3.)

While the rate of serious incidents involving intimate partner violence clearly declined between 1994 and 2011, the proportion of intimate partner violence incidents that were categorized as acts of serious violence remained roughly constant. Table 6.10 provides an overview of female victims of intimate partner violence between 1994 and 2011. As Table 6.10 shows, the proportion of female intimate partner violence victims who were victims of serious violence fluctuated between 27.5% and 42% during this span. In 2011 more than one-third (34.8%) of female intimate partner violence victims suffered some act of serious violence.

FOCUS ON FEMALE VICTIMS. Between 2002 and 2011, two-thirds (66.6%) of female intimate partner violence victims were physically attacked by the offender; a comparable

FIGURE 6.1

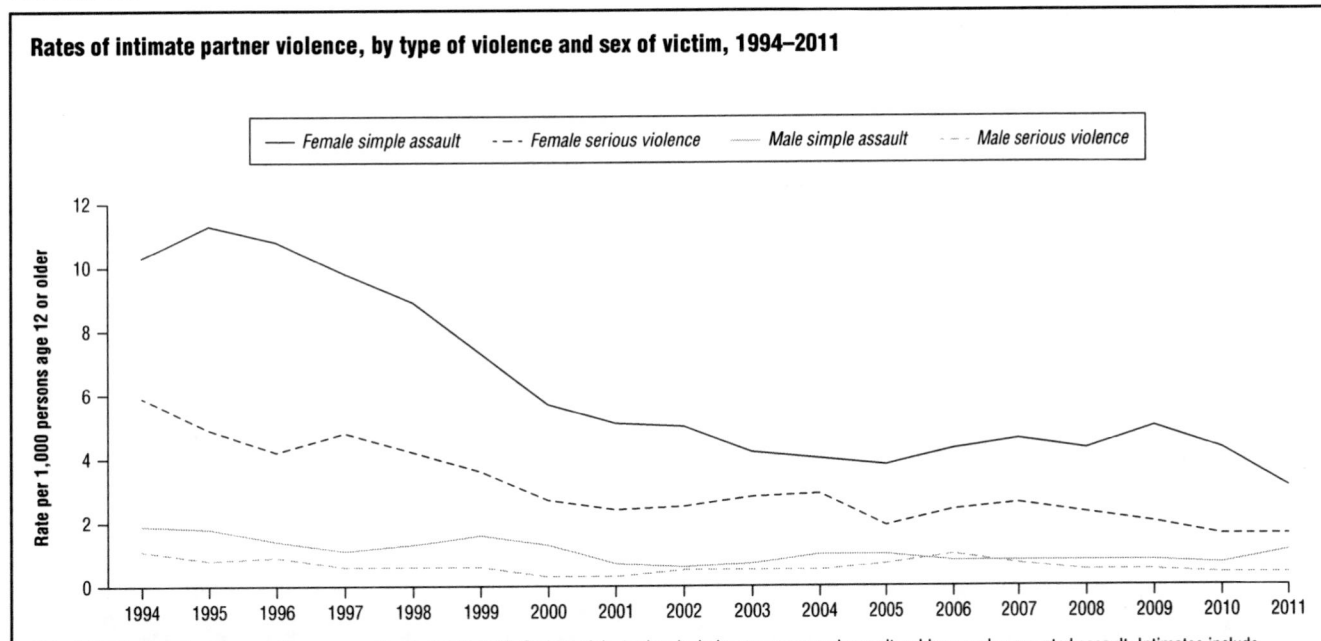

Rates of intimate partner violence, by type of violence and sex of victim, 1994–2011

— Female simple assault · · · Female serious violence — Male simple assault · · · Male serious violence

Note: Estimates based on 2-year rolling averages beginning in 1993. Serious violent crime includes rape or sexual assault, robbery, and aggravated assault. Intimates include current or former spouses, boyfriends, and girlfriends.

SOURCE: Shannan Catalano, "Figure 1. Rate of Intimate Partner Violence, by Victim's Sex, 1994–2011," in *Intimate Partner Violence: Attributes of Victimization, 1993–2011*, U.S. Department of Justice, Office of Justice Programs, Bureau of Justice Statistics, November 2013, http://www.bjs.gov/content/pub/pdf/ipvav9311.pdf (accessed July 16, 2014)

TABLE 6.9

Intimate partner violence, by sex of victim, 1993–2011

| | | | Female | | | | | | Male | | |
| | | | | Rate* | | | | | | Rate* | |
Year	Population	Total intimate partner violence	Overall	Serious violence	Simple assault	Population	Total intimate partner violence	Overall	Serious violence	Simple assault
1994	109,437,100	1,766,700	16.1	5.9	10.3	102,584,300	303,460	3.0	1.1	1.9
1995	110,590,240	1,785,590	16.1	4.9	11.3	103,518,050	272,450	2.6	0.8	1.8
1996	111,660,070	1,676,990	15.0	4.2	10.8	104,497,420	240,280	2.3	0.9	1.4
1997	112,710,280	1,644,100	14.6	4.8	9.8	105,826,410	185,650	1.8	0.6	1.1
1998	113,762,940	1,499,130	13.2	4.2	8.9	107,097,100	202,720	1.9	0.6	1.3
1999	115,100,630	1,250,570	10.9	3.6	7.3	108,124,040	229,510	2.1	0.6	1.6
2000	116,451,730	974,160	8.4	2.7	5.7	109,234,760	173,190	1.6	0.3	1.3
2001	117,564,090	882,720	7.5	2.4	5.1	110,445,860	112,450	1.0	0.3	0.7
2002	118,743,930	889,740	7.5	2.5	5.0	111,658,350	120,350	1.1	0.5	0.6
2003	121,306,110	852,220	7.0	2.8	4.2	114,141,510	132,810	1.2	0.5	0.7
2004	123,740,880	861,380	7.0	2.9	4.0	116,763,970	174,620	1.5	0.5	1.0
2005	124,886,860	718,590	5.8	1.9	3.8	118,217,640	205,270	1.7	0.7	1.0
2006	126,162,070	842,410	6.7	2.4	4.3	119,707,120	218,220	1.8	1.0	0.8
2007	127,494,730	922,380	7.2	2.6	4.6	121,294,250	183,150	1.5	0.7	0.8
2008	128,696,840	847,700	6.6	2.3	4.3	122,596,860	156,900	1.3	0.5	0.8
2009	129,617,960	914,480	7.1	2.0	5.0	123,556,100	157,050	1.3	0.5	0.8
2010	130,519,420	775,650	5.9	1.6	4.3	124,514,350	130,890	1.1	0.4	0.7
2011	131,212,660	620,850	4.7	1.6	3.1	125,539,420	191,540	1.5	0.4	1.1

*Rates calculated per 1,000 persons age 12 or older.
Note: Estimates based on 2-year rolling averages beginning in 1993. Serious violent crime includes rape or sexual assault, robbery, and aggravated assault. Intimates include current or former spouses, boyfriends, and girlfriends.

SOURCE: Shannan Catalano, "Appendix Table 1. Number and Rate of Intimate Partner Violence, by Victim's Sex, 1993–2011," in *Intimate Partner Violence: Attributes of Victimization, 1993–2011*, U.S. Department of Justice, Office of Justice Programs, Bureau of Justice Statistics, November 2013, http://www.bjs.gov/content/pub/pdf/ipvav9311.pdf (accessed July 16, 2014)

proportion of male intimate partner violence victims (64.6%) also suffered physical attacks during this span. (See Table 6.11.) Female victims of intimate partner vio-lence were far more likely to be threatened prior to a physical attack. As Table 6.11 shows, more than half (51.8%) of female victims were threatened before being

FIGURE 6.2

Rates of serious domestic violence, by victim-offender relationship, 1993–2012

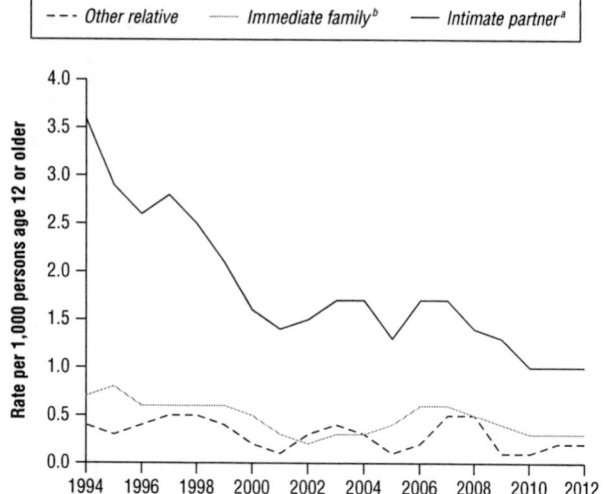

Note: Serious violent crime includes rape or sexual assault, robbery, and aggravated assault. Data are based on 2-year rolling averages beginning in 1993.
[a]Includes current or former spouses, boyfriends, and girlfriends.
[b]Includes parents, children, and siblings.

SOURCE: Jennifer L. Truman and Rachel E. Morgan, "Figure 3. Rate of Serious Domestic Violence, by Victim–Offender Relationship, 1993–2012," in *Nonfatal Domestic Violence, 2003–2012*, U.S. Department of Justice, Office of Justice Programs, Bureau of Justice Statistics, April 2014, http://www.bjs.gov/content/pub/pdf/ndv0312.pdf (accessed July 20, 2014)

FIGURE 6.3

Rates of simple assault domestic violence, by victim-offender relationship, 1993–2012

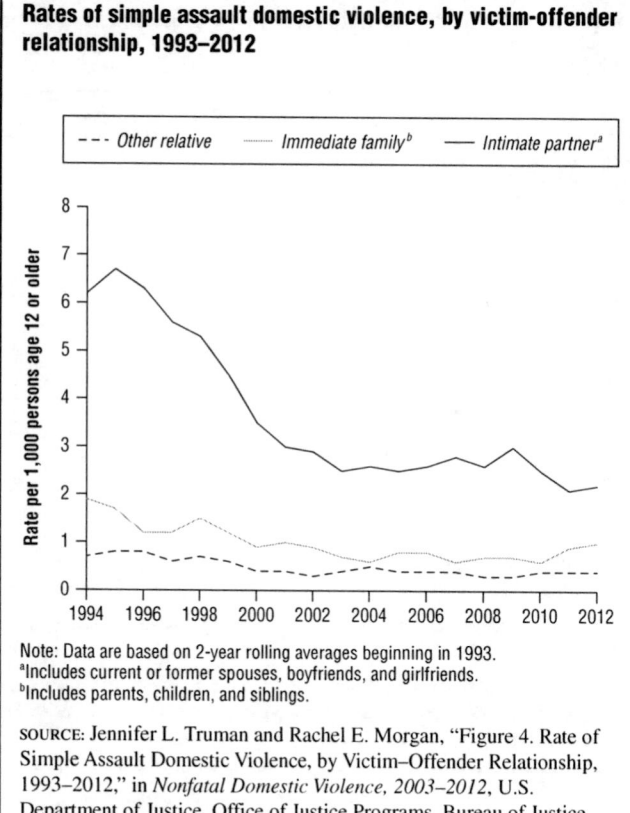

Note: Data are based on 2-year rolling averages beginning in 1993.
[a]Includes current or former spouses, boyfriends, and girlfriends.
[b]Includes parents, children, and siblings.

SOURCE: Jennifer L. Truman and Rachel E. Morgan, "Figure 4. Rate of Simple Assault Domestic Violence, by Victim–Offender Relationship, 1993–2012," in *Nonfatal Domestic Violence, 2003–2012*, U.S. Department of Justice, Office of Justice Programs, Bureau of Justice Statistics, April 2014, http://www.bjs.gov/content/pub/pdf/ndv0312.pdf (accessed July 20, 2014)

TABLE 6.10

Female victims of serious intimate partner violence, 1993–2011

Year	Total intimate partner violence	Percent Total	Percent Serious violence	Percent Simple assault
1994	1,766,700	100%	36.3	63.7
1995	1,785,590	100%	30.2	69.8
1996	1,676,990	100%	28.1	71.9
1997	1,644,100	100%	32.7	67.3
1998	1,499,130	100%	32.1	67.9
1999	1,250,570	100%	33.0	67.0
2000	974,160	100%	32.4	67.6
2001	882,720	100%	32.3	67.7
2002	889,740	100%	33.2	66.8
2003	852,220	100%	40.1	59.9
2004	861,380	100%	42.0	58.0
2005	718,590	100%	33.5	66.5
2006	842,410	100%	35.7	64.3
2007	922,380	100%	36.0	64.0
2008	847,700	100%	34.3	65.7
2009	914,480	100%	28.8	71.2
2010	775,650	100%	27.5	72.5
2011	620,850	100%	34.8	65.2

Note: Estimates based on 2-year rolling averages beginning in 1993. Serious violent crime includes rape or sexual assault, robbery, and aggravated assault. Intimates include current or former spouses, boyfriends, and girlfriends.

SOURCE: Shannan Catalano, "Appendix Table 3. Serious Intimate Partner Violence against Females, 1993–2011," in *Intimate Partner Violence: Attributes of Victimization, 1993–2011*, U.S. Department of Justice, Office of Justice Programs, Bureau of Justice Statistics, November 2013, http://www.bjs.gov/content/pub/pdf/ipvav9311.pdf (accessed July 22, 2014)

attacked by an intimate partner. By comparison, fewer than one-third (31.4%) of male victims of intimate partner violence were threatened prior to being physically attacked. In general, there is a strong correlation between being threatened and being physically attacked for female victims of intimate partner violence. As Figure 6.4 shows, between 1994 and 2011 the percentage of female intimate partner violence victims who were physically attacked ranged from 60% to 72%, and the proportion of female victims who were threatened prior to a physical attack ranged between 39% and 63%.

Table 6.11 also provides an overview of the types of physical attacks suffered by victims of intimate partner violence. Of the female victims of intimate partner violence who were physically attacked, 44.6% were struck, slapped, or knocked down; 36.1% were held, pushed, grabbed, tripped, or jumped; and 8.2% were sexually assaulted. Among male intimate partner violence victims who were physically attacked, 43.3% were hit, slapped, or knocked down, and 19.3% were struck by some sort of object. Less than 1% of male intimate partner violence victims who suffered physical attacks were sexually assaulted by their partner. As Table 6.12 shows, between 2002 and 2011 male victims of intimate

TABLE 6.11

Types of physical attacks against victims of violent victimization, by victim's sex and victim-offender relationship, 2002–11

	Female		Male	
	Intimate[a]	Nonintimate[b]	Intimate[a]	Nonintimate[b]
Victim was physically attacked	66.6%	40.3%	64.6%	40.1%
Offender threatened victim before attacking[c]	51.8%	33.6%	31.4%	39.4%
Type of attack				
Sexual violence	8.2%	5.3%	0.9%	0.2%
Shot at, stabbed, or hit with weapon	3.8	1.6	8.2	2.9
Hit by object held in hand or thrown	5.4	4.3	19.3	4.5
Hit, slapped, or knocked down	44.6	21.1	43.3	25.7
Grabbed, held, tripped, jumped, or pushed	36.1	16.5	14	15.1
Other type of attack	6.1	2.4	6.3	2.8
Average annual violent victimizations	805,700	2,336,830	173,960	3,365,420

[a]Includes former or current spouses, boyfriends, and girlfriends.
[b]Includes relatives, friends, neighbors, acquaintances, and strangers.
[c]Victims who were physically attacked were subsequently asked if the offender threatened them prior to the attack.
Note: Violent victimization includes rape, sexual assault, robbery, aggravated assault, and simple assault. Percentages for type of attack sum to more than the percentage of victims who were attacked because victims were able to select more than one response. Estimates include 3.4% to 9.7% missing data on whether the offender threatened the victim before attacking.

SOURCE: Shannan Catalano, "Table 3. Type of Physical Attack in Violent Victimization, by Victim's Sex and Victim-Offender Relationship, 2002–2011," in *Intimate Partner Violence: Attributes of Victimization, 1993–2011*, U.S. Department of Justice, Office of Justice Programs, Bureau of Justice Statistics, November 2013, http://www.bjs.gov/content/pub/pdf/ipvav9311.pdf (accessed July 22, 2014)

FIGURE 6.4

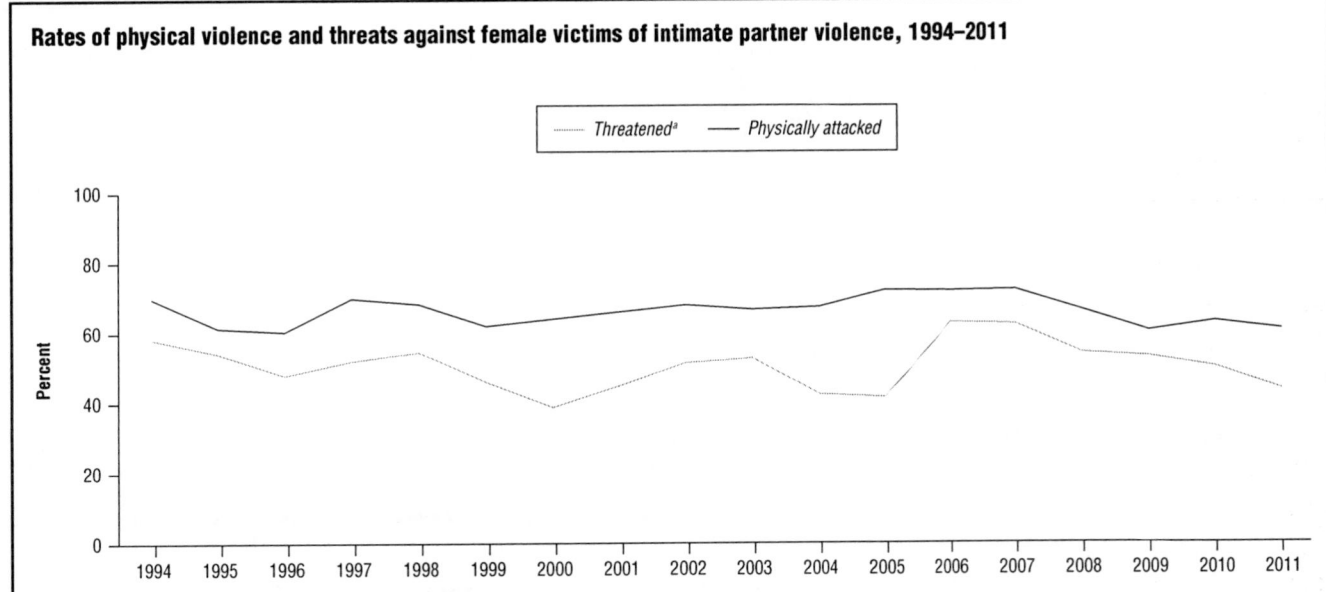

Rates of physical violence and threats against female victims of intimate partner violence, 1994–2011

[a]Victims who were physically attacked were subsequently asked if the offender threatened them prior to the attack.
Note: Estimates based on 2-year rolling averages beginning in 1993. Intimate partner violence includes rape or sexual assault, robbery, aggravated assault, and simple assault committed by current or former spouses, boyfriends, and girlfriends.

SOURCE: Shannan Catalano, "Figure 4. Physical Attacks and Threats in Intimate Partner Violence against Females, 1994–2011," in *Intimate Partner Violence: Attributes of Victimization, 1993–2011*, U.S. Department of Justice, Office of Justice Programs, Bureau of Justice Statistics, November 2013, http://www.bjs.gov/content/pub/pdf/ipvav9311.pdf (accessed July 22, 2014)

partner violence (27%) were considerably more likely than female intimate partner violence victims (17.6%) to be victimized in a way that involved some sort of weapon.

In intimate partner violence situations, female victims are more likely than male victims to suffer physical injury. As Table 6.13 shows, between 2002 and 2011 roughly half (49.7%) of female victims of intimate partner violence sustained injuries after being attacked; among male victims, 43.5% suffered injuries during this same period. Between 1994 and 2011 the proportion of female intimate partner violence victims who suffered injuries peaked between 2006 and 2007, when 60% of all female victims were physically injured. (See Figure 6.5.) This rate fell in subsequent years, dropping to 42% in 2011.

TABLE 6.12

Presence of weapons in violent victimizations, by victim's sex and victim-offender relationship, 2002–11

| | Female | | Male | |
	Intimate[a]	Nonintimate[b]	Intimate[a]	Nonintimate[b]
Total	**100%**	**100%**	**100%**	**100%**
No weapon	78.0%	72.7%	71.5%	67.6%
Any weapon	17.6%	20.0%	27.0%	24.4%
Firearm	4.7	6.6	0.8	8.5
Knife	6.2	5.6	11.1	6.6
Other weapon[c]	6.7	7.7	15.1	9.3
Did not know if offender had weapon	4.3%	7.3%	1.6%	8.0%
Average annual violent victimizations	805,700	2,336,830	173,960	3,365,420

[a]Includes former or current spouses, boyfriends, and girlfriends.
[b]Includes relatives, friends, neighbors, acquaintances, and strangers.
[c]Includes broken bottles, cookware, household objects, and unknown weapon types.
Note: Violent victimization includes rape or sexual assault, robbery, aggravated assault, and simple assault.

SOURCE: Shannan Catalano, "Table 4. Presence of Weapons, by Victim's Sex and Victim-Offender Relationship, 2002–2011," in *Intimate Partner Violence: Attributes of Victimization, 1993–2011*, U.S. Department of Justice, Office of Justice Programs, Bureau of Justice Statistics, November 2013, http://www.bjs.gov/content/pub/pdf/ipvav9311.pdf (accessed July 22, 2014).

TABLE 6.13

Types of physical injuries sustained by victims of violent victimization, by sex and victim-offender relationship, 2002–11

| | Female | | Male | |
	Intimate[a]	Nonintimate[b]	Intimate[a]	Nonintimate[b]
Total	**100%**	**100%**	**100%**	**100%**
No injury	50.3%	76.0%	56.5%	78.4%
Any injury	49.7%	24.0%	43.5%	21.6%
Serious injury	13.0	5.0	5.4	3.9
Sexual violence[c]	6.6	2.8	0.7	0.2
Gun shot, knife wounds	1.1	0.4	1.9	1.0
Internal injuries, unconciousness, broken bones	5.3	1.7	2.8	2.7
Bruises, cuts, or other injuries	45.7	20.9	40.7	19.8
Average annual violent victimizations	805,700	2,336,830	173,960	3,365,420

[a]Includes former or current spouses, boyfriends, or girlfriends.
[b]Includes relatives, friends, neighbors, acquaintances, and strangers.
[c]Sexual violence injuries includes rape, attempted rape, and sexual assault injuries.
Note: Violent victimization includes rape or sexual assault, robbery, aggravated assault, and simple assault. Percentages for type of injury sum to more than the percentage of victims injured because victims were able to select more than one response. Estimates include missing data ranging from 0.1% to 0.4% of injuries.

SOURCE: Shannan Catalano, "Table 5. Physical Injury, by Victim's Sex and Victim-Offender Relationship, 2002–2011," in *Intimate Partner Violence: Attributes of Victimization, 1993–2011*, U.S. Department of Justice, Office of Justice Programs, Bureau of Justice Statistics, November 2013, http://www.bjs.gov/content/pub/pdf/ipvav9311.pdf (accessed July 22, 2014).

Of the female victims who sustained physical injuries as a result of intimate partner violence between 2002 and 2011, nearly half (45.7%) suffered cuts, bruises, or other injuries; 13% suffered serious injuries as a result of a physical attack. (See Table 6.14.) As Table 6.14 shows, between 2002 and 2011 nearly one in five (18.2%) female victims of intimate partner violence received medical attention for injuries sustained in a physical attack; 8.2% received treatment at a hospital. By comparison, one in 10 (10.8%) male victims of intimate partner violence received treatment for injuries during that span, with 4.4% receiving hospital care. Between 1994 and 2011, the proportion of female intimate partner victims who received medical treatment following an attack reached a high point in 2003, when more than a quarter (27%) received medical attention for their injuries. (See Figure 6.6.)

The *NSCAW II Wave 3 Report: Wave 3 Tables* (June 2014, http://www.acf.hhs.gov/sites/default/files/opre/nscaw_wave_3_tables_june_2014_clean.pdf) is part of the second *National Survey of Child and Adolescent Well-Being (NSCAW-II)*, a longitudinal study created by the Office of Planning, Research, and Evaluation, a division of the Administration for Children and Families. The NSCAW-II is designed to provide a comprehensive analysis of the efficacy and impact of the child welfare system. As Cecilia Casanueva et al. report in *NSCAW II Wave 3 Report: Wave 3 Tables*, children who have become involved with the child welfare system often come from homes where domestic violence is prevalent. Table 6.15 provides an overview of NSCAW participants whose mothers demonstrated a need for domestic violence services between June 2011 and

FIGURE 6.5

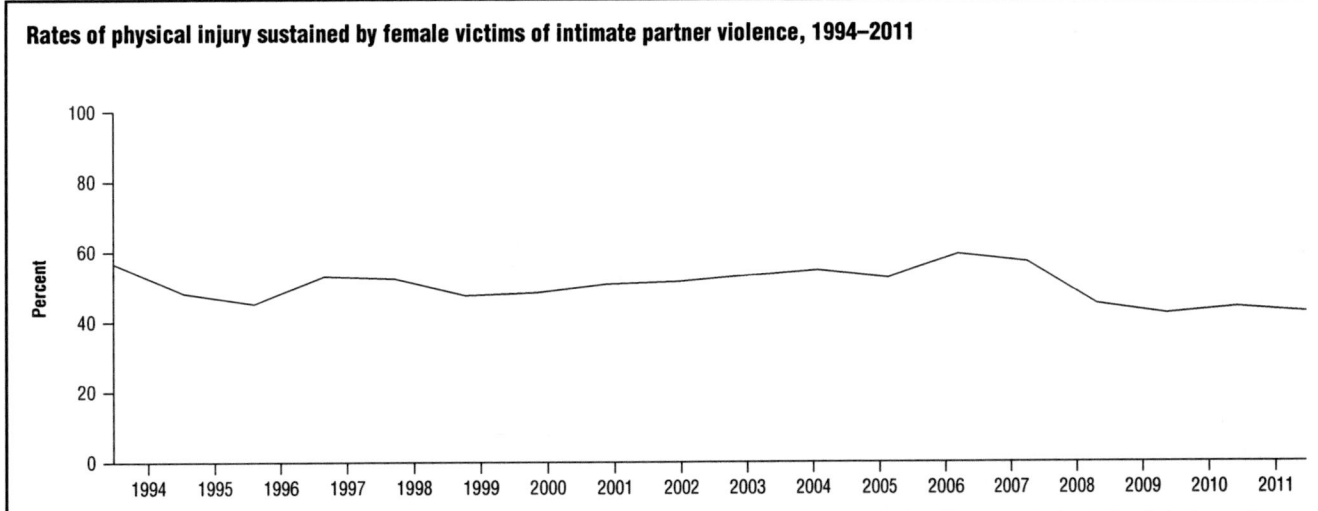

Rates of physical injury sustained by female victims of intimate partner violence, 1994–2011

Note: Estimates based on 2-year rolling averages beginning in 1993. Intimate partner violence includes rape or sexual assault, robbery, aggravated assault, and simple assault committed by current or former spouses, boyfriends, and girlfriends. Estimates include missing data on injuries ranging from 0.1% to 0.4%.

SOURCE: Shannan Catalano, "Figure 5. Physical Injury in Intimate Partner Violence against Females, 1994–2011," in *Intimate Partner Violence: Attributes of Victimization, 1993–2011*, U.S. Department of Justice, Office of Justice Programs, Bureau of Justice Statistics, November 2013, http://www.bjs.gov/content/pub/pdf/ipvav9311.pdf (accessed July 22, 2014).

TABLE 6.14

Medical treatment received by victims of violent victimization, by sex, victim-offender relationship, and site of treatment, 2002–11

	Female		Male	
	Intimate[a]	Nonintimate[b]	Intimate[a]	Nonintimate[b]
Total violent victimizations resulting in injury	49.7%	23.8%	43.5%	21.5%
No treatment	31.6%	14.0%	32.7%	12.0%
Any treatment	18.2%	9.8%	10.8%	9.6%
At scene, home, neighbor's or friend's house	8.3	3.5	6.1	3.4
Medical office, clinic, or health unit	1.5	1.9	0.2	1.1
Hospital setting	8.2	4.2	4.4	4.9
Another location	0.1	0.2	0.1	0.2
Average annual violent victimizations	805,700	2,336,830	173,960	3,365,420

[a]Includes former or current spouses, boyfriends, and girlfriends.
[b]Includes relatives, friends, neighbors, acquaintances, and strangers.
Note: Violent victimization includes rape or sexual assault, robbery, aggravated assault, and simple assault.

SOURCE: Shannan Catalano, "Table 6. Medical Treatment, by Victim's Sex and Victim-Offender Relationship, 2002–2011," in *Intimate Partner Violence: Attributes of Victimization, 1993–2011*, U.S. Department of Justice, Office of Justice Programs, Bureau of Justice Statistics, November 2013, http://www.bjs.gov/content/pub/pdf/ipvav9311.pdf (accessed July 22, 2014).

December 2012, when the Wave 3 data were collected. As Table 6.15 shows, 16.2% of all mothers involved in the study showed a need for social services related to domestic violence. African American mothers (19.8%) demonstrated the greatest need for these services, followed by Hispanic mothers (18.3%), and white mothers (13.5%).

NATIONAL INTIMATE PARTNER AND SEXUAL VIOLENCE SURVEY (2010)

The Centers for Disease Control and Prevention (CDC) is an agency within the U.S. Department of Health and Human Services. The CDC operates the National Center for Injury Prevention and Control, which is devoted to preventing violence and injuries. In 2010 the center, in collaboration with the Department of Justice's National Institute of Justice and the U.S. Department of Defense, conducted the National Intimate Partner and Sexual Violence Survey (NISVS), a comprehensive survey that collected information from adults about their experiences of sexual violence, stalking, and intimate partner violence. The results are summarized by Michele C. Black et al. in *National Intimate Partner and Sexual Violence Survey: 2010 Summary Report* (November 2011, http://www.cdc.gov/ViolencePrevention/pdf/NISVS_Report2010-a.pdf). This publication was the most comprehensive report of its kind as of November 2014.

FIGURE 6.6

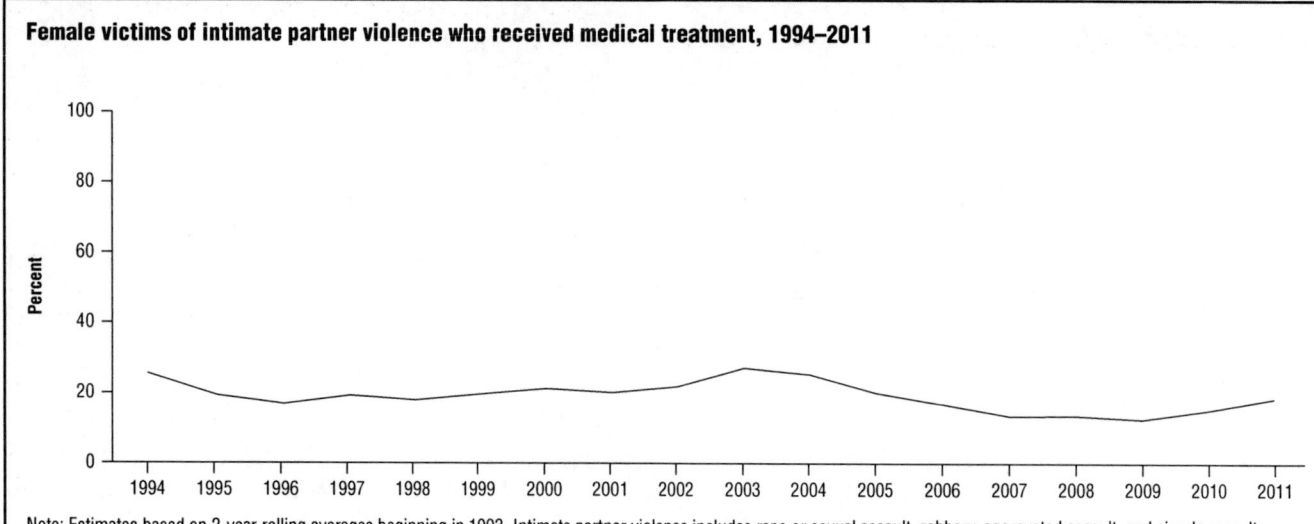

Female victims of intimate partner violence who received medical treatment, 1994–2011

Note: Estimates based on 2-year rolling averages beginning in 1993. Intimate partner violence includes rape or sexual assault, robbery, aggravated assault, and simple assault committed by current or former spouses, boyfriends, and girlfriends.

SOURCE: Shannan Catalano, "Figure 6. Medical Treatment of Female Victims of Intimate Partner Violence, 1994–2011," in *Intimate Partner Violence: Attributes of Victimization, 1993–2011*, U.S. Department of Justice, Office of Justice Programs, Bureau of Justice Statistics, November 2013, http://www .bjs.gov/content/pub/pdf/ipvav9311.pdf (accessed July 22, 2014)

TABLE 6.15

In-home mothers' need, referral to, and receipt of domestic violence services, by age and race and ethnicity, 2012

	Need for domestic violence services[a]	Referred to domestic violence services	Stayed in a shelter for battered women or received some other domestic violence services
	%	%	%
Total	16.2	3.8	1.3
Parent age (years)			
Under 20	9.2	3.0	0.0
20–29	17.3	3.0[b]	0.5
30–49	16.4	4.3[c]	1.7
50–59	6.0	0.8	0.6
60 and older	3.1	0.0	0.0
Parent race/ethnicity			
Black	19.8	3.6	1.3
White	13.5	4.0	1.2
Hispanic	18.3	2.8	1.2
Other	16.1	8.3	2.5

[a]Mothers were determined to be "in need of domestic violence services" if they met any one of three criteria: (1) caseworker report of a parent's need for domestic violence services at Wave 3, (2) a Conflicts Tactics Scale-2 (CTS-2) score indicating at least one incident of severe or less severe physical interpersonal violence suffered in the past 12 months, or (3) the mother's self-reported need ("a lot" or "somewhat") for domestic violence services in the past year, if she had not received any such services.
[b]Mothers 20 to 29 years old were significantly more likely to be referred for domestic violence services than mothers 50 to 59 years old.
[c]Mothers 30 to 49 years old were significantly more likely to be referred for domestic violence services than mothers 50 to 59 years old.
Note: The term "in-home mother" refers to the mothers of children living at home at Wave 3. Only permanent caregivers were asked about domestic violence services; responses here reflect only those of in-home mothers. Mothers who indicated that they had not ever received domestic violence services were included as not having received this service in the past 12 months. All analyses were on weighted NSCAW II Wave 3- data.

SOURCE: Adapted from Cecelia Casanueva et al., "Exhibit 22. In-Home Mothers' Need, Referral to, and Receipt of Domestic Violence Services in Past 12 Months (Wave 3)," in *NSCAW II Wave 3 Report: Wave 3 Tables*, U.S. Department of Health and Human Services, Administration for Children and Families, Office of Planning, Research, and Evaluation, June 5, 2014, http://www.acf.hhs.gov/sites/default/files/opre/nscaw_wave_3_tables_june_2014_clean.pdf (accessed July 22, 2014)

According to Black et al., the survey was conducted by telephone using a nationally representative sample of 16,507 adults (9,086 women and 7,421 men) in the United States who were aged 18 years and older, spoke English and/or Spanish, and were not living in institutional settings such as prisons, military bases, nursing homes, or college dormitories. The researchers considered intimate partners to be former or current "romantic or sexual partners." Intimate partners included couples who were cohabitating (living together) and not cohabitating. In addition, opposite sex and same-sex couples were included.

The NISVS provides a particularly comprehensive look at intimate partner violence because it covers not only physical and sexual violence but also other actions, such as psychological aggression, stalking, and control of reproductive or sexual health. Black et al. note that the survey included "a broad range of behaviorally specific questions to capture the full burden of physical, sexual, and psychological violence by an intimate partner, as well as stalking."

Terms and Definitions

The survey participants were asked about their lifetime experiences and previous 12-month experiences of being subjected to violent actions by their intimate partners. The assessed behaviors fell within five broad violence types:

- Sexual violence—rape (i.e., completed forced penetration, attempted penetration, and alcohol- or drug-facilitated completed penetration), being made to penetrate someone else, sexual coercion, unwanted sexual contact, and noncontact unwanted sexual experiences

- Physical violence—behaviors such as slapping, pushing, or shoving and being beaten, burned, or choked

- Psychological aggression—expressive aggression (such as name calling, insulting, or humiliating an intimate partner) and coercive control (behaviors intended to monitor and control or threaten an intimate partner)

- Stalking—a pattern of harassing or threatening tactics used by a perpetrator that is both unwanted and causes fear or safety concerns in the victim

- Control of reproductive or sexual health—behaviors such as refusing to wear a condom when requested to do so, trying to impregnate a partner who does not want to get pregnant, and trying to become pregnant by a partner who does not want a pregnancy to occur

In addition, survey participants provided demographic information about themselves and the intimate partners who acted violently against them. The participants were also asked detailed questions about the impacts on them of intimate partner violence and about the violent patterns of the perpetrators.

Rape, Physical Violence, and Stalking

As noted earlier, Black et al. define rape as including attempted and complete penetration. More specifically, the researchers provide the following examples of the actions that fall into this category for female and male victims:

- Female victims—unwanted vaginal, oral, or anal penetration through the use of threats of physical harm or through the use of physical force (such as being pinned or held down, or by the use of violence)

- Female victims—unwanted vaginal, oral, or anal penetration when the victims were drunk, high or otherwise drugged, or passed out and unable to consent

- Female victims—unwanted vaginal, oral, or anal penetration by a penis and unwanted vaginal or anal penetration by a male or female perpetrator using his or her fingers or an object

- Male victims—unwanted oral or anal penetration by a penis and unwanted anal penetration by a male or female perpetrator using his or her fingers or an object

FEMALE VICTIMS. Black et al. estimate that more than one-third (35.6%) of adult women in the United States have been victimized during their lifetime by an intimate partner using rape (9.4%), physical violence (32.9%), and/or stalking (10.7%). Overall, this sums to more than 42.4 million victims. In addition, 28.8% of women are believed to have experienced specific impacts from their lifetime experiences of intimate partner violence. (The effects and impacts of domestic violence are discussed in detail in Chapter 7.)

Nearly two-thirds (63.8%) of women who were victimized during their lifetime experienced only one of the three types of intimate partner violence. More than half (56.8%) experienced physical violence only, 4.4% experienced rape only, and 2.6% experienced stalking only. The remaining women were victimized by a combination of intimate partner violence types, including 12.5% who experienced rape, physical violence, and stalking during their lifetime.

Black et al. also provide lifetime prevalence percentages for rape, physical violence, and/or stalking broken down by the race and ethnicity of women victims. It should be noted that estimates are not available for races with small sample sizes. In descending order for each violence type, the percentages were:

- Rape, physical violence, and/or stalking—multiracial (53.8%), Native American or Alaskan Native (46%), non-Hispanic African American (43.7%), Hispanic (37.1%), non-Hispanic white (34.6%), and Asian or Pacific Islander (19.6%)

- Rape—multiracial (20.1%), non-Hispanic African American (12.2%), non-Hispanic white (9.2%), and Hispanic (8.4%)

- Physical violence—multiracial (50.4%), Native American or Alaskan Native (45.9%), non-Hispanic African American (40.9%), Hispanic (35.2%), and non-Hispanic white (31.7%)

- Stalking—multiracial (18.9%), non-Hispanic African American (14.6%), Hispanic (10.6%), and non-Hispanic white (10.4%)

MALE VICTIMS. According to Black et al., more than a quarter (32.3 million, or 28.5%) of the total U.S. adult male population have been victimized during their lifetime by an intimate partner using physical violence (28.2%) and/or stalking (2.1%). It should be noted that the sample size for rape was too small to provide a reliable national estimate. The 12-month prevalence among adult men for all three types of victimizations was 5%. The percentages by violence type were 4.7% for physical violence and 0.5% for stalking.

As Black et al. report, men were much more likely than women to experience only one of the three victimization types during their lifetime. Nearly all the victimized men (92.1%) experienced physical violence only. Another 6.3% experienced physical violence and stalking. The percentage of victimized men who experienced other combinations of the three violence types could not be reliably calculated.

Among male victims of rape, physical violence, and/ or stalking, nearly one out of seven (15%) were aged 11 to 17 years, and more than one-third (38.6%) were aged 18 to 24 years. Another 30.6% were aged 25 to 34 years. Overall, 84.2% of the male victims were 34 years old or younger when they first experienced intimate partner violence.

Black et al. break down the lifetime prevalence percentages for rape, physical violence, and/or stalking by the race and ethnicity of the male victims. It should be noted that estimates are not available for racial and ethnic groups with small sample sizes. In descending order for each violence type, the percentages were:

- Rape, physical violence, and/or stalking—Native American or Alaskan Native (45.3%), multiracial (39.3%), non-Hispanic African American (38.6%), non-Hispanic white (28.2%), and Hispanic (26.6%)

- Physical violence—Native American or Alaskan Native (45.3%), multiracial (38.8%), non-Hispanic African American (36.8%), non-Hispanic white (28.1%), Hispanic (26.5%), and Asian or Pacific Islander (8.4%)

- Stalking—non-Hispanic white (1.7%)

Sexual Violence

Within the category of sexual violence Black et al. include rape (as defined earlier) and other sexual acts described as follows:

- Being made to penetrate someone else—the perpetrator made or attempted to make the victim sexually penetrate someone without the victim's consent by threatening to physically harm the victim or using physical force against the victim (such as being pinned or held down, or by the use of violence). This includes being made to receive oral sex.

- Being made to penetrate someone else—the perpetrator made or attempted to make the victim sexually penetrate someone without the victim's consent, because the victim was drunk, high, drugged, or passed out and unable to consent. This includes being made to receive oral sex.

- Sexual coercion—unwanted sexual penetration of a victim who was coerced in a nonphysical way, such as through lies or emotional compulsion.

- Unwanted sexual contact—unwanted sexual experiences involving touch but not sexual penetration, such as being kissed in a sexual way or having sexual body parts fondled or grabbed.

- Noncontact unwanted sexual experiences—unwanted sexual experiences that do not involve any touching or penetration, including someone exposing their sexual body parts, flashing, or masturbating in front of the victim, someone making a victim show his or her body parts, someone making a victim look at or participate in sexual photos or movies, or someone harassing the victim in a public place in a way that made the victim feel unsafe.

FEMALE VICTIMS. As noted earlier, Black et al. estimate a 9.4% lifetime prevalence rate and a 0.6% 12-month prevalence rate for rape of adult women by intimate partners. The lifetime prevalence percentages by rape type were 6.6% for completed forced penetration, 2.5% for attempted forced penetration, and 3.4% for completed alcohol/drug-facilitated penetration. The percentages for lifetime prevalence of nonrape acts of sexual violence were 9.8% for sexual coercion, 6.4% for unwanted sexual contact, and 7.8% for noncontact unwanted sexual experiences. Sufficient data were available for the researchers to estimate 0.4% as the 12-month prevalence of completed forced penetration. The 12-month prevalence rates for specific types of nonrape sexual violence were 1.7% for sexual coercion, 0.5% for unwanted sexual contact, and 0.7% for noncontact unwanted sexual experiences.

MALE VICTIMS. According to Black et al., "too few men reported rape by an intimate partner to produce reliable prevalence estimates." However, estimated prevalence rates for overall nonrape sexual violence are 8% for lifetime prevalence and 2.5% for 12-month prevalence. In terms of specific sexually violent acts, sexual coercion had the highest lifetime prevalence at 4.2%, followed by noncontact unwanted sexual experiences (2.7%), unwanted sexual contact (2.6%), and being made to penetrate someone else (2.2%). The 12-month prevalence estimates were lower than the lifetime prevalence estimates, but again, sexual coercion was the most common type of nonrape sexual violence, at 1%. All the other types of sexual violence in this category had rates of less than 1%.

Physical Violence

Black et al. divide physical violence into two broad categories: slapping, pushing, or shoving and severe physical violence. The latter category includes actions that are particularly painful and/or injurious.

FEMALE VICTIMS. Overall, an estimated 36.2 million women have been slapped, pushed, or shoved by an intimate partner during their lifetime. This represents 30.3% of all adult U.S. women. Nearly as many women (29 million, or 24.3% of the total U.S. woman population) have experienced at least one form of severe physical violence. The lifetime prevalence rates for the five most commonly reported types of severe physical violence are: being slammed against something (17.2%), being hit with a fist or something hard (14.2%), being beaten (11.2%), being hurt by having hair pulled (10.4%), and being choked or suffocated (9.7%).

MALE VICTIMS. Black et al. estimate that 29.1 million men have been slapped, pushed, or shoved by an intimate partner during their lifetime. This represents 25.7% of all adult U.S. men. In addition, 15.6 million (13.8% of the total U.S. adult male population) men have experienced at least one form of severe physical violence. The lifetime prevalence rates for the five most commonly reported types of severe physical violence for male victims are: being hit with a fist or something hard (9.4%), being kicked (4.3%), being hurt by having hair pulled (2.9%), being attacked by a perpetrator armed with a knife or gun (2.8%), and being slammed against something (2.7%).

Stalking

As noted earlier, Black et al. define stalking as harassing or threatening actions that are unwanted and cause a victim to be afraid or otherwise concerned about his or her personal safety.

FEMALE VICTIMS. Black et al. estimate that 10.7% of U.S. adult women (or approximately 12.7 million women nationally) have been victimized by stalking by an intimate partner at some point during their life. The most commonly experienced stalking actions reported by victims were: receiving unwanted phone calls or text messages (77.4%) and having a current or former intimate partner show up unwanted at their home, workplace, or school (68.4%). In addition, more than one-third (37.4%) of the women said that during their lifetime they had been watched or followed by a current or former intimate partner. The estimated 12-month prevalence rate for stalking of female victims was 2.8%. This equates to approximately 3.3 million women nationally.

MALE VICTIMS. An estimated 2.4 million men have been the victims of stalking by an intimate partner at some point during their life. This equates to 2.1% of the total U.S. adult male population. Male stalking victims most commonly reported that they experienced unwanted phone calls or text messages (83.7%), were approached by a current or former intimate partner or experienced that person showing up unwanted at their home, workplace, or school (52.1%), and/or experienced being watched or followed by a current or former intimate partner (52.1%).

Psychological Aggression

Although physical and sexual forms of domestic violence typically receive the most attention from researchers, psychological aggression is another focus point. Black et al. divide acts of psychological aggression into two broad categories: expressive aggression (such as name calling and insulting behavior) and coercive control (such as overly controlling behaviors).

FEMALE VICTIMS. Black et al. find that psychological aggression by intimate partners is quite prevalent. Nearly half (48.4%) of adult women in the United States are estimated to have experienced it during their lifetime. This equates to about 57.6 million women nationally. The lifetime prevalence rates for expressive aggression (40.3%) and coercive control (41.1%) were nearly equal. The most frequently reported forms of psychological aggression were being called names, such as ugly or stupid (64.3%), and having one's whereabouts and movements monitored and questioned in a demanding fashion (61.7%). In addition, 58% of the women surveyed said they had been insulted, made fun of, or humiliated by an intimate partner, whereas 57.9% reported witnessing an intimate partner so angry that he or she "seemed dangerous."

MALE VICTIMS. Overall, an estimated 55.2 million men have at some point during their life experienced psychological aggression by an intimate partner. This value represents 48.8% of all adult U.S. men. The lifetime prevalence rates were 31.9% for expressive aggression and 42.5% for coercive control. The most frequently reported forms of psychological aggression were having one's whereabouts and movements monitored and questioned in a demanding fashion (63.1%) and being called names, such as ugly or stupid (51.6%). In addition, 42.4% of the men surveyed said they had been told by an intimate partner that they were a loser, a failure, or not good enough, and 40.4% reported witnessing an intimate partner so angry that he or she "seemed dangerous."

HOMICIDE TRENDS AND DOMESTIC VIOLENCE

Another source of data regarding the prevalence of domestic violence is the Federal Bureau of Investigation (FBI), because the agency compiles Uniform Crime Reports (UCR) that track the number of certain crimes committed in the United States based on reports from local law enforcement agencies. Crimes that are not reported to the police are not included in the UCR counts.

Selected UCR statistics are published annually by the FBI in the *Crime in the United States* series. In addition, the BJS uses UCR data in occasional reports on crime trends.

Fatal Domestic Violence Estimates, 2012

In *Crime in the United States*, the FBI focuses mostly on crime types, perpetrator characteristics, and agency actions, such as arrests; few data are available on the victim-offender relationships. However, the FBI does provide some limited information on the victim-offender relationships involved in homicides (i.e., murders). These data are useful in trying to establish the prevalence of fatal domestic violence.

The FBI indicates in *Crime in the United States, 2013* (November 2014, http://www.fbi.gov/about-us/cjis/ucr/crime-in-the-u.s/2013/crime-in-the-u.s.-2013) that 12,253 murders were reported to law enforcement agencies in 2013. The victim-offender relationship was known for 7,813 of the murders, or 64% of the total. The data provide the following counts of people murdered by family members or intimate partners:

- Women murdered by husbands (534)

- Men murdered by wives (108)

- People murdered by other family members (1,022)

- Women murdered by boyfriends (458)

- Men murdered by girlfriends (137)

These 2,259 murders account for 29% of the 7,813 homicides in 2013 in which the victim-offender relationship was known. It should be noted that the FBI specifies that the spousal categories include former spouses and common-law spouses (i.e., people whose spousal standing has been afforded by state laws that consider long-time cohabitating couples to have a spousal relationship). In addition, the FBI includes stepparents, stepchildren, and stepsiblings in its definition of family members. However, the FBI counts murders that occur within homosexual relationships as murders by acquaintances, rather than under the spousal or boyfriend/girlfriend categories. Thus, the number of homicides involving homosexual intimate partners is not specified. In 2013, 346 of the 7,813 homicides for which the victim-offender relationship was known were attributed to friends and 2,660 were attributed to acquaintances without further description of the relationships.

Homicide Trends, 1980–2008

In *Homicide Trends in the United States, 1980–2008: Annual Rates for 2009 and 2010* (November 2011, http://bjs.ojp.usdoj.gov/content/pub/pdf/htus8008.pdf), the most comprehensive homicide trends report published by the Bureau of Justice Statistics as of November 2014, Alexia Cooper and Erica L. Smith of the BJS discuss data obtained from the FBI's Supplementary Homicide Reports, which are compiled as part of the UCR program. The Supplementary Homicide Reports include some detailed information about homicide circumstances and victim-offender relationships. Cooper and Smith use the data to describe homicide trends between 1980 and 2008. They note that the victim-offender relationship was known in 63.1% of the homicides. All of the following discussion and related graphics present statistics for this subset of murders.

VICTIM-OFFENDER TRENDS. Overall, 10% of the homicides in which the victim-offender relationship was known involved spousal murder, 12.4% were homicides between other family members, and 6.3% involved girlfriend/boyfriend murder. Thus, 28.7% of the homicides during this period could be classified as domestic violence murders.

As Cooper and Smith report, between 1980 and 2008 females (41.5%) were nearly six times more likely than males (7.1%) to be the victims of intimate homicides. The distinction was less pronounced in murders involving other family members. In these cases females (16.7%) were only slightly more likely than males (10.9%) to be the victims. However, the predominance of female victims in these murder types stands in stark contrast to the gender breakdown in homicides that do not involve intimate partners or family members. Male victims outnumbered female victims in murders involving strangers (25.5% male victims compared with 11.9% female victims) and in cases where the perpetrators were acquaintances or otherwise known (56.4% male victims compared with 29.9% female victims). Thus, only in cases in which homicides were committed by intimate partners and other family members were females more often the victims than males.

Cooper and Smith also provide demographic data for the victims and perpetrators of murders involving intimate partners (spouses, former spouses, boyfriends, or girlfriends) and family members. In intimate homicides nearly half of the victims (48.5%) and offenders (47%) were in the age group 18 to 34 years. For murders involving family members, nearly one-third (32.8%) of the victims were aged 18 to 34 years; 50.5% of the perpetrators fell into this age group. Overall, victims of intimate partner homicide were predominantly female (63.7%) rather than male (36.3%), and male murderers (70.3%) were far more common than female murderers (29.7%) in these cases. The sex differences were less stark among victims of interfamilial (within the family) homicide, in that 54.7% of the victims were male and 45.3% of the victims were female. Again, males predominated among perpetrators (74.4%), compared with females (25.6%).

Between 1980 and 2008, whites accounted for slightly more than half of the parties involved in intimate homicides (55% of the victims and 54.2% of the offenders). African Americans made up 42.7% of the victims and 43.5% of the perpetrators, whereas other races accounted for 2.4% of the victims and 2.3% of the offenders. In interfamilial homicides whites also accounted for the majority of the victims and perpetrators (59.2% each). By comparison, African Americans made up 38.2% of the victims and 38.3% of the perpetrators, and other races accounted for 2% of the victims and 2.5% of the murderers.

INTIMATE PARTNER HOMICIDES. Of all homicide victims aged 12 years and older who were murdered between 1980 and 2008, 16% were killed by their intimate partners. Cooper and Smith note that in 1980 the majority (69.1%) of intimate homicides involved spousal murder. However, this percentage fell over time as boyfriend/girlfriend homicides became more prevalent. In 2008 fewer than half (46.7%) of the intimate homicides were spousal murders, whereas boyfriend/girlfriend murders accounted for 48.6% of the total, up from 26.8% in 1980. The changes over time in the victim-offender relationship of intimate homicides reflect the changes described in Chapter 1 for the makeup of intimate couples (that is, the trend away from marriage and toward other arrangements, such as cohabitation).

Far more females than males were murdered by intimate partners between 1980 and 2008. The percentage of males killed in intimate homicides declined from 10.4% in 1980 to 4.9% in 2008, a decrease of 53%. The percentage of females murdered by intimate partners dropped from 43% in 1980 to 38% in 1995. However, the percentage rose to 45% by 2008. Overall, in 1980 females were about four times more likely than males to be the victims of intimate homicide. By 2008 females were approximately nine times more likely than males to be the victims of intimate homicide.

White females were slightly more likely than African American females to be murdered by an intimate partner between 1980 and 2008. The two cohorts were roughly equal during the early 1980s, but white females predominated over the remainder of the period. On average, white women accounted for 44% of the victims in intimate homicides between 1980 and 2008. Intimate homicides of African American women declined from 43% in 1980 to 33% in 1995, but then climbed back up to 43% by 2008. In 1980 the percentage of African American male murder victims killed by an intimate partner was 13%. This value declined through 2008, when it was about 5%, the same percentage as for white males.

Guns were the most commonly used weapons on all intimate homicide victims between 1980 and 2008,

except for boyfriends murdered by their girlfriends and people murdered by a same-sex intimate partner. These homicides more frequently involved knives than guns. Guns were the murder weapons in a vast majority of the homicides in which ex-husbands were killed by ex-wives (83.6%), ex-wives were killed by ex-husbands (75%), wives were killed by husbands (66.7%), and husbands were killed by wives (66.1%).

INTERFAMILIAL HOMICIDES. Cooper and Smith also provide data on interfamilial homicides committed by various family members. It should be noted that spouses and ex-spouses are included in the same category; thus, there is some overlap between these data and the statistics presented earlier for intimate partner murders. Overall, spouses and ex-spouses were the perpetrators in just over half (52%) of interfamilial homicides in 1980. By 2008 this percentage had fallen to 37%. Parental murders of children made up 15% of the total in 1980 and climbed to 25% in 2008. Likewise, homicides in which children killed their parents increased from 10% in 1980 to 13% in 2008. The percentages of murders committed by siblings also rose, from 15% in 1980 to 18% in 2008. The rate of interfamilial homicides in which other family members were the perpetrators changed little during this period.

Cooper and Smith make the following general observations regarding interfamilial homicides between 1980 and 2008:

- Fathers were more likely than mothers to be murdered by one of their own children

- Sons aged 16 to 19 years old were most often the offenders when children killed their parents

- Brothers were more likely than sisters to be murdered by a sibling, and the perpetrators were usually brothers

- Approximately half of the brothers who murdered brothers were aged 16 to 30 years

- Sisters murdered by siblings were most often killed by brothers

Additional BJS Homicide Data

Although Cooper and Smith's findings represented the most extensive compilation of U.S. homicide statistics as of November 2014, the Bureau of Justice Statistics has produced subsequent reports offering additional data concerning spousal and interfamilial homicides. In *Intimate Partner Violence: Attributes of Victimization, 1993–2011*, Shannan Catalano provides an overview of homicides committed by intimate partners between 1993 and 2010. As Catalano notes, the percentage of female homicide victims who were killed by intimate partners rose steadily between 2008 and 2010. In 2008, 36.4% of female homicide victims were murdered by an intimate partner. In 2010 this figure rose to 39.3%. The percentage of male homicide victims who were killed by intimate partners rose from 2.7% in 2008 to 3% in 2009, before dropping to 2.8% in 2010. Overall, the total number of female homicide victims fell during this period, from 3,282 in 2008 to 3,032 in 2010. The number of male homicide victims also declined during this span, dropping from 12,296 in 2008 to 10,878 in 2010.

NATIONAL VIOLENCE AGAINST WOMEN SURVEY (1995–96)

As a joint effort of the Department of Justice's National Institute of Justice and the CDC, the National Violence against Women Survey (NVAWS) collected data about intimate and nonintimate partner violence in 1995–96. The NVAWS collected information from interviews with 8,000 men and 8,000 women to assess their experiences as victims of various types of violence, including domestic violence. The NVAWS asked survey respondents about physical assaults and rape, but excluded other sexual assaults, murders, and robberies.

In *Extent, Nature, and Consequences of Intimate Partner Violence: Findings from the National Violence against Women Survey* (July 2000, http://www.ncjrs.gov/pdffiles1/nij/181867.pdf), Patricia Tjaden and Nancy Thoennes of the Center for Policy Research in Denver, Colorado, find that intimate violence is pervasive in American society, with women suffering about three times as much of this violence as men. They estimate that in 1998, 22.3 million (22.1%) women had been physically assaulted by intimates during the course of their lifetime, whereas 6.9 million (7.4%) men had been physically assaulted by intimates during the course of their lifetime. Women were also more likely to become victims of rape, stalking, and physical assault by intimates than their male counterparts at some point during their lifetime. Furthermore, women physically assaulted by their partners averaged 6.9 assaults by the same person, as opposed to men, who averaged 4.4 assaults by the same person.

During the 12 months that preceded the interview, women also reported higher rates of rape, stalking, and physical assault than did men. Tjaden and Thoennes estimate based on NVAWS data that about 1.5 million (1.5%) of the surveyed women and 835,000 (0.9%) of the surveyed men reported that they had been raped and/or physically assaulted by a partner in the 12 months preceding the survey. In other words, approximately 4.8 million women and 2.9 million men are assaulted by a partner every year.

The rates of violence between intimate partners varied by race. Whereas 37.5% of Native Americans or Alaskan Natives reported violence, 29.1% of African Americans, 24.8% of whites, and 15% of Asian or Pacific Islanders reported having been victimized by an intimate partner during their lifetime.

Tjaden and Thoennes conclude that most partner abuse and violence is not reported to the police. Women reported 17.2% of rapes, 26.7% of physical assaults, and 51.9% of stalking incidents to police, whereas men reported 13.5% of physical assaults and 36.2% of stalking incidents. Many victims said they thought the police would not or could not do anything on their behalf. These expressions of helplessness and hopelessness (feeling that others in a position to assist would be unwilling or unable to do so) is a common characteristic shared by many victims of intimate partner violence.

As Tjaden and Thoennes report in *Full Report of the Prevalence, Incidence, and Consequence of Violence against Women* (November 2000, https://www.ncjrs.gov/pdffiles1/nij/183781.pdf), more than one in five (22.1%) of women surveyed reported experiencing intimate partner violence; by comparison, 7.4% of men interviewed reported being victims of intimate partner violence. Overall, intimate partner violence accounted for nearly two-thirds (64%) of all violent acts committed against women 18 years of age and older. As Tjaden and Thoennes note, women who were raped or assaulted by an intimate partner were considerably more likely to report sustaining an injury than women who were raped or assaulted by another category of assailant.

Violence Statistics in Same-Sex Relationships

Tjaden and Thoennes also find that same-sex couples who lived together reported experiencing far more intimate violence during their lifetime than heterosexual cohabitants. Among women, 39.2% of the same-sex cohabitants and 21.7% of the opposite-sex cohabitants reported being raped, physically assaulted, or stalked by a partner during their lifetime. Among men, the comparative percentages were 23.1% and 7.4%, respectively.

Although survey findings indicate that members of same-sex couples have experienced more intimate partner violence than have members of heterosexual couples, the reported violence does not necessarily occur within the same-sex relationship. When comparing intimate partner victimization rates among same-sex and opposite-sex cohabitants by the gender of the perpetrator, Tjaden and Thoennes find that 30.4% of the same-sex women cohabitants reported being victimized by a male partner sometime during their lifetime, whereas 11.4% reported being victimized by a female partner. The researchers conclude that same-sex cohabiting women were three times more likely to report being victimized by a male partner than by a female partner. In comparison, women who lived with men were nearly twice as likely to report being victimized by a male partner than same-sex cohabiting women were to report being victimized by a female partner.

According to Tjaden and Thoennes, male same-sex partners reported more partner violence than did men who lived with women. Approximately 23.1% of men who lived with men said they had been raped, sexually assaulted, or stalked by a male cohabitant, as opposed to just 7.4% of men who reported comparable experiences with female cohabitants. This finding confirms the widely held observation that violence and abuse in intimate partner relationships is primarily inflicted by men, whether the victimized partner is male or female.

CHAPTER 7
CAUSES, EFFECTS, AND PREVENTION OF DOMESTIC VIOLENCE

THEORIES ON THE CAUSES OF DOMESTIC VIOLENCE

It should be noted that many theories have been put forward to explain why domestic violence occurs. Each theory has its champions and critics. People who support certain theories can cite studies that include empirical research (research based on observation and measurement) as supporting evidence. In reality, no single theory can explain what causes people to act violently in certain situations. In fact, there can be considerable overlap between theories in certain elements, for example, the idea that society at large helps perpetuate violent behaviors. Because males have historically been the primary perpetrators of domestic violence, most theories tend to focus on male attitudes and behaviors. In addition, most theories focus on intimate partner violence, which as noted in previous chapters is domestic violence in which the offender is a former or current spouse, boyfriend, or girlfriend of the victim. Some of the most common types of theories are briefly described in this chapter.

Resource Theories

According to resource theories of domestic violence, the more resources (social, personal, and economic) a person can command, the more power he or she can potentially call on. The individual who is rich in terms of these resources has less need to use force in an open manner. By contrast, a person with little education, low job prestige and income, or poor interpersonal skills may use violence to compensate for a real or perceived lack of resources and to maintain dominance.

Learned Behavior Theories

Theories based on learned behavior view domestic violence as behavior that may be learned early in life by children who experience domestic violence in their home and consider it to be "normal." As these children grow up, they may receive societal feedback that seems to

support the notion that violent behavior within relationships is acceptable. In addition, people who engage in domestic violence may learn that it achieves the desired results and has no negative consequences to them, thus, reinforcing its usefulness in their mind.

Feminist Theories

Feminist theories of violence against women emphasize that patriarchal structures of gender-based inequalities of power in society are at the root of the problem. That is, the violence, rather than being an individual psychological problem, is instead an expression of male domination of females. Pointing to history, some feminist researchers see wife abuse as a natural consequence of women's second-class status in society. In the feminist view, violence against women includes a variety of control tactics that are meant to control women.

Evan Stark furthers this view by positing in *Coercive Control: The Entrapment of Women in Personal Life* (2007) that "anti-hitting" campaigns are useless because men continue to attempt to control their partners. According to Stark, domestic violence is not about violence, but about women's fundamental right to self-determination, and as a result he suggests that intimate partner violence is a violation of human rights. Stark also notes that there are many female abusers of both males and other females; however, he opines that "there is no counterpart in men's lives to women's entrapment by men in personal life due to coercive control."

Psychological and Personality Theories

Some analysts believe that perpetrator psychological and personality disorders contribute to domestic violence behaviors. In *Domestic Violence* (January 2007, http://www.popcenter.org/problems/pdfs/domestic_violence.pdf), Rana Sampson notes that possible disorders and problems include posttraumatic stress, poor impulse control, low self-esteem, and substance abuse.

Control and Power Motivations

Many theories posit the desire for control and power in a relationship as a major motivation for people who use violence against their intimate partners. Stark argues in *Coercive Control* that intimate partner violence is best understood as part of men's attempts to destroy women's autonomy and assert patriarchal power in relationships and that physical violence must be seen as one aspect of a power dynamic that also includes economic and emotional measures of control. Control motivations often feature prominently in the domestic violence definitions that are crafted by government agencies and nonprofit organizations. For example, in "Domestic Violence" (2014, http://www.justice.gov/ovw/domestic-violence), the Office on Violence against Women, a part of the U.S. Department of Justice (DOJ), notes, "We define domestic violence as a pattern of abusive behavior in any relationship that is used by one partner to gain or maintain power and control over another intimate partner."

Champions of control theories as the cause of domestic violence sometimes stress the role of societal beliefs and practices as a contributing factor. These people believe that society in some ways condones and even fosters violence against certain classes of people, including women and children. The National Coalition against Domestic Violence states in its "Mission Statement and Purpose" (2014, http://www.ncadv.org/aboutus.php) that it "believes violence against women and children results from the use of force or threat to achieve and maintain control over others in intimate relationships, and from societal abuse of power and domination in the forms of sexism, racism, homophobia, classism, anti-Semitism, able-bodyism, ageism and other oppressions."

RISK FACTORS FOR DOMESTIC VIOLENCE

The risk factors for domestic violence are gleaned from empirical studies conducted by researchers who examine demographic or relationship factors associated with domestic violence cases to compare prevalence rates between different population subsets. Researchers do differ in their definitions of domestic violence and in the types of cases or victims that they assess. Nevertheless, their studies give valuable clues about what types of victims are most at risk for experiencing domestic violence.

In "Making Sociological Sense out of Trends in Intimate Partner Violence" (*Violence against Women*, vol. 10, no. 6, June 2004), Joseph H. Michalski of the University of Western Ontario indicates that key risk factors of domestic violence include:

- Social isolation of the couple

- Separate peer support networks

- Inequality between partners

- Lack of relational distance, or a high degree of intimacy within a couple

- The centralization of authority—in other words, patriarchal dominance within a family

- Exposure to violence and violent networks

Sarah Romans et al. of the University of Toronto find in "Who Is Most at Risk for Intimate Partner Violence?: A Canadian Population-Based Study" (*Journal of Interpersonal Violence*, vol. 22, no. 12, December 2007) that risk factors for intimate partner violence include a younger age; being divorced, separated, or single; having children living in the household; and having poor physical health. A lower income or minority status puts women, but not men, at a higher risk for intimate partner violence. Still, Romans et al. explain that classification is not exclusive. Just about anyone, rich or poor, male or female, may be a victim of domestic violence.

Some studies have assessed the relationship between socioeconomic status and domestic violence prevalence. For example, the 1985 National Family Violence Resurvey, which surveyed 6,002 households, showed that serious physical acts of wife abuse were more likely to occur in poorer homes. In the survey, families living at or below the poverty level had a rate of marital violence 500% greater than more affluent families. Deborah N. Pearlman et al. of Brown University find in "Neighborhood Environment, Racial Position, and Risk of Police-Reported Domestic Violence: A Contextual Analysis" (*Public Health Reports*, vol. 118, no. 1, January–February 2003) a complex but strong relationship between poverty and domestic violence and speculate that one explanation for the increased risk of domestic violence in poorer neighborhoods might be differences in law enforcement availability and practices; that is, economically deprived communities might have less police notification, attention, and documentation.

Risk Factors for Fatal Domestic Violence

In "How Can Practitioners Help an Abused Woman Lower Her Risk of Death?" (*National Institute of Justice Journal*, no. 250, November 2003), Carolyn Rebecca Block of the Illinois Criminal Justice Information Authority investigates what factors present in abusive relationships might indicate that a threat of violence will escalate to homicide. She finds that certain types of past violence directed against female intimates indicate an increased risk of homicide, especially choking. She also finds that recently abused women are more likely to be killed. Half of women who were killed in 1995 and 1996 by their partners had experienced violence in the previous 30 days before the survey. Increasingly, frequent violent incidents pose a higher risk of homicide.

Jacquelyn C. Campbell et al. evaluate in "Assessing Risk Factors for Intimate Partner Homicide" (*National Institute of Justice Journal*, no. 250, November 2003) the risk factors among abused women for being killed by their intimate partners. The researchers find that abused women whose abusers owned guns and who had threatened to kill them were at a high risk of being killed by their intimate partners. Other high-risk factors for homicide include extreme jealousy, attempts to choke, and marital rape.

Substance Abuse as a Risk Factor

Although researchers generally do not consider alcohol and drug use to be the cause of violence, they find that it can contribute to, accelerate, or increase aggression. A variety of data sources establish a correlation (a complementary or parallel relationship) between substance abuse and violence, but a correlation does not establish a causation.

According to the National Institute on Alcohol Abuse and Alcoholism in *Alcohol and Intimate Partner Violence* (March 2005, http://pubs.niaaa.nih.gov/publications/Social/Module8IntimatePartnerViolence/Module8.html), "alcohol is not a clearly identified direct cause of IPV [intimate partner violence], though it clearly is a correlate and may be a contributing factor." Substance abuse may promote or provoke domestic violence, but both may also be influenced by other factors, such as environmental, biological, and situational stressors. Based on available research, it remains unclear whether substance abuse is a key factor in most domestic violence incidents. As Jennifer M. Reingle et al. note in "On the Pervasiveness of Event-Specific Alcohol Use, General Substance Use, and Mental Health Problems as Risk Factors for Intimate Partner Violence" (*Journal of Interpersonal Violence*, vol. 29, no. 16, November 2014), whereas alcohol and marijuana abuse are often associated with higher rates of intimate partner violence, other factors, notably mental health issues such as depression and personality disorders, are also prevalent in domestic violence situations.

Although anecdotal evidence suggests that alcohol and drugs appear to be linked to violence and abuse, in controlled studies the connection is not as clear. Richard J. Gelles and Mary M. Cavanaugh suggest in "Association Is Not Causation: Alcohol and Other Drugs Do Not Cause Violence" (Donileen R. Loseke, Richard J. Gelles, and Mary M. Cavanaugh, eds., *Current Controversies on Family Violence*, 2005) that substance abuse is not a cause of family violence; rather, it is often used as an excuse for family violence. Gelles and Cavanaugh argue that although substantial evidence has linked alcohol and drug use to violence, there is little scientific evidence that alcohol or other drugs, such as cocaine, have pharmacological properties that produce violent and abusive

behavior. The researchers maintain that alcoholism may be associated with intimate violence but that it is not a primary cause of the violence. They cite experiments using college students as subjects that have found that when the students thought they were consuming alcohol, they acted more aggressively than if they were told they had been given nonalcoholic drinks. According to Gelles and Cavanaugh, it is the expectation of the effects of alcohol that influences behavior, not the actual liquor consumed.

In "Risky Mix: Drinking, Drug Use, and Homicide" (*National Institute of Justice Journal*, no. 250, November 2003), a study of patterns of alcohol and drug use in murders and attempted murders of women by their partners, Phyllis Sharps et al. show a relationship between substance use and violence. They find that in the year before the violent incident, female victims used alcohol and drugs less frequently and consumed smaller amounts than did their male partners. Sharps et al. also note that during the homicide or attempted homicide 31.3% of perpetrators consumed alcohol, 12.6% used drugs, and 26.2% used both. Nearly three out of 10 (29.9%) homicide or attempted homicide perpetrators used neither alcohol nor drugs. In contrast, perpetrators who abused their partners without attempting to kill them consumed alcohol 21% of the time, drugs 6.7% of the time, and both 5.8% of the time. Nearly two-thirds (65.8%) of perpetrators who abused their partners without attempting to kill them used neither alcohol nor drugs. Sharps et al. conclude that increased substance use results in more serious violence. Martie P. Thompson and J. B. Kingree of Clemson University agree. They find in "The Roles of Victim and Perpetrator Alcohol Use in Intimate Partner Violence Outcomes" (*Journal of Interpersonal Violence*, vol. 21, no. 2, February 2006) that alcohol use among male batterers led to a significant increase in the likelihood that their partners would suffer injury in a violent incident.

Although most studies focus on substance abuse by the offenders in domestic violence cases, research also finds that women with substance abuse problems are at higher risk of being victimized by their intimate partners. In "Working at the Intersection of Domestic Violence, Substance Abuse and Mental Health: Creating Trauma-Informed Services and Organizations" (March 29, 2012, http://www.nationalcenterdvtraumamh.org/wp-content/uploads/2012/01/March-29-Mental-Health-Pre-Con-Flyer.pdf), Carole Warshaw of the National Center on Domestic Violence, Trauma, and Mental Health cites studies showing that women who are treated for substance abuse problems in outpatient and inpatient settings are at higher risk than other women for domestic violence. According to Warshaw, batterers take advantage of, or even exacerbate, substance abuse issues in their female partners to better exert control over them.

Childhood and Youth Victimization as a Risk Factor

Research demonstrates a relationship between having experienced violence as a child or youth and being further victimized or becoming an abuser later in life.

Shelby A. Kaura and Craig M. Allen of Iowa State University note in "Dissatisfaction with Relationship Power and Dating Violence Perpetration by Men and Women" (*Journal of Interpersonal Violence*, vol. 19, no. 5, May 2004), a study of 352 male and 296 female undergraduate college students, that witnessing parental violence was the strongest predictor of perpetrating dating violence. The National Institute of Justice finds in *Violence against Women: Identifying Risk Factors* (November 2004, https://www.ncjrs.gov/pdffiles1/nij/197019.pdf) exceedingly high rates of abuse during college, especially of women who had been victimized in childhood or adolescence. During their first year of college, 23% of women who had not been victimized in the past were victimized physically, sexually, or both. By contrast, 32% of women who had been victimized in childhood, 42% of women who had been victimized in adolescence, and 66% of women who had been victimized in both childhood and adolescence were abused during their first year of college.

The National Institute of Justice also looks at whether adults who experienced sexual abuse or domestic violence had been abused in childhood or adolescence. Over a quarter (28%) of adults who had not been abused before reaching adulthood were sexually abused as adults, whereas 75% of those who had been abused in childhood and adolescence were sexually abused as adults. Sixty percent of women who had not been abused in childhood or adolescence experienced some domestic violence in adulthood, whereas 97% of women who had been sexually abused in childhood and adolescence experienced some domestic violence in adulthood.

DATING VIOLENCE IN ADOLESCENCE. Dating violence encompasses physical, sexual, or psychological violence in a dating relationship. Experiencing dating violence puts victims at a greater risk for engaging in risky sexual behavior, anorexia nervosa (intense fear of becoming fat even when dangerously underweight) or bulimia (recurrent episodes of binge eating followed by purging to prevent weight gain), substance abuse, and suicide. It can also be an indicator that an adolescent is at risk for victimization in intimate relationships in adulthood.

Carl D. Maas et al. explore in "Childhood Predictors of Teen Dating Violence Victimization" (*Violence and Victims*, vol. 25, no. 2, 2010) the relationship between child maltreatment and domestic violence and teen dating violence. The researchers examined data from the Raising Healthy Children project, a longitudinal study (a study of the same group of people over time) of students in a suburban school district in the Pacific Northwest. They find a strong association between child maltreatment and dating violence victimization for female adolescents. In addition, witnessing intimate partner violence in childhood also puts girls at greater risk for dating violence. However, Maas et al. also note that strong bonds between parents and children provide a protective effect against teen dating violence victimization.

Mireille Cyr, Pierre McDuff, and John Wright of the Université de Montréal examined dating violence among a group of adolescent girls who had been sexually abused as children and reported their findings in "Prevalence and Predictors of Dating Violence among Adolescent Female Victims of Child Sexual Abuse" (*Journal of Interpersonal Violence*, vol. 21, no. 8, August 2006). Dating violence was more prevalent among these young women than other studies had found in a general population of female adolescents. Nearly half of the sexually abused teens reported that they had experienced physical violence in a dating relationship in the previous year. Certain characteristics of the abuse the girls had suffered made it even more likely for them to be the victims of physical violence, namely if the sexual abuse included penetration or physical violence. Cyr, McDuff, and Wright argue that sexually abused youth have difficulties with intimate relationships, including a fear of intimacy and ambivalent attachment, that might explain the higher levels of dating violence among this group.

The Centers for Disease Control and Prevention (CDC) in its Youth Risk Behavior Survey questions students in grades nine to 12 on their experiences of dating violence and forced sexual intercourse. In 2013 about one out of 10 (10.3%) students said they had been hit, slapped, or physically hurt on purpose by their boyfriend or girlfriend during the past year. (See Table 7.1.) Female students (13%) were considerably more likely to say they had experienced dating violence than were male students (7.4%). Students in grades 11 and 12 had higher rates of dating violence than did students in grade nine and 10, possibly because older students are more likely to go on dates. The overall rates by race and ethnicity were 9.7% for white students, 10.3% for African American students, and 10.4% for Hispanic students. Students were also asked if they had ever been "physically forced" to engage in sexual activity. As shown in Table 7.1, 10.4% had experienced this type of abuse in 2013. The rate for female students (14.4%) was more than twice as high as for male students (6.2%). Younger female students were more likely than older female students to have experienced an incident of sexual dating violence. The overall rates by race and ethnicity were 8.9% for African

American students, 9.8% for white students, and 11.5% for Hispanic students.

Table 7.2 shows previous Youth Risk Behavior Survey results for these same two questions. From 1999 to 2011 between 8.8% and 9.9% of students said they had been hit, slapped, or physically hurt on purpose by their boyfriend or girlfriend during the past year. In addition, from 2001 to 2011 between 7.4% and 9% students self-reported being physically forced to have unwanted sexual intercourse at some point during their life.

TABLE 7.1

Percentage of high school students who experienced dating violence and sexual dating violence, by sex, race and Hispanic origin, and grade, 2013

	Physical dating violence			Sexual dating violence		
	Female	Male	Total	Female	Male	Total
Category	%	%	%	%	%	%
Race/ethnicity						
White*	12.9	6.4	9.7	14.6	4.8	9.8
Black*	12.3	8.2	10.3	8.8	8.9	8.9
Hispanic	13.6	7.0	10.4	16.0	6.7	11.5
Grade						
9	11.9	5.7	8.8	15.7	5.9	10.9
10	13.4	6.4	10.0	15.9	5.0	10.5
11	12.4	8.2	10.4	12.0	7.3	9.7
12	13.9	9.5	11.7	13.9	6.4	10.2
Total	**13.0**	**7.4**	**10.3**	**14.4**	**6.2**	**10.4**

*Non-Hispanic.

Notes: Among the 73.9% of students nationwide who dated or went out with someone during the 12 months before the survey. Including being hit, slammed into something, or injured with an object or weapon on purpose by someone they were dating or going out with. One or more times during the 12 months before the survey. Including kissing, touching, or being physical forced to have sexual intercourse when they did not want to by someone they were dating or going out with.

SOURCE: Adapted from Laura Kann et al., "Table 21. Percentage of High School Students Who Experienced Physical Dating Violence and Sexual Dating Violence, by Sex, Race/Ethnicity, and Grade—United States, Youth Risk Behavior Survey, 2013," in "Youth Risk Behavior Surveillance—United States, 2013," *MMWR*, vol. 62, no. 4, June 13, 2014, http://www.cdc.gov/mmwr/pdf/ss/ss6304.pdf (accessed July 17, 2014)

EFFECTS OF DOMESTIC VIOLENCE

There are often urgent and long-term physical and mental health consequences of domestic violence. Short-term physical consequences include mild to moderate injuries, such as broken bones, bruises, and cuts. More serious medical problems include sexually transmitted diseases, miscarriages, premature labor, and injury to unborn children, as well as damage to the central nervous system sustained as a result of blows to the head, including traumatic brain injuries, chronic headaches, and loss of vision and hearing. The medical consequences of abuse may go unreported because women are reluctant to disclose abuse as the cause of their injuries, and health professionals are uncomfortable inquiring about it.

Kristie A. Thomas et al. explain in "Intersections of Harm and Health: A Qualitative Study of Intimate Partner Violence in Women's Lives" (*Violence against Women*, vol. 14, no. 11, November 2008) that on the one hand intimate partner violence produces adverse health effects in victims, in addition to worsening already compromised health. On the other hand, ill health increases women's dependence on the abuser. The researchers conducted qualitative interviews with female volunteers from eight Philadelphia, Pennsylvania, social service agencies. They find that there was a high correlation between intimate partner violence and adverse health effects, including headaches, high blood pressure, drug and alcohol abuse, chronic pain, and embarrassing scars. Thomas et al. conclude that "the pathways linking [intimate partner violence] and health are often bidirectional and cyclical, ultimately resulting in compromised health quality over the long term."

In "Does Physical Intimate Partner Violence Affect Sexual Health" (*Trauma, Violence, and Abuse*, vol. 8, no. 2, April 2007), Ann L. Coker of the University of Texas Health Science Center undertook a systematic review of studies that looked at whether domestic violence affected women's sexual health. Coker finds that a causal connection could be made between intimate partner violence

TABLE 7.2

Trends in the prevalence of violent behavior against high school students by dates and intimate partners, 1991–2011

	1991	1993	1995	1997	1999	2001	2003	2005	2007	2009	2011	Changes from 1991–2011*	Changes from 2009–2011
Hit, slapped, or physically hurt on purpose by their boyfriend or girlfriend (during the 12 months before the survey)	NA	NA	NA	NA	8.8	9.5	8.9	9.2	9.9	9.8	9.4	No change, 1999–2011	No change
Ever physically forced to have sexual intercourse (when they did not want to)	NA	NA	NA	NA	NA	7.7	9.0	7.5	7.8	7.4	8.0	No change, 2001–2011	No change

*Based on trend analyses using a logistic regression model controlling for sex, race/ethnicity, and grade.
NA = Not available.

SOURCE: Adapted from "Trends in the Prevalence of Behaviors That Contribute to Violence National YRBS: 1991–2011," in *Youth Risk Behavior Surveillance System (YRBSS)*, U.S. Department of Health and Human Services, Centers for Disease Control and Prevention, Division of Adolescent and School Health, undated, http://www.cdc.gov/healthyyouth/yrbs/pdf/us_violence_trend_yrbs.pdf (accessed July 23, 2014)

and unplanned pregnancies and abortions, sexually transmitted infections, sexual dysfunction (e.g., lack of sexual pleasure), and sexual risk taking (e.g., failure to use condoms or partner nonmonogamy).

Abused women are also at risk for health problems that are not directly caused by the abuse. Jacquelyn Campbell et al. compare in "Intimate Partner Violence and Physical Health Consequences" (*Archives of Internal Medicine*, vol. 162, no. 10, May 27, 2002) the physical health problems of abused women to a control group of women who had never suffered abuse. The researchers find that abused women suffered 50% to 70% more gynecological, central nervous system, and stress-related problems. Examples of stress-related problems included chronic fear, headaches, back pain, gastrointestinal disorders, appetite loss, and increased incidence of viral infections such as colds. Although women who most recently suffered physical abuse reported the most health problems, Campbell et al. find evidence that abused women remain less healthy over time. Other scholars have identified a range of both mental and physical health issues suffered by female victims of intimate partner violence. As Laura E. Watkins et al. observe in "The Longitudinal Impact of Intimate Partner Aggression and Relationship Status on Women's Physical Health and Depression Symptoms" (*Journal of Family Psychology*, vol. 28, no. 5, October 2014), the presence of both physical and psychological health problems was particularly prevalent among younger women who remained in relationships with abusive partners.

Post-traumatic Stress Disorder

Women who have been abused are at risk for developing post-traumatic stress disorder (PTSD). According to the National Institutes of Health in "Post-traumatic Stress Disorder" (2014, http://www.nimh.nih.gov/health/publications/anxiety-disorders/index.shtml#pub4), PTSD symptoms include startling easily, emotional numbness (especially in relationships), irritability or aggressiveness, avoidance of situations that are similar to the traumatic event, and reliving the trauma in flashbacks and nightmares.

The development of PTSD may lead to some of the adverse health outcomes associated with intimate partner violence. Studies such as Mary Ann Dutton et al.'s "Intimate Partner Violence, PTSD, and Adverse Health Outcomes" (*Journal of Interpersonal Violence*, vol. 21, no. 7, July 2006) and Stephanie J. Woods's "Intimate Partner Violence and Post-traumatic Stress Disorder Symptoms in Women: What We Know and Need to Know" (*Journal of Interpersonal Violence*, vol. 20, no. 4, April 2005) show that victims of intimate partner violence have up to five times a greater likelihood of having or developing PTSD, as well as a host of other mental health problems

such as depression and substance abuse. Some researchers estimate that between 31% and 84% of all battered women develop PTSD. The more severe the violence, the higher the likelihood that a woman will develop the disorder.

In "Intimate Partner Violence and Posttraumatic Stress Disorder among High-Risk Women: Does Pregnancy Matter?" (*Violence against Women*, vol. 16, no. 4, April 2010), Caroline C. Stampfel, Derek A. Chapman, and Andrea E. Alvarez used data from the Chicago Women's Health Risk Study to evaluate the prevalence of PTSD among women who had experienced intimate partner violence. The researchers find that African American women who were victims of intimate partner violence had the highest rates of PTSD and that pregnancy exacerbated the potential for the development of the disorder. Ninety percent of African American women who were victims of intimate partner violence had PTSD, and 95% of African American women who were both victims of intimate partner violence and pregnant had PTSD. Hispanic women, however, were less likely to have PTSD if they were pregnant. Stampfel, Chapman, and Alvarez also report that negative pregnancy outcomes were more likely among women with PTSD than among women without PTSD.

According to Dutton et al., PTSD "appears to be a linchpin in the relationship between exposure to violence and negative health outcomes." The researchers postulate that PTSD, which has been shown to lead to negative health behaviors, has consequences on battered women's health. These consequences may result from not adhering to a doctor's instructions or from specific coping strategies to deal with PTSD. In addition, biological responses to PTSD may contribute to an increase in blood pressure or a suppression of the immune system.

Researchers have found that women exhibit a range of psychological responses to the traumatic impact of intimate partner violence. In "Impact of Intimate Partner Violence on Women's Mental Health" (*Journal of Family Violence*, vol. 29, no. 7, October 2014), Gunnur Karakurt, Douglas Smith, and Jason Whiting assess the mental health status of women living in domestic abuse shelters. According to Karakurt, Smith, and Whiting, women seeking mental health services for domestic violence can be divided into three basic categories. Whereas one segment of female domestic violence victims expresses a readiness to sever their relationships with their abusers, some women become primarily fixated on the psychological damage they have incurred as a result of abuse, and the remaining victims express feelings of guilt for their perceived role in causing the domestic violence situation to arise in the first place.

As discussed in Chapter 3, children living in domestic violence situations also suffer a range of negative outcomes. On one level, these consequences revolve around questions of physical health. In "Impacts of Domestic Violence on Child Growth and Nutrition: A Conceptual Review of the Pathways of Influence" (*Social Science & Medicine*, vol. 72, no. 9, May 2011), Kathryn M. Yount, Ann M. DiGirolamo, and Usha Ramakrishnan note that violence against young mothers can impact the physical development of their children by interfering with their basic nutritional and dietary needs. In the long term, domestic violence can also have a profound impact on the psychological well-being of children who have been exposed to abusive situations. In many cases, these negative effects stem from a child's fundamental inability to comprehend domestic violence. As Victoria Thornton writes in "Understanding the Emotional Impact of Domestic Violence on Young Children" (*Educational & Child Psychology*, vol. 31, no. 1, March 2014), small children lack the intellectual and emotional tools to process their feelings in the aftermath of an abusive situation. According to Thornton, the failure to express these feelings adequately can often lead to long-term emotional struggles.

PREVENTING DOMESTIC VIOLENCE

The United States has a two-pronged approach to preventing domestic violence. One prong is the criminal justice system, which investigates and prosecutes people who violate criminal laws, including laws against domestic violence. Chapter 1 describes federal and state legislation that establishes the legal basis for dealing with abusers. Additional information about the role of the criminal justice system is presented in Chapter 9. This chapter will focus on preventive measures of other forms, including those facilitated by government agencies that are devoted to public health and welfare and private organizations that work to prevent domestic violence in society. Some of the key elements of prevention include increasing public awareness about domestic violence (e.g., through education campaigns) and providing victim services, such as domestic violence hotlines and emergency shelters for victims.

INCREASING PUBLIC AWARENESS

As noted earlier, domestic violence was historically considered to be a private matter settled within families. The secrecy surrounding this type of violence made it easier for society at large to believe that domestic violence was not particularly common or problematic. Greater public awareness has been achieved in part through the higher priority paid to domestic violence cases in the legal and criminal justice system. This has opened many cases to the public eye through media coverage, particularly when the victims or perpetrators are celebrities, such as movie stars or famous sports figures. Since the 1990s dozens of domestic violence accusations involving celebrities have received media coverage. In most cases, the charges are dropped by the alleged victims and never reach a courtroom. Famous people involved in these cases include the boxer Floyd Mayweather Jr. (1977–); the actor Charlie Sheen (1965–); and the singers Chris Brown (1989–), Rihanna (1988–), Whitney Houston (1963–2012), and Bobby Brown (1969–).

In recent years the National Football League (NFL) has come under particularly intense scrutiny for the high number of domestic violence incidents involving its players. As Michael Martinez reports in "NFL's Past Penalties for Domestic Violence 'a Different Story'" (CNN.com, September 16, 2014), between 2000 and 2014, 85 NFL players were arrested on domestic violence charges. The most controversial domestic violence case involving an NFL player occurred in February 2014, when Baltimore Ravens running back Ray Rice (1987—) was arrested for assaulting his girlfriend, Janay Palmer, at an Atlantic City casino. The incident gained national attention days later, when celebrity news outlet TMZ aired video footage that showed Rice dragging an unconscious Palmer out of an elevator. The NFL's decision to suspend Rice for two games sparked further outrage among a number of women's groups and anti–domestic violence organizations, who decried the punishment as inadequate. Facing mounting criticism in August 2014, the league announced harsher rules governing domestic violence incidents involving its players, increasing the penalty for a first offense to a six-game suspension. On September 8, 2014, less than two weeks after the NFL introduced its new code of conduct, TMZ released additional video footage from inside the casino elevator, which clearly showed Rice punching Palmer in the face. That same day, the Baltimore Ravens terminated Rice's contract and the league suspended him indefinitely (the suspension was later overturned in court). Despite these actions, the league remained under fire in the media for its overall handling of the case.

Public Health Campaigns

In *Breaking the Silence—Public Health's Role in Intimate Partner Violence Prevention* (May 17, 2012, http://www.cdc.gov/cdcgrandrounds/archives/2012/june2012.htm), the CDC provides information about programs and activities that are facilitated by the agency to aid in the prevention of intimate partner violence. Besides data collection and research projects, the CDC operates two key programs: Domestic Violence Prevention Enhancement and Leadership through Alliances (DELTA) and Dating Matters.

The agency notes in "Domestic Violence Prevention Enhancement and Leadership through Alliances (DELTA)" (November 14, 2013, http://www.cdc.gov/ViolencePrevention/DELTA/index.html) that the DELTA program is devoted to reducing the incidence of new cases of intimate partner violence. The program was established during the 1990s, when the federal government began funding Coordinated Community Responses (CCRs) in local communities. According to the CDC, the CCRs involve entities from law enforcement, public health, and the nonprofit sector and focus on "providing services to victims, holding batterers accountable, and reducing the number of recurring assaults." In 2002 the agency began funding the DELTA program to focus on the following prevention strategies:

- Preventing first-time perpetration and first-time victimization

- Reducing the risk factors that are associated with intimate partner violence

- Promoting protective factors that reduce the likelihood of intimate partner violence

- Implementing evidence-supported strategies that incorporate behavior and social change theories

- Evaluating prevention strategies and using results to form future plans

According to the CDC, state domestic violence coalitions use DELTA funding to support local CCRs that are involved in projects such as preventing teen dating violence, supporting healthy relationship development, and preventing first-time perpetration of domestic violence by men and boys.

In the fact sheet "Affordable Care Act Rules on Expanding Access to Preventive Services for Women" (June 28, 2013, http://www.hhs.gov/healthcare/facts/fact sheets/2011/08/womensprevention08012011a.html), the U.S. Department of Health and Human Services (HHS) notes that under the Patient Protection and Affordable Care Act of 2010 medical insurance plans that were initiated or renewed after August 2012 must cover interpersonal and domestic violence screening and counseling services for all adolescent and adult women at no charge to them. The Affordable Care Act includes major reforms to the nation's health care system including greatly expanded preventive programs. According to the HHS, the new screening and counseling requirement should aid in the detection and treatment of abused women.

Victim Services

One of the most common victim services is the operation of domestic violence hotlines by government entities and private organizations. For example, the National Domestic Violence Hotline (2014, http://www.thehotline.org) was established in 1996 as part of the Violence against Women Act of 1994. The hotline is available 24 hours a day, seven days a week. The operators who answer the phone can provide informational

materials on battering intervention, the criminal justice system, sexual assault, and other issues, as well as crisis intervention and safety planning. Referrals to local service providers are also available. According to the National Domestic Violence Hotline, between 1996 and 2013 the hotline provided assistance to 3.4 million people seeking help for domestic violence and dating violence issues. In 2013 the hotline received a total of 331,078 contacts; of these, 264,415 were incoming calls, 55,610 were online chats, and 11,053 were texts.

A new innovation in victim services technology is the availability of application (app) software for mobile computerized devices such as smartphones and tablets. For example, in August 2012 the communications corporation Verizon Wireless introduced the HopeLine app. The company notes in "HopeLine from Verizon Introduces Mobile App for Android Smartphones and Tablets" (August 3, 2012, http://news.verizonwireless.com/news/2012/08/pr2012-08-02c.html) that the app allows users to connect directly to resources, such as the National Domestic Violence Hotline. In addition, the app provides access to an online community through which people can share stories, photos, and videos and learn about domestic violence services.

There are thousands of victim service agencies around the country that help domestic violence victims. The "Directory of Crime Victim Services" (2014, http://ovc.ncjrs.org/findvictimservices/search.asp), operated by the DOJ's Office for Victims of Crime, includes an extensive online directory of more than 10,000 programs. Online visitors can search for crime victim services in a particular state. For example, a search for resources in California yields nearly 1,000 services available to domestic violence victims. The directory also lists resources that are located in some other countries and services that are provided through the U.S. military.

Besides law enforcement and other criminal justice agencies, the directory includes government and private agencies that offer the following types of services to domestic violence victims:

- In-person information about and referrals to available services and support organizations

- Assistance in filing crime victim compensation claims with appropriate agencies

- Support, assistance, and advocacy as victims navigate the criminal justice process, including postsentencing services and support

- Crisis counseling, including in-person crisis intervention, hotline counseling, emotional support, and guidance, provided by advocates, counselors, mental health professionals, or peers

- Emergency financial assistance, including cash out-lays for needs such as transportation, food, clothing, and emergency housing

- Emergency assistance in certain legal matters, such as filing of temporary restraining orders, injunctions, and other protective orders

- Follow-up contact via telephone, in-person meetings, or written communications to offer emotional support and check on a victim's progress

- Coordination and provision of supportive group activities, including social support services

- Personal advocacy services, such as accompanying victims to the hospital; intervening with employers, creditors, and others on behalf of victims; and assisting in filing insurance claims and for programs, such as public assistance, workers' compensation, or unemployment benefits, as appropriate

- Safety planning for stalking victims to help reduce the chances of physical or emotional harm from stalkers

- Shelters and safe houses that offer short- and long-term housing and related support services for victims and families after a victimization

- Professional, psychological, psychiatric, or other therapy or counseling-related evaluation and treatment for individuals, couples, and family members affected by victimization

- Transportation services to and from victim service agencies

The Bureau of Justice Statistics (BJS), an office within the U.S. Department of Justice, publishes annual data on domestic violence through its *Criminal Victimization* series and oversees the National Crime Victimization Survey (NCVS), a leading source of victimization statistics. The BJS also manages an online database, the NCVS Victimization Analysis Tool (NVAT), which provides additional statistics on domestic violence in the United States. Besides calculating prevalence rates for various types of domestic violence, the BJS assesses the relationships between victims and perpetrators in domestic violence situations, as well as the rates at which victims of domestic violence seek medical attention or other victim services.

Table 7.3 provides an overall breakdown of violent victimizations between 2003 and 2012. Most victims of intimate partner violence do not end up receiving victim services. (See Table 7.3.) For example, of the 810,794 victims of intimate partner violence in 2012, only 227,300, or 28%, received victim services following the incident. Although this pattern has generally also proven true for victims of rape or sexual assault, in recent years the proportion of rape or sexual assault victims who

received victim services has seen a sudden rise. In 2003, 134,478 individuals were raped or sexually assaulted by an intimate partner; of these, 28,674 (21%) received victim services. (See Table 7.4.) Of the 64,412 cases of intimate partner rape or sexual assault that were recorded in 2012, nearly two-thirds of the victims (39,638, or 62%) went on to receive victim services.

Table 7.5 provides a breakdown of victims who received medical treatment for injuries related to domestic violence incidents between 2003 and 2012. Of the 810,794 victims of intimate partner violence in 2012, 486,920 (60%) reported no injury following the incident, 193,699 (24%) were injured but not treated, and 130,175 (16%) were treated for an injury. (See Table 7.5.) Victims of rape or sexual assault are far more likely to sustain injuries than other victims of intimate partner violence. Of the 64,412 victims who were raped or sexually assaulted by an intimate partner in 2012, nearly three-quarters (46,392, or 72%) were reported as sustaining injuries; however, only 6,975 victims (15% of those injured; 11% of victims of this type of violence) received some form of medical treatment. (See Table 7.6.)

Why Do Abused Women Stay?

One complicated issue for people who are devoted to preventing domestic violence is that victims sometimes choose to stay in violent relationships. This begs the question: Why do victims stay? Some authors and advocates believe this question implies that there is something wrong with the victims for staying, rather than placing the blame where it belongs: on the abusers. Ola W. Barnett of Pepperdine University argues in "Why Battered Women Do Not Leave, Part 1: External Inhibiting Factors within Society" (*Trauma, Violence, and Abuse*, vol. 1, no. 4, October 2000) that better questions might be: "Why does he beat her?" or "Why does society let him get away with it?" or "What can be done to stop him?" Nevertheless, researchers have focused their efforts on determining the motivations that drive victims, particularly women, to stay in abusive relationships.

WOMEN'S REASONS TO STAY. Women stay in abusive relationships for a variety of reasons. A major reason women stay is their economic dependency on their batterer. Many women feel they are better off with a violent husband than facing the challenge of raising children on their own. Some harbor deep feelings for their abusive partner and believe that over time they can change their partner's behavior. Others mistakenly interpret their abuser's efforts to control their life as expressions of love. Some frequently reported practical considerations include:

- The women have at least one dependent child who must be cared for

- The women are unemployed

TABLE 7.3

Violent victimizations, by victim-offender relationship, type of victimization, and victim services status, 2003–12

Crime type	2003	2004	2005	2006	2007	2008	2009	2010	2011	2012
Violent victimization	7,679,050	6,726,060	6,947,795	8,430,430	6,814,183	6,393,471	5,669,237	4,935,983	5,812,523	6,842,593
Intimates	1,040,285	1,031,721	816,006	1,305,249	905,810	1,103,392	1,039,650	773,434	850,772	810,794
Services received from victim service agencies	284,308	297,761	198,909	281,045	261,604	240,625	217,766	179,200	136,650	227,300
No services received from victim service agencies	746,862	720,818	613,323	1,024,205	641,433	862,767	816,060	588,985	687,562	571,060
Other relatives	440,634	402,467	426,284	558,407	501,907	454,603	343,020	356,129	504,135	448,598
Services received from victim service agencies	48,456	79,467	44,074	72,067	42,288	103,397!	32,192!	65,493	98,815	48,375
No services received from victim service agencies	389,574	323,001	382,211	472,819	456,886	347,182	259,374	286,381	401,192	395,057
Well-known/casual acquaintances	2,596,812	2,267,162	2,356,241	2,661,522	1,997,175	1,781,331	1,756,014	1,573,294	1,779,618	2,263,252
Services received from victim service agencies	375,444	192,241	241,004	131,423	185,473	117,579	116,849	125,725	127,146	214,089
No services received from victim service agencies	2,208,746	2,070,063	2,108,625	2,525,332	1,806,263	1,651,546	1,639,164	1,445,512	1,628,526	2,039,402
Stranger	3,107,181	2,672,238	2,829,598	3,184,058	2,706,132	2,154,770	2,165,849	1,812,303	2,146,307	2,710,114
Services received from victim service agencies	184,275	137,505	131,079	162,685	116,067	74,153	86,549	35,277!	103,639	57,636
No services received from victim service agencies	2,922,906	2,534,733	2,692,957	3,014,495	2,590,066	2,063,254	2,065,653	1,762,695	2,031,405	2,603,245
Do not know relationship	346,484	268,558	361,855	506,652	448,275	486,084	217,989	288,667	240,956	371,910
Services received from victim service agencies	34,350!	10,575!	25,115!	27,612!	13,584!	37,100!	12,176!	13,638!	19,326!	10,053!
No services received from victim service agencies	305,324	254,111	321,009	465,480	422,566	431,443	194,488	259,214	216,374	355,561
Do not know number of offenders	147,654	83,914	157,809	214,541	254,885	413,292	139,707	132,156	290,736	228,660
Services received from victim service agencies	3,019!	4,311!	32,778!	11,162!	14,767!	4,017!	—	6,019!	12,648!	3,501!
No services received from victim service agencies	141,517	79,603	114,015	197,311	237,461	395,569	122,292	121,178	211,167	219,040
Serious violent victimization	2,395,954	2,290,845	2,258,400	3,149,814	2,242,721	1,998,697	1,969,921	1,694,835	1,854,837	2,084,691
Intimates	498,467	334,623	311,475	535,611	306,986	398,306	250,475	268,780	262,658	270,239
Services received from victim service agencies	183,771	127,069	111,033	139,378	90,492	72,473	41,680	70,495	39,075	84,628
No services received from victim service agencies	314,696	204,866	196,667	396,232	213,720	325,833	206,303	196,350	223,584	184,010
Other relatives	152,182	132,619	113,790	254,037	283,009	185,741	94,760	111,251	106,379	140,837
Services received from victim service agencies	16,517!	49,433!	20,661!	36,642!	24,463!	16,954!	17,510!	28,605!	18,680!	11,301!
No services received from victim service agencies	135,664	83,187	93,129	206,527	258,547	168,788	42,471!	78,390	85,212	129,535
Well-known/casual acquaintances	588,591	739,743	529,824	853,719	501,995	445,012	648,287	462,152	483,669	459,981
Services received from victim service agencies	108,942	53,395	95,781	39,682	46,336!	44,434	105,049!	64,259	50,095!	54,989
No services received from victim service agencies	479,649	684,364	430,924	812,654	453,421	397,060	543,238	395,836	428,680	400,312
Stranger	957,750	966,386	1,096,475	1,259,605	937,792	709,102	821,534	721,671	803,761	1,020,398
Services received from victim service agencies	52,634	60,698	47,325	105,035	56,320	43,811	22,941!	15,721!	60,819	35,605
No services received from victim service agencies	905,116	905,687	1,049,150	1,154,570	881,472	652,925	784,946	695,423	735,299	974,289
Do not know relationship	132,730	74,175	152,888	176,216	141,219	157,134	121,315	93,777	112,302	106,332
Services received from victim service agencies	6,524!	5,256!	17,833!	18,083!	—	12,718!	5,160!	2,933!	15,158!	10,053!
No services received from victim service agencies	122,015	68,920	122,424	147,597	136,759	134,800	111,904	85,362	95,622	93,411
Do not know number of offenders	66,235	43,300	53,948	70,626	71,720	103,401	33,550!	37,205!	86,067	86,904
Services received from victim service agencies	—	4,311!	6,828!	7,277!	11,314!	4,017!	—	2,118!	8,289!	3,501!
No services received from victim service agencies	66,235	38,989	42,286	57,281	60,406	99,385	33,550!	30,127!	72,513	79,209
Simple assault	5,283,096	4,435,215	4,689,395	5,280,616	4,571,462	4,394,774	3,699,316	3,241,148	3,957,686	4,757,902
Intimates	541,818	697,098	504,532	769,639	598,824	705,086	789,175	504,654	588,113	540,555
Services received from victim service agencies	100,537	170,692	87,876	141,666	171,111	168,152	176,086	108,705	97,575	142,671
No services received from victim service agencies	432,166	515,952	416,656	627,972	427,713	536,934	609,757	392,635	463,978	387,049
Other relatives	288,452	269,848	312,494	304,370	218,897	268,862	248,260	244,878	397,755	307,761
Services received from victim service agencies	31,939	30,034	23,413!	35,426	17,826!	86,443!	14,682!	36,888!	80,135!	37,074
No services received from victim service agencies	253,909	239,814	289,082	266,292	198,339	178,394	216,903	207,990	315,979	265,522

TABLE 7.3

Violent victimizations, by victim–offender relationship, type of victimization, and victim services status, 2003–12 [CONTINUED]

Crime type	2003	2004	2005	2006	2007	2008	2009	2010	2011	2012
Well-known/casual acquaintances	**2,008,221**	**1,527,419**	**1,826,417**	**1,807,803**	**1,495,180**	**1,336,318**	**1,107,727**	**1,111,143**	**1,295,949**	**1,803,271**
Services received from victim service agencies	266,502	138,846	145,223	91,741	139,138	73,146	11,800!	61,467	77,052	159,100
No services received from victim service agencies	1,729,098	1,385,699	1,677,701	1,712,678	1,352,843	1,254,486	1,095,927	1,049,676	1,199,846	1,639,089
Stranger	**2,149,431**	**1,705,852**	**1,733,123**	**1,924,453**	**1,768,340**	**1,445,668**	**1,344,315**	**1,090,632**	**1,342,546**	**1,689,717**
Services received from victim service agencies	131,641	76,807	83,754	57,651	59,747	30,342!	63,608!	19,556!	42,820	22,031!
No services received from victim service agencies	2,017,790	1,629,046	1,643,807	1,859,925	1,708,593	1,410,329	1,280,707	1,067,272	1,296,106	1,628,957
Do not know relationship	**213,754**	**194,383**	**208,968**	**330,436**	**307,055**	**328,949**	**96,674**	**194,890**	**128,654**	**265,577**
Services received from victim service agencies	27,826!	5,319!	7,282!	9,529!	13,584!	24,382!	7,016!	10,704!	4,168!	—
No services received from victim service agencies	183,309	185,191	198,584	317,883	285,807	296,643	82,584	173,852	120,752	262,151
Do not know number of offenders	**81,419**	**40,614!**	**103,861**	**143,915**	**183,165**	**309,891**	**106,156**	**94,952**	**204,669**	**141,756**
Services received from victim service agencies	3,019!	—	25,950!	3,885!	3,453!	—	—	3,901!	4,359!	—
No services received from victim service agencies	75,283	40,614!	71,729	140,030	177,055	296,185	88,742	91,051	138,654	139,831

—Estimate is equal to 0 sample cases.

!Interpret data with caution, based on 10 or fewer sample cases or the coefficient of variation is greater than 50%.

Notes: Detail may not sum to total due to rounding and/or missing data. Due to methodological changes in the 2006 National Crime Victimization Survey, use caution when comparing 2006 criminal victimization estimates to other years.

source: "Number of Violent Victimizations, Serious Violent Victimizations, and Simple Assaults by Victim–Offender Relationship and Victim Services, 2003–2012," in *NCVS Victimization Analysis Tool (NVAT)*, U.S. Department of Justice, Office of Justice Programs, Bureau of Justice Statistics, July 23, 2014, http://www.bjs.gov/index.cfm?ty=nvat (accessed July 23, 2014)

TABLE 7.4

Rapes and sexual assaults, by victim-offender relationship and victim services status, 2003–12

Crime type	2003	2004	2005	2006	2007	2008	2009	2010	2011	2012
Rape/sexual assault	325,311	255,769	207,760	463,598	248,277	349,691	305,574	268,574	244,188	346,830
Intimates	134,478	59,669	66,750	157,698	55,110	103,675	43,198	109,205	44,155	64,412
Services received from victim service agencies	28,674!	26,871!	8,208!	65,485!	17,767!	43,444!	10,297!	44,809!	8,240!	39,638!
No services received from victim service agencies	105,805!	32,798	58,542	92,213	37,343	60,231!	32,901!	64,396!	35,915	24,774!
Other relatives	33,301!	5,596!	11,853!	7,397!	6,529!	24,670!	34,779!	12,921!	1,721!	3,458!
Services received from victim service agencies	9,134!	2,879!	—	—	—	5,219!	—	12,921!	—	3,458!
No services received from victim service agencies	24,166!	2,717!	11,853!	7,397!	6,529!	19,451!	—	—	1,721!	—
Well-known/casual acquaintances	95,418	78,441	60,813	152,255	81,968	90,611	187,848	97,817	117,760	162,288
Services received from victim service agencies	19,363!	18,057!	25,103!	3,440!	14,700!	10,590!	8,787!	39,914!	29,515!	29,061!
No services received from victim service agencies	76,055	60,384	35,711!	148,815	65,029	80,022	179,061	57,902	88,245	133,228
Stranger	58,978	91,802	59,982	134,929	77,477	76,907	36,586	43,167	72,807	59,126
Services received from victim service agencies	5,813!	20,865!	9,103!	24,969!	19,158!	3,108!	—	3,560!	15,240!	3,103!
No services received from victim service agencies	53,165	70,936	50,879	109,960	58,318	73,798	36,586	39,607	57,567	52,246
Do not know relationship	3,135!	17,170!	5,375!	11,320!	13,823!	9,346!	3,163!	5,464!	4,835!	17,174
Services received from victim service agencies	—	2,814!	—	—	—	2,892!	—	—	—	—
No services received from victim service agencies	3,135!	14,356!	5,375!	11,320!	13,823!	6,454!	3,163!	5,464!	4,835!	17,174!
Do not know number of offenders	—	3,092!	2,987!	—	13,370!	44,483!	—	—	2,911!	40,372!
Services received from victim service agencies	—	—	—	—	8,042!	4,017!	—	—	2,911!	—
No services received from victim service agencies	—	3,092!	2,987!	—	5,329!	40,466!	—	—	—	40,372!

—Estimate is equal to 0 sample cases.
!Interpret data with caution, based on 10 or fewer sample cases or the coefficient of variation is greater than 50%.
Notes: Detail may not sum to total due to rounding and/or missing data. Due to methodological changes in the 2006 National Crime Victimization Survey, use caution when comparing 2006 criminal victimization estimates to other years.

SOURCE: "Number of Rape/Sexual Assaults by Victim-Offender Relationship and Victim Services, 2003–2012," in *NCVS Victimization Analysis Tool (NVAT)*, U.S. Department of Justice, Office of Justice Programs, Bureau of Justice Statistics, July 23, 2014, http://www.bjs.gov/index.cfm?ty=nvat (accessed July 23, 2014)

- The women lack a support system, for example, their parents are distant, unable, or unwilling to help

- The women may fear losing mutual friends and the support of family, especially in-laws

- The women have no property that is solely their own

- The women lack access to cash, credit, or other financial resources

- If the women leave, then they risk being charged with desertion and losing their children and joint assets

- Women may face a decline in living standards for themselves and their children, and the children, especially older ones, may resent this reduced living standard

- The women and/or their children may be in poor health

In "'We Don't Have Time for Social Change': Cultural Compromise and the Battered Woman Syndrome" (*Gender and Society*, vol. 17, no. 5, October 2003), Bess Rothenberg of Clemson University argues that women are victimized and coerced into staying in violent relationships by a combination of different forces. According to Rothenberg, women are victimized first and foremost by violent abusers; second, by a society that sanctions the right of men to hit women and socializes women into staying in abusive relationships; third, by representatives of institutions who are in a position to help but who instead ignore the plight of battered women (e.g., doctors, police, the criminal justice system, clergy, and therapists); and fourth, by the everyday realities of being a woman in a patriarchal system that expects women to raise children and denies them access to education, job skills, and good employment.

Similarly, in "Victims of Chronic Dating Violence: How Women's Vulnerabilities Link to Their Decisions to Stay" (*Family Relations*, vol. 54, no. 2, April 2005), April L. Few and Karen H. Rosen examine why women stay in abusive dating relationships and describe a combination of "relational" and "situational" vulnerabilities that work together to influence a woman's decision to stay. They define relational vulnerabilities as one's beliefs about what behaviors and interactions are normal in an intimate relationship. Situational vulnerabilities refer to the degree to which a woman was experiencing stress at the beginning of the abusive relationship (either as a consequence of life changes or as a consequence of feeling like one is getting too old for marriage or parenthood). Few and Rosen find that an accumulation of vulnerabilities, combined with lacking protective factors such as a high self-esteem, a social support system, and healthy coping skills, made it more likely that a woman would stay in a chronically abusive dating relationship.

TABLE 7.5

Violent victimizations, by victim-offender relationship, type of victimization, and injury and medical treatment status, 2003–12

Crime type	2003	2004	2005	2006	2007	2008	2009	2010	2011	2012
Violent victimization	**7,679,050**	**6,726,060**	**6,947,795**	**8,430,430**	**6,814,183**	**6,393,471**	**5,669,237**	**4,935,983**	**5,812,523**	**6,842,593**
Intimates	**1,040,285**	**1,031,721**	**816,006**	**1,305,249**	**905,810**	**1,103,392**	**1,039,650**	**773,434**	**850,772**	**810,794**
Not injured	458,807	469,987	375,134	481,470	490,532	655,364	604,905	431,806	569,855	486,920
Not treated for injury	274,275	380,870	261,570	660,217	309,492	297,608	332,745	175,653	188,499	193,699
Treated at scene, home, medical office, or other location	307,203	180,864	179,302	163,563	105,786	150,420	102,000	165,974	92,418	130,175
Other relatives	**440,634**	**402,467**	**426,284**	**558,407**	**501,907**	**454,603**	**343,020**	**356,129**	**504,135**	**448,598**
Not injured	245,914	228,089	306,988	353,011	268,267	328,052	237,219	250,478	298,142	276,341
Not treated for injury	157,970	130,014	83,376	115,123	70,124	63,489	64,647	58,292	91,563	81,466
Treated at scene, home, medical office, or other location	36,750	44,364	35,920!	90,273	163,516	63,061	41,155	44,510	114,430	90,791
Well-known/casual acquaintances	**2,596,812**	**2,267,162**	**2,356,241**	**2,661,522**	**1,997,175**	**1,781,331**	**1,756,014**	**1,573,294**	**1,779,618**	**2,263,252**
Not injured	2,047,938	1,733,624	1,914,564	1,965,928	1,579,088	1,428,360	1,362,438	1,264,429	1,318,565	1,852,448
Not treated for injury	312,027	314,144	282,976	493,327	285,173	222,771	272,537	156,346	286,207	250,193
Treated at scene, home, medical office, or other location	236,848	216,858	158,702	202,267	132,914	130,199	121,039	152,519	174,846	160,611
Stranger	**3,107,181**	**2,672,238**	**2,829,598**	**3,184,058**	**2,706,132**	**2,154,770**	**2,165,849**	**1,812,303**	**2,146,307**	**2,710,114**
Not injured	2,530,680	2,027,807	2,208,657	2,469,966	2,105,304	1,756,549	1,712,201	1,357,845	1,730,944	2,163,554
Not treated for injury	339,275	359,568	320,075	348,710	279,204	206,093	238,183	256,033	200,459	308,346
Treated at scene, home, medical office, or other location	237,226	284,863	300,867	365,383	321,625	192,127	215,465	198,425	214,904	238,215
Do not know relationship	**346,484**	**268,558**	**361,855**	**506,652**	**448,275**	**486,084**	**217,989**	**288,667**	**240,956**	**371,910**
Not injured	245,027	210,947	257,243	428,649	385,545	424,444	142,937	237,558	196,770	315,250
Not treated for injury	63,932!	29,337!	47,706!	45,161	36,893	24,660!	14,872!	28,656!	26,105!	28,506!
Treated at scene, home, medical office, or other location	37,525	28,274!	52,703	30,369!	22,704!	33,038!	52,702	22,453!	12,511!	21,667!
Do not know number of offenders	**147,654**	**83,914**	**157,809**	**214,541**	**254,885**	**413,292**	**139,707**	**132,156**	**290,736**	**228,660**
Not injured	121,483	70,682	125,995	177,667	225,608	349,711	125,462	104,039	247,597	170,724
Not treated for injury	8,176!	8,921!	14,431!	8,705!	18,159!	63,581!	8,072!	20,810!	8,313!	10,495!
Treated at scene, home, medical office, or other location	17,995!	4,311!	17,383!	28,169!	11,118!	—	6,173!	7,307!	34,825!	47,441!
Serious violent victimization	**2,395,954**	**2,290,845**	**2,258,400**	**3,149,814**	**2,242,721**	**1,998,697**	**1,969,921**	**1,694,835**	**1,854,837**	**2,084,691**
Intimates	**498,467**	**334,623**	**311,475**	**535,611**	**306,986**	**398,306**	**250,475**	**268,780**	**262,658**	**270,239**
Not injured	211,689	125,898	54,779	208,383	134,990	141,140	91,069	88,514	121,745	99,847
Not treated for injury	63,576	97,145	122,331	255,036	114,718	153,410	120,419	60,756	86,733	98,807
Treated at scene, home, medical office, or other location	223,201	111,580	134,365	72,191	57,278	103,756	38,987	119,510	54,181	71,585
Other relatives	**152,182**	**132,619**	**113,790**	**254,037**	**283,009**	**185,741**	**94,760**	**111,251**	**106,379**	**140,837**
Not injured	55,709	47,087	91,533	166,455	129,647	149,780	58,370!	71,161	90,692	81,385
Not treated for injury	80,639!	58,767!	12,860!	39,476!	11,663!	3,387!	16,031!	15,904!	5,236!	20,639!
Treated at scene, home, medical office, or other location	15,834!	26,765!	9,396!	48,107!	141,699!	32,574!	20,359!	24,186!	10,451!	38,813
Well-known/casual acquaintances	**588,591**	**739,743**	**529,824**	**853,719**	**501,995**	**445,012**	**648,287**	**462,152**	**483,669**	**459,981**
Not injured	354,177	522,131	372,879	570,711	376,762	317,454	414,712	306,304	270,341	339,562
Not treated for injury	136,000	117,015	55,283	179,336	77,365	67,720	148,821	53,336	112,256	68,260
Treated at scene, home, medical office, or other location	98,415	100,597	101,662	103,673	47,868	59,839	84,753	102,512	101,073	52,159
Stranger	**957,750**	**966,386**	**1,096,475**	**1,259,605**	**937,792**	**709,102**	**821,534**	**721,671**	**803,761**	**1,020,398**
Not injured	683,419	680,283	785,121	889,925	637,897	467,249	555,738	470,259	562,860	697,624
Not treated for injury	119,196	92,606	154,334	128,185	111,082	117,115	100,838	126,390	77,395	167,838
Treated at scene, home, medical office, or other location	155,135	193,497	157,019	241,495	188,813	124,738	164,958	125,022	163,506	154,935
Do not know relationship	**132,730**	**74,175**	**152,888**	**176,216**	**141,219**	**157,134**	**121,315**	**93,777**	**112,302**	**106,332**
Not injured	88,508	52,533	98,441	130,760	122,526	107,932	77,237	69,490	71,062	68,025
Not treated for injury	9,536!	6,191!	22,607!	25,593!	15,561!	18,277!	—	9,993!	23,158!	10,153!
Treated at scene, home, medical office, or other location	34,686!	15,451!	31,840!	19,863!	—	30,926!	39,301!	14,294!	12,511!	21,667!

TABLE 7.5

Violent victimizations, by victim-offender relationship, type of victimization, and injury and medical treatment status, 2003–12 [CONTINUED]

Crime type	2003	2004	2005	2006	2007	2008	2009	2010	2011	2012
Do not know number of offenders	**66,235**	**43,300**	**53,948**	**70,626**	**71,720**	**103,401**	**33,550!**	**37,205!**	**86,067**	**86,904**
Not injured	48,713	34,291	30,849!	37,186!	45,859	51,918	21,446!	20,950!	48,331	36,075
Not treated for injury	2,546!	4,698!	5,716!	8,705!	14,744!	51,483!	5,931!	8,948!	2,911!	3,388!
Treated at scene, home, medical office, or other location	14,976!	4,311!	17,383!	24,734!	11,118!	—	6,173!	7,307!	34,825!	47,441!
Simple assault	**5,283,096**	**4,435,215**	**4,689,395**	**5,280,616**	**4,571,462**	**4,394,774**	**3,699,316**	**3,241,148**	**3,957,686**	**4,757,902**
Intimates	**541,818**	**697,098**	**504,532**	**769,639**	**598,824**	**705,086**	**789,175**	**504,654**	**588,113**	**540,555**
Not injured	247,117	344,089	320,356	273,087	355,542	514,224	513,836	343,292	448,110	387,073
Not treated for injury	210,699	283,725	139,239	405,180	194,774	144,197	212,326	114,897	101,767	94,892
Treated at scene, home, medical office, or other location	84,001	69,284	44,937	91,371	48,508	46,664	63,013	46,465	38,237	58,590
Other relatives	**288,452**	**269,848**	**312,494**	**304,370**	**218,897**	**268,862**	**248,260**	**244,878**	**397,755**	**307,761**
Not injured	190,205	181,002	215,455	186,557	138,619	178,272	178,848	179,318	207,450	194,956
Not treated for injury	77,331	71,247	70,516	75,647	58,461	60,102	48,616	42,387	86,327	60,827
Treated at scene, home, medical office, or other location	20,917!	17,599!	26,524!	42,166!	21,817!	30,487!	20,796!	20,324!	103,979	51,978!
Well-known/casual acquaintances	**2,008,221**	**1,527,419**	**1,826,417**	**1,807,803**	**1,495,180**	**1,336,318**	**1,107,727**	**1,111,143**	**1,295,949**	**1,803,271**
Not injured	1,693,761	1,211,493	1,541,684	1,395,218	1,202,326	1,110,907	947,725	958,126	1,048,225	1,512,885
Not treated for injury	176,027	197,129	227,693	313,991	207,808	155,051	123,716	103,010	173,951	181,933
Treated at scene, home, medical office, or other location	138,433	116,261	57,040	98,594	85,046	70,360	36,286!	50,007	73,773	108,452
Stranger	**2,149,431**	**1,705,852**	**1,733,123**	**1,924,453**	**1,768,340**	**1,445,668**	**1,344,315**	**1,090,632**	**1,342,546**	**1,689,717**
Not injured	1,847,261	1,347,524	1,423,536	1,580,041	1,467,407	1,289,299	1,156,463	887,586	1,168,083	1,465,930
Not treated for injury	220,079	266,962	165,740	220,525	168,121	88,979	137,346	129,642	123,064	140,508
Treated at scene, home, medical office, or other location	82,091	91,367	143,847	123,888	132,812	67,390	50,507	73,403	51,398	83,279
Do not know relationship	**213,754**	**194,383**	**208,968**	**330,436**	**307,055**	**328,949**	**96,674**	**194,890**	**128,654**	**265,577**
Not injured	156,519	158,414	158,802	297,889	263,019	316,512	65,700	168,068	125,708	247,225
Not treated for injury	54,396!	23,147!	25,099!	19,568!	21,332!	6,383!	14,872!	18,663!	2,947!	18,353!
Treated at scene, home, medical office, or other location	2,839!	12,823!	20,864!	10,506!	22,704!	2,111!	13,401!	8,160!	—	—
Do not know number of offenders	**81,419**	**40,614!**	**103,861**	**143,915**	**183,165**	**309,891**	**106,156**	**94,952**	**204,669**	**141,756**
Not injured	72,770	36,391!	95,145	140,481	179,749	297,793	104,016	83,090	199,267	134,649
Not treated for injury	5,630!	4,223!	8,715!	—	3,415!	12,098!	2,140!	11,862!	5,402!	7,106!
Treated at scene, home, medical office, or other location	3,019!	—	—	3,434!	—	—	—	—	—	—

—Estimate is equal to 0 sample cases.

!Interpret data with caution, based on 10 or fewer sample cases or the coefficient of variation is greater than 50%.

Notes: Detail may not sum to total due to rounding and/or missing data. Due to methodological changes in the 2006 National Crime Victimization Survey, use caution when comparing 2006 criminal victimization estimates to other years.

SOURCE: "Number of Violent Victimizations, Serious Violent Victimizations, and Simple Assaults by Victim-Offender Relationship and Medical Treatment for Physical Injuries, 2003–2012," in *NCVS Victimization Analysis Tool (NVAT)*, U.S. Department of Justice, Office of Justice Programs, Bureau of Justice Statistics, July 23, 2014, http://www.bjs.gov/index.cfm?ty=nvat (accessed July 23, 2014)

TABLE 7.6

Rapes and sexual assaults, by victim-offender relationship and injury and medical treatment status, 2003–12

Crime type	2003	2004	2005	2006	2007	2008	2009	2010	2011	2012
Rape/sexual assault	**325,311**	**255,769**	**207,760**	**463,598**	**248,277**	**349,691**	**305,574**	**268,574**	**244,188**	**346,830**
Intimates	**134,478**	**59,669**	**66,750**	**157,698**	**55,110**	**103,675**	**43,198**	**109,205**	**44,155**	**64,412**
Not injured	55,048!	8,467!	10,965!	11,419!	13,251!	14,811!	28,067!	9,533!	15,524!	18,020!
Not treated for injury	15,281!	20,946!	27,882!	123,119	28,676!	81,291!	6,427!	14,190!	27,169!	39,417!
Treated at scene, home, medical office, or other location	64,150!	30,256!	27,904!	23,160!	13,183!	7,573!	8,703!	85,482!	1,463!	6,975!
Other relatives	**33,301!**	**5,596!**	**11,853!**	**7,397!**	**6,529!**	**24,670!**	**34,779!**	**12,921!**	**1,721!**	**3,458!**
Not injured	2,346!	5,596!	4,604!	—	6,529!	19,451!	34,779!	10,866!	1,721!	3,458!
Not treated for injury	30,954!	—	7,249!	7,397!	—	—	—	2,055!	—	—
Treated at scene, home, medical office, or other location	—	—	—	—	—	5,219!	—	—	—	—
Well-known/casual acquaintances	**95,418**	**78,441**	**60,813**	**152,255**	**81,968**	**90,611**	**187,848**	**97,817**	**117,760**	**162,288**
Not injured	38,017	51,676	21,327!	98,347	47,503	57,720	110,808!	66,428	62,622	120,667
Not treated for injury	32,509!	14,177!	17,443!	33,010!	28,396!	23,598!	69,942!	19,271!	55,138	27,096!
Treated at scene, home, medical office, or other location	24,892!	12,587!	22,043!	20,898!	6,069!	9,294!	7,098!	12,118!	—	14,526!
Stranger	**58,978**	**91,802**	**59,982**	**134,929**	**77,477**	**76,907**	**36,586**	**43,167**	**72,807**	**59,126**
Not injured	29,472!	62,659	30,975!	100,622	37,532	34,516!	22,140!	26,102!	37,162!	50,697
Not treated for injury	16,004!	10,070!	15,230!	14,582!	17,738!	31,717!	3,974!	11,443!	16,965!	8,429!
Treated at scene, home, medical office, or other location	13,502!	19,073!	13,777!	19,724!	22,206!	10,673!	10,472!	5,623!	18,680!	—
Do not know relationship	**3,135!**	**17,170!**	**5,375!**	**11,320!**	**13,823!**	**9,346!**	**3,163!**	**5,464!**	**4,835!**	**17,174!**
Not injured	3,135!	14,546!	5,375!	3,797!	13,823!	6,454!	3,163!	5,464!	1,572!	6,817!
Not treated for injury	—	—	—	7,523!	—	—	—	—	—	2,829!
Treated at scene, home, medical office, or other location	—	2,624!	—	—	—	2,892!	—	—	3,263!	7,528!
Do not know number of offenders	**—**	**3,092!**	**2,987!**	**—**	**13,370!**	**44,483!**	**—**	**—**	**2,911!**	**40,372!**
Not injured	—	3,092!	—	—	5,329!	4,378!	—	—	2,911!	2,154!
Not treated for injury	—	—	2,987!	—	8,042!	40,105!	—	—	—	38,218!
Treated at scene, home, medical office, or other location	—	—	—	—	—	—	—	—	—	—

—Estimate is equal to 0 sample cases.

!Interpret data with caution, based on 10 or fewer sample cases or the coefficient of variation is greater than 50%.

Notes: Detail may not sum to total due to rounding and/or missing data. Due to methodological changes in the 2006 National Crime Victimization Survey, use caution when comparing 2006 criminal victimization estimates to other years.

SOURCE: "Number of Rape/Sexual Assaults by Victim-Offender Relationship and Medical Treatment for Physical Injuries, 2003–2012," in *NCVS Victimization Analysis Tool (NVAT)*, U.S. Department of Justice, Office of Justice Programs, Bureau of Justice Statistics, July 23, 2014, http://www.bjs.gov/index.cfm?ty=nvat (accessed July 23, 2014)

In "Why Battered Women Do Not Leave, Part 2: External Inhibiting Factors—Social Support and Internal Inhibiting Factors" (*Trauma, Violence, and Abuse*, vol. 2, no. 1, January 2001), Barnett outlines several internalized socialization beliefs (normal, learned beliefs about how society and relationships work) as well as psychological factors induced by trauma that serve as obstacles to battered women leaving their abuser. Barnett emphasizes that many of these beliefs are detrimental to all women, but battered women are particularly vulnerable. For example, some women turn to romantic relationships for a sense of self-worth. When an adult woman values her ability to form a relationship with a male partner over other characteristics, losing the relationship may seem worse than staying and enduring the abuse. Battered women tend to hold some distorted beliefs that keep them in abusive relationships. Common distorted thought patterns among battered women include a belief that violence is commonplace and not abusive, a belief that they caused the abuse, a lack of recognition that children are harmed more by witnessing intimate partner violence than by living with a single parent, and a belief that they can and should help the abuser to change.

In "The Role of Female Behavior and Attributions in Predicting Behavioral Responses to Hypothetical Male Aggression" (*Violence against Women*, vol. 16, no. 6, June 2010), Deborah L. Rhatigan and Alison M. Nathanson of the University of Tennessee, Knoxville, studied whether college women sometimes attribute abusive behavior to positive attributes and therefore choose to stay with their partners. The researchers asked 293 college women to read descriptions of scenes that involved conflict and abusive behavior. The women were then asked to describe the motives of the abuser and state whether or not they would leave him. Rhatigan and Nathanson find that some women interpreted male abuse as evidence of loving feelings. Women who made these "positive" attributions had lower scores of self-esteem, and they were much less likely to say that they would leave the relationship than women who attributed the behavior to negative motives.

Victimized women may fear that attempting to end an abusive relationship will lead to even worse violence. Research shows this fear of reprisal is well founded. Lenore E. Walker explains in *Terrifying Love: Why Battered Women Kill and How Society Responds* (1989) that batterers often panic when they think women are going to end the relationship. In the personal stories women told Walker, they repeatedly related that after calling the police or asking for a divorce, their partners' violence escalated.

Walker observes that in an abusive relationship it is often the man who is desperately dependent on the relationship. Battered women are likely to feel that the batterer's

sanity and emotional stability are their responsibility, that they are their partner's only link to the normal world. Walker indicates that almost 10% of abandoned batterers committed suicide when their partners left them.

It appears, however, that more batterers become homicidal than suicidal. Barnett emphasizes in "Why Battered Women Do Not Leave, Part 1" that evidence consistently demonstrates that after women leave abusive partners they often continue to be assaulted, stalked, and threatened and that leaving provokes some batterers to kill their partners. Block concurs in "How Can Practitioners Help an Abused Woman Lower Her Risk of Death?" that an attempt to leave can escalate domestic violence. She finds that 45% of homicides of a woman by a man were in response to the woman trying to leave her abusive partner.

Walker claims in *The Battered Woman* (1979) that abused women suffer from a constellation of symptoms—the so-called battered-woman syndrome—that keeps them from leaving abusive partners. She argues that a psychological condition known as "learned helplessness" plays a significant role in keeping women in abusive relationships. Although Walker believes, as do other multiple-victimization theorists, that women are victims of a patriarchal society and institutions that fail to advocate for abused women, she also emphasizes the psychological problems women develop in response to abuse.

The concept of learned helplessness was articulated by Martin E. P. Seligman. In *Helplessness: On Depression, Development, and Death* (1992), Seligman describes how he conducted an experiment in which he taught dogs to fear the sound of a bell. He did so by restraining dogs, ringing the bell, and then subjecting the dogs to a painful (but not dangerous) shock. This process was repeated several times.

Next, to test the effectiveness of the training, Seligman placed the dogs in a cage that had an electrified floor on one side, an unelectrified floor on the other side, and a wall that separated the two parts of the cage. The wall was low enough that the dogs could jump over it if they wished. Seligman placed the dogs on the electrified floor, rang the bell, and administered shocks through the floor. He expected that the dogs would jump over the wall to the unelectrified floor. However, most of the dogs did not. Seligman theorized this was because their earlier experience, where they had been shocked with no possibility of escape, had taught them that they were helpless.

Seligman called this learned helplessness. He and other psychologists theorize that this condition also occurs in humans, with similar effects. In *Battered Woman*, Walker contends that battered women have learned through their life experiences that they are helpless to escape or avoid violence. These battered women are conditioned to believe that they cannot predict their safety and that nothing can be done to fundamentally change their situation. They become passive, submissive, depressed, overwhelmingly fearful, and psychologically paralyzed. Walker emphasizes that although they do not respond with total helplessness, they narrow their choices, choosing the ones that seem to have the greatest likelihood of success.

WHAT CAN A WOMAN DO?

In "Understanding Women's Responses to Domestic Violence" (*Qualitative Social Work*, vol. 2, no. 3, September 2003), Kate Cavanagh of the University of Glasgow gathers qualitative data from interviews with the female partners of violent men to illustrate that battered women try to end the violence in their relationships in many ways, even if they stay. She finds that women worked to stop the violence by talking with their partner about the violence, developing strategies for avoiding the violence (e.g., being affectionate or feigning agreement with the abuser), challenging the violence (e.g., fighting back, orally or physically), telling other people about the violence, and leaving (usually temporarily) the relationship. Cavanagh argues that abused women almost always actively fight the abuse: "At some points in time the struggle to change took second place to the struggle to survive but not even women subjected to the extremes of abuse totally 'gave up.'"

For their landmark book *Intimate Violence* (1988), Richard J. Gelles and Murray A. Straus interviewed 192 women who suffered minor violence and 140 women who suffered severe violence and asked which long-range strategies they used to avoid violence. Fifty-three percent of the minor-violence victims and 69% of the severe-violence victims learned to avoid issues they thought would anger their partner. Others learned to read a change in their partner's facial expressions or body language as one of the first signs of impending abuse. Avoidance worked for about 68% of those women who suffered minor abuse, but this tactic was successful for less than one-third of the more severely abused victims.

Gelles and Straus find that 70% of battered women had left their spouse in the year preceding the interview. However, only about half of those who left reported that this was a "very effective" method of ending the abuse. In fact, for one out of eight women it only made things worse. Batterers put incredible pressure on their partner to return. Often, when the women returned they were abused more severely than before, as revenge or because the men learned that, once again, they could get away with this behavior. Women who returned also risked losing the aid of personal and public support systems because these people perceived that their help or advice was useless or ignored.

Silke Meyer of the University of Queensland notes in "Seeking Help to Protect the Children?: The Influence of Children on Women's Decisions to Seek Help When Experiencing Intimate Partner Violence" (*Journal of Family Violence*, vol. 25, no. 8, November 2010) that the single biggest predictor of a battered woman leaving an abusive relationship was whether the woman perceived that her children would have to witness violence if she stayed. In fact, the presence of children was the key predictor of the woman's likelihood of reporting abuse to the police; no other victim characteristic examined, including education, household income, marriage, or language spoken in the home, made her more likely to do so. Interestingly, pregnancy had no effect on help-seeking behaviors of any kind. Silke points out that the reasons why children's presence increased help-seeking have yet to be examined.

By contrast, Hee Yun Lee, Eonju Park, and Elizabeth Lightfoot of the University of Minnesota find in "When Does a Battered Woman Seek Help from the Police? The Role of Battered Women's Functionality" (*Journal of Family Violence*, vol. 25, no. 2, April 2010) that most victims of intimate partner violence seek help from the police at least once after a violent incident. The researchers conducted a telephone survey of 111 women in four cities who were recruited through social service agencies that provide services to victims of domestic violence. Lee, Park, and Lightfoot note that certain women were more likely to seek help from the police, including those who were more severely injured and those who were participating in social functions such as child-rearing and relationships with family and friends. In addition, battered women who were in shorter term relationships were more likely than women who were in longer term relationships to seek help from the police.

Just Say "No"

Many researchers believe there is real truth to the statement that men abuse because they can. A wife who will not permit herself to be beaten from the first act of minor abuse, such as a slap or push, is the most successful in stopping it. Gelles and Straus note in *Intimate Violence* that simply eliciting a promise to stop was by far the most effective strategy women could undertake, especially in cases of minor violence. Threatening to divorce or leave the home worked in about 40% of the minor-abuse cases, but this strategy worked in less than 5% of the severe-abuse situations. Physically fighting back was the least successful method. It worked in less than 2% of the minor-abuse cases and in less than 1% of the severe-abuse cases.

CHAPTER 8
RAPE AND STALKING

One of the difficulties inherent in the analysis of rape and stalking data is that neither of these crimes has a recognized standard definition. In its narrowest definition, rape includes only sexual acts that involve penetration of female victims by male perpetrators. Broader definitions include a wider variety of sexual acts committed against both female and male victims. Likewise, stalking encompasses various behaviors that are considered to be harassing and threatening, but do not involve direct violent contact. Law enforcement agencies use specific legal definitions for rape and stalking that are spelled out in criminal codes. For example, the Federal Bureau of Investigation (FBI) compiles rape data as part of its Uniform Crime Reports program, but only offenses known to police are included, and offenders are not categorized by their relationships to the victims. National victim surveys are far more informative for assessing the prevalence of rape and stalking because the surveys typically include incidents not reported to law enforcement and provide data about victim-offender relationships.

RAPE

Rape is an act of sexual violence by one person against another. It is an act of power that aims to hurt at the most intimate level. Rape is a violation, whether it occurs at the hands of a stranger or within the home at the hands of an abusive husband or partner.

National Crime Victimization Survey

Chapter 6 describes the National Crime Victimization Survey (NCVS), which is an annual survey overseen by the Bureau of Justice Statistics (BJS) within the U.S. Department of Justice (DOJ). The NCVS includes a nationally representative sample of people aged 12 years and older who are asked about their experiences of being victimized by certain crimes within the previous six months. The victimizations include both those reported and not reported to the police. The BJS publishes summary

results in its annual *Criminal Victimization* series. The agency also operates a searchable database of historical NCVS results that is accessible online using the NCVS Victimization Analysis Tool (http://bjs.ojp.usdoj.gov/index.cfm?ty=nvat). The NCVS crime set includes rape and sexual assault as defined as follows:

- Rape—forced sexual intercourse including both psychological coercion as well as physical force. Forced sexual intercourse means vaginal, anal or oral penetration by the offender (s). This category also includes incidents where the penetration is from a foreign object such as a bottle. Includes attempted rapes, male as well as female victims, and both heterosexual and homosexual rape. Attempted rape includes verbal threats of rape.

- Sexual assault—a wide range of victimizations, separate from rape or attempted rape. These crimes include attacks or attempted attacks generally involving unwanted sexual contact between victim and offender. Sexual assaults may or may not involve force and include such things as grabbing or fondling. Sexual assault also includes verbal threats.

The BJS considers domestic violence as violence involving intimate partners or family members. In terms of victim-offender relationships, the following specific terms are used:

- Intimate partners—spouses or ex-spouses, boyfriends or ex-boyfriends, and girlfriends or ex-girlfriends

- Other relatives—parents or stepparents, children or stepchildren, brothers or sisters, and other relatives

Table 8.1 provides a breakdown of victim-offender relationships in rapes and sexual assaults based on NCVS data between 2008 and 2012. Well-known and casual acquaintances committed the largest number (162,288) of the victimizations in 2012 and made up 47% of the

TABLE 8.1

Rapes and sexual assaults, by victim-offender relationship, 2008–12

Crime type	2008	2009	2010	2011	2012
Rape/sexual assault	349,691	305,574	268,574	244,188	346,830
Intimates	103,675	43,198	109,205	44,155	64,412
Other relatives	24,670!	34,779!	12,921!	1,721!	3,458!
Well-known/casual acquaintances	90,611	187,848	97,817	117,760	162,288
Stranger	76,907	36,586	43,167	72,807	59,126
Do not know relationship	9,346!	3,163!	5,464!	4,835!	17,174!
Do not know number of offenders	44,483!	—	—	2,911!	40,372!

Notes: Detail may not sum to total due to rounding and/or missing data.
—Estimate is equal to 0 sample cases.
!Interpret data with caution, based on 10 or fewer sample cases or the coefficient of variation is greater than 50%.

SOURCE: Adapted from "Number of Rape/Sexual Assaults by Victim-Offender Relationship, 2008–2012," in *NCVS Victimization Analysis Tool (NVAT)*, U.S. Department of Justice, Office of Justice Programs, Bureau of Justice Statistics, July 17, 2014, http://www.bjs.gov/index.cfm?ty=nvat (accessed July 17, 2014)

total. Intimate partners committed the second largest group of victimizations (64,412, or 19% of the total). Victimizations by strangers (59,126 victimizations, or 17%) and by other relatives (3,458 victimizations, or 1%) made up 18% of the total victimizations in 2012. In 17% of the victimizations, the offender-victim relationship (17,174) or the number of offenders (40,372) was unknown.

White offenders account for the highest proportion of rapes or sexual assaults involving an intimate partner. Of the 64,412 incidences of intimate partner rape or sexual assault in 2012, more than four-fifths (53,044, or 82%) were committed by white offenders. (See Table 8.2.) By comparison, of the 810,794 cases of intimate partner violence in 2012, 532,320 (66%) involved white offenders. (See Table 8.3.)

Table 8.4 provides a breakdown of weapon use during rapes and sexual assaults between 2008 and 2012. As Table 8.4 shows, no record of weapon use exists for cases of rape or sexual assault involving intimate partners or other relatives in 2012. Of the 162,288 rapes and sexual assaults committed by people who were either well-known to the victim or were casual acquaintances with the victim that year, roughly one-third (53,566, or 33%) involved the use of some sort of weapon.

VICTIMIZATIONS NOT REPORTED TO THE POLICE. In *Criminal Victimization, 2013* (September 2014, http://www.bjs.gov/content/pub/pdf/cv13.pdf), Jennifer L. Truman and Lynn Langton of the BJS examine data to determine which types of crimes were the least likely to be reported by victims to the police in 2004, 2012, and 2013. As Truman and Langton report, on average slightly fewer than half (45.6%) of all violent crimes were reported to the police in 2013. The rate at which crimes were reported varied considerably among types of violent crimes. For example, about one-third (34.8%) of all rape and sexual assault cases were reported to the police in 2013. By comparison, well

over half (57%) of all cases of intimate partner violence were reported to the police in 2013.

National Intimate Partner and Sexual Violence Survey (2010)

As noted in Chapter 6, the National Intimate Partner and Sexual Violence Survey (NISVS) was conducted in 2010 and included a representative sample of 16,507 adults (9,086 women and 7,421 men) in the United States who were aged 18 years and older. The survey was overseen by the Centers for Disease Control and Prevention, an agency within the U.S. Department of Health and Human Services. The surveyors asked about physical and sexual victimizations, psychological aggression, stalking, and control of reproductive or sexual health. Michele C. Black et al. summarize the survey results in *National Intimate Partner and Sexual Violence Survey: 2010 Summary Report* (November 2011, http://www.cdc.gov/ViolencePrevention/pdf/NISVS_Report2010-a.pdf). Table 8.5 lists the types of questions that were asked of survey participants to ascertain their victimization experiences with sexual violence and stalking.

Sexually violent experiences were divided into the following categories:

- Noncontact unwanted sexual experiences

- Unwanted sexual contact

- Sexual coercion

- Being made to penetrate someone else (males only)

- Rape (i.e., completed forced penetration, attempted penetration, and alcohol/drug-facilitated completed penetration; specific actions that were classified as rape are described in Chapter 6)

Black et al. note that the NISVS was different from many other surveys about sexual victimization because it questioned men about being made to penetrate someone else. They indicate that "being made to penetrate is a form

TABLE 8.2

Rapes and sexual assaults, by victim-offender relationship and race and Hispanic origin, 2003–12

Crime type	2003	2004	2005	2006	2007	2008	2009	2010	2011	2012
Rape/sexual assault	325,311	255,769	207,760	463,598	248,277	349,691	305,574	268,574	244,188	346,830
Intimates	134,478	59,669	66,750	157,698	55,110	103,675	43,198	109,205	44,155	64,412
Non-Hispanic white	121,530!	57,397	30,835!	114,688	55,110	91,857!	19,537!	105,541!	23,708!	53,044!
Non-Hispanic black	7,020!	—	23,937!	36,866!	—	8,416!	20,623!	—	2,925!	1,289!
Non-Hispanic American Indian/Alaskan Native	—	—	—	—	—	—	—	—	—	3,530!
Non-Hispanic Asian/Native Hawaiian/other Pacific Islander	—	—	—	—	—	—	—	3,664!	—	—
Non-Hispanic two or more races	—	—	2,839!	3,182!	—	3,402!	3,038!	—	—	3,445!
Hispanic	5,928!	2,272!	9,139!	2,962!	—	—	—	—	17,521!	3,104!
Other relatives	33,301!	5,596!	11,853!	7,397!	6,529!	24,670!	34,779!	12,921!	1,721!	3,458!
Non-Hispanic white	30,954!	5,596!	4,604!	—	2,070!	22,183!	34,779!	4,786!	—	3,458!
Non-Hispanic black	—	—	7,249!	2,681!	—	2,487!	—	4,025!	—	—
Non-Hispanic American Indian/Alaskan Native	—	—	—	—	—	—	—	—	—	—
Non-Hispanic Asian/Native Hawaiian/other Pacific Islander	2,346!	—	—	—	—	—	—	—	—	—
Non-Hispanic two or more races	—	—	—	—	—	—	—	—	—	—
Hispanic	—	—	—	4,716!	4,459!	—	—	4,110!	1,721!	—
Well-known/casual acquaintances	95,418	78,441	60,813	152,255	81,968	90,611	187,848	97,817	117,760	162,288
Non-Hispanic white	82,172	49,958	35,658	106,876	44,870	59,080	170,738!	66,041	84,835	66,034
Non-Hispanic black	7,659!	28,482!	14,904!	27,346!	6,609!	9,340!	13,297!	24,410!	17,031!	14,139!
Non-Hispanic American Indian/Alaskan Native	—	—	—	—	11,179!	—	—	—	1,190!	21,818!
Non-Hispanic Asian/Native Hawaiian/other Pacific Islander	—	—	2,641!	5,417!	—	3,356!	—	—	—	43,665!
Non-Hispanic two or more races	2,810!	—	2,987!	3,227!	12,742!	5,535!	—	2,895!	—	3,445!
Hispanic	2,777!	—	4,624!	9,388!	6,567!	13,301!	3,813!	4,470!	14,703!	13,187!
Stranger	58,978	91,802	59,982	134,929	77,477	76,907	36,586	43,167	72,807	59,126
Non-Hispanic white	42,927	57,206	32,396!	103,587	65,154	40,242!	23,430!	19,971!	45,782	45,192
Non-Hispanic black	9,327!	20,491!	5,574!	20,831!	9,064!	27,757!	4,881!	3,578!	12,745!	3,849!
Non-Hispanic American Indian/Alaskan Native	—	—	—	3,814!	—	—	—	—	—	—
Non-Hispanic Asian/Native Hawaiian/other Pacific Islander	—	—	—	—	—	4,153!	—	—	—	3,103!
Non-Hispanic two or more races	6,725!	2,710!	—	—	—	—	—	—	—	—
Hispanic	—	11,394!	22,011!	6,697!	3,258!	4,754!	8,274!	19,618!	14,280!	6,982!

TABLE 8.2

Rapes and sexual assaults, by victim-offender relationship and race and Hispanic origin, 2003–12 [CONTINUED]

Crime type	2003	2004	2005	2006	2007	2008	2009	2010	2011	2012
Do not know relationship	**3,135!**	**17,170!**	**5,375!**	**11,320!**	**13,823!**	**9,346!**	**3,163!**	**5,464!**	**4,835!**	**17,174!**
Non-Hispanic white	—	11,952!	5,375!	7,343!	13,823!	6,935!	—	3,391!	1,572!	10,357!
Non-Hispanic black	—	—	—	—	—	2,411!	—	—	3,263!	—
Hispanic	3,135!	5,218!	—	3,976!	—	—	3,163!	2,073!	—	6,817!
Do not know number of offenders	**—**	**3,092!**	**2,987!**	**—**	**13,370!**	**44,483!**	**—**	**—**	**2,911!**	**40,372!**
Non-Hispanic white	—	3,092!	2,987!	—	8,042!	1,967!	—	—	2,911!	40,372!
Non-Hispanic black	—	—	—	—	—	6,427!	—	—	—	—
Non-Hispanic American Indian/Alaskan Native	—	—	—	—	5,329!	—	—	—	—	—
Hispanic	—	—	—	—	—	36,088!	—	—	—	—

—Estimate is equal to 0 sample cases.
!Interpret data with caution, based on 10 or fewer sample cases or the coefficient of variation is greater than 50%.
Notes: Detail may not sum to total due to rounding and/or missing data. Due to methodological changes in the 2006 National Crime Victimization Survey, use caution when comparing 2006 criminal victimization estimates to other years.

SOURCE: "Number of Rape/Sexual Assaults by Victim-Offender Relationship and Race/Hispanic Origin-Expanded Categories, 2003–2012," in *NCVS Victimization Analysis Tool (NVAT)*, U.S. Department of Justice, Office of Justice Programs, Bureau of Justice Statistics, July 23, 2014, http://www.bjs.gov/index.cfm?ty=nvat (accessed July 23, 2014)

TABLE 8.3

Violent victimizations, by victim-offender relationship and race and Hispanic origin, 2003–12

Crime type	2003	2004	2005	2006	2007	2008	2009	2010	2011	2012
Violent victimization	7,679,050	6,726,060	6,947,795	8,430,430	6,814,183	6,393,471	5,669,237	4,935,983	5,812,523	6,842,593
Intimates	1,040,285	1,031,721	816,006	1,305,249	905,810	1,103,392	1,039,650	773,434	850,772	810,794
Non-Hispanic white	778,986	630,034	521,230	807,541	643,732	873,903	701,481	539,133	643,683	532,320
Non-Hispanic black	94,451	174,897	71,847	203,988	171,848	85,930	188,423	140,101	82,599!	164,701
Non-Hispanic American Indian/Alaskan Native	10,927!	61,959!	42,840!	15,088!	—	—	—	4,535!	23,315!	6,522!
Non-Hispanic Asian/Native Hawaiian/other Pacific Islander	2,300!	27,387!	—	31,522!	9,096!	9,769!	7,375!	21,015!	8,545!	—
Non-Hispanic two or more races	72,590!	17,549!	63,762!	108,830	30,557!	30,539!	19,411!	17,866!	4,718!	28,461!
Hispanic	81,031	119,895	116,328	138,281	50,577!	103,249	122,960	50,783	87,913	78,789
Other relatives	440,634	402,467	426,284	558,407	501,907	454,603	343,020	356,129	504,135	448,598
Non-Hispanic white	339,276	287,492	310,765	380,022	289,403	309,530	265,041	224,169	409,105	304,999
Non-Hispanic black	35,047	33,705!	51,255!	77,783	153,199!	36,454!	35,018!	39,250	39,846	61,253
Non-Hispanic American Indian/Alaskan Native	3,702!	30,591!	—	30,716!	—	67,710!	3,414!	8,650!	7,190!	—
Non-Hispanic Asian/Native Hawaiian/other Pacific Islander	2,346!	—	—	7,300!	4,585!	3,529!	—	7,352!	3,394!	5,503!
Non-Hispanic two or more races	17,591!	18,954!	11,163!	14,054!	26,160!	17,737!	3,837!	19,782!	8,691!	3,705!
Hispanic	42,672	31,726	53,101	48,532	28,559!	19,643!	35,711!	56,926	35,910	73,139
Well-known/casual acquaintances	2,596,812	2,267,162	2,356,241	2,661,522	1,997,175	1,781,331	1,756,014	1,573,294	1,779,618	2,263,252
Non-Hispanic white	1,953,865	1,688,421	1,727,646	1,772,900	1,308,500	1,344,869	1,224,250	1,159,011	1,068,410	1,526,150
Non-Hispanic black	281,323	308,660	313,915	402,315	307,177	199,191	228,098	183,406	394,577	336,063
Non-Hispanic American Indian/Alaskan Native	11,792!	26,233!	3,372!	15,436!	34,064	19,413!	19,590!	26,933!	11,171!	34,568!
Non-Hispanic Asian/Native Hawaiian/other Pacific Islander	24,081!	34,801!	31,615!	63,129!	38,637!	27,108!	48,175!	5,772!	30,970!	63,752!
Non-Hispanic two or more races	72,019	64,064	120,080	83,985	70,108	32,301!	18,572!	36,727!	60,955	28,343!
Hispanic	253,733	144,983	159,612	323,757	238,689	158,449	217,328	161,447	213,535	274,377
Stranger	3,107,181	2,672,238	2,829,598	3,184,058	2,706,132	2,154,770	2,165,849	1,812,303	2,146,307	2,710,114
Non-Hispanic white	2,109,731	2,014,807	1,865,080	2,106,015	1,906,041	1,349,137	1,337,225	978,639	1,262,227	1,728,361
Non-Hispanic black	470,559	261,698	382,718	466,592	298,268	389,123	397,169	373,781	219,494	325,040
Non-Hispanic American Indian/Alaskan Native	45,189!	43,545!	31,859!	32,611!	31,883!	22,915!	38,935!	59,422!	15,820!	19,509!
Non-Hispanic Asian/Native Hawaiian/other Pacific Islander	60,733	46,608	65,248	116,397	33,160!	70,073	33,536!	84,919	75,688	124,005
Non-Hispanic two or more races	53,918!	37,180	63,256	1,02,304	113,076	33,055!	34,621	48,207	108,241	43,060
Hispanic	367,050	268,400	421,438	360,139	323,704	290,468	324,363	267,335	464,837	470,139

TABLE 8.3

Violent victimizations, by victim-offender relationship and race and Hispanic origin, 2003–12 [CONTINUED]

Crime type	2003	2004	2005	2006	2007	2008	2009	2010	2011	2012
Do not know relationship	**346,484**	**268,558**	**361,855**	**506,652**	**448,275**	**486,084**	**217,989**	**288,667**	**240,956**	**371,910**
Non-Hispanic white	220,672	182,233	232,847	320,317	265,417	332,029	92,498	184,135	119,802	113,096
Non-Hispanic black	68,392	30,531!	74,773	89,748	58,295	58,562	41,381!	46,771!	52,107	177,858
Non-Hispanic American Indian/Alaskan Native	4,910!	—	—	—	—	—	—	—	—	4,240!
Non-Hispanic Asian/Native Hawaiian/other Pacific Islander	—	4,063!	18,818!	11,112!	3,294!	18,184!	4,264!	5,769!	3,865!	20,340!
Non-Hispanic two or more races	19,002!	—	—	12,685!	19,242!	6,617!	—	3,238!	—	3,084!
Hispanic	33,507	51,732	35,418!	72,790	102,027	70,693	79,845	48,755	65,183	53,291
Do not know number of offenders	**147,654**	**83,914**	**157,809**	**214,541**	**254,885**	**413,292**	**139,707**	**132,156**	**290,736**	**228,660**
Non-Hispanic white	87,356	45,608	93,585	99,506	193,512	289,663	113,520	97,084	216,502	146,489
Non-Hispanic black	26,130!	27,727!	18,129!	53,746!	9,105!	53,841	11,128!	3,501!	23,551!	26,258!
Non-Hispanic American Indian/Alaskan Native	—	5,880!	—	—	5,329!	3,550!	—	7,080!	—	2,520!
Non-Hispanic Asian/Native Hawaiian/other Pacific Islander	3,316!	—	3,854!	—	2,437!	3,167!	3,407!	—	17,125!	—
Non-Hispanic two or more races	4,239!	—	6,442!	—	16,264!	4,047!	6,265!	5,937!	5,501!	30,707!
Hispanic	26,613!	4,698!	35,799!	61,290!	28,238!	59,024!	5,386!	18,555!	28,057!	22,686!

—Estimate is equal to 0 sample cases.

!Interpret data with caution, based on 10 or fewer sample cases or the coefficient of variation is greater than 50%.

Notes: Detail may not sum to total due to rounding and/or missing data. Due to methodological changes in the 2006 National Crime Victimization Survey use caution when comparing 2006 criminal victimization estimates to other years.

SOURCE: "Number of Violent Victimizations by Victim-Offender Relationship and Race/Hispanic Origin-Expanded Categories, 2003–2012," in *NCVS Victimization Analysis Tool (NVAT)*, U.S. Department of Justice, Office of Justice Programs, Bureau of Justice Statistics, July 23, 2014, http://www.bjs.gov/index.cfm?ty=nvat (accessed July 23, 2014)

TABLE 8.4

Rapes and sexual assaults, by victim-offender relationship and weapon use, 2008–12

Crime type	2008	2009	2010	2011	2012
Rape/sexualassault	349,691	305,574	268,574	244,188	346,830
Intimates	103,675	43,198	109,205	44,155	64,412
Yes, offender had weapon	—	3,383!	45,387!	2,925!	—
No, offender did not have weapon	100,299	39,815	63,818!	32,818	64,412
Do not know if offender had weapon	3,376!	—	—	8,412!	—
Other relatives	24,670!	34,779!	12,921!	1,721!	3,458!
No, offender did not have weapon	24,670!	34,779	12,921!	1,721!	3,458!
Well-known/casual acquaintances	90,611	187,848	97,817	117,760	162,288
Yes, offender had weapon	2,732!	45,124!	10,223!	2,891!	53,566!
No, offender did not have weapon	75,693	142,724!	83,889	104,002	103,856
Do not know if offender had weapon	12,186!	—	3,705!	10,866!	4,866!
Stranger	76,907	36,586	43,167	72,807	59,126
Yes, offender had weapon	—	—	5,268!	2,609!	—
No, offender did not have weapon	54,279!	30,302!	25,566!	61,719	42,687
Do not know if offender had weapon	22,628!	6,284!	12,333!	8,478!	16,439!
Do not know relationship	9,346!	3,163!	5,464!	4,835!	17,174!
Yes, offender had weapon	—	—	5,464!	—	3,317!
No, offender did not have weapon	9,346!	3,163!	—	4,835!	11,028!
Do not know if offender had weapon	—	—	—	—	2,829!
Do not know number of offenders	44,483!	—	—	2,911!	40,372!
Yes, offender had weapon	—	—	—	—	38,218!
No, offender did not have weapon	44,483!	—	—	2,911!	2,154!

Notes: Detail may not sum to total due to rounding and/or missing data.
—Estimate is equal to 0 sample cases.
!Interpret data with caution, based on 10 or fewer sample cases or the coefficient of variation is greater than 50%.

SOURCE: Adapted from "Number of Rape/Sexual Assaults by Victim-Offender Relationship and Weapon Use, 2008–2012," in *NCVS Victimization Analysis Tool (NVAT)*, U.S. Department of Justice, Office of Justice Programs, Bureau of Justice Statistics, July 17, 2014, http://www.bjs.gov/index.cfm?ty=nvat (accessed July 17, 2014)

of sexual victimization distinct from rape that is particularly unique to males and, to our knowledge, has not been explicitly measured in previous national studies."

Rape and Sexual Assault Demographics

Table 8.6 provides a breakdown by race and age of rape and sexual assault victims between 2008 and 2012. In 2012 there were 346,830 cases of rape and sexual assault in the United States. The highest number of rapes and sexual assaults occurred among victims between the ages of 35 and 49 years old, who accounted for more than one-third (129,993, or 37%) of all cases that year. (See Table 8.6.) Individuals between the ages of 25 and 34 accounted for 70,615 (20%) of all rape and sexual assault victims in 2012; individuals between the ages of 18 and 20 accounted for 62,079 victims (18%), and individuals between the ages of 12 and 14 accounted for 26,606 victims (8%) of rape and sexual assault that year. Of the 346,830 victims of rape and sexual assault in 2012, 215,570 (62%) were female and 131,259 (38%) were male. (See Table 8.7.)

Of the 346,830 cases of rape and sexual assault recorded in the NCVS Victimization Analysis Tool in 2012, 204,887 (59%) occurred in areas with populations of fewer than 100,000 residents. This rate varied by the age group of the victims. For example, of the 26,606 rape and sexual assault victims who were between the ages of 12 and 14 that year, 23,148 (87%) were victimized in areas where the population was under 100,000. By comparison, in 2012 fewer than half of all rape and sexual assault victims between the ages of 18 and 20 (27,320 out of 62,079, or 44%) were victimized in areas with fewer than 100,000 residents. (See Table 8.8.) A breakdown of rapes and sexual assaults in 2012 by region and victim's age is presented in Table 8.9.

As Janet L. Lauritsen and Nicole White report in *Seasonal Patterns in Criminal Victimization Trends* (June 2014, http://www.bjs.gov/content/pub/pdf/spcvt.pdf), rates of intimate partner violence, rape, and sexual assault tend to rise in the summer. Between 1993 and 2010, cases of rape and sexual assault saw the most substantial increases in the summers of 1999, 2001, 2006, and 2008. (See Figure 8.1.) In cases of intimate partner violence that occurred during that span, the most noticeable spikes took place in the summers of 1993, 1994, and 2006. (See Figure 8.2.)

National Violence against Women Survey

The National Violence against Women Survey (NVAWS) was conducted in 1995 and 1996 and included

TABLE 8.5

Questions about sexual violence asked during the National Intimate Partner and Sexual Violence Survey, 2010

Sexual violence

How many people have ever...	• exposed their sexual body parts to you, flashed you, or masturbated in front of you?
	• made you show your sexual body parts to them? Remember, we are only asking about things that you didn't want to happen.
	• made you look at or participate in sexual photos or movies?
How many people have ever...	• harassed you while you were in a public place in a way that made you feel unsafe?
	• kissed you in a sexual way? Remember, we are only asking about things that you didn't want to happen.
	• fondled or grabbed your sexual body parts?
When you were drunk, high, drugged, or passed out and unable to consent, how many people ever...	• had vaginal sex with you? By vaginal sex, we mean that (if female: a man or boy put his penis in your vagina) (if male: a woman or girl made you put your penis in her vagina)?
	• (if male) made you perform anal sex, meaning that they made you put your penis into their anus?
	• made you receive anal sex, meaning they put their penis into your anus?
	• made you perform oral sex, meaning that they put their penis in your mouth or made you penetrate their vagina or anus with your mouth?
	• made you receive oral sex, meaning that they put their mouth on your (if male: penis) (if female: vagina) or anus?
How many people have ever used physical force or threats to physically harm you to make you...	• have vaginal sex?
	• (if male) perform anal sex?
	• receive anal sex?
	• make you perform oral sex?
	• make you receive oral sex?
	• put their fingers or an object in your (if female: vagina or) anus?
How many people have ever used physical force or threats of physical harm to...	• (if male) try to make you have vaginal sex with them, but sex did not happen?
	• try to have (if female: vaginal) oral, or anal sex with you, but sex did not happen?
How many people have you had vaginal, oral, or anal sex with after they pressured you by...	• doing things like telling you lies, making promises about the future they knew were untrue, threatening to end your relationship, or threatening to spread rumors about you?
	• wearing you down by repeatedly asking for sex, or showing they were unhappy?
	• using their authority over you, for example, your boss or your teacher?

Stalking tactics

How many people have ever...	• watched or followed you from a distance, or spied on you with a listening device, camera, or GPS [global positioning system]?
	• approached you or showed up in places, such as your home, workplace, or school when you didn't want them to be there?
	• left strange or potentially threatening items for you to find?
	• sneaked into your home or car and did things to scare you by letting you know they had been there?
	• left you unwanted messages? This includes text or voice messages.
	• made unwanted phone calls to you? This includes hang-up calls.
	• sent you unwanted emails, instant messages, or sent messages through websites like MySpace or Facebook?
	• left you cards, letters, flowers, or presents when they knew you didn't want them to?

SOURCE: Adapted from Michele C. Black et al., "Appendix C. Victimization Questions," in *National Intimate Partner and Sexual Violence Survey: 2010 Summary Report*, U.S. Department of Health and Human Services, Centers for Disease Control and Prevention, National Center for Injury Prevention and Control, December 14, 2011, http://www.cdc.gov/ViolencePrevention/pdf/NISVS_Report2010-a.pdf (accessed July 23, 2014)

16,000 adult participants split evenly between men and women. Although the survey is much older than those already described, the NVAWS results are of particular note because they provide information about victim attitudes and reactions after the violent experiences.

In *Extent, Nature, and Consequences of Rape Victimization: Findings from the National Violence against Women Survey* (January 2006, http://www.ncjrs.gov/pdffiles1/nij/210346.pdf), the most recent report of its kind as of November 2014, Patricia Tjaden and Nancy Thoennes of the Center for Policy Research in Denver, Colorado, use NVAWS data to estimate that 302,091 women are raped each year and that 17.7 million women have been raped during their lifetime, compared with 92,748 men who are raped each year and 2.8 million men who have been raped during their lifetime. Native American or Alaskan Native women were estimated to have the highest rate of having been raped during their lifetime (34.1%),

followed by African American women (18.8%), non-Hispanic white women (17.9%), Hispanic women (11.9%), and Asian or Pacific Islander women (6.8%).

Tjaden and Thoennes find that most female victims of rape had been raped by a current or former intimate partner. Just over one out of five (21.5%) had been raped by a date or former date, 20.2% by a spouse or former spouse, and 4.3% by a cohabitating partner or former partner. Male victims tended to be raped by acquaintances (40.3%). Only 4.1% of males had been raped by a spouse or former spouse, 3.7% by a current or former cohabitating partner, and 2.7% by a date or former date. In fact, Tjaden and Thoennes note that 7.7% of all women, but only 0.4% of all men, had ever been raped by a current or former intimate partner.

JUSTICE SYSTEM OUTCOMES. Tjaden and Thoennes find that the overwhelming majority of rapes went unreported to the police and that women raped by intimate

TABLE 8.6

Rapes and sexual assaults, by age and race and Hispanic origin, 2008–12

Crime type	2008	2009	2010	2011	2012
Rape/sexual assault	349,691	305,574	268,574	244,188	346,830
12 to 14	20,770!	35,538!	32,781!	3,961!	26,606!
Non-Hispanic white	17,367!	35,538!	9,832!	3,961!	19,512!
Non-Hispanic black	—	—	18,491!	—	—
Hispanic	3,403!	—	4,458!	—	7,094!
15 to 17	35,633!	19,692!	20,531!	20,995!	12,060!
Non-Hispanic white	25,441!	14,810!	12,218!	13,792!	—
Non-Hispanic black	5,438!	4,881!	3,843!	4,032!	3,656!
Non-Hispanic Asian/Native Hawaiian/other Pacific Islander	—	—	—	—	4,904!
Hispanic	4,754!	—	4,470!	3,171!	3,500!
18 to 20	52,398!	9,918!	13,790!	44,029	62,079
Non-Hispanic white	12,294!	9,918!	10,126!	25,943!	46,111
Non-Hispanic black	4,017!	—	—	12,740!	2,629!
Non-Hispanic American Indian/Alaskan Native	—	—	—	—	3,530!
Non-Hispanic Asian/Native Hawaiian/other Pacific Islander	—	—	3,664!	—	—
Non-Hispanic two or more races	—	—	—	—	6,890!
Hispanic	36,088!	—	—	5,347!	2,920!
21 to 24	34,497!	120,398!	68,769!	28,419!	16,344!
Non-Hispanic white	9,609!	116,586!	65,473!	14,323!	12,395!
Non-Hispanic black	15,998!	—	—	9,074!	—
Non-Hispanic Asian/Native Hawaiian/other Pacific Islander	3,356!	—	—	—	—
Non-Hispanic two or more races	5,535!	—	—	—	—
Hispanic	—	3,813!	3,296!	5,022!	3,950!
25 to 34	50,686!	33,337!	53,734	41,496	70,615
Non-Hispanic white	30,573!	5,774!	30,649	30,863!	63,783!
Non-Hispanic black	15,960!	20,623!	7,566!	3,263!	2,116!
Non-Hispanic Asian/Native Hawaiian/other Pacific Islander	4,153!	—	4,025!	—	—
Hispanic	—	6,940!	11,495!	7,370!	4,716!
35 to 49	135,725	62,198	74,763	46,755	129,993
Non-Hispanic white	120,469	55,338!	62,440!	33,431	54,254!
Non-Hispanic black	5,040!	2,488!	2,875!	6,856!	5,739!
Non-Hispanic American Indian/Alaskan Native	—	—	—	—	21,818!
Non-Hispanic Asian/Native Hawaiian/other Pacific Islander	—	—	—	—	41,864!
Non-Hispanic two or more races	—	—	2,895!	—	—
Hispanic	10,215!	4,371!	6,553!	6,468!	6,318!
50 to 64	10,707!	16,021!	—	23,959!	21,788!
Non-Hispanic white	3,429!	5,760!	—	6,869!	15,058!
Non-Hispanic black	7,278!	7,098!	—	—	5,137!
Non-Hispanic American Indian/Alaskan Native	—	—	—	1,190!	—
Hispanic	—	3,163!	—	15,900!	1,593!
65 or older	9,275!	8,471!	4,206!	34,573!	7,344!
Non-Hispanic white	3,082!	4,760!	4,206!	29,625!	7,344!
Non-Hispanic black	3,108!	3,711!	—	—	—
Hispanic	3,085!	—	—	4,948!	—

—Estimate is equal to 0 sample cases.
!Interpret data with caution, based on 10 or fewer sample cases or the coefficient of variation is greater than 50%.
Notes: Detail may not sum to total due to rounding and/or missing data.

SOURCE: "Number of Rape/Sexual Assaults by Age and Race/Hispanic Origin-Expanded Categories, 2008–2012," in *NCVS Victimization Analysis Tool (NVAT)*, U.S. Department of Justice, Office of Justice Programs, Bureau of Justice Statistics, July 23, 2014, http://www.bjs.gov/index.cfm?ty=nvat (accessed July 23, 2014)

partners were less likely to report rapes to the police than were women raped by nonintimate partners. Only 18% of women raped by intimates reported the rape, compared with 20.9% of women raped by nonintimates. Of the women who did not report the rape to the police, 22.1% said they were too afraid of the rapist, 18.1% said they

TABLE 8.7

Rapes and sexual assaults, by victim's sex and race and Hispanic origin, 2008–12

Crime type	2008	2009	2010	2011	2012
Rape/sexual assault	**349,691**	**305,574**	**268,574**	**244,188**	**346,830**
Male	39,589!	19,816!	15,020!	34,804!	131,259
Non-Hispanic white	23,834!	13,425!	12,947!	13,243!	54,093!
Non-Hispanic black	8,942!	2,488!	—	5,344!	3,849!
Non-Hispanic American Indian/Alaskan Native	—	—	—	—	21,818!
Non-Hispanic Asian/Native Hawaiian/other Pacific Islander	—	—	—	—	41,864!
Hispanic	6,813!	3,902!	2,073!	16,217!	9,635!
Female	310,102	285,758	253,555	209,384	215,570
Non-Hispanic white	198,429	235,060	181,998	145,565	164,363
Non-Hispanic black	47,896	36,313!	32,774!	30,620!	15,428!
Non-Hispanic American Indian/Alaskan Native	—	—	—	1,190!	3,530!
Non-Hispanic Asian/Native Hawaiian/other Pacific Islander	7,509!	—	7,689!	—	4,904!
Non-Hispanic two or more races	5,535!	—	2,895!	—	6,890!
Hispanic	50,732!	14,385!	28,199!	32,008	20,455!

—Estimate is equal to 0 sample cases.
!Interpret data with caution, based on 10 or fewer sample cases or the coefficient of variation is greater than 50%.
Notes: Detail may not sum to total due to rounding and/or missing data.

SOURCE: "Number of Rape/Sexual Assaults by Sex and Race/Hispanic Origin-Expanded Categories, 2008–2012," in *NCVS Victimization Analysis Tool (NVAT)*, U.S. Department of Justice, Office of Justice Programs, Bureau of Justice Statistics, July 23, 2014, http://www.bjs.gov/index.cfm?ty=nvat (accessed July 23, 2014)

were too ashamed, 17.7% said it was a minor incident, 12.6% said the police could not do anything, and 11.9% said the police would not believe them. Almost one out of 10 (8.6%) said it was because the perpetrator was a husband, family member, or friend.

When women did call the police, the police took a report 75.9% of the time, and in 9.9% of the cases the police did nothing. In 43.3% of the reported cases the perpetrator was arrested or detained. The perpetrator was prosecuted in 37% of reported cases, and 46.2% of those prosecutions resulted in a conviction. Of those convicted rapists, 24% did not go to jail.

MARITAL RAPE

Historically, wives were considered to be the property of the husband, and therefore rape of a wife was viewed as impossible. No husband still living with his wife was prosecuted for marital rape in the United States until 1978, and at that time marital rape was a crime in only five states, as reported by Jennifer A. Bennice and Patricia A. Resick of the University of Missouri, St. Louis, in "Marital Rape: History, Research, and Practice" (*Trauma, Violence, and Abuse*, vol. 4, no. 3, July 2003). By 1993 marital rape under some conditions was recognized in all 50 states.

ACQUAINTANCE RAPE

As shown in Table 8.1, NCVS data indicate that 162,288 rapes and sexual assaults in 2012 were by well-

known or casual acquaintances of the victims. This number accounts for nearly half (47%) of the 346,830 total rapes and sexual assaults for that year. Calculating percentages for the other years shown in Table 8.1 provides the following shares for well-known or casual acquaintances: 2008 (26%), 2009 (61%), 2010 (36%), and 2011 (48%). Thus, this perpetrator group accounted for roughly a fourth to more than half of all rapes and sexual assaults each year.

Date Rape

As noted earlier, intimate partners are commonly defined as current or former spouses, boyfriends or ex-boyfriends, and girlfriends or ex-girlfriends. Although a spousal relationship has a legal definition, the distinction between a boyfriend/girlfriend and a dating acquaintance is far less clear-cut. However, in general, date rape is considered to be a form of acquaintance rape (as opposed to intimate partner rape), especially if the perpetrator and victim have not known one another for long and the abuse begins early in the relationship. Date rape is typically discussed by researchers in association with older teenagers and young people in their 20s.

HIGH SCHOOL RAPE. Table 8.10 provides a breakdown of high school students who have ever been forced to engage in sexual intercourse, by grade, sex, and race. As Table 8.10 shows, in 2013 more than one in 10 high school girls (10.5%) reported that they had been forced to have sexual intercourse at some point in their lives; by comparison, 4.2% of high school boys reported ever

TABLE 8.8

Rapes and sexual assaults, by victim's age and population size, 2008–12

Crime type	2008	2009	2010	2011	2012
Rape/sexual assault	**349,691**	**305,574**	**268,574**	**244,188**	**346,830**
12 to 14	20,770!	35,538!	32,781!	3,961!	26,606!
Not a place	12,879!	—	—	—	3,458!
Under 100,000	—	35,538!	9,654!	3,961!	23,148!
100,000–249,999	4,488!	—	—	—	—
250,000–499,999	—	—	4,636!	—	—
1 million or more	3,403!	—	18,491!	—	—
15 to 17	35,633!	19,692!	20,531!	20,995!	12,060!
Not a place	20,507!	5,572!	6,187!	—	—
Under 100,000	15,127!	5,238!	9,874!	20,995!	4,904!
100,000–249,999	—	8,882!	4,470!	—	—
500,000–999,999	—	—	—	—	3,656!
1 million or more	—	—	—	—	3,500!
18 to 20	52,398!	9,918!	13,790!	44,029	62,079
Not a place	—	—	7,051!	11,204!	12,373!
Under 100,000	47,609!	5,135!	6,739!	28,146!	27,320!
100,000–249,999	4,789!	—	—	3,006!	8,121!
250,000–499,999	—	4,784!	—	—	11,289!
500,000–999,999	—	—	—	1,674!	—
1 million or more	—	—	—	—	2,976!
21 to 24	34,497!	120,398!	68,769!	28,419!	16,344!
Not a place	3,600!	51,427!	5,116!	—	—
Under 100,000	9,365!	61,728!	60,004!	20,855!	9,247!
100,000–249,999	—	—	3,649!	3,725!	—
250,000–499,999	21,533!	—	—	—	7,097!
500,000–999,999	—	7,244!	—	3,839!	—
25 to 34	50,686!	33,337!	53,734	41,496	70,615
Not a place	2,487!	—	5,857!	11,747!	—
Under 100,000	31,146!	20,116!	18,613!	11,148!	50,131!
100,000–249,999	7,410!	3,038!	14,813!	15,274!	5,056!
250,000–499,999	9,644!	—	—	—	8,913!
500,000–999,999	—	1,988!	7,265!	1,721!	—
1 million or more	—	8,195!	7,186!	1,607!	6,515!
35 to 49	135,725	62,198	74,763	46,755	129,993
Not a place	67,731!	6,706!	—	11,984!	—
Under 100,000	49,282!	51,935!	62,275!	30,841	70,890!
100,000–249,999	7,138!	3,557!	3,705!	3,930!	9,280!
250,000–499,999	1,967!	—	—	—	38,761!
500,000–999,999	—	—	—	—	8,826!
1 million or more	9,608!	—	8,782!	—	2,237!
50 to 64	10,707!	16,021!	—	23,959!	21,788!
Not a place	1,679!	2,604!	—	—	2,958!
Under 100,000	5,126!	6,319!	—	5,287!	13,389!
100,000–249,999	3,902!	7,098!	—	11,184!	—
500,000–999,999	—	—	—	—	1,593!
1 million or more	—	—	—	7,488!	3,849!
65 or older	9,275!	8,471!	4,206!	34,573!	7,344!
Not a place	—	4,760!	—	2,818!	—
Under 100,000	6,193!	—	2,987!	26,807!	5,858!
100,000–249,999	3,082!	—	1,219!	—	—
250,000–499,999	—	—	—	—	1,487!
1 million or more	—	3,711!	—	4,948!	—

—Estimate is equal to 0 sample cases.

!Interpret data with caution, based on 10 or fewer sample cases or the coefficient of variation is greater than 50%.

Notes: Detail may not sum to total due to rounding and/or missing data.

SOURCE: "Number of Rape/Sexual Assaults by Age and Population Size, 2008–2012," in *NCVS Victimization Analysis Tool (NVAT)*, U.S. Department of Justice, Office of Justice Programs, Bureau of Justice Statistics, July 23, 2014, http://www.bjs.gov/index.cfm?ty=nvat (accessed July 23, 2014)

having been forced to engage in sexual intercourse. Female Hispanic high school students (12.2%) reported the highest rate of forced sexual intercourse, followed by female African American high school students (11.5%) and female white high school students (9.1%). Among all female high school students in 2013, 10th graders (11.8%) had the highest proportion of girls who had ever been forced to have sexual intercourse. (See Table 8.10.)

Table 8.11 shows percentages of high school students by state and major urban school district who have ever been forced to engage in sexual intercourse. In 2013 Arkansas (11.6%) and Wyoming (11.6%) had the highest rates of high school students who had ever been forced to have sexual intercourse; New Hampshire (5.7%) had the lowest percentage of high school students who had ever been forced to have sexual intercourse. Missouri (15.4%) and Arkansas (15.3%) reported the highest percentages of

TABLE 8.9

Rapes and sexual assaults, by victim's age and geographical region, 2008–12

Crime type	2008	2009	2010	2011	2012
Rape/sexual assault	349,691	305,574	268,574	244,188	346,830
12 to 14	20,770!	35,538!	32,781!	3,961!	26,606!
Northeast	12,879!	—	18,491!	—	3,458!
Midwest	4,488!	—	—	—	12,292!
South	3,403!	35,538!	4,458!	—	7,539!
West	—	—	9,832!	3,961!	3,317!
15 to 17	35,633!	19,692!	20,531!	20,995!	12,060!
Northeast	—	4,000!	—	—	3,500!
Midwest	11,907!	—	—	13,792!	3,656!
South	18,813!	10,453!	15,519!	7,202!	4,904!
West	4,914!	5,238!	5,012!	—	—
18 to 20	52,398!	9,918!	13,790!	44,029	62,079
Northeast	—	—	—	13,747!	—
Midwest	12,853!	4,784!	10,126!	16,228!	29,243!
South	3,457!	—	3,664!	3,560!	13,366!
West	36,088!	5,135!	—	10,494!	19,470!
21 to 24	34,497!	120,398!	68,769!	28,419!	16,344!
Northeast	3,356!	—	16,610!	—	—
Midwest	22,007!	116,586!	43,747!	9,719!	2,068!
South	3,600!	3,813!	5,116!	16,995!	7,097!
West	5,535!	—	3,296!	1,705!	7,179!
25 to 34	50,686!	33,337!	53,734	41,496	70,615
Northeast	—	9,984!	7,613!	5,226!	6,091!
Midwest	3,302!	—	3,391!	11,088!	11,115!
South	39,974!	7,251!	10,458!	10,562!	3,254!
West	7,410!	16,102!	32,272	14,620!	50,155!
35 to 49	135,725	62,198	74,763	46,755	129,993
Northeast	28,060!	38,103!	6,896!	9,677!	5,468!
Midwest	44,439!	8,476!	8,764!	5,910!	36,667!
South	57,578!	2,488!	2,875!	25,347!	13,631!
West	5,648!	13,131!	56,227!	5,821!	74,227!
50 to 64	10,707!	16,021!	—	23,959!	21,788!
Northeast	—	7,098!	—	3,989!	6,807!
Midwest	3,429!	2,604!	—	—	2,555!
South	3,376!	6,319!	—	18,461!	4,109!
West	3,902!	—	—	1,509!	8,317!
65 or older	9,275!	8,471!	4,206!	34,573!	7,344!
Northeast	—	2,033!	2,987!	2,818!	—
Midwest	3,108!	—	—	26,807!	5,858!
South	—	6,438!	—	4,948!	—
West	6,167!	—	1,219!	—	1,487!

—Estimate is equal to 0 sample cases.
!Interpret data with caution, based on 10 or fewer sample cases or the coefficient of variation is greater than 50%.
Notes: Detail may not sum to total due to rounding and/or missing data.

SOURCE: "Number of Rape/Sexual Assaults by Age and Region, 2008–2012," in *NCVS Victimization Analysis Tool (NVAT)*, U.S. Department of Justice, Office of Justice Programs, Bureau of Justice Statistics, July 23, 2014, http://www.bjs.gov/index.cfm?ty=nvat (accessed July 23, 2014)

female high school students who had ever been forced to engage in sexual intercourse, whereas Maryland (8.6%) and Wyoming (8%) had the highest proportions of male high school students who had ever been forced to have sex. Among large urban school districts, Duval County, Florida (11.5%; greater Jacksonville), reported the highest percentage of high school students who had ever been forced to have sex, followed by Palm Beach County, Florida (11.3%), Detroit, Michigan (10.8%), and Memphis, Tennessee (10.7%).

Dating violence is not limited to forced sexual intercourse. Table 8.12 provides an overview of high school students who experienced either physical dating violence or sexual dating violence in 2013, by state and urban school district. As Table 8.12 shows, Louisiana (14.8%) had the highest rate of physical dating violence among high school students that year, followed by Arkansas (13.8%), Georgia (12.4%), and New York (12.1%). Hawaii (13.8%) reported the highest rate of sexual dating violence among high school students in 2013. As Table 8.13 shows, sexual harassment among students also poses a serious problem for public school administrators in the United States. During the 2009–10 school year, 3.2% of all U.S. public schools reported experiencing incidents of sexual harassment involving students. (See Table 8.13.)

COLLEGE RAPE. In *The Sexual Victimization of College Women* (December 2000, http://www.ncjrs.gov/pdffiles1/nij/182369.pdf), the most comprehensive survey of college women regarding sexual victimization available as of October 2014, Bonnie S. Fisher, Francis T. Cullen, and Michael G. Turner find a disturbingly high rate of rapes among college women. Their study was

FIGURE 8.1

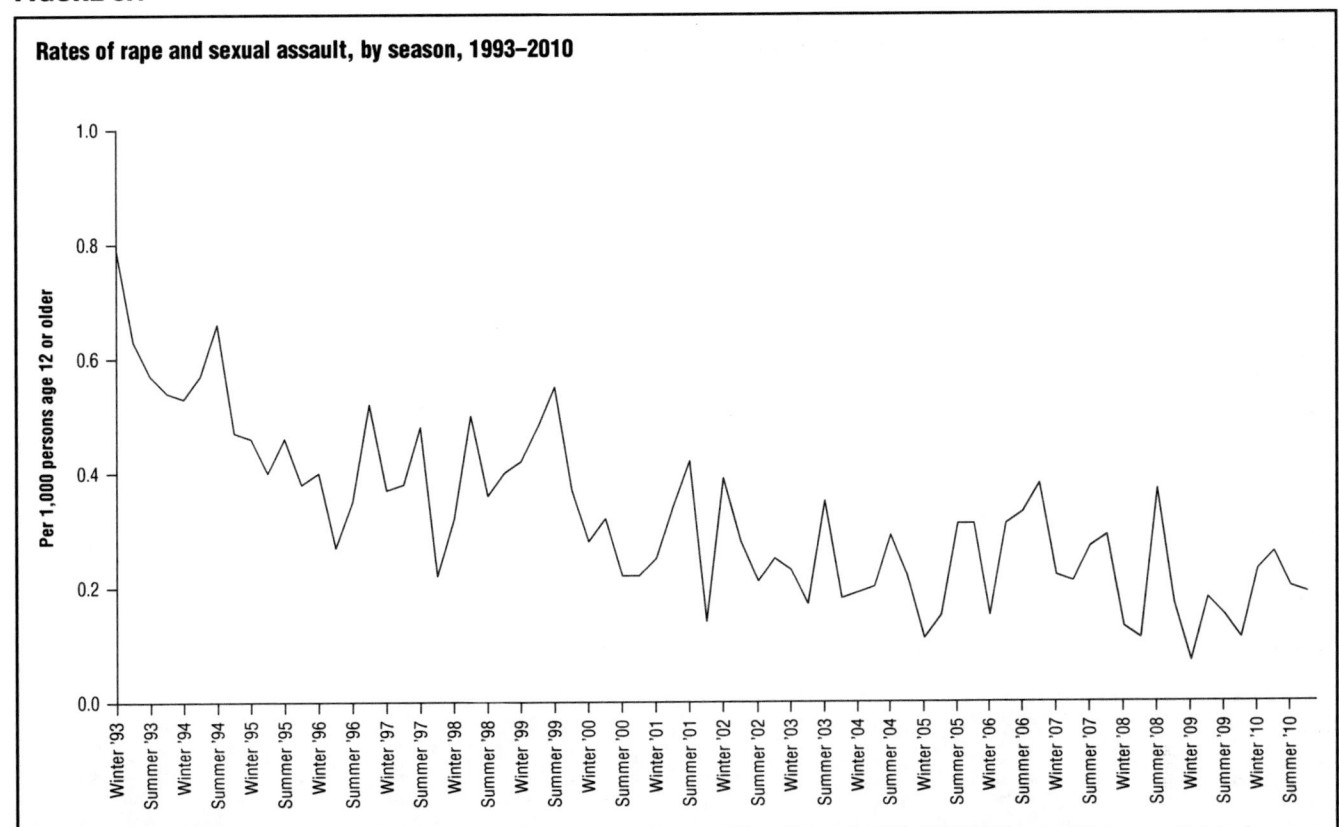

Rates of rape and sexual assault, by season, 1993–2010

SOURCE: Janet L. Lauritsen and Nicole White, "Figure 7. Seasonal Rates of Rape and Sexual Assault, 1993–2010," in *Seasonal Patterns in Criminal Victimization Trends*, U.S. Department of Justice, Office of Special Programs, Bureau of Justice Statistics, June 2014, http://www.bjs.gov/content/pub/pdf/spcvt.pdf (accessed July 23, 2014)

based on a national telephone survey of 4,446 randomly selected women attending colleges and universities during the fall of 1996. Respondents were asked between late February and early May 1997 if they had experienced sexual victimization "since school began in fall 1996." During this seven- to 10-month period, 2.8% of the women had experienced either an attempted or completed rape. The researchers suggest that the data show that 4.9% of college women are victimized during a given calendar year and that the percentage of attempted or completed rape victimizations of college women during their college careers approaches one in four. Fisher, Cullen, and Turner conclude that although the 2.8% figure might "seem" low, "from a policy perspective, college administrators might be disturbed to learn that for every 1,000 women attending their institutions, there may well be 35 incidents of rape in a given academic year.... For a campus with 10,000 women, this would mean the number of rapes could exceed 350."

Fisher, Cullen, and Turner also asked respondents about other types of sexual victimization. They find that 1.7% of their sample had been victims of completed sexual coercion (unwanted sexual penetration with the threat of punishment or the promise of reward), 1.3% had been victims of attempted sexual coercion, 1.9% had been victims of unwanted completed sexual contact with force or the threat of force, and 1.8% had been victims of completed sexual contact without physical force. Smaller percentages of women had been sexually threatened.

Fisher, Cullen, and Turner also find that fewer than 5% of the rapes and attempted rapes had been reported to the police and that even smaller percentages of other types of sexual victimization had been reported. These percentages confirm other researchers' findings, including those of Bonnie S. Fisher et al. in "Reporting Sexual Victimization to the Police and Others: Results from a National-Level Study of College Women" (*Criminal Justice and Behavior*, vol. 30, no. 1, February 2003), that students overwhelmingly do not report acquaintance rapes or attempted rapes. According to the Centers for Disease Control and Prevention, the term *hidden rape* is sometimes used to describe this finding of widespread unreported and underreported sexual assault. Anecdotal reports from college and university administrators suggest that many female students who have been raped not only fail to report the offense but also drop out of school.

Steven Lawyer et al. examined the prevalence of drug- and alcohol-related sexual assaults among college women and published their results in "Forcible, Drug-Facilitated,

FIGURE 8.2

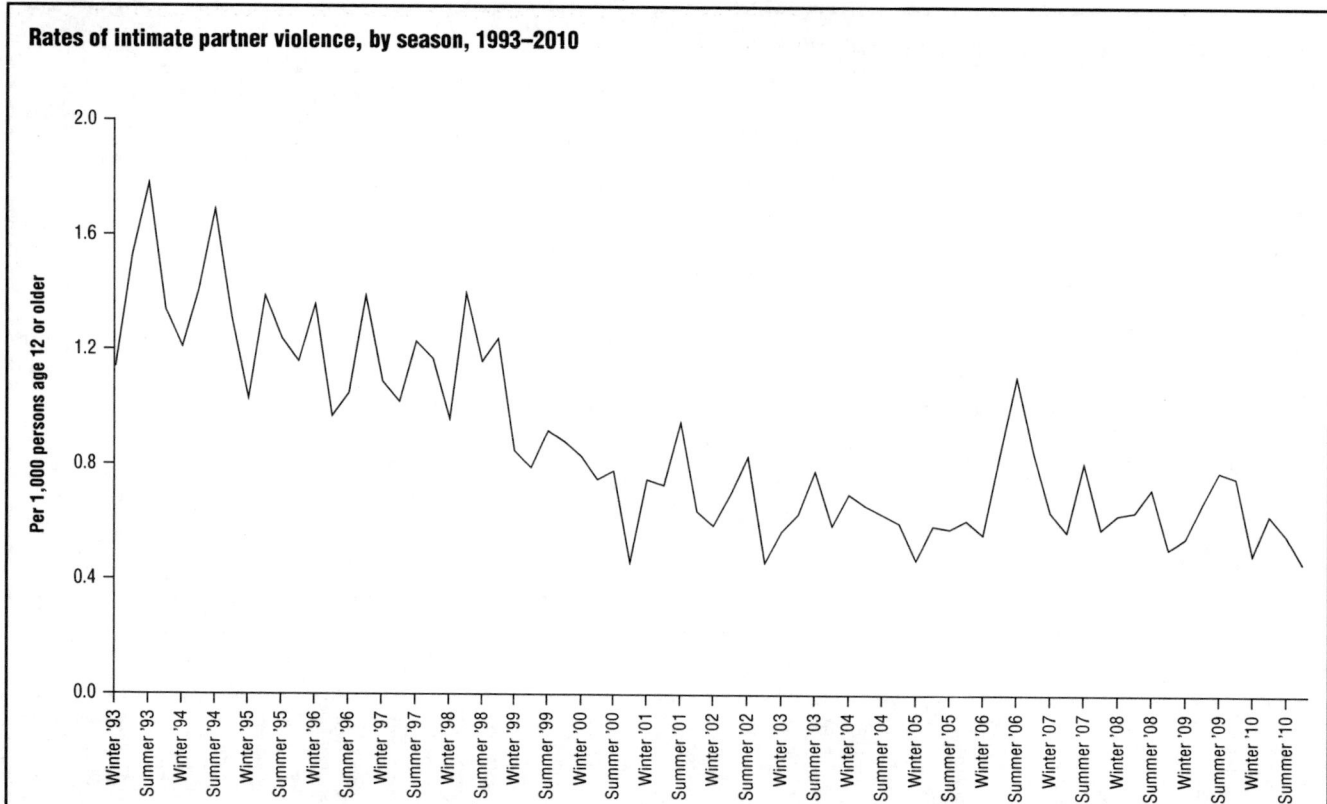

Rates of intimate partner violence, by season, 1993–2010

SOURCE: Janet L. Lauritsen and Nicole White, "Figure 12. Seasonal Rates of Intimate Partner Violence, 1993–2010," in *Seasonal Patterns in Criminal Victimization Trends*, U.S. Department of Justice, Office of Special Programs, Bureau of Justice Statistics, June 2014, http://www.bjs.gov/content/pub/pdf/spcvt.pdf (accessed July 23, 2014)

TABLE 8.10

Percentage of high school students who have ever been forced to have sexual intercourse, by sex, grade, and race and Hispanic origin, 2013

Category	Female %	Male %	Total %
Race/ethnicity			
White*	9.1	3.1	6.1
Black*	11.5	5.2	8.4
Hispanic	12.2	5.2	8.7
Grade			
9	8.3	3.8	6.1
10	11.8	2.8	7.2
11	10.5	4.7	7.7
12	11.2	5.5	8.4
Total	**10.5**	**4.2**	**7.3**

*Non-Hispanic.
Note: Refers to students who were forced to have sexual intercouse against their will.

SOURCE: Adapted from Laura Kann et al., "Table 19. Percentage of High School Students Who Were Ever Physically Forced to Have Sexual Intercourse, by Sex, Race/Ethnicity, and Grade—United States, Youth Risk Behavior Survey, 2013," in "Youth Risk Behavior Surveillance—United States, 2013," *MMWR*, vol. 62, no. 4, June 13, 2014, http://www.cdc.gov/mmwr/pdf/ss/ss6304.pdf (accessed July 23, 2014)

and Incapacitated Rape and Sexual Assault among Undergraduate Women" (*Journal of American College Health*, vol. 58, no. 5, March–April 2010). The researchers recruited 314 college women who reported that they had been sexually assaulted during the spring of 2004. The researchers find that 5.4% of the female students reported a forcible sexual assault or rape and that 29.6% reported a drug-related sexual assault or rape. Most (84.6%) of the drug-related sexual assaults were preceded by voluntary consumption of drugs or alcohol, but 15.4% were due to involuntary incapacitation. Lawyer et al. conclude that drug-related sexual assaults and rapes are extremely common on college campuses.

Table 8.14 offers a breakdown of the number of sexual offenses that occurred at U.S. colleges and universities between 2001 and 2011. As Table 8.14 shows, there were a total of 3,344 incidents involving forced sexual activity at degree-granting postsecondary institutions in 2011; more than two-thirds of these incidents (2,378, or 71%) occurred in residence halls. Nearly half (1,630, or 49%) of all incidents involving forced sexual activity that year were reported at four-year public institutions.

Table 8.15 shows rates of forced sexual activity at U.S. postsecondary institutions between 2001 and 2011. Incidents involving forced sexual activity at colleges and universities reached their highest level in 2011, when there were nearly 2.2 incidents per 10,000 students

TABLE 8.11

Percentage of high school students who have ever been forced to have sexual intercourse, by sex, state, and select metropolitan areas, 2013

Site	Female %	Male %	Total %
State surveys			
Alabama	13.0	7.4	10.2
Alaska	13.2	5.3	9.3
Arizona	14.2	7.1	10.6
Arkansas	15.3	7.6	11.6
Connecticut	11.6	6.8	9.2
Delaware	9.9	5.4	7.7
Florida	8.9	5.6	7.2
Georgia	—*	—	—
Hawaii	11.1	5.5	8.4
Idaho	12.7	4.1	8.3
Illinois	11.6	7.9	9.8
Kansas	9.8	4.9	7.3
Kentucky	11.9	7.2	9.6
Louisiana	—	—	—
Maine	10.5	4.7	7.6
Maryland	11.5	8.6	10.2
Massachusetts	—	—	—
Michigan	11.0	6.3	8.7
Mississippi	11.9	6.2	9.1
Missouri	15.4	5.2	10.2
Montana	11.9	5.7	8.7
Nebraska	11.4	5.9	8.6
Nevada	14.0	7.6	10.9
New Hampshire	7.9	3.3	5.7
New Jersey	11.3	5.5	8.4
New Mexico	10.2	5.4	7.7
New York	—	—	—
North Carolina	12.8	5.1	8.9
North Dakota	11.1	4.5	7.7
Ohio	11.2	4.3	7.5
Oklahoma	9.5	2.9	6.1
Rhode Island	9.7	7.0	8.5
South Carolina	13.3	6.6	10.0
South Dakota	9.6	5.4	7.5
Tennessee	14.2	6.7	10.4
Texas	12.9	7.0	9.9
Utah	8.9	5.9	7.4
Vermont	10.9	4.4	7.6
Virginia	—	—	—
West Virginia	11.9	3.8	7.7
Wisconsin	—	—	—
Wyoming	15.1	8.0	11.6
Median	11.5	5.6	8.6
Range	(7.9–15.4)	(2.9–8.6)	(5.7–11.6)
Large urban school district surveys			
Baltimore, MD	9.0	9.9	9.8
Boston, MA	11.6	7.3	9.5
Broward County, FL	9.8	5.4	7.5
Charlotte-Mecklenburg, NC	11.6	4.7	8.4
Chicago, IL	8.8	8.3	8.8
Detroit, MI	10.8	10.5	10.8
District of Columbia	11.1	6.8	9.2
Duval County, FL	13.4	9.4	11.5
Houston, TX	11.8	7.6	9.9
Los Angeles, CA	10.2	6.3	8.2
Memphis, TN	12.5	8.8	10.7
Miami-Dade County, FL	9.9	4.6	7.3
Milwaukee, WI	—	—	—

attending degree-granting institutions. The rate was higher at institutions with residence halls, where there were 3.1 incidents of forced sexual activity per 10,000 students. In general, the number of incidents involving forcible sexual activity remained roughly the same between 2001 and 2011. (See Figure 8.3.)

TABLE 8.11

Percentage of high school students who have ever been forced to have sexual intercourse, by sex, state, and select metropolitan areas, 2013 [CONTINUED]

Site	Female %	Male %	Total %
New York City, NY	—	—	—
Orange County, FL	12.6	6.5	9.8
Palm Beach County, FL	13.5	9.4	11.3
Philadelphia, PA	10.2	7.2	8.7
San Bernardino, CA	8.5	4.4	6.4
San Diego, CA	8.9	6.0	7.5
San Francisco, CA	—	—	—
Seattle, WA	8.6	7.9	8.3
Median	10.5	7.2	9.0
Range	(8.5–13.5)	(4.4–10.5)	(6.4–11.5)

*Non-Hispanic.

Note: Refers to students who were forced to have sexual intercouse against their will.

SOURCE: Adapted from Laura Kann et al., "Table 20. Percentage of High School Students Who Were Ever Physically Forced to Have Sexual Intercourse, by Sex—Selected U.S. Sites, Youth Risk Behavior Survey, 2013," in "Youth Risk Behavior Surveillance—United States, 2013," *MMWR*, vol. 62, no. 4, June 13, 2014, http://www.cdc.gov/mmwr/pdf/ss/ss6304.pdf (accessed July 23, 2014).

FRATERNITIES AND ATHLETICS. In 2006 an African American stripper hired for a Duke University lacrosse team party accused three white male players of raping her in a bathroom. The university's president canceled the rest of the lacrosse team's season. The case set off racial tensions in Durham, North Carolina, where the woman accuser was a student at North Carolina Central University, a historically black college. Although the charges against all three students were dropped in April 2007, a national discussion about athletes on campus and rape had been set in motion.

The relationship between athletics, fraternities, and rape is not a new dynamic. Several studies find that peer support of violence and social ties with abusive peers are predictors of abuse against women. In addition, training for violent occupations such as athletics and the military can "spill over" into personal life. Athletic training is sex-segregated, promotes hostile attitudes toward rivals, and rewards athletes for physically dominating others. Todd W. Crosset et al. report in "Male Student-Athletes and Violence against Women: A Survey of Campus Judicial Affairs Offices" (*Violence against Women*, vol. 2, no. 2, June 1996) on data that they gathered from the judicial affairs offices of the 10 Division I schools with the largest athletic programs. Although male student athletes made up just 3% of the student population, they accounted for 35% of the reported perpetrators.

In "Dating Aggression, Sexual Coercion, and Aggression-Supporting Attitudes among College Men as a Function of Participation in Aggressive High School Sports" (*Violence against Women*, vol. 12, no. 5, May 2006), Gordon B. Forbes et al. indicate that participation

TABLE 8.12

Percentage of high school students who have ever experienced physical dating violence and sexual dating violence, by sex, state, and select metropolitan areas, 2013

Site	Physical dating violence			Sexual dating violence		
	Female	Male	Total	Female	Male	Total
	%	%	%	%	%	%
State surveys						
Alabama	12.9	10.2	11.6	13.7	7.2	10.6
Alaska	11.3	6.2	9.1	16.6	5.7	11.4
Arizona	—*	—	—	—	—	—
Arkansas	14.8	11.6	13.8	15.2	9.7	12.8
Connecticut	10.1	7.9	9.0	15.5	7.3	11.1
Delaware	10.7	6.8	8.9	12.3	8.4	10.4
Florida	10.6	9.1	9.9	13.1	7.7	10.5
Georgia	12.9	11.6	12.4	—	—	—
Hawaii	12.3	8.8	11.1	18.4	8.0	13.8
Idaho	11.8	6.3	9.1	—	—	—
Illinois	13.7	8.5	11.1	16.7	6.5	11.6
Kansas	9.4	5.9	7.8	11.6	4.0	7.8
Kentucky	11.8	7.6	9.8	13.1	6.4	9.8
Louisiana	16.1	12.6	14.8	—	—	—
Maine	11.1	6.8	9.0	—	—	—
Maryland	12.0	9.7	11.1	13.8	9.0	11.7
Massachusetts	—	—	—	—	—	—
Michigan	11.0	6.6	8.8	14.1	5.5	9.8
Mississippi	13.4	7.3	10.4	12.7	8.3	10.4
Missouri	11.6	7.4	9.6	—	—	—
Montana	11.0	6.6	8.8	15.6	6.4	11.1
Nebraska	10.0	5.3	7.6	15.6	4.7	10.1
Nevada	12.4	9.1	10.9	17.1	7.2	12.2
New Hampshire	9.1	5.8	7.4	14.8	5.0	10.2
New Jersey	—	—	—	—	—	—
New Mexico	11.0	7.7	9.4	12.6	7.3	10.0
New York	12.4	11.7	12.1	14.2	9.3	11.8
North Carolina	12.2	6.2	9.4	14.5	5.1	9.8
North Dakota	11.9	7.3	9.7	—	—	—
Ohio	—	—	—	13.4	6.1	9.7
Oklahoma	11.3	5.7	8.4	13.9	5.5	9.5
Rhode Island	9.4	7.3	8.4	12.0	5.2	8.8
South Carolina	13.1	7.5	10.4	13.7	7.0	10.4
South Dakota	9.6	6.0	7.8	15.8	5.3	10.5
Tennessee	10.8	8.4	9.6	14.4	6.9	10.8
Texas	12.5	7.4	9.9	14.5	7.9	11.1
Utah	7.7	6.1	7.0	15.1	6.4	10.8
Vermont	11.4	9.0	10.2	—	—	—
Virginia	13.5	8.1	10.9	—	—	—
West Virginia	13.8	8.0	10.8	13.4	4.2	8.7
Wisconsin	10.3	6.7	8.5	15.7	4.0	9.6
Wyoming	12.6	7.4	10.3	15.7	6.7	11.5
Median	11.7	7.4	9.6	14.4	6.5	10.5
Range	(7.7–16.1)	(5.3–12.6)	(7.0–14.8)	(11.6–18.4)	(4.0–9.7)	(7.8–13.8)
Large urban school district surveys						
Baltimore, MD	9.4	10.1	10.0	4.6	12.9	9.2
Boston, MA	10.6	6.4	8.5	14.3	7.4	10.7
Broward County, FL	9.5	5.8	7.6	14.5	4.3	9.5
Charlotte-Mecklenburg, NC	11.1	6.0	8.8	11.5	5.6	8.9
Chicago, IL	14.5	9.5	12.3	10.2	7.3	9.1
Detroit, MI	8.4	8.8	8.8	7.9	7.4	8.0
District of Columbia	15.0	8.0	12.0	10.5	7.3	9.3
Duval County, FL	16.4	12.7	14.9	—	—	—
Houston, TX	13.5	7.2	11.0	12.4	8.4	10.9
Los Angeles, CA	7.4	7.2	7.4	15.3	7.5	11.3
Memphis, TN	14.4	10.7	12.8	12.3	8.8	10.7
Miami-Dade County, FL	10.7	6.6	8.7	10.4	8.1	9.4
Milwaukee, WI	17.7	15.7	16.8	—	—	—
New York City, NY	10.3	10.4	10.5	9.9	11.3	10.8
Orange County, FL	9.7	6.7	8.5	13.7	5.8	10.1
Palm Beach County, FL	14.8	10.5	12.5	14.4	11.6	13.0

in aggressive male sports in high school is a risk factor in perpetrating dating violence in college. In a study of 147 men, the researchers find that men who had been involved in aggressive sports in high school engaged in more psychological and physical aggression and sexual coercion in their dating relationships. They were also more accepting of violence, caused their sexual partners more physical injury, and were more hostile toward

TABLE 8.12

Percentage of high school students who have ever experienced physical dating violence and sexual dating violence, by sex, state, and select metropolitan areas, 2013 [CONTINUED]

	Physical dating violence			Sexual dating violence		
	Female	Male	Total	Female	Male	Total
Site	%	%	%	%	%	%
Philadelphia, PA	—	—	—	—	—	—
San Bernardino, CA	9.9	6.9	8.3	12.5	6.8	9.5
San Diego, CA	7.9	6.5	7.4	15.2	6.4	11.0
San Francisco, CA	11.1	8.9	10.3	12.3	6.8	9.9
Seattle, WA	8.4	8.8	8.7	—	—	—
Median	10.6	8.4	9.4	12.3	7.4	9.9
Range	(7.4–17.7)	(5.8–15.7)	(7.4–16.8)	(4.6–15.3)	(4.3–12.9)	(8.0–13.0)

*Not available.

Notes: Among students who dated or went out with someone during the 12 months before the survey. Including being hit, slammed into something, or injured with an object or weapon on purpose by someone they were dating or going out with. One or more times during the 12 monthsbefore the survey. Including kissing, touching, or being physical forced to have sexual intercourse when they did not want to by someone they were dating or going out with.

SOURCE: Adapted from Laura Kann et al., "Table 22. Percentage of High School Students Who Experienced Physical Dating Violence and Sexual Dating Violence, by Sex—Selected U.S. Sites, Youth Risk Behavior Survey, 2013," in "Youth Risk Behavior Surveillance—United States, 2013," *MMWR*, vol. 62, no. 4, June 13, 2014, http://www.cdc.gov/mmwr/pdf/ss/ss6304.pdf (accessed July 23, 2014).

women. According to Forbes et al., the results indicate "that participation in aggressive high school sports is one of the multiple developmental pathways leading to relationship violence."

DATE RAPE DRUGS. Some drugs are known as date rape drugs because they are used by perpetrators to render victims incapable of resisting sexual attacks. One such date rape drug is Rohypnol, which is a hypnotic sedative 10 times more powerful than Valium. Rohypnol has been used to obtain nonconsensual sex from many women. When mixed in a drink, it causes memory impairment, confusion, and drowsiness. A woman may be completely unaware of a sexual assault until she wakes up the following morning. The only way to determine if a victim has been given Rohypnol is to test for the drug within two or three days of the rape, and few hospital emergency departments routinely screen for this drug. Health educators, high school guidance counselors, resident advisers at colleges, and scores of newspaper and magazine articles advise women not to accept drinks at parties or to leave drinks sitting unattended.

Rohypnol is legally prescribed outside of the United States for short-term treatment of severe sleep disorders, but it is neither manufactured nor approved for sale in the United States. In addition, its use (as is the use of other controlled substances) to facilitate a violent act, such as a rape, is against the law. The importation of the drug was banned in March 1996, and the U.S. Customs and Border Protection began seizing quantities of Rohypnol at U.S. borders. In response to reported abuse, the manufacturers reformulated the drug as green tablets that can be detected in clear liquids and are visible in the bottom of a cup.

Three other drugs are also used as date rape pills. Gamma hydroxybutyric acid (also known as "liquid ecstasy") enhances the effects of alcohol, which reduces the drinker's inhibitions. It also causes a form of amnesia. Ketamine hydrochloride (also known as "Special K") is an animal tranquilizer that is used to impair a person's natural resistance impulses. Another dangerous date rape drug is a combination of ecstasy and Viagra (a prescription drug that is used to treat erectile dysfunction); this combination is dubbed "sextasy." According to media reports, the drugs are taken together by male teens because Viagra offsets impotence, which is a potential side effect of ecstasy use. Public health officials are alarmed by this off-label use of Viagra and fear that it may contribute to increased rates of sexually transmitted diseases and sexual assault.

Dean G. Kirkpatrick et al. interviewed 5,000 women between the ages of 18 and 86, 2,000 of whom were currently attending college. In *Drug-Facilitated, Incapacitated, and Forcible Rape: A National Study* (July 2007, http://www.ncjrs.gov/pdffiles1/nij/grants/219181.pdf), the researchers report that 18% of all women had been raped during their lifetime and that 11.5% of college women had been raped during their lifetime. The researchers indicate that more college women than women in the general population had experienced either drug-assisted rapes (in which the perpetrator purposely administered drugs or alcohol to assault the victim) or drug-facilitated rapes (in which the perpetrator took advantage of the victim's voluntary intoxication to assault her). During their lifetime, 6.4% of college women and 5% of women in the general population had experienced these types of rape.

Combating Sexual Violence on Campus

In recent years, advocacy groups and government agencies have become increasingly active in confronting

TABLE 8.13

Percentage of public schools reporting sexual harassment of students by other students, by school size, setting, racial and ethnic composition, and other categories, select years 2003–10

	Happens at least once a week[a]
Year and school characteristic	Student sexual harassment of other students
All schools	
2003–04	4.0
2005–06	3.5
2007–08	3.0
2009–10 All schools	**3.2**
School level[b]	
Primary	1.8!
Middle	6.1
High school	3.2
Combined	7.5!
Enrollment size	
Less than 300	4.5!
300–499	2.4!
500–999	2.6
1,000 or more	4.7
Locale	
City	3.6!
Suburban	2.6
Town	2.9!
Rural	3.6
Percent combined enrollment of black, Hispanic, Asian/Pacific Islander, and American Indian/Alaska Native students	
Less than 5 percent	4.5!
5 percent to less than 20 percent	1.8!
20 percent to less than 50 percent	2.6
50 percent or more	4.1!
Percent of students eligible for free or reduced–price lunch	
0–25	2.6
26–50	3.2
51–75	3.2!
76–100	3.9!
Student/teacher ratio[c]	
Less than 12	4.2!
12–16	2.4
More than 16	3.6
Prevalence of violent incidents[d]	
No violent incidents	‡
Any violent incidents	4.1

TABLE 8.13

Percentage of public schools reporting sexual harassment of students by other students, by school size, setting, racial and ethnic composition, and other categories, select years 2003–10 [CONTINUED]

!Interpret data with caution. The coefficient of variation (CV) for this estimate is between 30 and 50 percent
‡Reporting standards not met. Either there are too few cases for a reliable estimate or the coefficient of variation (CV) is 50 percent or greater.
[a]Includes schools that reported the activity happens either at least once a week or daily.
[b]Primary schools are defined as schools in which the lowest grade is not higher than grade 3 and the highest grade is not higher than grade 8. Middle schools are defined as schools in which the lowest grade is not lower than grade 4 and the highest grade is not higher than grade 9. High schools are defined as schools in which the lowest grade is not lower than grade 9 and the highest grade is not higher than grade 12. Combined schools include all other combinations of grades, including K–12 schools.
[c]Student/teacher ratio was calculated by dividing the total number of students enrolled in the school by the total number of full-time-equivalent (FTE) teachers. Information regarding the total number of FTE teachers was obtained from the Common Core of Data (CCD), the sampling frame for SSOCS.
[d]"Violent incidents" include rape or attempted rape sexual battery other than rape physical attack or fight with or without a weapon, threat of physical attack or fight with or without a weapon, and robbery with or without a weapon.
Note: Responses were provided by the principal or the person most knowledgeable about crime and safety issues at the school. "At school" was defined for respondents to include activities that happen in school buildings, on school grounds, on school buses, and at places that hold school-sponsored events or activities. Respondents were instructed to respond only for those times that were during normal school hours or when school activities or events were in session, unless the survey specified otherwise.

SOURCE: Adapted from Simone Robers et al., "Table 7.1. Percentage of Public Schools Reporting Selected Discipline Problems That Occurred at School, by Frequency and Selected School Characteristics: Selected Years, 1999–2000 through 2009–10," in *Indicators of School Crime and Safety: 2013*, U.S. Department of Education, National Center for Education Statistics, U.S. Department of Justice, Office of Justice Programs, Bureau of Justice Statistics, June 2014, http://www.bjs.gov/content/pub/pdf/iscs13.pdf (accessed July 23, 2014)

the problem of sexual violence at the nation's postsecondary institutions. One specific area of reform has focused on improving the ways that colleges and universities report incidents of rape and sexual assault. Claire Groden reports in "Campus Rape Victims Find a Voice" (Time .com, August 8, 2013) that rape and sexual assault is "notoriously underreported" at American institutions of higher learning. According to Groden, between one-fifth and one-quarter of all female college students experience sexual assault, rape, or attempted rape at some point before completing their degree. However, statistics provided by most colleges and universities fail to reflect this reality. For example, Groden notes that in 2011 the University of Southern California reported a total of only 15

cases of rape or sexual assault, despite having a student body of 40,000.

By early 2013 the federal government began taking more aggressive measures to hold colleges and universities accountable. The Violence against Women Reauthorization Act, which was signed into law in March 2013, includes a stipulation known as the Campus Sexual Violence Act provision, which requires all institutions participating in federal financial aid programs to provide detailed reporting of all on-campus incidences of rape, sexual assault, domestic violence, and stalking. Furthermore, Groden notes that at the beginning of the 2013–14 academic year, nearly 30 schools, including Dartmouth College, the University of Southern California, and Princeton University, were under federal investigation for violations related to the underreporting of sexual violence on campus. According to Scott Neuman, in "55 Colleges, Universities under Investigation for Abuse Claims" (NPR.org, May 1, 2014), by May 2014 the number of institutions under investigation had climbed to 55 colleges and universities nationwide.

In January 2014 President Barack Obama (1961–) announced the formation of the White House Task Force to Protect Students from Sexual Assault, a new agency

TABLE 8.14

Forcible and nonforcible sex offenses at degree-granting postsecondary institutions, by type of institution, 2001–11

Control and level of institution and type of incident	Number of incidents										2011		
	2001	2002	2003	2004	2005	2006	2007	2008	2009	2010	Total	In residence hall	At other locations
All institutions													
Sex offenses—forcible	2,201	2,327	2,595	2,667	2,674	2,670	2,694	2,639	2,544	2,919	3,344	2,378	966
Sex offenses—nonforcible	461	261	60	27	42	43	40	35	65	33	45	16	29
Public 4-year													
Sex offenses—forcible	1,245	1,278	1,358	1,482	1,398	1,400	1,425	1,317	1,214	1,460	1,630	1,151	479
Sex offenses—nonforcible	207	113	28	16	25	15	23	12	40	15	17	7	10
Nonprofit 4-year													
Sex offenses—forcible	820	914	1,048	1,026	1,088	1,080	1,065	1,083	1,102	1,220	1,406	1,132	274
Sex offenses—nonforcible	113	81	14	5	6	10	8	16	11	8	13	6	7
For-profit 4-year													
Sex offenses—forcible	4	4	8	5	4	12	12	9	9	22	29	13	16
Sex offenses—nonforcible	13	1	2	0	1	0	2	0	1	1	0	0	0
Public 2-year													
Sex offenses—forcible	118	118	160	142	175	167	181	210	205	208	261	72	189
Sex offenses—nonforcible	119	61	14	6	10	16	7	7	12	8	15	3	12
Nonprofit 2-year													
Sex offenses—forcible	2	7	6	3	8	3	9	16	8	7	11	8	3
Sex offenses—nonforcible	2	2	0	0	0	1	0	0	0	0	0	0	0
For-profit 2-year													
Sex offenses—forcible	12	6	15	9	1	8	2	4	6	2	7	2	5
Sex offenses—nonforcible	7	3	2	0	0	1	0	0	1	1	0	0	0

Note: Sex offenses, forcible includes any sexual act directed against another person forcibly and/or against that person's will. Sex offense, nonforcible includes only statutory rape or incest. Degree-granting institutions grant associate's or higher degrees and participate in Title IV federal financial aid programs. Crimes, arrests, and referrals include incidents involving students, staff, and on-campus guests. Excludes off-campus crimes and arrests even if they involve college students or staff.

SOURCE: Adapted from Simone Robers et al., "Table 22.1. On-Campus Crimes, Arrests, and Referrals for Disciplinary Action at Degree-Granting Postsecondary Institutions, by Location of Incident, Control and Level of Institution, and Type of Incident: 2001 through 2011," in *Indicators of School Crime and Safety: 2013*, U.S. Department of Education, National Center for Education Statistics, U.S. Department of Justice, Office of Justice Programs, Bureau of Justice Statistics, June 2014, http://www.bjs.gov/content/pub/pdf/iscs13.pdf (accessed July 23, 2014)

designed to provide support for victims of on-campus sexual violence. The initial findings of the task force were published in *Not Alone: The First Report of the White House Task Force to Protect Students from Sexual Assault* (April 2014, https://www.notalone.gov/assets/report.pdf). Among the task force's key recommendations is a requirement that schools conduct an "evidence-based survey" on sexual violence by 2016. By establishing greater openness about the reality of sexual violence on campus, the task force asserts, college administrations will become better equipped to combat the issue. "A mandate for schools to periodically conduct a climate survey," the task force states, "will change the national dynamic: with a better picture of what's really happening on campus, schools will be able to more effectively tackle the problem and measure the success of their efforts."

Another key development in the movement to end sexual violence on college campuses followed in September 2014, when California implemented a law clarifying the legal definition of consensual sex. Bill Chappell reports in "California Enacts 'Yes Means Yes' Law, Defining Sexual Consent" (NPR.org, September 29, 2014) that the new law requires individuals to establish specific verbal consent before engaging in sexual activities. Furthermore, the law states that affirmative consent cannot be obtained in situations when a person is either sleeping or intoxicated. The law also requires California's colleges and universities to implement more stringent policies relating to sexual assault and domestic violence cases on campus.

International Concerns about Rape

Historically, because women have been viewed as the possessions of their fathers and husbands, sexual abuse of a woman has been considered to be a violation of a man's property rights rather than a violation of a woman's human rights. However, primarily through the efforts of women's advocacy groups worldwide, in most countries rape is no longer viewed as a violation of family honor but as an abuse and violation of women as well as a crime.

TABLE 8.15

Forcible and nonforcible sex offenses at degree-granting postsecondary institutions, per 10,000 full-time-equivalent students and type of institution, 2001–11

Control and level of institution and type of incident	Number of incidents per 10,000 full-time-equivalent (FTE)[1] students											2011	
	Total, institutions with and without residence halls											Institutions with residence halls	Institutions without residence halls
	2001	2002	2003	2004	2005	2006	2007	2008	2009	2010	Total		
All institutions													
Sex offenses—forcible	1.885	1.896	2.051	2.056	2.058	2.001	1.969	1.898	1.712	1.901	2.171	3.099	0.405
Sex offenses—nonforcible	0.395	0.213	0.047	0.021	0.032	0.032	0.029	0.025	0.044	0.021	0.029	0.030	0.028
Public 4-year													
Sex offenses—forcible	2.408	2.374	2.452	2.634	2.448	2.409	2.390	2.151	1.892	2.217	2.427	2.633	0.403
Sex offenses—nonforcible	0.400	0.210	0.051	0.028	0.044	0.026	0.039	0.020	0.062	0.023	0.025	0.026	0.016
Nonprofit 4-year													
Sex offenses—forcible	3.169	3.410	3.790	3.617	3.784	3.694	3.587	3.586	3.561	3.835	4.325	4.628	0.748
Sex offenses—nonforcible	0.437	0.302	0.051	0.018	0.021	0.034	0.027	0.053	0.036	0.025	0.040	0.033	0.118
For-profit 4-year													
Sex offenses—forcible	0.151	0.121	0.196	0.095	0.082	0.179	0.159	0.162	0.125	0.265	0.354	1.544	0.075
Sex offenses—nonforcible	0.492	0.030	0.049	0.000	0.021	0.000	0.026	0.000	0.014	0.012	0.000	0.000	0.000
Public 2-year													
Sex offenses—forcible	0.344	0.324	0.435	0.383	0.480	0.454	0.484	0.538	0.483	0.479	0.619	1.234	0.469
Sex offenses—nonforcible	0.347	0.167	0.038	0.016	0.027	0.044	0.019	0.018	0.028	0.018	0.036	0.048	0.032
Nonprofit 2-year													
Sex offenses—forcible	0.516	1.793	1.638	0.877	2.325	0.983	3.622	5.841	3.042	2.798	3.320	10.280	0.820
Sex offenses—nonforcible	0.516	0.512	0.000	0.000	0.000	0.328	0.000	0.000	0.000	0.000	0.000	0.000	0.000
For-profit 2-year													
Sex offenses—forcible	0.645	0.309	0.674	0.373	0.042	0.347	0.087	0.149	0.171	0.052	0.191	1.718	0.141
Sex offenses—nonforcible	0.376	0.154	0.090	0.000	0.000	0.043	0.000	0.000	0.028	0.026	0.000	0.000	0.000

Notes: Although crimes, arrests, and referrals include incidents involving students, staff, and campus guests, they are expressed as a ratito FTE students because comprehensive FTE counts of all these groups are not available. Sex offenses, forcible includes any sexual act directed against another person forcibly and/or against that person's will. Sex offense, nonforcible includes only statutroy rape or incest. Degree-granting institutions grant associate's or higher degrees and participate in Title IV federal financial aid programs. Crimes, arrests, and referrals include incidents involving students, staff, and on-campus guests. Excludes off-campus crimes and arrests even if they involve college students or staff.

SOURCE: Adapted from Simone Robers et al., "Table 22.2. On-Campus Crimes, Arrests, and Referrals for Disciplinary Action per 10,000 Full-Time-Equivalent (FTE) Students at Degree-Granting Postsecondary Institutions, by whether Institution Has Residence Halls, Control and Level of Institution, and Type of Incident: 2001 through 2011," in *Indicators of School Crime and Safety: 2013*, U.S. Department of Education, National Center for Education Statistics, U.S. Department of Justice, Office of Justice Programs, Bureau of Justice Statistics, June 2014, http://www.bjs.gov/content/pub/pdf/iscs13.pdf (accessed July 23, 2014)

The United Nations (UN) has taken a firm stance on violence against women and children worldwide. The UN Declaration on the Elimination of Violence against Women (December 20, 1993, http://www.un.org/documents/ga/res/48/a48r104.htm) specifically names marital rape, sexual abuse of female children, selling women into slavery or prostitution, and other acts of sexual violence against women in its condemnation of "any act of gender-based violence that results in, or is likely to result in, physical, sexual or psychological harm or suffering to women, including threats of such acts, coercion or arbitrary deprivation of liberty, whether occurring in public or in private life."

In February 2012 the UN Security Council released the statement "Security Council Presidential Statement Condemns Sexual Violence in Conflict, Post-conflict Situations, Urges Complete, Immediate Cessation of Such Acts" (February 23, 2012, http://www.un.org/News/Press/docs/2012/sc10555.doc.htm) to reaffirm its commitment to the implementation of five previous resolutions it has issued related to violence against women. The statement was spurred by the council's review of the report "Conflict-Related Sexual Violence" (January 13, 2012, http://www.unhcr.org/refworld/docid/4f27a19c2.html), which details "incidents, trends, and patterns of sexual violence in armed conflict and post-conflict situations, including the deliberate targeting of civilians for sexual violence." In particular, the report singles out armed militia groups and former and current armed forces active in various African countries as "credibly suspected of committing or being responsible for patterns of rape and other forms of sexual violence."

The UN News Centre notes in "Senior UN Official Condemns 'Alarming' Reports of Sexual Violence in Mali" (April 10, 2012, http://www.un.org/apps/news/story.asp?NewsID=41734) that Margot Wallström, the special representative of the Secretary-General on Sexual Violence in Conflict, had "strongly condemned the reported acts of sexual violence committed against Malian women

FIGURE 8.3

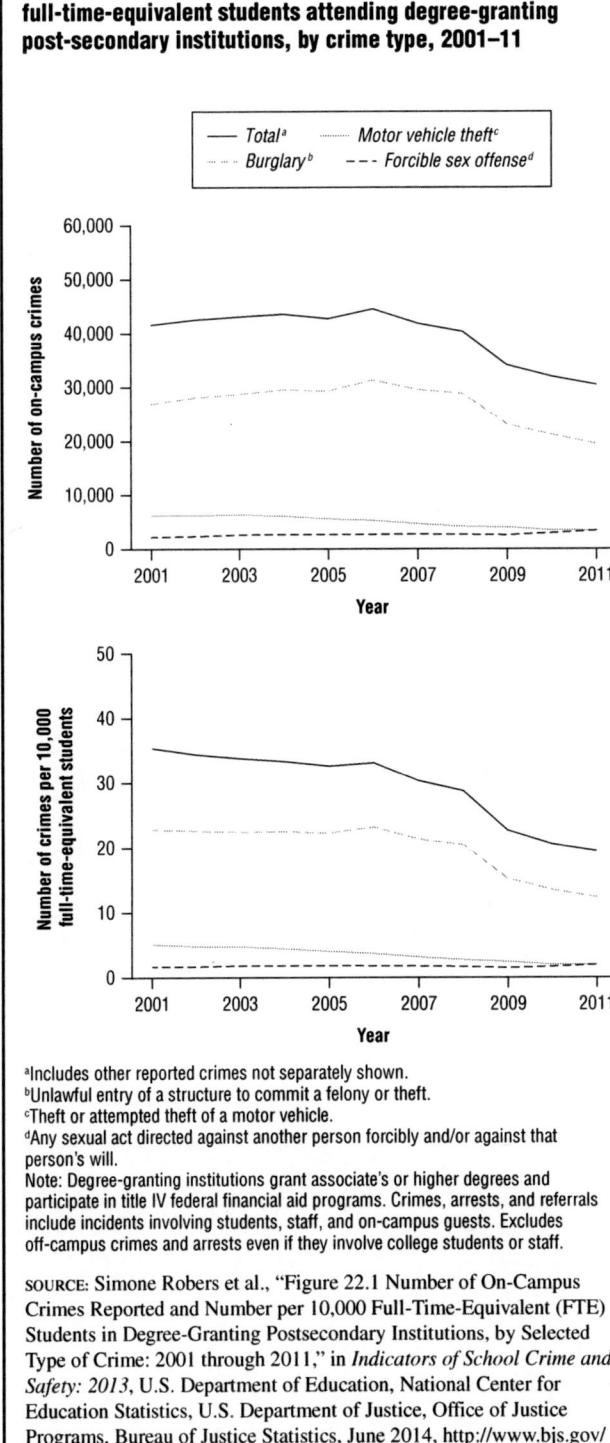

Number of on-campus crimes reported and number per 10,000 full-time-equivalent students attending degree-granting post-secondary institutions, by crime type, 2001–11

[a]Includes other reported crimes not separately shown.
[b]Unlawful entry of a structure to commit a felony or theft.
[c]Theft or attempted theft of a motor vehicle.
[d]Any sexual act directed against another person forcibly and/or against that person's will.
Note: Degree-granting institutions grant associate's or higher degrees and participate in title IV federal financial aid programs. Crimes, arrests, and referrals include incidents involving students, staff, and on-campus guests. Excludes off-campus crimes and arrests even if they involve college students or staff.

SOURCE: Simone Robers et al., "Figure 22.1 Number of On-Campus Crimes Reported and Number per 10,000 Full-Time-Equivalent (FTE) Students in Degree-Granting Postsecondary Institutions, by Selected Type of Crime: 2001 through 2011," in *Indicators of School Crime and Safety: 2013*, U.S. Department of Education, National Center for Education Statistics, U.S. Department of Justice, Office of Justice Programs, Bureau of Justice Statistics, June 2014, http://www.bjs.gov/content/pub/pdf/iscs13.pdf (accessed July 23, 2014)

and girls." Mali is a country in western Africa that in early 2012 was cast into political and social turmoil by a violent civil war. The UN notes that it has received allegations of "abductions, public rapes and subjecting women and girls to acts of sexual violence in front of family members." Wallström warned the warring parties that "acts of conflict-related sexual violence can constitute war crimes or crimes against humanity for which combatants and their commanders will be held to account."

STALKING

Stalking is generally defined as harassment or threatening behavior that involves repeated visual or physical proximity; nonconsensual communication; verbal, written, or implied threats; or a combination of these acts that would cause a reasonable person fear. Stalking is a series of actions that can escalate from legal but annoying acts, such as following or repeatedly phoning a victim, to violent and even fatal actions.

National Intimate Partner and Sexual Violence Survey (2010)

Black et al. note that for purposes of the NISVS, stalking was defined as "a pattern of harassing or threatening tactics used by a perpetrator that is both unwanted and causes fear or safety concerns in the victim." Table 8.5 lists the types of questions that were asked of survey participants to ascertain their victimization experiences with stalking. Perpetrator tactics include watching or following victims, leaving unwanted messages, making unwanted telephone calls, and approaching victims at their home, workplace, or school when the victims do not want the perpetrators to be at these places.

According to Black et al., 16.2% of U.S. women and 5.2% of U.S. men have been stalked during their lifetime. This equates to 19.3 million women and 5.9 million men. The 12-month prevalence rates were 4.3% for women and 1.3% for men. As Black et al. report, the lifetime prevalence percentages of stalking victimizations broken down by the race and ethnicity of the female victims were: multiracial (30.6%), Native American or Alaskan Native (22.7%), non-Hispanic African American (19.6%), non-Hispanic white (16%), and Hispanic (15.2%). For men, the breakdown was 6% for non-Hispanic African Americans and 5.1% each for non-Hispanic whites and Hispanics. No estimates could be obtained for other ethnic and racial groups because of small sample sizes.

Figure 8.4 shows the lifetime prevalence for female victims for various types of stalking tactics. More than three-quarters (78.8%) of the victims had received unwanted phone calls, voice messages, text messages, or hang-up calls. More than half (57.6%) of the victims said they had been approached by their stalkers at their home or workplace or their stalkers had showed up at these places, and more than one-third (38.6%) of the victims reported being watched or followed. Lower percentages of female victims indicated they had received unwanted gifts (26.4%), had experienced their stalkers sneaking into their home or car (22.9%), had received unwanted e-mails or messages (12.9%), or had been left strange items by their stalkers (12.2%).

The distribution of stalking tactics was very similar for male stalking victims. (See Figure 8.5.) Three-fourths (75.9%) of them had received unwanted phone calls of some sort. More than four out of 10 (43.5%) said they had been approached by their stalkers at their home or workplace or their stalkers had showed up at these places. Slightly less than one-third (31%) of the victims reported having been watched or followed. Lower percentages of male victims indicated they had experienced their stalkers sneaking into their home or car (16.6%), had received unwanted e-mails or messages (12.3%), had received unwanted gifts (11.6%), or had been left strange items by their stalkers (9%).

Figure 8.6 provides information about the offender-victim relationship for female stalking victims. About two-thirds (66.2%) of the victims identified their stalkers as intimate partners (i.e., former or current spouses, boyfriends, or girlfriends). Another 24% of the victims said their stalkers were acquaintances. This category includes

FIGURE 8.4

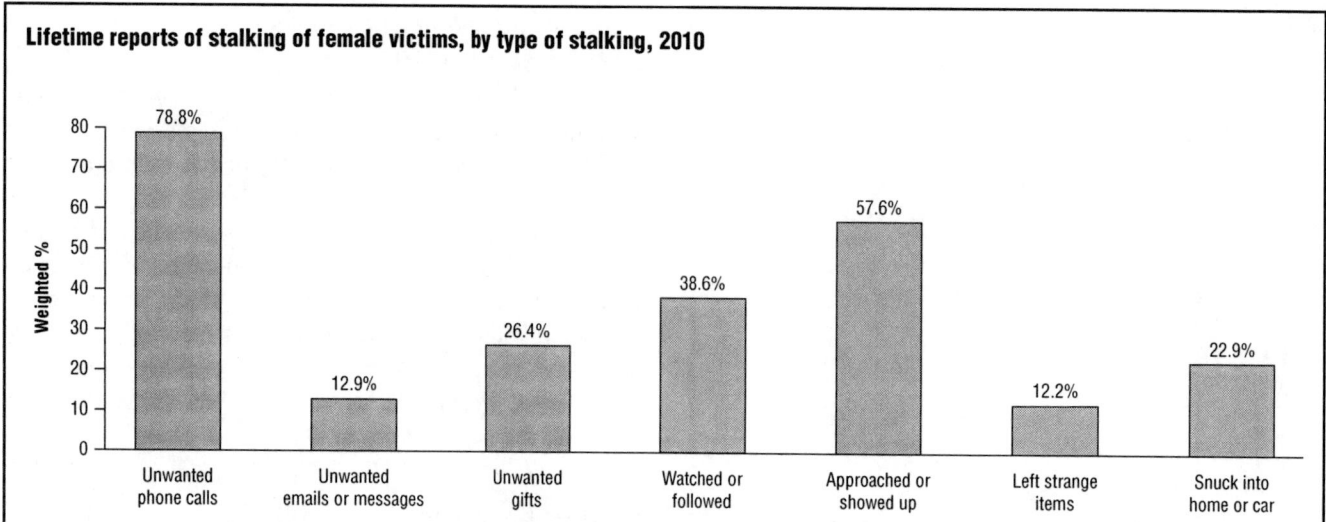

Lifetime reports of stalking of female victims, by type of stalking, 2010

SOURCE: Michele C. Black et al., "Figure 3.1. Lifetime Reports of Stalking among Female Victims by Type of Tactic Experienced—NISVS 2010," in *National Intimate Partner and Sexual Violence Survey: 2010 Summary Report*, U.S. Department of Health and Human Services, Centers for Disease Control and Prevention, National Center for Injury Prevention and Control, December 14, 2011, http://www.cdc.gov/ViolencePrevention/pdf/NISVS_Report2010-a.pdf (accessed July 23, 2014)

FIGURE 8.5

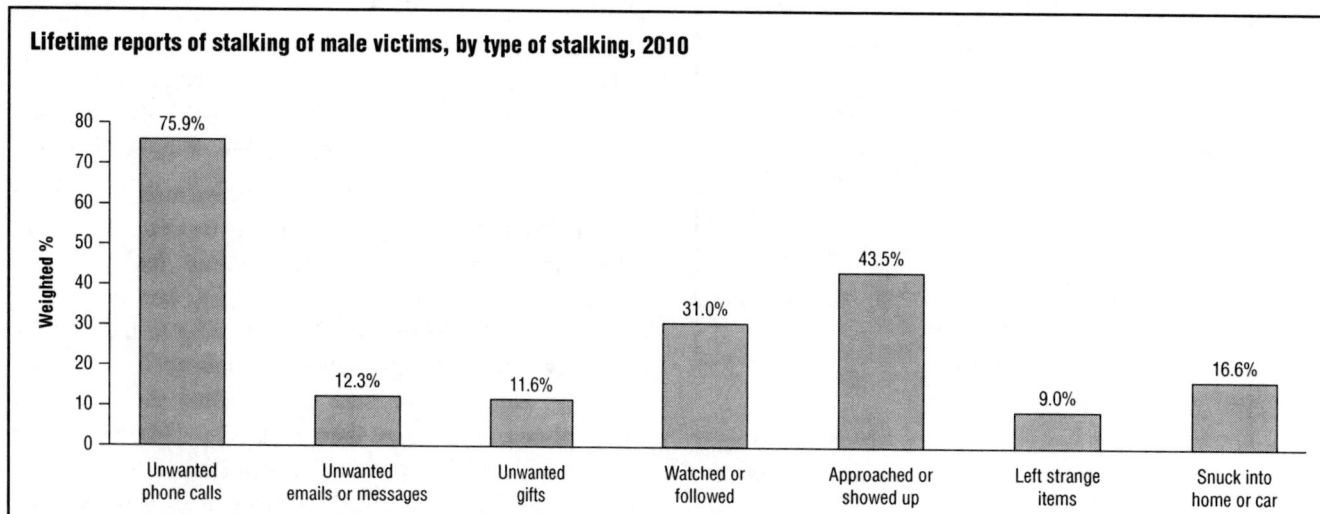

Lifetime reports of stalking of male victims, by type of stalking, 2010

SOURCE: Michele C. Black et al., "Figure 3.2. Lifetime Reports of Stalking among Male Victims by Type of Tactic Experienced—NISVS 2010," in *National Intimate Partner and Sexual Violence Survey: 2010 Summary Report*, U.S. Department of Health and Human Services, Centers for Disease Control and Prevention, National Center for Injury Prevention and Control, December 14, 2011, http://www.cdc.gov/ViolencePrevention/pdf/NISVS_Report2010-a.pdf (accessed July 23, 2014)

friends, neighbors, family friends, first dates, people briefly known, and people not known well by the victims. Strangers were blamed for stalking by 13.2% of the female victims. In addition, 6.8% of the victims indicated their stalkers were family members, and 2.5% said their stalkers were people of authority. Overall, 86.8% of the female victims knew their stalkers.

According to Black et al., 76% of the female victims said that during their lifetime they had been stalked by only one perpetrator. Another 17% reported having been stalked by two perpetrators, and 7.1% indicated three or more stalkers. The vast majority (82.5%) of female stalking victims said they had been stalked during their lifetime by only male perpetrators. Another 8.8% said their stalkers had been only female, and 4.6% reported having had both male and female stalkers.

The offender-victim relationships for lifetime victimizations by male stalking victims are shown in Figure 8.7. Approximately four out of 10 (41.4%) victims said their stalkers were intimate partners, whereas 40% identified their stalkers as acquaintances. Another 19% of the male victims indicated they had been stalked by strangers, and

5.3% said their stalkers were family members. Overall, 81% of the male victims knew their stalkers.

Black et al. indicate that 82.2% of the male victims said that during their lifetime they had been stalked by only one perpetrator. Nearly one out of 10 (9.6%) reported having had two stalkers. Male victims were almost as likely to have been stalked during their lifetime by males only (44.3%) as by females only (46.7%). Another 5.5% of the men said they had been stalked by both male and female perpetrators.

INTIMATE PARTNER STALKING. According to Black et al., an estimated 12.7 million women (or 10.7% of the adult female U.S. population) have been stalked by an intimate partner during their lifetime. The 12-month prevalence among adult women for stalking was 2.8%. The lifetime prevalence percentages of stalking victimizations broken down by the race and ethnicity of the female victims were: multiracial (18.9%), non-Hispanic African American (14.6%), Hispanic (10.6%), and non-Hispanic white (10.4%).

In addition, Black et al. estimate that 2.4 million adult men (or 2.1% of the adult male U.S. population)

FIGURE 8.6

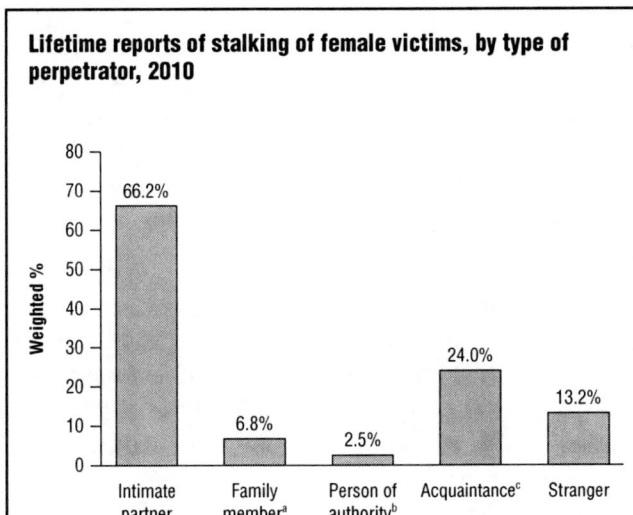

Lifetime reports of stalking of female victims, by type of perpetrator, 2010

Note: Relationship is based on respondents' reports of their relationship at the time the perpetrator first committed any violence against them.
[a]Includes immediate and extended family members.
[b]Includes, for example: boss, supervisor, superior in command, teacher, professor, coach, clergy, doctor, therapist, and caregiver.
[c]Includes friends, neighbors, family friends, first date, someone briefly known and people not known well.

SOURCE: Michele C. Black et al., "Figure 3.3. Lifetime Reports of Stalking among Female Victims by Type of Perpetrator—NISVS 2010," in *National Intimate Partner and Sexual Violence Survey: 2010 Summary Report*, U.S. Department of Health and Human Services, Centers for Disease Control and Prevention, National Center for Injury Prevention and Control, December 14, 2011, http://www.cdc.gov/ViolencePrevention/pdf/NISVS_Report2010-a.pdf (accessed July 23, 2014)

FIGURE 8.7

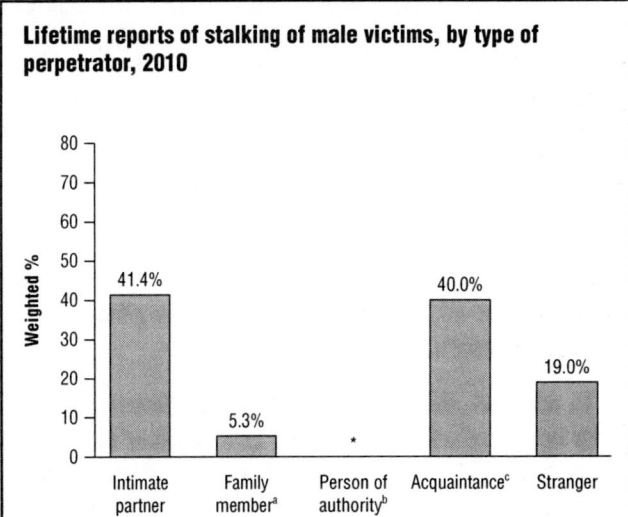

Lifetime reports of stalking of male victims, by type of perpetrator, 2010

Note: Relationship is based on respondents' reports of their relationship at the time the perpetrator first committed any violence against them.
[a]Includes immediate and extended family members.
[b]Includes, for example: boss, supervisor, superior in command, teacher, professor, coach, clergy, doctor, therapist, and caregiver.
[c]Includes friends, neighbors, family friends, first date, someone briefly known and people not known well.
*Estimate is not reported.

SOURCE: Michele C. Black et al., "Figure 3.4. Lifetime Reports of Stalking among Male Victims by Type of Perpetrator—NISVS 2010," in *National Intimate Partner and Sexual Violence Survey: 2010 Summary Report*, U.S. Department of Health and Human Services, Centers for Disease Control and Prevention, National Center for Injury Prevention and Control, December 14, 2011, http://www.cdc.gov/ViolencePrevention/pdf/NISVS_Report2010-a.pdf (accessed July 23, 2014)

have been stalked by an intimate partner during their lifetime. The 12-month prevalence of stalking victimization of adult men was 0.5%. This equates to about 519,000 men nationally based on the U.S. adult male population. The lifetime prevalence percentage for non-Hispanic white men was 10.4%. The researchers were unable to determine the percentages for other racial and ethnic groups due to small sample sizes.

Supplemental Victimization Survey

In 2006 the DOJ's Office on Violence against Women funded the Supplemental Victimization Survey (SVS) as a supplement to the NCVS to explore the extent and nature of stalking in the United States. Shannan Catalano of the BJS indicates in *Stalking Victims in the United States—Revised* (September 2012, http://bjs.ojp .usdoj.gov/content/pub/pdf/svus_rev.pdf) that the survey included 65,270 participants aged 18 years and older who were interviewed during the first six months of 2006 about experiences that had occurred during the previous 12 months. The SVS classified an individual as a stalking victim if he or she had been the recipient of one of the following seven harassing behaviors on at least two separate occasions:

- Received unwanted phone calls
- Received unsolicited or unwanted letters or e-mails
- Was followed or spied on
- Found the stalker showing up at places without a legitimate reason
- Found the stalker waiting at places for him or her
- Received unwanted items, presents, or flowers
- Had information posted or had rumors spread about him or her on the Internet, in a public place, or by word of mouth

In addition, the victims had to have "feared for their safety or that of a family member as a result of the course of conduct or have experienced additional threatening behaviors that would cause a reasonable person to feel fear." According to Catalano, these criteria were based on federal and state criminal laws that cover stalking. Survey participants who reported experiencing conduct consistent with stalking, but who did not meet the fear criteria, were classified as being victims of harassment, rather than as victims of stalking.

Overall, Catalano estimates that 3.3 million adults aged 18 years and older were stalked during a 12-month period in 2005 to 2006. This represents 1.5% of the adult U.S. population. The percentage was higher for females (2.2%) than for males (0.8%) and gradually decreased with age; that is, individuals aged 18 to 19 years had the

highest rate, at 2.9%. The percentages decreased with increasing household income, in that people making $7,499 or less annually had the highest rate of 3.3%. On a racial and ethnic basis, the highest 12-month prevalence was among people of two or more races (4.1%). Marital status also played a factor. Divorced or separated individuals (3.3%) and those who had never married (2.4%) had the highest prevalence of stalking.

According to Catalano, the most common stalking behaviors were as follows (the percentages add up to more than 100% because the victims were allowed to name multiple behaviors):

- 66.7% of victims experienced unwanted phone calls and messages
- 36.3% of victims had rumors spread about them
- 34.4% of victims were spied on or followed
- 31.6% of victims experienced a stalker showing up at places where they were
- 30.7% received unwanted letters and e-mails
- 29.3% found a stalker waiting for them
- 12.5% received unwanted presents

Stalking victims were also asked how long the stalking had lasted. The largest share (39.3%) said it had lasted six months or less and 16.9% said the duration was between seven and 11 months. Another 13.4% of victims reported they had been stalked for one year, 9% said two years, 4.6% said three years, and 2.8% said four years. Just over one out of 10 (11.1%) victims had been stalked for five or more years. The remaining 2.9% did not know how long the stalking had taken place.

As Catalano reports, 69.9% of the stalking victims knew their stalkers. More than a quarter (28.1%) of the victims identified their stalkers as current or former intimate partners (i.e., spouses, boyfriends, or girlfriends). Another 41.8% of the victims said their stalkers were other known people, including friends, roommates, work or school colleagues, relatives, or other acquaintances. Only 9% of the victims were stalked by strangers. The remaining 21% of the victims either had unknown victim-offender relationships (14.2%) or could not identify a single offender as the stalker (6.8%).

Anti-stalking Legislation

All 50 states and the District of Columbia have laws that make stalking a crime, but whether it is a felony or a misdemeanor varies by state. In addition, how much fear or distress the victim must experience before the behavior is considered to be stalking varies considerably. In 2000 the National Center for Victims of Crime and the Office on Violence against Women created the Stalking Resource Center. The center maintains the website "Criminal Stalking Laws" (http://www.victimsofcrime.org/our-programs/stalking-resource-center/stalking-laws/criminal-stalking-laws-by-state), at which visitors can access state stalking laws. For example, according to the Stalking Resource Center (http://www.victimsofcrime.org/our-programs/stalking-resource-center/stalking-laws/criminal-stalking-laws-by-state/california), as of November 2014 California Penal Code Section 646.9 set forth the definition and penalties for stalking as: "Any person who willfully, maliciously, and repeatedly follows or willfully and maliciously harasses another person and who makes a credible threat with the intent to place that person in reasonable fear for his or her safety, or the safety of his or her immediate family is guilty of the crime of stalking, punishable by imprisonment in a county jail for not more than one year, or by a fine of not more than one thousand dollars ($1,000), or by both that fine and imprisonment, or by imprisonment in the state prison." There are stricter penalties for perpetrators who are convicted of stalking while subject to restraining orders and under other circumstances.

In 1996 the Interstate Stalking Punishment and Prevention Act, which is part of the National Defense Authorization Act of 1997, made interstate stalking a felony. This federal statute addresses cases that cross state lines. In the past interstate offenses were difficult for state law enforcement agencies to take action against. In 2005 the Violence against Women Act was renewed, which criminalized stalking by surveillance and expanded the definition of "accountable harm" to include substantial emotional harm to the victim.

Cyberstalking

Cyberstalking (online harassment and threats that can escalate to frightening and even life-threatening offline violence) is a relatively recent phenomenon. Brian H. Spitzberg and Greg Hoobler note in "Cyberstalking and the Technologies of Interpersonal Terrorism" (*New Media and Society*, vol. 4, no. 1, February 2002), a study of college students, that almost one-third of students responded that they had experienced some degree of computer-based harassment and pursuit. The researchers state that "it stands to reason that if there are classes of people who elect, or are driven obsessively, to pursue intimacy with others that these pursuers will seek whatever means are available that might increase their access to the objects of their pursuit, and that people's increasing exposure on and through the computer will make them more accessible as victims."

In January 2006 a federal anticyberstalking law was signed into law by President George W. Bush (1946–) as part of the reauthorized Violence against Women Act. It prohibited anyone from using a telephone or telecommunications device (including a computer) "without disclosing his identity and with intent to annoy, abuse, threaten, or harass any person."

Although the extent of the problem is difficult to measure, by 1999 cyberstalking had generated enough concern to warrant the report *Cyberstalking: A New Challenge for Law Enforcement and Industry* (August 1999) by the U.S. attorney general. The attorney general's report cautions that although cyberstalking does not involve physical contact, it should not be considered less dangerous than physical stalking. In *Stalking and Domestic Violence: Report to Congress* (May 2001, http://www.ncjrs.gov/pdffiles1/ojp/186157.pdf), the DOJ compares the similarities and differences between offline and online stalking. Most stalking cases, offline and online, involve stalking by former intimate partners, although there are cases of stranger stalking in each. Stalking victims, offline and online, are most often women, whereas stalkers are most often men. Most stalkers are motivated by a desire to control the victim.

The DOJ also notes major differences. Cyberstalking is actually easier for the stalker than offline stalking; the online environment lowers barriers to harassment and threats. Offline stalking, for example, requires the perpetrator to be in the same area as the victim, whereas cyberstalkers can be anywhere. In addition, the online environment makes it easy for a cyberstalker to "encourage third parties to harass or threaten a victim." For example, a stalker can impersonate a victim online and post inflammatory messages, causing others to send threatening messages back to the victim.

Cyberstalking is increasingly used by perpetrators of intimate partner violence. According to Cynthia Southworth et al. in "Intimate Partner Violence, Technology, and Stalking" (*Violence against Women*, vol. 13, no. 8, August 2007), the same technologies that have provided victims of intimate partner violence access to information, resources, and social support have also led to "disinhibited communication, online harassment, and stalking technology." The researchers note that because of technology, stalkers are finding it even easier to monitor the whereabouts and activities of their victims. Among other uses of technology, stalkers can tap telephone lines and intercept cell phone and cordless phone calls, implement caller ID services to locate victims, use global positioning system devices to track victims, install spyware and keystroke logging hardware to track victims' computer use, and employ hidden wireless cameras to spy on victims.

CYBERSTALKING CASES IN THE NEWS. The attorney general's report recounts many serious instances of cyberstalking that attracted attention in the media and among policy makers. The first successful prosecution under California's cyberstalking law was in Los Angeles, where a 50-year-old man stalked a 28-year-old woman who had refused his advances. He posted her name, address, and telephone number online along with messages saying that she wanted to be raped. The Internet posts prompted men to knock on the woman's door, often during the night, in the hopes of fulfilling the fantasy her stalker had posted. In April 1999 the accused pleaded guilty to stalking and solicitation of sexual assault and was sentenced to a six-year prison term.

In July 2002 the CBS News program *48 Hours* investigated a lethal case of cyberstalking that shocked the nation. In 1999 a 20-year-old New Hampshire resident named Amy Boyer was killed by a cyberstalker she had met, but never befriended or dated, years earlier in the eighth grade. Unknown to Boyer, her stalker had apparently obsessed over her for years and had constructed a website that described his stalking of Boyer and his plans to kill her. He used an investigation service to discover where she worked and ambushed her as she left, shooting her and then killing himself. Boyer's death inspired her parents to speak out and champion anticyberstalking laws.

Cyberstalkers sometimes "meet" their victims on social networking sites such as MySpace and Facebook. In one such case reported by Levi Pulkkinen in "Convicted Cyberstalker Back at It, Prosecutors Claim" (SeattlePI.com, August 15, 2010), 23-year-old William Thomas Pritchard met a 17-year-old girl on MySpace. When he asked her to send him nude photos of herself, she refused. Pritchard soon began sending nude photos of himself to her. He also tried contacting her friends to obtain personal information about her and even went to a job fair that she was attending with her high school classmates. Frustrated by her refusals, he threatened to kill her and then carve his name in her chest. Pritchard was arrested in August 2010. Court records indicate that he had already been convicted twice before of cyberstalking. According to Pulkkinen in "Cyberstalker Who Terrorized Teen Sentenced" (SeattlePI.com, March 3, 2011), Prichard was convicted and sentenced to five and a half years in prison.

Because of the global reach of the Internet, cyberstalking is not limited to a nation's physical borders. One notable case of international cyberstalking involved Colin Mak Yew Loong, a Singaporean man accused of harassing several musicians from around the world between 2005 and 2013. One of Mak's victims was aspiring American opera singer Leandra Ramm (1984–), who developed post-traumatic stress disorder as a result of Mak's actions, forcing her to abandon her career. Although Ramm's initial attempts to press charges against Mak proved difficult due to the complexities of international law, she was eventually able to bring the case before a Singapore court. Mak was found guilty on a number of charges, including harassment and sending threatening e-mails, and sentenced to three years in jail. As Katharine Quarmby notes in "How the Law Is Standing Up to Cyberstalking" (Newsweek.com, August 13, 2014), with the verdict Mak became the first person to be convicted in a case of global cyberstalking.

LAW ENFORCEMENT AND CYBERSTALKING. According to Robert D'Ovidio and James Doyle in "A Study on Cyberstalking" (*FBI Law Enforcement Bulletin*, vol. 72, no. 3, March 2003), cyberstalking presents some unique law enforcement challenges. Offenders are often able to use the anonymity of online communication to avoid detection and accountability for their actions. Appropriate interventions and recourse are unclear because often the stalker and his victim have never been in physical proximity to one another. Complicating the situation, the identity of the stalker may be difficult to determine. Furthermore, many law enforcement agencies are unprepared to investigate cyberstalking cases because they lack the expertise and training. The attorney general's report finds that some victims had been advised by law enforcement agents to simply "turn off their computers" or to "come back if the cyberstalkers confront or threaten them offline."

Furthermore, some state and local law enforcement agencies are frustrated in their efforts to track down cyberstalkers by the limits of their statutory authority. For example, the Cable Communications Policy Act of 1984 bars the release of cable subscriber information to law enforcement agencies without advance notice to the subscriber and a court order. Because a growing number of Internet users receive services via cable, the act inadvertently grants those wishing to remain anonymous for purposes of cyberstalking some legal protection from investigation. The attorney general's report calls for modifications to the act to include provisions that help law enforcement agents gain access to the identifying information they need while maintaining privacy safeguards for cable customers. Spitzberg and Hoobler note that "it may be ironic that to combat the risks of cyberstalking, law enforcement may need the very tools of electronic surveillance and intrusion that are currently the source of many citizens' fundamental fears of privacy invasion."

The National Conference of State Legislatures (NCSL) operates the website "State Cyberstalking and

Cyberharassment Laws" (December 5, 2013, http://www.ncsl.org/issues-research/telecom/cyberstalking-and-cyberharassment-laws.aspx), which provides information on state legislation that deals with cyberstalking. The NCSL defines cyberstalking as "the use of the Internet, email or other electronic communications to stalk, and generally refers to a pattern of threatening or malicious behaviors." It also notes that what distinguishes cyberstalking from more benign forms of cyberharassment is that cyberstalking poses a "credible threat of harm." According to the organization, as of December 2013 all 50 states had passed laws prohibiting cyberstalking, cyberharassment, or both.

CHAPTER 9
DOMESTIC VIOLENCE, LAW ENFORCEMENT, AND COURT RESPONSES TO DOMESTIC VIOLENCE

DOMESTIC VIOLENCE AND LAW ENFORCEMENT

Historically, family disturbance calls were not taken seriously by law enforcement, which reflects society's attitude about domestic violence at the time. For example, during the mid-1960s Detroit, Michigan, police dispatchers were instructed to screen out family disturbance calls unless they suspected "excessive" violence. A 1975 police guide, *The Function of the Police in Crisis Intervention and Conflict Management*, taught officers to avoid making an arrest at all costs and to discourage the victim from pressing charges by emphasizing the consequences of testifying in court, the potential of lost income, and other detrimental aspects of prosecution.

Changes in society's tolerance for domestic violence mean that these approaches to domestic violence no longer enjoy official support (although they may still influence the actions of individual officers). By 2008 every state had moved to authorize probable cause arrests (arrest before the completion of the investigation of the alleged violation or crime) without a warrant in domestic violence cases. (A warrant is a written legal document authorizing a police officer to make a search, seizure, or arrest.) Many police departments have adopted pro-arrest or mandatory arrest policies. Pro-arrest strategies include a range of sanctions from issuing a warning, to mandated treatment, to prison time.

The police are often an abuse victim's initial contact with the judicial system, which makes the response by the police particularly important. The manner in which the police handle a domestic violence complaint will likely color the way the victim views the entire judicial system. Not surprisingly, when the police project the blame for intimate partner violence on victims, the victims may be reluctant to report further abuse.

Reporting Domestic Violence to the Police

Domestic violence incidents come to the attention of the police via reports from the victims themselves, from witnesses to the violence, and from people who learn about the victimization after it occurs. As explained in Chapter 1, some states require medical personnel to report suspected or known abuse cases involving adults to law enforcement agencies.

The Bureau of Justice Statistics (BJS) is an agency within the U.S. Department of Justice (DOJ). Since 1972 the BJS has conducted the National Crime Victimization Survey (NCVS), an annual survey that measures the levels of victimization resulting from criminal activity in the United States. It should be noted that only victimizations against people aged 12 years and older are included. The most recent NCVS data are discussed by Jennifer L. Truman and Lynn Langton in *Criminal Victimization, 2013* (September 2014, http://www.bjs.gov/content/pub/pdf/cv13.pdf).

As shown in Table 9.1, at most half (44.2% to 50.3%) of all violent crime victimizations compiled in the 2004, 2012, and 2013 NCVS surveys were reported by the victims to the police. The reporting rates were slightly higher (54.9% to 56.9%) for domestic violence victimizations and for the subset of domestic violence victimizations that were intimate partner victimizations (53.3% to 57%). The latter are victimizations committed by current or former spouses, boyfriends, or girlfriends. For rape or sexual assault, the overall reporting rate reached 34.8% in 2013, up from 29.3% in 2004 and 28.2% in 2012. In 2013 the reporting rate for domestic cases involving serious violence (rape, sexual assault, robbery, or aggravated assault) was nearly two-thirds (65.3%) and for serious intimate partner violence, the reporting rate was 60.4%.

Table 9.2 compares violent victimizations reported and not reported to police in terms of victimization rates

TABLE 9.1

Crime victimizations reported to the police, by crime type, 2004, 2012, and 2013

Type of crime	2004	2012	2013
Violent crime[a]	**50.3%**	**44.2%**	**45.6%**
Rape/sexual assault	29.3	28.2	34.8
Robbery	60.6	55.9	68.0‡
Assault	50.1	43.7	43.4
Aggravated assault	69.8	62.4	64.3
Simple assault	43.9	39.7	38.5
Domestic violence[b]	56.6	54.9	56.9
Intimate partner violence[c]	56.4	53.3	57.0
Stranger violence	54.4	48.9	49.6
Violent crime involving injury	60.8	58.6	55.5
Serious violent crime[d]	**62.8%**	**54.4%**	**61.0%**
Serious domestic violence[b]	69.7	60.9	65.3
Serious intimate partner violence[c]	69.1	55.4	60.4
Serious stranger violence	67.9	54.8	61.9
Serious violent crime involving weapons	68.5	56.3	65.7
Serious violent crime involving injury	69.0	56.1	66.2
Property crime[e]	**39.2%**	**33.5%**	**36.1%†**
Household burglary	53.3	54.8	57.3
Motor vehicle theft	85.6	78.6	75.5
Theft	32.4	26.4	28.6†

†Significant change from 2012 to 2013 at the 95% confidence level.
‡Significant change from 2012 to 2013 at the 90% confidence level.
[a]Excludes homicide because the NCVS is based on interviews with victims and therefore cannot measure murder.
[b]Includes victimization committed by intimate partners and family members.
[c]Includes victimization committed by current or former spouses, boyfriends, or girlfriends.
[d]Includes rape or sexual assault, robbery, and aggravated assault.
[e]Includes household burglary, motor vehicle theft, and theft.

SOURCE: Jennifer L. Truman and Lynn Langton, "Table 6. Percent of Victimizations Reported to Police, by Type of Crime, 2004, 2012, and 2013," in *Criminal Victimization, 2013*, U.S. Department of Justice, Office of Justice Programs, Bureau of Justice Statistics, September 2014, http://www.bjs.gov/content/pub/pdf/cv13.pdf (accessed November 14, 2014)

(number of violent victimizations per 1,000 people aged 12 years and older) for 2004, 2012, and 2013. In 2013 the victimization rate for domestic violence incidents reported to the police was 2.4 victimizations per 1,000 people aged 12 years and older; the rate for serious domestic violence incidents was 1.1 victimizations per 1,000 people aged 12 years and older. For domestic violence incidents not reported to the police in 2013, the victimization rate was 1.7 victimizations per 1,000 people aged 12 years and older; the rate for serious domestic violence incidents that were not reported was 0.6 per 1,000 people aged 12 years and older.

Table 9.3 presents the reporting data between 2008 and 2012 broken down by victim-offender relationship. The two offender categories involved in domestic violence cases are intimates and other relatives. Overall, NCVS data indicate that nearly 1.3 million domestic violence victimizations took place in 2012. The 55% that were reported to the police included 431,959 intimate partner victimizations and 259,793 victimizations by other relatives. The 45% that were not reported to the police included 350,758 intimate partner victimizations

and 186,183 victimizations by other relatives. It should be noted that for another 17,253 victimizations by intimate partners, the survey participants did not know if the victimizations were or were not reported to the police. However, this number made up less than 1.4% of the total domestic violence victimizations during 2012.

OUTCOME OF POLICE INTERVENTION

During the early 1970s it was legal for the police to make probable cause arrests without a warrant for felonies, but only 14 states permitted it for misdemeanors. Because the crime of simple assault (assault without a weapon that results in minor injuries) and battery is a misdemeanor in most states, family violence victims were forced to initiate their own criminal charges against a batterer. By 2008, however, all states authorized warrantless probable cause misdemeanor arrests in domestic violence cases. Regardless, more than half of the states have added qualifiers, such as visible signs of injury or a report of the violence within eight hours of the incident. Most state codes authorizing warrantless arrests require police to inform victims of their rights, which include the acquisition of protection orders and referral to emergency and shelter facilities and transportation.

Mandatory Arrests

Arrest gained popularity as a tactic after the publication of the first in a series of six studies funded by the National Institute of Justice known as the Spouse Assault Replication Program. All the studies were designed to explain how arrest in domestic violence cases could serve as a deterrent to future violence. Lawrence W. Sherman and Richard A. Berk, the authors of the influential first study in the series, "The Specific Deterrent Effects of Arrest for Domestic Assault" (*American Sociological Review*, vol. 49, April 1984), found that "the arrest intervention certainly did not make things worse and may well have made things better."

Although Sherman and Berk cautioned about generalizing the results of a small study dealing with a single police department in which few police officers properly followed the test procedure, they concluded that in instances of domestic violence an arrest is advisable except in cases where it would be clearly counterproductive. At the same time, Sherman and Berk recommended allowing the police a certain amount of flexibility when making decisions about individual situations, on the premise that police officers must be permitted to rely on professional judgment based on experience.

Sherman and Berk's study had a tremendous impact on police practices, even though J. David Hirschel, Ira W. Hutchison III, and Charles W. Dean explain in "The Failure of Arrest to Deter Spouse Abuse" (*Journal of Research in Crime and Delinquency*, vol. 29, no. 1,

TABLE 9.2

Rate of crime victimizations reported and not reported to the police, by crime type, 2004, 2012, and 2013

Type of crime	Reported to police			Not reported to police		
	2004	2012	2013	2004	2012	2013
Violent crime[a]	**14.0**	**11.5**	**10.6**	**13.6**	**14.0**	**12.2**
Rape/sexual assault	0.3	0.4	0.4	0.7	0.9	0.7
Robbery	1.5	1.6	1.7	1.0	1.2	0.8‡
Assault	12.1	9.6	8.5	11.8	11.9	10.7
Aggravated assault	4.1	2.4	2.4	1.8	1.3	1.3
Simple assault	8.0	7.2	6.1	10.1	10.6	9.5
Domestic violence[b]	3.4	2.6	2.4	2.5	2.0	1.7
Intimate partner violence[c]	2.4	1.6	1.6	1.8	1.3	1.2
Stranger violence	6.0	5.1	3.9‡	4.9	5.0	3.8‡
Violent crime involving injury	5.0	3.5	3.4	3.1	2.4	2.6
Serious violent crime[d]	**6.0**	**4.3**	**4.5**	**3.5**	**3.5**	**2.8**
Serious domestic violence[b]	1.3	1.0	1.1	0.6	0.6	0.6
Serious intimate partner violence[c]	1.0	0.6	0.8	0.4	0.4	0.5
Serious stranger violence	2.7	2.1	1.7	1.3	1.7	1.0†
Serious violent crime involving weapons	4.7	3.0	2.9	2.1	2.3	1.5†
Serious violent crime involving injury	2.4	1.6	1.9	1.1	1.2	0.9
Property crime	**65.7**	**52.2**	**47.4†**	**100.0**	**101.9**	**83.1†**
Burglary	16.6	16.4	14.8	14.1	13.2	10.9†
Motor vehicle theft	7.9	4.0	3.9	1.3	1.1	1.2
Theft	41.2	31.9	28.7†	84.6	87.7	71.0†

Note: Victimization rates are per 1,000 persons age 12 or older for violent crime and per 1,000 households for property crime.
†Significant change from 2012 to 2013 at the 95% confidence level.
‡Significant change from 2012 to 2013 at the 90% confidence level.
[a]Excludes homicide because the NCVS is based on interviews and therefore cannot measure murder.
[b]Includes victimization committed by intimate partners and family members.
[c]Includes victimization committed by current or former spouses, boyfriends, or girlfriends.
[d]Includes rape or sexual assault, robbery, and aggravated assault.

SOURCE: Jennifer L. Truman and Lynn Langton, "Table 7. Rates of Victimizations Reported and Not Reported to Police, by Type of Crime, 2004, 2012, and 2013," in *Criminal Victimization, 2013*, U.S. Department of Justice, Office of Justice Programs, Bureau of Justice Statistics, September 2014, http://www.bjs.gov/content/pub/pdf/cv13.pdf (accessed November 14, 2014)

February 1992) that the five other Spouse Assault Replication Program studies found that arrest had little or no effect on domestic violence recurrence. Some police departments have adopted a presumptive arrest policy. This policy means that an arrest should be made unless clear and compelling reasons exist not to arrest. Presumptive arrest provisions forbid officers from basing the decision to arrest on the victim's preference or on a perception of the victim's willingness to testify or participate in the proceedings. Proponents point out that arresting an offender gives the victim a respite from fear and an opportunity to look for help. Furthermore, they claim it prevents bias in arrests.

By the 1990s as many as one out of three police departments had adopted a mandatory arrest policy in domestic abuse cases. According to David Eitle of Florida International University in "The Influence of Mandatory Arrest Policies, Police Organizational Characteristics, and Situational Variables on the Probability of Arrest in Domestic Violence Cases" (*Crime and Delinquency*, vol. 51, no. 4, October 2005), mandatory police arrest policies do result in more arrests when the police are called to the scene of a domestic assault. In addition, he notes that these policies reduce somewhat the overrepresentation of African Americans among those being

arrested. However, do these arrests reduce violence against women?

Some studies suggest that mandatory arrest policies have positive effects. For example, Jacquelyn C. Campbell et al. explain in "Risk Factors for Femicide in Abusive Relationships: Results from a Multisite Case Control Study" (*American Journal of Public Health*, vol. 93, no. 7, July 2003) that previous arrest for battering actually decreased women's risk of being subsequently killed by the batterer. According to Christopher D. Maxwell, Joel H. Garner, and Jeffrey A. Fagan in "The Effects of Arrest on Intimate Partner Violence: New Evidence from the Spouse Assault Replication Program" (July 2001, http://www.ncjrs.gov/pdffiles1/nij/188199.pdf), the arrest of batterers is consistently related to subsequent reduced aggression against their intimate partner.

However, Debra Houry, Sudha Reddy, and Constance Parramore of Emory University suggest in "Characteristics of Victims Coarrested for Intimate Partner Violence" (*Journal of Interpersonal Violence*, vol. 21, no. 11, November 2006) that some battered women's advocates do not support mandatory arrest. They fear that poor and minority families are treated more harshly than middle-class families and that if the police arrive and

TABLE 9.3

Violent victimizations, by reporting to the police and victim-offender relationship, 2008–12

Crime type	2008	2009	2010	2011	2012
Violent victimization	**6,393,471**	**5,669,237**	**4,935,983**	**5,812,523**	**6,842,593**
Intimates	**1,103,392**	**1,039,650**	**773,434**	**850,772**	**810,794**
Yes, reported to the police	628,132	593,148	511,195	508,254	431,959
No, did not report to the police	471,141	443,171	262,239	337,389	350,758
Do not know	4,119!	3,331!	—	—	17,243!
Other relatives	**454,603**	**343,020**	**356,129**	**504,135**	**448,598**
Yes, reported to the police	293,810	159,243	240,023	297,260	259,793
No, did not report to the police	160,793	174,142	116,106	200,157	186,183
Do not know	—	9,635!	—	6,718!	—
Well-known/casual acquaintances	**1,781,331**	**1,756,014**	**1,573,294**	**1,779,618**	**2,263,252**
Yes, reported to the police	705,808	611,294	547,503	791,548	808,448
No, did not report to the police	1,048,537	1,136,866	1,006,180	933,866	1,428,133
Do not know	26,986!	7,854!	17,554!	43,066!	26,671!
Stranger	**2,154,770**	**2,165,849**	**1,812,303**	**2,146,307**	**2,710,114**
Yes, reported to the police	970,883	913,704	992,012	1,029,016	1,324,977
No, did not report to the police	1,156,701	1,229,605	805,335	1,090,328	1,302,507
Do not know	27,186!	22,540!	14,956!	26,962!	46,780
Do not know relationship	**486,084**	**217,989**	**288,667**	**240,956**	**371,910**
Yes, reported to the police	218,066	123,491	157,914	134,274	122,224
No, did not report to the police	260,590	90,766	125,271	104,815	246,318
Do not know	3,296!	—	5,482!	—	3,368!
Do not know number of offenders	**413,292**	**139,707**	**132,156**	**290,736**	**228,660**
Yes, reported to the police	149,025	96,842	73,978!	87,181	71,601
No, did not report to the police	259,638	36,446!	58,178	126,981	150,711
Do not know	4,629!	—	—	57,431!	2,154!

Notes: Detail may not sum to total due to rounding and/or missing data.
—Estimate is equal to 0 sample cases.
!Interpret data with caution, based on 10 or fewer sample cases or the coefficient of variation is greater than 50%.

SOURCE: Adapted from "Number of Violent Victimizations by Victim-Offender Relationship and Reporting to the Police, 2008–2012," in *NCVS Victimization Analysis Tool (NVAT)*, U.S. Department of Justice, Office of Justice Programs, Bureau of Justice Statistics, July 17, 2014, http://www.bjs.gov/index.cfm?ty=nvat (accessed July 17, 2014)

both spouses are bloodied by the fight, both will be arrested, forcing the children into foster care. In fact, Mary A. Finn and Pamela Bettis of Georgia State University state in "Punitive Action or Gentle Persuasion: Exploring Police Officers' Justifications for Using Dual Arrest in Domestic Violence Cases" (*Violence against Women*, vol. 12, no. 3, March 2006) that "mandatory and preferred arrest policies may be resulting in a backlash for victims who are arrested along with their batterers.... Officers justified arrest of both parties, citing that such was required by law and the desire to force both parties to obtain counseling for their relationship."

Victoria Frye, Mary Haviland, and Valli Rajah examine some of the unintended consequences of the mandatory arrest law in New York City and report their findings in "Dual Arrest and Other Unintended Consequences of Mandatory Arrest in New York City: A Brief Report" (*Journal of Family Violence*, vol. 22, no. 6, August 2007). Frye, Haviland, and Rajah find that no arrest remained a significant problem, despite the mandatory arrest legislation, and that the police disproportionately failed to arrest abusers of poor women. At the same time, arrest of the victims (both dual arrests and retaliatory arrests) accounted for 34% of police-related calls to the helpline. In spite of these findings, Frye, Haviland, and Rajah conclude that mandatory arrest laws do have a positive impact on domestic violence. Regardless, they call for further police training and better supervision to reduce the problems of no arrest and victim arrest that result from mandatory arrest laws. Amy M. Zelcer outlines possible alternatives to mandatory arrest laws in "Battling Domestic Violence: Replacing Mandatory Arrest Laws with a Trifecta of Preferential Arrest, Officer Education, and Batterer Treatment Programs" (*American Criminal Law Review*, vol. 51, no. 2, Spring 2014). Zelcer recommends an integrated approach to police intervention in domestic violence situations, one that grants victims some degree of decision-making power in determining whether an arrest should be made, combined with improved officer training and expanded therapeutic opportunities for abusers.

EMPOWERING VICTIMS. Indeed, innovative programs that team social services with the police have shown some promise in empowering women to report violence to the police. In "The Efficacy of a Police-Advocacy Intervention for Victims of Domestic Violence: 12 Month

Follow-up Data" (*Violence against Women*, vol. 16, no. 4, April 2010), Carla Smith Stover et al. of Yale University evaluate a New Haven, Connecticut, program, Domestic Violence Home Visit Intervention, that provides home visits immediately after a domestic violence incident and for several follow-up visits over the subsequent year. The visits are conducted by a partnership of a police officer who has received specialized training in domestic violence and its effects on children and by a victim advocate who is trained in basic domestic violence issues, crisis intervention, legal issues, and social service responses. Stover et al. find that although the level of domestic violence for both the visited women and the control group were similar, women involved in the program were more likely than women in the control group to call the police to report domestic disputes in the year following the initial incident. Women who received the home visits were also much more likely to use court-based services and mental health services for their children.

PROTECTION ORDERS

What Are They?

An abuse victim in any state may go to court to obtain a protection order. Also referred to as "restraining orders" or "injunctions," civil orders of protection are legally binding court orders that prohibit an individual who has committed an act of domestic violence from further abusing the victim. Although the terms are often used interchangeably, restraining orders usually refer to short-term or temporary sanctions, whereas protection orders have longer duration and may be permanent. These orders generally prohibit harassment, contact, communication, and physical proximity to the victim. Protection orders are common and readily obtained, but they are not always effective.

Petitioners may file for protection orders in circumstances other than violent physical abuse, including sexual assault, marital rape, harassment, emotional abuse, and stalking. Protection orders are valid for varying lengths of time depending on the state. Protection orders give victims an option other than filing a criminal complaint. Issued quickly, usually within 24 hours, they provide safety for the victim by barring or evicting the abuser from the household. Statutes in most states make violating a protection order a matter of criminal contempt, a misdemeanor, or even a felony. However, this judicial protection has little meaning if the police do not maintain records and follow through with arrest should the abuser violate the order.

The "full faith and credit" provision of the Violence against Women Act of 1994 was passed to establish nationwide enforcement of protection orders in courts throughout the country. States, territories, and tribal lands were ordered to honor protection orders issued in other jurisdictions, although the act did not mandate how these orders were to be enforced. According to Christina DeJong and Amanda Burgess-Proctor of Michigan State University in "A Summary of Personal Protection Order Statutes in the United States" (*Violence against Women*, vol. 12, no. 1, January 2006), most states have amended their domestic violence codes or statutes to reflect this new requirement, although the states vary widely on how easy it is for battered women to get their protection orders enforced. Courts and law enforcement agencies in most states have access to electronic registries of protection orders, both to verify the existence of an order and to assess whether violations have occurred.

PROTECTION ORDERS FOR BATTERED MEN. In "Do Judicial Responses to Restraining Order Requests Discriminate against Male Victims of Domestic Violence?" (*Journal of Family Violence*, vol. 24, no. 8, November 2009), Henry J. Muller, Sarah L. Desmarais, and John M. Hamel examine a random sample of petitions for protection orders against intimate partners in California to determine whether battered men had the same access to protection orders as did battered women. The researchers indicate that judges were about 13 times more likely to grant a request for a protection order to a female victim against her male intimate partner than to a male victim against his female partner, especially in cases involving low-level violence.

Effects of Protection Orders

In "Protection Orders and Intimate Partner Violence: An 18-Month Study of 150 Black, Hispanic, and White Women" (*American Journal of Public Health*, vol. 94, no. 4, April 2004), Judith McFarlane et al. report on their study of the "types and frequencies of intimate partner violence" before and after victims had applied for a two-year protection order against an intimate partner. The researchers interviewed 150 women over an 18-month period to determine whether protection orders diminished violence. Although 44% of the women who had been granted a protection order reported at least one violation of the order, the researchers find significant reductions in physical assaults, stalking, and threats of assault over time among all women who applied for a protection order, even if they had not been granted the order. McFarlane et al. hypothesize that it was not the protection order itself that led to the diminished violence but the contact with the criminal justice system that exposed the battering to public view.

Other researchers have linked a number of positive psychological effects to the use of protection orders in domestic violence cases. Caroline Vaile Wright and Dawn M. Johnson report in "Encouraging Legal Help Seeking for Victims of Intimate Partner Violence: The

Therapeutic Effects of the Civil Protection Order" (*Journal of Traumatic Stress*, vol. 25, no. 6, December 2012) that protection orders have been shown to alleviate symptoms of post-traumatic stress disorder and other emotional disorders in residents of shelters for battered women. Jane K. Stoever also notes the psychological benefits of protection orders in "Enjoining Abuse: The Case for Indefinite Domestic Violence Protection Orders" (*Vanderbilt Law Review*, vol. 67, no. 4, May 2014). Citing the prevalence of longer court orders in business disputes and other legal areas involving property, Stoever argues that extending standard protection orders for domestic violence cases would enable victims to achieve greater physical and emotional distance from their abusers.

LANDMARK LEGAL DECISIONS

Before the 1962 landmark case *Self v. Self* (58 Cal. 2d 683), when the California Supreme Court ruled that "one spouse may maintain an action against the other for battering," women had no legal recourse against abusive partners. The judicial system had tended to view wife abuse as a matter to be resolved within the family. Maintaining that "a man's home is his castle," the federal government traditionally had been reluctant to violate the sanctity of the home. Furthermore, many legal authorities persisted in "blaming the victim," maintaining that the wife was, to some degree, responsible for her own beating by somehow inciting her husband to lose his temper. Yet even after *Self v. Self*, turning to the judicial system for help was still unlikely to bring assistance to or result in justice for victims of spousal abuse. Jurisdictions throughout the United States continued to ignore the complaints of battered women until the late 1970s.

This section summarizes the outcomes of several landmark cases that not only helped define judicial responsibility but also shaped the policies and practices aimed at protecting the victims of domestic violence.

Baker v. City of New York

Sandra Baker was estranged from her husband. In July 1955 the local domestic relations court issued a protective order directing her husband, who had a history of serious mental illness, "not to strike, molest, threaten, or annoy" his wife. Baker called the police the following October when her husband created a disturbance at the family home. When a police officer arrived, she showed him the court order. The officer told her it was "no good" and "only a piece of paper" and refused to take any action.

Baker went to the domestic relations court and told her story to a probation officer. While making a phone call, she saw her husband in the corridor. She went to the probation officer and told him her husband was in the

corridor. She asked if she could wait in his office because she was "afraid to stand in the room with him." The probation officer told her to go to the waiting room. Minutes later, her husband shot and wounded her.

Baker sued the city of New York, claiming that the city owed her more protection than she was given. The New York State Supreme Court Appellate Division, in *Baker v. City of New York* (25 A.D.2d 770 [1966]), agreed that the city of New York failed to fulfill its obligation. The court found that she was "a person recognized by the order of protection as one to whom a special duty was owed ... and peace officers had a duty to supply protection to her." Neither the police officer nor the probation officer had fulfilled this duty, and both were found guilty of negligence. Because the officers were representatives of the city of New York, Baker had the right to sue the city.

Equal Protection

Another option women have used in response to unchecked violence and abuse is to sue the police for failing to intervene, alleging that their constitutional rights to liberty and equal protection under the law were violated by the lack of police response. The equal protection clause of the 14th Amendment provides that no state shall "deny to any person within its jurisdiction the equal protection of the laws." This clause prohibits states from arbitrarily classifying individuals by group membership. If a woman can prove that a police department has a gender-based policy of refusing to arrest men who abuse their wives, she can claim that the policy is based on gender stereotypes and therefore violates the equal protection clause.

THURMAN V. CITY OF TORRINGTON. Between October 1982 and June 1983 Tracey Thurman repeatedly called the Torrington, Connecticut, police to report that her estranged husband was threatening both her life and her child's life. The police ignored her requests for help no matter how often she called or how serious the situation became. At one point her husband attacked her in view of the police and was arrested. Thurman obtained protection and restraining orders against him after this incident. However, when her husband later came to her home and threatened her again, in violation of his probation and the court orders, police refused to intervene.

On June 10, 1983, Thurman's husband came to her home. She called the police. He then stabbed her repeatedly in the chest, neck, and throat. A police officer arrived 25 minutes later but did not arrest her husband, despite the attack. Three more police officers arrived. The husband went into the house and brought out their child and threw him down on his bleeding mother. The officers still did not arrest him. Although Thurman was on the stretcher waiting to be placed in the ambulance, her husband came at her again. Only at that point did the police take him into custody. Thurman later sued the city of Torrington, claiming she was denied equal protection under the law.

In *Thurman v. City of Torrington* (595 F.Supp. 1521 [D. Conn. 1984]), the U.S. District Court for Downstate Connecticut agreed, stating:

> City officials and police officers are under an affirmative duty to preserve law and order, and to protect the personal safety of persons in the community.... This duty applies equally to women whose personal safety is threatened by individuals with whom they have or have had a domestic relationship as well as to all other persons whose personal safety is threatened.... A police officer may not ... "automatically decline to make an arrest simply because the assaulter and his victim are married to each other." ... Such inaction on the part of the officer is a denial of the equal protection of the laws.

There could be no question, the court concluded, that the city of Torrington, through its police department, had "condoned a pattern or practice of affording inadequate protection, or no protection at all, to women who have complained of having been abused by their husbands or others with whom they have had close relations." Therefore, the police had failed in their duty to protect Thurman and deserved to be sued.

In "Maimed Wife Strikes Blow for Justice" (ChicagoTribune.com, May 18, 1986), Dick Polman notes that Thurman was left partially paralyzed by the attack and received a $1.9 million settlement from the local police department.

Due Process

The due process clause of the 14th Amendment provides that no state can "deprive any person of life, liberty, or property, without due process of law; nor deny to any person within its jurisdiction the equal protection of the laws." It does not, however, obligate the state to protect citizens from harm or provide services that would protect them. Rather, a state may create special conditions in which that state has constitutional obligations to particular citizens because of a special relationship between the state and the individual. Abused women have used this argument to claim that being under a protection order puts them in a special relationship.

MACIAS V. HIDE. During the 18 months before Maria Teresa Macias's estranged husband, Avelino Macias, murdered her at her place of work in April 1996, Maria had filed 22 complaints with the Sonoma County Sheriff's Department in California. In the months before her death, Avelino sexually abused Maria, broke into her home, and terrorized and stalked her. Maria's family filed a wrongful death lawsuit against the Sonoma County Sheriff's Department, accusing the department of failing to provide Maria equal protection under the law and of discriminating against her as a Hispanic and a woman.

The U.S. District Court for the Northern District of California dismissed the case because Judge D. Lowell Jensen (1928–) said there was no connection between Maria's murder and how the sheriff's department had responded to her complaints. In *Macias v. Hide* (No. 99-15662 [2000]), the U.S. Court of Appeals for the Ninth Circuit reversed the earlier decision and ruled that the lawsuit could proceed with the discovery phase and pretrial motions. Judge Arthur L. Alarcón (1925–) of the U.S. Court of Appeals for the Ninth Circuit conveyed the unanimous opinion of the court when he wrote, "It is well established that 'there is no constitutional right to be protected by the state against being murdered by criminals or madmen.' There is a constitutional right, however, to have police services administered in a nondiscriminatory manner—a right that is violated when a state actor denies such protection to disfavored persons."

After this decision the case proceeded to trial. In June 2002 Sonoma County agreed to pay $1 million to Maria's family to settle the case. The settlement agreement did not include an admission of any wrongdoing by the county. Nevertheless, domestic violence activists lauded the result.

TOWN OF CASTLE ROCK, COLORADO V. GONZALES. The U.S. Supreme Court reaffirmed in 2005 that governments are not required to offer citizens protection from violent abusers. According to the case *Town of Castle Rock, Colorado v. Gonzales* (No. 04-278 [2005]), Jessica Gonzales's three children were taken from her home by her estranged husband in violation of a protection order. When she alerted the police and repeatedly asked them for assistance, they made no effort to find the children or to enforce the state's mandatory arrest law. The children were killed later that night. Gonzales sued the town, arguing that by failing to respond to her calls the police had violated her right to due process of law, and the case eventually reached the U.S. Supreme Court. In its review, the court found in June 2005 that "Colorado law has not created a personal entitlement to enforcement of restraining orders" and that the state's law did not really require arrest in all cases, but actually left considerable discretion in the hands of the police. So even though the Castle Rock police made a tragically incorrect decision in this case, they did not do so in violation of Gonzales's due process rights.

KEY DOMESTIC VIOLENCE LEGISLATION

Although appealing to the judicial system for help will not solve all the problems an abused woman faces, the reception a battered woman can expect from the system (police, prosecutors, and courts) improved markedly during the late 20th century. The Violence against

Women Act (VAWA), which was signed into law by President Bill Clinton (1946–) in September 1994, did much to help. The act simultaneously strengthened prevention and prosecution of violent crimes against women and provided law enforcement officials with the tools they needed to prosecute batterers. Although the system is imperfect, legal authorities became far more likely to view abuse complaints as legitimate and serious than they had in the past.

The Violence against Women Act

As noted in Chapter 1, the VAWA was originally passed in 1994 and was amended and reauthorized in 2000, 2005, and 2013.

CIVIL RIGHTS ISSUES. The original VAWA included provisions declaring that violent crimes against women motivated by gender violate victims' federal civil rights, giving victims access to federal courts for redress. In 2000 the civil rights section of the act was tested in the U.S. Supreme Court. Christy Brzonkala, an 18-year-old freshman at Virginia Polytechnic Institute and State University, was violently attacked and raped by two men, Antonio Morrison and James Crawford, in September 1994. Brzonkala did not immediately report the rape, and no physical evidence of the rape was preserved. Two months later she filed a complaint with the school; after learning that the college took limited action against the two men, she withdrew from the school and sued her assailants for damages in federal court.

Brzonkala's case reached the Supreme Court in 2000. Briefs in favor of giving victims of gender-motivated violence access to federal courts were filed by dozens of groups (such as the American Medical Women's Association, the National Association of Human Rights Workers, the National Coalition against Domestic Violence, and the National Women's Health Network) as well as by law scholars and human rights experts. However, in May 2000 the Supreme Court ruled 5–4 in *United States v. Morrison et al.* (529 U.S. 598) that Congress could not enact a law giving victims of gender-motivated violence access to federal civil rights remedies. The majority opinion emphasized that "the Constitution requires a distinction between what is truly national and what is truly local," and it ruled that the violent assault of Brzonkala was local.

In October 2000 Congress responded to the Supreme Court decision by passing new legislation, the Victims of Trafficking and Violence Protection Act. The new legislation included the titles Strengthening Law Enforcement to Reduce Violence against Women, Strengthening Services to Victims of Violence, Limiting the Effects of Violence on Children, and Strengthening Education and Training to Combat Violence against Women. The act allocated $3.3 billion over five years to fund support services for victims of violence and for educational outreach programs on dating violence, rape, and stalking via the Internet. The act also funded new programs for transitional housing and expanded protections for immigrant women. The new act did not mention women's civil rights.

ISSUES AFFECTING IMMIGRANT WOMEN. In "The Facts on Immigrant Women and Domestic Violence" (2014, https://www.futureswithoutviolence.org/userfiles/file/Children_and_Families/Immigrant.pdf), Futures without Violence explains that abuse of immigrant women is a problem in the United States. Immigrant women may be at increased risk for various reasons, including a cultural background that teaches them to defer to their husband. Many foreign-born women cannot speak English and do not know their rights in the United States. Others have no resources or support systems to turn to for help. Some of the distinctive ways that battered immigrant women are abused include threats of being reported to the U.S. Citizenship and Immigration Services, being deported, being reported for working "under the table," or withdrawing their petition to legalize their immigration status.

U.S. immigration laws have unintentionally contributed to the problem of abuse among immigrant women. The Immigration Marriage Fraud Amendment Act was passed in 1986 in an attempt to prevent immigrants from illegally obtaining resident status through a sham marriage to a U.S. citizen. The amendment requires that spouses, usually husbands, petition for conditional resident status for an undocumented mate. Conditional status lasts a minimum of two years, during which time the couple must remain married. If the marriage dissolves, the immigrant loses conditional status and may be deported. As a result, some wives can become prisoners of an abusive husband for as long as the husband controls their conditional resident status. Even though the law was amended by the Immigration Act of 1990 to permit a waiver of conditional status if the immigrant could prove battery or extreme cruelty, the initial filing for conditional status was still in the hands of the husband.

Reauthorized in 2005, the VAWA provides a way for immigrant women to petition for residency status for themselves and for their children without their husband's knowledge. In addition, the act provides a way for canceling deportation proceedings against battered immigrant women by waiving deportation and allowing them the opportunity to become lawful permanent residents of the United States. These processes are described by William A. Kandel of the Congressional Research Service in *Immigration Provisions of the Violence against Women Act (VAWA)* (May 15, 2012, http://www.fas.org/sgp/crs/misc/R42477.pdf). Kandel notes, "Noncitizen victims of domestic violence who seek to permanently reside in the United States face a precarious situation because their legal immigration status often depends upon remaining married. In addition, research on domestic violence indicates that foreign nationals married to U.S. citizens or lawful permanent residents (LPR) possess factors that increase their risk of spousal abuse compared to U.S. citizens." As Kandel notes, 98,192 VAWA petitions on behalf of immigrant women were processed between 1997 and 2011, and three-fourths of them were approved. These protections for immigrant women who are victims of domestic violence were subsequently extended with the passage of the Violence against Women Reauthorization Act of 2013.

During the first decade of the 21st century new policies and programs for immigrant victims emerged throughout the country, especially in cities with large immigrant populations. To improve the communication between immigrants and the criminal justice system, authorities have made special efforts to reach immigrant victims by hiring multicultural criminal justice staffs and providing informational materials in a variety of languages. Police representatives also attend meetings of immigrant groups, and members of the immigrant community are encouraged to serve as representatives on citizen police committees.

The most effective programs that assist immigrant women acknowledge the multiple pressures these women face during their efforts to become oriented and assimilated into American culture and society. Along with cultural shock and language barriers, many immigrant women confront racism, class prejudice, and sexism. Fear of authority and the absence of social networks and support services compound the problem. Finally, recognizing that many women are brought to the United States in circumstances that increase the likelihood of victimization (such as mail-order brides, child care workers, or prostitutes) is an important step in stemming the crisis and addressing the crime of domestic violence. According to Marianne Sullivan et al. in "Participatory Action Research in Practice: A Case Study in Addressing Domestic Violence in Nine Cultural Communities" (*Journal of Interpersonal Violence*, vol. 20, no. 8, August 2005), including battered immigrant women in the development of experimental programs that address battering in their communities is crucial to guarantee the success of those programs.

Domestic Violence Gun Ban

Federal law includes batterers convicted of domestic violence crimes and those with domestic violence protection orders filed against them among the people who are prohibited from owning or carrying guns. Since 1994, all federally licensed gun dealers must run background checks on gun purchasers. The Federal Bureau of Investigation breaks down in "National Instant Criminal Background Check System (NICS) Operations 2013" (January 2014, http://www.fbi.gov/about-us/cjis/nics/reports/2013-operations-report) the major reasons reported for denying gun purchases between November 30, 1998, and December 31, 2013. Of the 1,075,781 total denials, 106,735 (9.9% of the total) were denied for "misdemeanor crime of domestic violence conviction." Another 45,220 denials (4.2% of the total) were denied for "protection/restraining order for domestic violence."

Loopholes in state and federal laws allow batterers to purchase guns despite the federal ban. In many states private gun owners can sell their firearms without background checks. In addition, many states keep incomplete records of domestic violence offenders and orders of protection. Still other evidence suggests that some gun dealers knowingly allow people who are not legally eligible to purchase firearms to buy them through a third party. However, Elizabeth Richardson Vigdor and James A. Mercy report in "Do Laws Restricting Access to Firearms by Domestic Violence Offenders Prevent Intimate Partner Homicide?" (*Evaluation Review*, vol. 30, no. 3, June 2006) that the rates for female intimate partner homicide decline by 7% after a state passes a law restricting access to firearms by individuals subjected to a restraining order, although they see no decline in the rates of homicides that result from restricting access to firearms by individuals convicted of a misdemeanor.

DIFFICULTIES IN THE COURT SYSTEM

An appeal to the U.S. judicial system should be an effective method of obtaining justice. For domestic violence victims, however, this has not always been the case. In the past, ignorance, social prejudices, and uneven attention from the criminal justice system all tended to underestimate the severity and importance of the problem. Over time, society has become significantly less tolerant of domestic violence, and laws in many states criminalize behavior that was previously considered to be acceptable.

Intimate partner abuse cases are often complicated by evidence problems because domestic violence usually takes place behind closed doors. The volatile and unpredictable emotions and motivations influencing the behavior of both the abuser and the victim may not always fit neatly into the organized and systematic framework of legal case presentation. Finally, the varying training mandates to ensure that prosecutors and judges are better informed about the social and personal costs of domestic violence, along with society's changing attitudes toward abuse, influence the responses of the judicial system.

Willingness of Victims to Prosecute

One of the most formidable problems in prosecuting abusers is the victim's reluctance to cooperate. Although many abused women have the courage to initiate legal proceedings against their batterer, some are later reluctant to cooperate with the prosecution because of their emotional attachment to their abuser. Other reasons for their reluctance are fear of retaliation by their abuser, mistrust or lack of information about the criminal justice system, or fear of the demands of court appearances. In addition, a victim might choose not to move forward with the prosecution for economic reasons if, for example, the batterer is her husband and the primary income earner for the family. Religious convictions and family influence can also cause victims to drop the charges.

Factors Associated with Prosecutors' Charging Decisions in Domestic Violence Cases

In "Modeling Prosecutors' Charging Decisions in Domestic Violence Cases" (*Crime and Delinquency*, vol. 52, no. 3, July 2006), John L. Worrall, Jay W. Ross, and Eric S. McCord investigate what factors influenced the decisions of prosecutors to charge a batterer and what factors influenced the decisions of prosecutors to pursue a misdemeanor or a felony charge. They collected data on 245 domestic violence cases that were filed by police officers; examined the impact of characteristics of the victim, the offender, and the offense; and determined how these characteristics influenced the prosecutors' charging decisions.

Worrall, Ross, and McCord find that prosecutors were more likely to charge offenders if they had been arrested or if they had inflicted serious injuries on the victim. The researchers indicate that criminal charges were more likely to be filed against a male batterer than against a female batterer. They also note that if the victim supported prosecution, felony charges were more likely to be filed against the batterer.

Court Case Outcomes

Erica L. Smith and Donald J. Farole Jr. of the BJS analyzed 3,750 intimate partner violence cases in the courts of 16 metropolitan areas to determine their outcomes and reported the results in *Profile of Intimate Partner Violence Cases in Large Urban Counties* (October 2009, http://bjs.ojp.usdoj.gov/content/pub/pdf/pipvcluc.pdf). The researchers find that 84% of these cases involved a female victim and a male defendant. Most defendants were charged with either simple assault (78%) or aggravated assault (12%).

According to Smith and Farole, 56% of all domestic violence cases filed with the courts resulted in conviction. Another 33% of cases were dismissed. Three-quarters (75.3%) of those convicted served a jail sentence, 7.4% went to prison, and 17.3% were put on probation.

Smith and Farole note that certain characteristics of intimate partner violence cases were associated with different adjudication outcomes. For example, 56.4% of

convictions were in cases in which a third party had witnessed the assault. Forty percent of convictions were in cases in which a child was present at the time of the assault; in cases that were dismissed or resulted in acquittal, a child was present only 30.8% of the time. Cases resulting in convictions had a higher incidence of defendant use of alcohol or drugs than did dismissed or acquitted cases (34.7% and 29%, respectively). Certain factors were found to increase the odds of a conviction, including a defendant's formal statement (2 times more likely to result in conviction), the presence of witnesses (1.7 times more likely to result in conviction), a history of abuse (1.7 times more likely to result in conviction), physical evidence had been obtained (1.5 times more likely to result in conviction), and the victim was injured during the incident (1.3 times more likely to result in conviction).

TREATMENT FOR MALE BATTERERS

Rather than serving a prison term, some convicted batterers enter treatment programs. As a requirement of probation, courts may order a batterer into an intervention program. According to Bethany J. Price and Alan Rosenbaum in "Batterer Intervention Programs: A Report from the Field" (*Violence and Victims*, vol. 24, no. 6, 2009), intervention programs have proliferated because the batterers are typically charged with misdemeanors, which do not justify a prison term; victims usually do not want the perpetrator jailed; and these programs allow the perpetrators to continue earning a livelihood. Price and Rosenbaum find in their survey of programs that most of the programs focus on education with a psychotherapeutic component, averaging about 40 hours in length, and often include anger management and alcohol and substance abuse components. Regardless of an intervention program's philosophy or methods, program directors and criminal justice professionals generally monitor offenders' behavior closely. Most batterers enter intervention programs after having been charged by the police with a specific incident of abuse.

The criminal justice system categorizes offenders based on their potential danger, history of substance abuse, psychological problems, and risk of dropout and rearrest. Ideally, interventions focus on the specific type of batterer and the approach that will most effectively produce results, such as linking a substance abuse treatment program with a batterer intervention program. Other program approaches focus on specific sociocultural characteristics, such as poverty, race, ethnicity, and age. Shelly Jackson argues in "Analyzing the Studies" (Shelly Jackson et al., *Batterer Intervention Programs: Where Do We Go from Here?* June 2003, http://www.ncjrs.gov/pdffiles1/nij/195079.pdf) that the effectiveness of batterer intervention programs might improve if the programs were seen "as part of a broader criminal justice and community response to domestic violence that includes arrest, restraining orders, intensive monitoring of batterers, and changes to social norms that may inadvertently tolerate partner violence."

In addition, other researchers have identified specific behavioral issues associated with certain extreme cases of intimate partner violence. As Mark D. Thomas, Larry W. Bennett, and Charles Stoops observe in "The Treatment Needs of Substance Abusing Batterers: A Comparison of Men Who Batter Their Female Partners" (*Journal of Family Violence*, vol. 28, no. 2, February 2013), violent behavior is both more prevalent and more extreme among batterers who struggle with alcohol and drug abuse. Thomas, Bennett, and Stoops also analyze the connection between substance abuse in batterers and a range of other behavioral issues, including trauma and borderline personality disorder. As the authors note, treatment for batterers struggling with substance abuse must also address the question of chemical dependency in order to be effective.

Program Dropout Rates

Batterers leave a program either because of successful completion or because they are asked to leave. The reasons for termination include failure to cooperate, nonpayment of fees, revocation of parole or probation, failure to attend group sessions regularly, or violation of program rules. Successful completion of a program means that the offender has attended the required sessions and accomplished the program's objectives. With court-mandated clients a final report is also made to probation officials. To be successful, batterer intervention programs must have the support of the criminal justice system, which includes coordinated efforts between police, prosecutors, judges, victim advocates, and probation officers.

Dropout rates in battering programs are high, even though courts have ordered most clients to attend. Several studies, such as that by Jennifer Rooney and R. Karl Hanson in "Predicting Attrition from Treatment Programs for Abusive Men" (*Journal of Family Violence*, vol. 16, no. 2, June 2001), record varying dropout rates, some finding that as many as 90% of the men who begin short-term treatment programs do not complete them.

High dropout rates in batterer intervention programs make it difficult to evaluate their success. Evaluations based on men who complete these programs focus on a select group of highly motivated men who likely do not reflect the composition of the group when it began. Because a follow-up is not conducted with program dropouts (often the men most likely to continue their violence) research generally fails to accurately indicate the success or failure of a given treatment program. Andrew Day et al. note in "Programs for Men Who Perpetrate

Domestic Violence: An Examination of the Issues Underlying the Effectiveness of Intervention Programs" (*Journal of Family Violence*, vol. 24, no. 3, April 2009) that the success of batterer intervention programs in reducing violence is generally much lower than in other established intervention programs. The researchers theorize that batterer intervention programs have difficulty linking theories of causation of domestic violence to intervention strategies and to stages of change in perpetrators; thus, these "program integrity issues" lead to poor outcomes. Day et al. conclude, "There would appear to be a need to further develop intervention approaches for perpetrators of domestic violence, both in terms of greater sophistication in how domestic violence is understood, identifying the needs of treatment participants, and delivering programs in ways that are engaging and motivating for men to change."

Certain characteristics are generally related to dropout rates. Bruce Dalton of the University of South Carolina indicates in "Batterer Characteristics and Treatment Completion" (*Journal of Interpersonal Violence*, vol. 16, no. 12, December 2001) that the level of threat that the batterer perceived from the referral source (e.g., the court) was, surprisingly, not related to program completion. Unemployment was the one characteristic most consistently related to dropping out of treatment. Dalton theorizes that these men had both trouble paying for the treatment and a lower investment in the "official social order." Loretta J. Stalans and Magnus Seng of Loyola University Chicago find similar results in "Identifying Subgroups at High Risk of Dropping out of Domestic Batterer Treatment: The Buffering Effects of a High School Education" (*International Journal of Offender Therapy and Comparative Criminology*, vol. 51, no. 2, April 2007). The researchers note that the following groups had a 60% dropout rate or higher: batterers who were aggressive in general, not only in the family setting; high school dropouts who were also ordered into substance abuse treatment; and unemployed offenders who were also ordered into substance abuse treatment.

Recidivism Rates

Recidivism (the tendency to relapse to old ingrained patterns of behavior) is a well-documented problem among people in intimate partner violence treatment programs. In "Predictors of Criminal Recidivism among Male Batterers" (*Psychology Crime and Law*, vol. 10, no. 4, December 2004), R. Karl Hanson and Suzanne Wallace-Capretta examine the risk factors that were associated with the recidivism of 320 male batterers within a five-year follow-up period. Of those men, 25.6% recidivated with a battering offense. Risk factors included being young, having an unstable lifestyle, being a substance abuser, and having a criminal history. Batterers were not deterred by expectations of social or legal negative consequences. However, maintaining positive relationships with community treatment providers was associated with deterrence of future battering. Rodney Kingsnorth of California State University, Sacramento, notes in "Intimate Partner Violence: Predictors of Recidivism in a Sample of Arrestees" (*Violence against Women*, vol. 12, no. 10, October 2006) that risk factors for recidivism during an 18-month period included use of a weapon, prior arrests (for domestic violence or other offenses), and the presence of a protective order.

According to Matthew T. Huss and Anthony Ralston of Creighton University in "Do Batterer Subtypes Actually Matter? Treatment Completion, Treatment Response, and Recidivism across a Batterer Typology" (*Criminal Justice and Behavior*, vol. 35, no. 6, June 2008), men who only expressed violent behaviors in the context of their families were much more likely to complete batterer intervention programs than men who were generally violent or antisocial or who had personality disorders. Because of the higher treatment completion rates, these men were less likely to batter again. However, all men who completed treatment reported reductions in violence toward their partner.

In "The Effects of Domestic Violence Batterer Treatment on Domestic Violence Recidivism: The Chesterfield County Experience" (*Criminal Justice and Behavior*, vol. 30, no. 1, February 2003), Jill A. Gordon and Laura J. Moriarty of Virginia Commonwealth University study the effects of batterer treatment on recidivism. The researchers find that attending treatment had no impact on recidivism when comparing the treatment group as a whole with the experimental group. In "Intervention Programs for Perpetrators of Intimate Partner Violence: Conclusions from a Clinical Research Perspective" (*Public Health Reports*, vol. 121, no. 4, July–August 2006), Christopher I. Eckhardt et al. concur in their review of the literature concerning batterer intervention programs and recidivism rates. However, Gordon and Moriarty also indicate that among the treatment group, the more sessions a batterer completed, the less likely he was to batter again. Batterers who completed all sessions were less likely to be rearrested for domestic violence than were batterers who had not completed all sessions.

Still, as Huss and Ralston note, "even small reductions in rates of domestic violence can have a substantial impact in tens of thousands of women's lives." Therefore, research continues into how to identify batterers who are most likely to benefit from batterer intervention programs. As the Washington State Institute for Public Policy reports in "What Works to Reduce Recidivism by Domestic Violence Offenders?" (January 2013, http://www.wsipp.wa.gov/ReportFile/1119/Wsipp_What-Works-to-Reduce-Recidivism-by-Domestic-Violence-Offenders_Full-Report.pdf), a study of five group-based batterer treatment programs proved effective in reducing incidences of domestic violence recidivism by 33 percent. As the authors note, however, these programs varied significantly in method and approach, making it difficult to determine which course of treatment ultimately proves most effective.

IMPORTANT NAMES AND ADDRESSES

ABA Center on Children and the Law
1050 Connecticut Ave. NW, Ste. 400
Washington, DC 20036
(202) 662-1720
1-800-285-2221
FAX: (202) 662-1755
URL: http://www.americanbar.org/groups/
child_law.html

ABA Commission on Domestic & Sexual Violence
1050 Connecticut Ave. NW, Ste. 400
Washington, DC 20005-1019
(202) 662-1000
URL: http://www.americanbar.org/groups/
domestic_violence.html

ACLU Women's Rights Project
125 Broad St., 18th Fl.
New York, NY 10004
(212) 549-2500
URL: http://www.aclu.org/womens-rights

Bureau of Justice Statistics
U.S. Department of Justice
810 Seventh St. NW
Washington, DC 20531
(202) 307-0765
E-mail: askbjs@usdoj.gov
URL: http://www.ojp.usdoj.gov/bjs/

Center for Effective Discipline
327 Groveport Pike
Canal Winchester, OH 43110
(614) 834-7946
FAX: (614) 321-6308
URL: http://www.stophitting.com/

Center for Women Policy Studies
1776 Massachusetts Ave. NW, Ste. 450
Washington, DC 20036
(202) 872-1770
FAX: (202) 296-8962
E-mail: cwps@centerwomenpolicy.org
URL: http://www.centerwomenpolicy.org/

Centers for Disease Control and Prevention
1600 Clifton Rd.
Atlanta, GA 30329-4027
1-800-232-4636
URL: http://www.cdc.gov/

Child Welfare Information Gateway
1250 Maryland Ave. SW, Eighth Fl.
Washington, DC 20024
1-800-394-3366
E-mail: info@childwelfare.gov
URL: http://www.childwelfare.gov/

Child Welfare League of America
1726 M St. NW, Ste. 500
Washington, DC 20036
(202) 688-4200
FAX: (202) 833-1689
E-mail: cwla@cwla.org
URL: http://www.cwla.org/

Children's Bureau
Administration for Children and Families
U.S. Department of Health and Human Services
370 L'Enfant Promenade SW
Washington, DC 20447
1-800-394-3366
URL: http://www.acf.hhs.gov/programs/cb/

Children's Defense Fund
25 E St. NW
Washington, DC 20001
1-800-233-1200
E-mail: cdfinfo@childrensdefense.org
URL: http://www.childrensdefense.org/

Crimes against Children Research Center
University of New Hampshire
15 Academic Way
125 McConnell Hall
Durham, NH 03824
(603) 862-1888
FAX: (603) 862-1122
E-mail: doreen.cole@unh.edu
URL: http://www.unh.edu/ccrc/

Institute on Violence, Abuse, and Trauma
10065 Old Grove Rd.
San Diego, CA 92131
(858) 527-1860
FAX: (858) 527-1743
E-mail: ivat@alliant.edu
URL: http://ivatcenters.org/

International Society for Prevention of Child Abuse and Neglect
13123 E. 16th Ave., Ste. B390
Aurora, Colorado 80045
(303) 864-5220
FAX: (303) 864-5222
E-mail: ispcan@ispcan.org
URL: http://www.ispcan.org/

National Center for Missing and Exploited Children
Charles B. Wang International Children's Bldg.
699 Prince St.
Alexandria, VA 22314-3175
(703) 224-2150
1-800-843-5678
FAX: (703) 224-2122
URL: http://www.missingkids.com/

National Center for Prosecution of Child Abuse
National District Attorneys Association
99 Canal Center Plaza, Ste. 330
Alexandria, VA 22314
(703) 549-9222
FAX: (703) 836-3195
URL: http://www.ndaa.org/ncpca.html

National Center for Victims of Crime
2000 M St. NW, Ste. 480
Washington, DC 20036
(202) 467-8700
FAX: (202) 467-8701
URL: http://www.victimsofcrime.org/

National Clearinghouse for the Defense of Battered Women
125 S. Ninth St., Ste. 302
Philadelphia, PA 19107

(215) 351-0010
1-800-903-0111
URL: http://www.ncdbw.org/

**National Coalition against Domestic
Violence**
One Broadway, Ste. B210
Denver, CO 80203
(303) 839-1852
FAX: (303) 831-9251
E-mail: mainoffice@ncadv.org
URL: http://www.ncadv.org/

**National Council on Child Abuse
and Family Violence**
1025 Connecticut Ave. NW, Ste. 1000
Washington, DC 20036
(202) 429-6695
FAX: (202) 521-3479
E-mail: info@nccafv.org
URL: http://www.nccafv.org/

**National Domestic Violence
Hotline**
PO Box 161810
Austin, TX 78716
(512) 453-8117
1-800-799-7233
URL: http://www.thehotline.org/

National Runaway Safeline
3080 N. Lincoln Ave.
Chicago, IL 60657
(773) 880-9860
1-800-786-2929
FAX: (773) 929-5150
URL: http://www.1800runaway.org/

**Office for Victims of Crime
U.S. Department of Justice**
810 Seventh St. NW, Eighth Fl.
Washington, DC 20531
(202) 307-5983
FAX: (202) 514-6383
URL: http://www.ojp.usdoj.gov/ovc/

**Office of Juvenile Justice and
Delinquency Prevention**
810 Seventh St. NW
Washington, DC 20531
(202) 307-5911
URL: http://www.ojjdp.gov/

**Office on Violence against Women
U.S. Department of Justice**
145 N St. NE, Ste. 10W.121
Washington, DC 20530
(202) 307-6026
FAX: (202) 305-2589

E-mail: ovw.info@usdoj.gov
URL: http://www.justice.gov/ovw

Prevent Child Abuse America
228 S. Wabash Ave., 10th Fl.
Chicago, IL 60604
(312) 663-3520
1-800-244-5373
FAX: (312) 939-8962
E-mail: mailbox@preventchildabuse.org
URL: http://www.preventchildabuse.org/

Rape, Abuse, and Incest National Network
1220 L St. NW, Ste. 505
Washington, DC 20005
(202) 544-1034
1-800-656-4673
FAX: (202) 544-3556
E-mail: info@rainn.org
URL: http://www.rainn.org/

**Survivors Network of Those Abused
by Priests**
PO Box 6416
Chicago, IL 60680-6416
(312) 455-1499
1-877-762-7432
FAX: (312) 455-1498
E-mail: bdorris@snapnetwork.org
URL: http://www.snapnetwork.org/

RESOURCES

The U.S. Department of Health and Human Services (HHS) is a major source of national information about issues related to family violence. The HHS agencies consulted for this book include the Children's Bureau and the Office of Planning, Research, and Evaluation (OPRE) within the Administration for Children and Families and the National Center for Health Statistics and the National Center for Injury Prevention and Control within the Centers for Disease Control and Prevention.

The U.S. Department of Justice compiles and publishes large amounts of data on crime and victimizations. Agencies that provided data include the Bureau of Justice Statistics, the Federal Bureau of Investigation, the National Institute of Justice, and the Office of Juvenile Justice and Delinquency Prevention. The Federal Interagency Forum on Child and Family Statistics is a group of 22 federal government agencies that are involved in research and activities related to children and families. The U.S. Government Accountability Office and the Congressional Research Service are also important sources of information about government programs and policies.

Four studies in the National Incidence Study of Child Abuse and Neglect were conducted by the private research company Westat under contract to the OPRE. Two key resources at educational institutions were the Crimes against Children Research Center at the University of New Hampshire and the National Scientific Council on the Developing Child, a project of the Center on the Developing Child at Harvard University. Criminal law information was obtained from the National Center for Prosecution of Child Abuse, a project of the National District Attorneys Association. In addition, the U.S. Conference of Catholic Bishops was a valuable source of information.

Many journals published useful articles on child maltreatment and domestic violence that were used in the preparation of this book. They include *Child Abuse and Neglect, Child Maltreatment, Children and Youth Services Review, Criminal Justice and Behavior, Journal of Adolescent Health, Journal of Child Sexual Abuse, Journal of Clinical Psychology, Journal of Consulting and Clinical Psychology, Journal of Counseling Psychology, Journal of the American Academy of Child and Adolescent Psychology, Journal of the American Academy of Psychiatry and the Law, Journal of the American Medical Association, Journal of Family Violence, Journal of Interpersonal Violence, Journal of Perinatal Medicine, Journal of Psychiatric & Mental Health Nursing, National Institute of Justice Journal, National Survey of Child and Adolescent Well-Being Research Brief, Pediatrics, Proceedings of the National Academy of Sciences, Violence against Women,* and *Violence and Victims.*

INDEX

C

H

Hammon v. Indiana, 98
Harm standard, 36, 75
Head Start program, 46
Health insurance, 15, 132
Health issues. *See* Medical issues
Healthcare workers and reporting laws,
    12–13
Hearndon, Paula, 99
Hearndon v. Graham, 99
Hearsay evidence, 97–98
Hide, Macias v., 177
High school rape, 152–153, 156*t*, 157*t*,
    158*t*–159*t*
High schools, sexual harassment in, 160
Hippocampal volume and child abuse, 61
Home visit interventions, 174
Homicides. *See* Fatalities
HopeLine app, 132
Hostile Hallways surveys, 83
Hotlines, 11, 23, 131, 132
Household composition. *See* Living
    arrangements
Housing, 15
Houston, Whitney, 131
Hyperarousal, 64–65

I

Immigrants, 178–179
Immigration Act of 1990, 178
Immigration Marriage Fraud Amendment
    Act, 178
In re Gault, 91
In the Interest of R.A.S., 98
"Incest exception," 100–101
Income. *See* Socioeconomic status
Indiana, Hammon v., 98
Injuries
    domestic violence, 133, 134*t*–135*t*
    rape and sexual assault, 139*t*
    violent victimization, 105, 106(*t*6.5),
        113–114, 114(*t*6.13), 115*f*, 137*t*–138*t*
Interfamilial homicides, 121
International issues
    cyberstalking, 168
    rape, 161–163
Internet
    child pornography, 100
    cyberstalking, 167–169
    sexual predators, 85
Interstate Stalking Punishment and
    Prevention Act, 167
Intervention
    child abuse prevention through, 38–43
    domestic violence, 174–175
    domestic violence offender treatment,
        180–182
Interviewing techniques, 95–96
Intimate partner stalking, 165–166

Intimate partner violence
    cyberstalking, 167
    degree of violence and victim-offender
        relationship, 106(*t*6.3)
    female victimization, characteristics of,
        110–115
    female victims of serious intimate
        partner violence, 112*t*
    homicides, 119–122
    injuries and medical treatment, 105,
        106(*t*6.5), 114(*t*6.13), 115*f*, 115*t*, 116*f*
    locations, 107*t*
    National Intimate Partner and Sexual
        Violence Survey, 115–119
    offenders, treatment of, 180–182
    physical attack types, 113*f*
    physical violence and threats against
        female victims, 113*f*
    rape and sexual assault, 136*t*, 139*t*,
        143–144, 144*t*, 145*t*–146*t*, 149*t*
    rates, by sex of victims, 111*f*, 111*t*
    reporting, 171–172
    by season, 156*f*
    serious domestic violence rates,
        112(*f*6.2)
    by sex, degree of violence, and victim-
        offender relationship, 106(*t*6.4)
    simple assault domestic violence rates,
        112(*f*6.3)
    trends, 107–110
    violent victimization types, 137*t*–138*t*,
        147*t*–148*t*
    weapons use, 106–107, 108*t*–110*t*,
        114(*t*6.12)
Investigations, child abuse, 31–32,
    34(*t*2.11), 38, 54*t*–55*t*

J

Jensen, D. Lowell, 177
Justice Research and Statistics Association,
    11–12
Justice system
    child abuse intervention, 38–39, 38–40
    child abuse prosecution, 93
    child sexual abuse prosecution, 93–96
    child welfare system, 39*f*
    children's rights, 91–92
    criminal *vs.* civil child abuse cases, 10
    domestic violence cases, 179–180
    domestic violence victim services, 132
    duplicate victims, 92*t*
    funding the child welfare system, 46
    jurisdiction and social changes, 2–3
    rape case outcomes, 150–152
    recovered memories and statutes of
        limitations, 98–100
    See also Legal issues and legislation

K

Kaiser Permanente, 79
Kempe, C. Henry, 12
Ketamine hydrochloride, 159

L

Law, Bernard, 83
Law enforcement
    cyberstalking, 168–169
    domestic violence, 141, 171–177
Learned behavior theories of domestic
    violence, 125
Learned helplessness, 140–141
Legal issues and legislation
    anticyberstalking laws, 167, 168–169
    anti-stalking legislation, 166–167
    Cable Communications Policy Act, 168
    Campus Sexual Violence Act, 160
    child abuse definitions, 9–10
    child pornography, 100
    child sexual abuse, 84–85
    domestic violence legislation, 11–12
    domestic violence victim services, 133
    family preservation, 41
    federal laws, 4–5, 9
    foster care hearings, 40
    "incest exception," 100–101
    key domestic violence legislation, 177–179
    mandatory reporting of child abuse, 38
    National Survey of Child and Adolescent
        Well-Being, 49
    prenatal drug exposure, 101
    reporting laws, 12–13
    Violence against Women
        Reauthorization Act, 160
    See also Justice system
Lesbian, gay, bisexual, and transgendered
    persons, 11
"Liquid ecstasy," 159
Living arrangements
    changes in, 1–2, 2*f*
    child abuse risk factors, 48
    child sexual abuse effects, 89
    child sexual abuse victims, 76
    of children, by demographic
        characteristics, 6*t*–8*t*
    children's economic status by, 9*t*–10*t*
    children's well-being indicators, 14*t*
    emotional and behavioral problems
        risks, 51*t*
    National Incidence Study of Child Abuse
        and Neglect, 37
    National Survey of Child and Adolescent
        Well-Being, 56*t*
    poverty, 14, 16*f*
    re-reports of maltreatment, 59*t*
Local government, 46
Locations of violent victimization, 105, 107*t*
Low-income families. *See* Poverty;
    Socioeconomic status

M

Macias v. Hide, 177
Mak Yew Loong, Colin, 168
Mali, 163

Mandatory arrests, 172–174

Mandatory reporting, 37–38, 85

Marital rape, 152

Marital status

 caregivers, 56*t*

 household types by, 2*f*

 parental marital status, 6*t*–8*t*

 stalking victims, 166

 violent victimization rates, 18*t*

Marriage fraud, 178

Maryland v. Craig, 97

Massachusetts, 100

Maternal, Infant, and Early Childhood Home visiting Program, 46

Mayweather, Floyd, Jr., 131

McKnight, Regina, 101

McKnight, State v., 101

Medicaid, 46

Medical issues

 child abuse risk factors, 15, 49

 child abuse victims in need of health care, 50, 52(*t*3.4)

 domestic violence injuries, 133, 134*t*–135*t*

 female victims of intimate partner violence, 116*f*

 injuries from violent victimization, 105, 106(*t*6.5), 115*t*, 137*t*–138*t*

 rape and sexual assault, 139*t*

 women victims of domestic violence, 129–130

Memory issues, 86, 98–100

Men

 domestic violence offender treatment, 180–182

 protection orders, 175

 stalking victims, 164(*f*8.5), 165(*f*8.7)

 See also Gender

Mental health

 child abuse effects, 57–58, 70–71

 child abuse offenders, 49

 child abuse risk factors, 50–51

 child sexual abuse effects, 88, 89

 need for treatment among surveyed parents, 58*t*

Mindfulness-based therapy, 79

Minnesota Student Surveys, 81

Mitchell, Bugh v., 98

Morrison, Antonio, 178

Morrison et al., United States v., 11

Mothers, 116*t*, 141

N

National Association to Protect Children, 100

National Center for Prosecution of Child Abuse, 10, 97, 99

National Center for Victims of Crime, 166

National Child Abuse and Neglect Data System. *See Child Maltreatment* (Children's Bureau)

National Child Abuse Prevention Month, 46

National Coalition for Child Protection Reform, 42

National Conference of State Legislatures, 38, 99, 168–169

National Crime Victimization Survey

 child sexual abuse, 80–81

 domestic violence reporting, 171–172

 female victimization characteristics, 110–115

 intimate partner violence trends, 107–110

 rape and sexual assault, 143–144, 144*t*, 149, 153*t*

 terms and definitions, 103–104

 victim services, 133, 134*t*–135*t*

 victim-offender relationship, 16

 violent victimization, 104–107, 105(*t*6.1), 105(*t*6.2)

National Defense Authorization Act, 167

National Domestic Violence Hotline, 132

National Football League, 131

National Incidence Study of Child Abuse and Neglect

 child abuse risk factors, 47–49

 data collection, 34–35

 sexual abuse, 74–76

 socioeconomic risk factors, 55–56

 victim demographics, 36–37

National Institute of Justice, 172

National Intimate Partner and Sexual Violence Survey

 domestic violence, 115–119

 public health issues, 13

 rape, 144, 149

 sexual violence questions, 150*t*

 stalking, 163–166

National Survey of Adolescents, 79–80

National Survey of Child and Adolescent Well-Being

 aggression and neglect, 60*t*

 arrests of adolescents, 52(*t*3.3)

 behavior problems as child abuse effect, 67–68

 caregiver demographics, 56*t*

 child abuse risk factors, 49–52, 51*t*, 52*t*, 54*t*–55*t*

 child service needs, 52(*t*3.4)

 child sexual abuse, 76

 data collection, 29–31

 demographics of children represented in, 33(*t*2.10)

 developmental problems, children with, 50*t*

 domestic violence, 114–115, 116*t*

 emotional and behavioral issues, children risks, 51*t*

 investigations, 34(*t*2.11)

investigations and dispositions, 31–32

 mental health treatment needs among parents, 58*t*

 neurobiological effects of child abuse, 59–60

 relationship issues as child abuse effect, 69–70

 re-reports of maltreatment, 59*t*

 self-reported violence, aggression, and neglect, 32–33, 34(*t*2.12), 35*t*

 sexual activity and pregnancy, adolescent girls', 53*f*, 53*t*

 substance abuse treatment needs among parents, 57*t*

National Survey of Children's Exposure to Violence, 80, 81

National Violence against Women Survey, 122–123, 149–152

Native Americans, 11

Neglect

 fatalities, 67(*f*3.6), 67(*f*3.7)

 National Incidence Study of Child Abuse and Neglect, 37

 National Survey of Child and Adolescent Well-Being, 35*t*

 offenders, 27

 state law definitions, 10

 tiers and types, 32*f*, 32*t*

Neurobiological effects

 child abuse, 59–61, 63–64

 child sexual abuse, 87

New York v. Ferber, 100

Nontraditional families, 1

Nutrition programs, 46

O

Obama, Barack, 160–161

O'Connor, Sandra Day, 97

Offenders

 celebrities, 22, 131

 child abuse fatalities, 28

 child abuse offender demographics, 26–27, 30*t*, 31*f*

 child abuse offenders, by maltreatment type, 31*t*

 child abuse risk factors, 49

 child sexual abuse, 76

 educators, 82–83

 National Incidence Study of Child Abuse and Neglect, 37

 notorious offenders, 84–85

 priests, 83–84, 100

 rape, 144

 treatment, 180–182

 See also Victim-offender relationship

Office of Family Assistance, 46

Office on Violence against Women, 11, 167

Ohio v. Roberts, 97–98

Operation Sunflower, 100

Outcomes
  child abuse cases, 31–32
  child protective service case, 43–46, 44*t*
  domestic violence cases, 172–175, 180

P

Parents
  child abuse risk factor, 48–49
  family preservation and reunification, 40–42
  homicides, 121
  National Survey of Child and Adolescent Well-Being, 35(*t*2.14), 57*t*
  self-reported aggression against children, 33
  termination of parental rights, 39–40
Paterno, Joe, 84
Patient Protection and Affordable Care Act, 132
Pennsylvania State University, 84–85
People v. Espinoza, 98
People v. Vigil, 98
Perpetrators. *See* Offenders
Personal Responsibility and Work Opportunity Reconciliation Act, 29, 49
Personality theory of domestic violence, 125
Physical abuse
  National Intimate Partner and Sexual Violence Survey, 117–119
  National Survey of Child and Adolescent Well-Being, 35*t*, 60*t*
  polyvictims, 19
  state law definitions, 10
Physicians, child sexual abuse by, 84
Polyvictims, 19–20, 21*f*
Population, 13, 15*f*
Pornography, child, 100
Post-traumatic stress disorder, 71, 88, 130
Poverty
  children living in poverty, 16*f*
  domestic violence risk factors, 126
  family structure, 9*t*–10*t*
  proactive child abuse prevention, 46
  See also Socioeconomic status
Power issues, 126
Prenatal drug exposure, 101
Prescription psychotropic medications, 71
Prevention
  child abuse, 38–43
  college rape, 159–161
  proactive child abuse prevention, 46
  stalking, 166–167
Priests, 83–84, 100
Pritchard, William Thomas, 168
Professionals
  child sexual abuse by, 82–85, 100
  reporting requirements for, 12–13
Prosecution
  child abuse, 93
  child sexual abuse, 93–96
  domestic violence cases, 179–180

Protecting Domestic Violence and Stalking Victims Act, 11
Protection orders, 175–176
Protective custody, 38
Psychological aggression, 119
Psychological issues
  cycle of violence theory, 68–69
  domestic violence causes, 125
  domestic violence effects, 130–131
  foster care, children in, 70
  protection orders, 175–176
  reasons women stay in abusive relationships, 140–141
  sports and fraternities and dating violence, 157–159
  treatment of adult victims of child sexual abuse, 79
Psychotropic medications, 71
Public awareness campaigns, 46
Public health issues
  children's status, 13–15
  children's well-being indicators, 14*t*
  domestic violence prevention, 131–132
Public opinion on corporal punishment, 22
Public schools, sexual harassment in, 160

R

Race/ethnicity
  adolescent victims of child sexual abuse, 79–80
  aggression and neglect victims, 60*t*
  arrests among adolescents, 52(*t*3.3)
  child abuse fatalities, 26
  child abuse offenders, 27, 31*f*
  child abuse victims, 26, 27*t*–28*t*
  child population, 13, 15*f*
  child sexual abuse, 75–76, 79
  children's living arrangements, 6*t*–8*t*
  cycle of violence theory, 69
  dating violence, 128–129, 129(*t*7.1)
  developmental problems, children with, 49, 50*t*
  disclosure of child sexual abuse, 81
  domestic violence, 17, 115
  domestic violence services for mothers of child abuse victims, 116*t*
  emotional and behavioral problems, children risks, 51*t*
  foster care, 40, 41*t*, 42*t*
  high school rape, 153, 156*t*
  homicide and domestic violence, 121
  intimate partner violence, 117–118, 122
  National Incidence Study of Child Abuse and Neglect, 36
  National Survey of Child and Adolescent Well-Being, 33(*t*2.10), 35*t*, 56*t*
  polyvictims, 19
  poverty, 14, 16*f*
  rape and sexual assault, 145*t*–146*t*, 150, 151*t*, 152*t*

removal of children from homes, 41
re-reports of maltreatment, 59*t*
sexual harassment in public schools, 160
stalking victims, 163
teen birth rates, 3*t*–4*t*, 5*f*
teen pregnancy, 2
violent victimization, 18*t*, 147*t*–148*t*
Radiology, 12
Ramm, Leandra, 168
Rape and sexual assault
  age of victims and population size, 153*t*
  of child abuse victims, 50
  civil rights issues, 178
  college on-campus crimes reported, 163*f*
  college rape, 154–159, 161*t*, 162*t*
  college rape prevention, 159–161
  date rape drugs, 159
  geographical region, 154*t*
  high school rape, 152–154, 156*t*, 157*t*
  injury and medical treatment status, 139*t*
  international concerns about, 161–163
  justice system outcomes, 150–152
  marital rape, 152
  National Crime Victimization Survey, 103–104, 143–144
  National Intimate Partner and Sexual Violence Survey, 117–119, 144, 149
  National Survey of Child and Adolescent Well-Being, 35*t*
  National Violence against Women Survey, 149–152
  race/ethnicity of victims, 145*t*–146*t*, 151*t*
  rates, by season, 155*f*
  sex and race/ethnicity of victims, 152*t*
  state law definitions, 10
  victim services status, 136*t*
  victim-offender relationships, 144*t*
  weapon use, 149*t*
R.A.S., In the Interest of, 98
Ravens, Baltimore, 131
Reasons women stay in abusive relationships, 133, 136, 140–141
Recidivism, domestic violence, 181–182
Recovered memories, 98–100
Referrals, child abuse, 23–24, 24*f*
Relationship effects of child abuse, 69–70
Reliability of children's testimony, 95–96
Removal of child abuse victims, 39
Reporting
  child abuse reporting laws, 12–13, 37–38
  Child Maltreatment data, 23–24, 25*t*
  child sexual abuse, 84–85, 93, 93*t*
  college on-campus crimes, 163*f*
  college sexual violence, 160
  crime victimization not reported, by crime type, 173*t*
  domestic violence, 13, 171–172
  prenatal drug exposure, 101

V

Vachss, Andrew, 100
Vatican, 84
Verizon Wireless, 132
Viable fetuses and prenatal drug exposure, 101
Victim services
  domestic violence, 116*t*, 132–133,
    134*t*–135*t*, 174–175
  rape and sexual assault victims, 136*t*
Victim-offender relationship
  child abuse, 26
  child abuse fatalities, 28, 33(*t*2.9)
  child sexual abuse, 76, 80, 86
  crime types, 17*t*
  disclosure of child sexual abuse, 81–82
  domestic violence, 16, 17*f*, 19*f*, 104–105
  homicide and domestic violence, 120–121
  injuries and medical treatment from
    violent victimization, 106(*t*6.5),
    114(*t*6.13), 115*t*
  National Crime Victimization Survey,
    143–144, 144*t*
  National Incidence Study of Child Abuse
    and Neglect, 37
  National Intimate Partner and Sexual
    Violence Survey, 144, 149
  National Violence against Women
    Survey, 150
  physical attack types, 113*f*
  rape and sexual assault, by injury and
    medical treatment status, 139*t*
  rape and sexual assault, by race/
    ethnicity, 145*t*–146*t*
  rape and sexual assault, by victim
    services status, 136*t*
  rape and sexual assault, by weapon
    use, 149*t*
  serious domestic violence rates by,
    112(*f*6.2)
  simple assault domestic violence rates,
    112(*f*6.3)
  stalking, 164–166, 165*f*
  violent victimization, 18*t*, 105(*t*6.2)
  violent victimization, by crime type, 17*t*
  violent victimization, by degree of
    violence, 106(*t*6.3)
  violent victimization, by type and injury
    and medical treatment status,
    137*t*–138*t*
  violent victimization, by type and race/
    ethnicity, 147*t*–148*t*
  violent victimization, by victim age,
    20(*t*1.9)
  violent victimization, by victim services
    status, 134*t*–135*t*
  violent victimization, reporting of, 174*t*
  violent victimization among children,
    20(*t*1.8)
  violent victimization resulting in injury
    and medical treatment, 106(*t*6.5)

weapons used in violent victimization,
    114(*t*6.12)
Victims
  adolescent child abuse victims, 61*f*
  adolescent child sexual abuse victims,
    79–80
  adult child sexual abuse victims, 78–79
  child abuse victims' legal rights, 91–92
  Child Maltreatment data, 25–26
  child sexual abuse, 93*t*, 94*t*
  child sexual abuse effects, 85–89,
    86*t*, 87*t*
  child sexual abuse victim
    demographics, 75
  crime victimization not reported, by
    crime type, 173*t*
  crime victimization reported to the
    police, 172*t*
  cycle of violence theory, 68–69
  domestic violence among parents of
    child abuse victims, 60*f*
  domestic violence effects, 129–131
  domestic violence prosecution, 179–180
  domestic violence responses, 141
  domestic violence risk factors, 127–128
  domestic violence victim demographics,
    16–18
  intimate partner violence, 122
  National Incidence Study of Child Abuse
    and Neglect, 36–37
  polyvictims, 19–20
  rape and sexual assault, by race/
    ethnicity, 151*t*
  rape and sexual assault, by sex and race/
    ethnicity, 152*t*
  reasons women stay in abusive
    relationships, 133, 136, 140–141
Victims of Trafficking and Violence
  Protection Act, 11, 178
Videotaping of children's testimony, 97
Vigil, People v., 98
Violence against Women Act
  civil rights issues, 178
  federal domestic violence legislation, 11
  immigrants, 178–179
  protection orders, 175
  victim services, 132
Violence against Women Reauthorization
  Act, 160, 167, 179
Violence escalation, 140
Violent victimization
  crime victimization not reported, by
    crime type, 173*t*
  crime victimization reported to the
    police, 172*t*
  cycle of violence theory, 68–69
  degree of violence and victim-offender
    relationship, 106(*t*6.3)
  female victimization, characteristics of,
    110–115

female victims of serious intimate
    partner violence, 112*t*
  high school students, 152–154
  injuries, 106(*t*6.5), 115*f*
  locations, 105, 107*t*
  medical treatment, 115*t*, 116*f*
  National Crime Victimization Survey,
    103–107
  physical attacks, 113*f*, 113*t*
  reporting, by victim-offender
    relationship, 174*t*
  by sex, degree of violence, and victim-
    offender relationship, 106(*t*6.4)
  by sex of victims, 111*f*, 111*t*
  by type, victim-offender relationship,
    and injury and medical treatment
    status, 137*t*–138*t*
  by type, victim-offender relationship,
    and race/ethnicity, 147*t*–148*t*
  weapons used, 106–107, 108*t*–110*t*
Virginia Polytechnic Institute, 11, 178

W

Wallström, Margot, 162–163
Washington, Crawford v., 98
Washington, Davis v., 98
Weapons
  domestic violence gun ban, 179
  fatal domestic violence risk factors, 127
  intimate partner homicides, 121
  rape and sexual assault, 144, 149*t*
  violent victimization, 106–107,
    108*t*–110*t*, 113, 114(*t*6.12)
Welfare services, 4–5, 46
Well-being indicators, 13–15, 14*t*
Wheeler v. United States, 94
White House Task Force to Protect Students
  from Sexual Assault, 160–161
Whitner, Cornelia, 101
Whitner v. South Carolina, 101
Widom, Cathy S., 68
Wilson, Rilya, 42–43
Witnesses. *See* Testimony, children's
Women
  domestic violence and sexual health,
    129–130
  domestic violence responses, 141
  empowering domestic violence victims,
    174–175
  physical violence and threats against,
    113*f*
  reasons for staying in abusive
    relationships, 133, 136, 140–141
  stalking victims, 164(*f*8.4), 165(*f*8.6)
  See also Gender
Women, Infants, and Children program, 46

Y

Youth Risk Behavior Survey, 128–129